A GRAMMAR OF ASSENT

John Henry Cardinal Newman

<<<<<<<<<<<<<<<<<<<<<<<>>>>>>>>>>>>>>>>>>>>

AN ESSAY IN AID OF

A GRAMMAR
OF ASSENT

*Non in dialectâ complacuit Deo salvum facere
populum suum*   ST. AMBROSE

NEW EDITION, EDITED WITH A PREFACE AND INTRODUCTION BY

CHARLES FREDERICK HARROLD

1947

LONGMANS, GREEN AND CO

NEW YORK • LONDON • TORONTO

LONGMANS, GREEN AND CO., INC.
55 FIFTH AVENUE, NEW YORK 3

LONGMANS, GREEN AND CO. LTD.
OF PATERNOSTER ROW
43 ALBERT DRIVE, LONDON, S.W. 19
NICOL ROAD, BOMBAY 1
17 CHITTARANJAN AVENUE, CALCUTTA 13
36A MOUNT ROAD, MADRAS 2

LONGMANS, GREEN AND CO.
215 VICTORIA STREET, TORONTO 1

A GRAMMAR OF ASSENT

NEW EDITION

DESIGNED BY ROBERT JOSEPHY

Printed in the United States of America
VAN REES PRESS • NEW YORK

PREFACE

BETWEEN 1868 and 1881, Newman was engaged intermittently in bringing out a carefully checked and revised edition of his collected works. Only thirty-six of the final forty volumes appeared under his hand. The *Grammar of Assent*, like many of Newman's other works, underwent certain stylistic corrections and alterations. The present edition of that work presents the text as Newman presumably wished it ultimately to appear. I may assure the reader at once that in none of the alterations in wording or phrasing has Newman's argument or illustration varied basically, or even interestingly, from the original text of 1870. In fact, in some cases it is difficult to conjecture just what improvement Newman believed he was achieving in re-casting a phrase, or substituting a word which is no more expressive than the original. In no cases, however, did Newman reduce the rhetorical power of his earlier expression. Unlike his contemporary, Walter Pater, he seems always to have known when an alteration was, or was not, an improvement.

By the time Newman ceased work on his collected writings, about 1882, the *Grammar of Assent* had gone through five editions; numerous reprints, of course, followed later, and the book was published in French (Paris, 1907) and in German (Munich, 1921). In spite of its technicalities, at least for the uninitiated reader, in spite of its refusal to oversimplify or to put extremely subtle ideas in deceptively simple language, Newman's volume continues to reach a wide public, and also to attract scholars and thinkers who wish to fathom the depths of Newman's thought and to observe that thought in relation to past and to present religious thinking.

This edition, unlike the first, contains the three Notes, two of which were added in 1880 and 1882; Note I remains undated. Probably the most important Note is number II, "On the alternative intellectually between Atheism and Catholicity," especially in its bearing upon certain elements of Newman's arguments in the text.

In the preparation of this edition, in the exacting labors of collating texts, and in numerous other ways, I have been greatly aided by my wife, Elizabeth Hebblewhite Harrold.

Charles Frederick Harrold

The Ohio State University
Columbus, Ohio
April 26, 1946

CONTENTS

ix

INTRODUCTION

O NE DAY in August 1866, while Newman and his good friend Ambrose St. John were vacationing "up at Glion over the Lake of Geneva," a thought suddenly struck Newman that the problem of inference and assent in connection with religious faith might be solved not by beginning with certitude but by contrasting assent with inference. He tells us that the problem had been "teasing him for these twenty or thirty years." The fact that he had originally planned to begin his treatise with an analysis of certitude reveals at once that his projected book was intended not to convert, not to argue anyone into agreeing with him, but merely to enable the believer to understand what it means to hold a belief, religious or non-religious. We may observe, incidentally, that Newman's resolve to start with the difference between inference and assent accounts in large measure for the fact that the *Grammar of Assent* has one of the least attractive, one of the most forbiddingly abstruse, opening chapters, of all books of like substance and influence.

The *Grammar of Assent* was the culmination of many years of thought and expression on the mental and emotional and other processes that result in belief. The central thought in Newman's argument, that assent or belief is arrived at not primarily by logic or demonstration, but by "the whole man" —his feelings, memories, associations, etc.—goes back as far as his book on *The Arians of the Fourth Century* (1833). There his stress was principally on the power of "imagination" to persuade men that the external world exists exactly as the senses report that it does. There Newman was struck by the mysticism of the Alexandrians, by their disdain for the sensuous and inferential approach to truth. Later, his entrance into the Roman Catholic Church was motivated not merely by the vast array of argument which fills his *Essay on Development* (1845), but by "the convergence of innumerable probabilities" which, in his particular "right state of heart," told overwhelmingly in favor of his belief in the Roman Church. Even earlier, in the *Lectures on Justification* (1838), he had written of faith as "an original means of knowledge, not resolvable into sense, or the faculty of reason, confirmed indeed by experience, as they are, but founded on a supernaturally implanted instinct, an instinct developed by religious obedience." Here he uses the word "instinct" in precisely the way he does in the *Grammar,* in a way, we may add, which misleads many of his present-day readers, but which was not nearly so confusing to Catholic readers of 1870. Also, in his famous Tamworth Reading-Room articles for *The Times* (1841), he had brilliantly stated his conviction that "man is *not* a reasoning animal; he is a seeing, feeling, contemplating, acting animal," a creature endowed with will and moral judgment. Here, too, Newman exhibits his relative contempt for logic; here also appears his admirably expressed statement of the primacy of conscience in reaching a sound judgment or a belief. But it is in the *Oxford University Sermons* (1843) that we see Newman deliberately engaged on "an exploring expedition" to determine the nature of faith and reason, to show the grounds on which the (logically) untrained believer justifiably holds his belief, namely, through "implicit" or unconscious reasoning, against a background of a "right state of heart." In these sermons Newman is convinced that conscience gives us a glimpse of reality behind the physical world so piercing and compelling that we place it on a level with our knowledge of the external world as derived through reason and the five senses. He is sure that logic is inadequate to a complete statement of our mental process, since so much of our reasoning is done subconsciously, mingling memories, emotions, associations with its strictly ratiocinative elements. Yet it is all this complex of conscious and subconscious activity that propels a man toward an assent. Again, "the whole man reasons," not just the "mind."

We may note also that in one of the Dublin lectures, "A Form of Infidelity of the Day" (1854), Newman anticipated a later view that religious knowledge cannot be considered as at all "scientific," but rather as a menace to further true (secular) knowledge. Newman was a too well-educated Catholic to leave unchallenged the "modern" notion of belief as mere sentiment, or of theology as a mere tissue of deductively arrived-at conclusions in matters in which logical reasoning never reaches results that all men can accept. The *Grammar of Assent* is an "essay in aid" in the direction of logically understood beliefs. It is an "essay" in the eighteenth-century meaning of that term, an "attempt," in a very informal manner, to meet the charges of skeptics and the ignorance of believers. It is an attempt to show that the modern mind is not violating itself in certain acts of assent that transcend logic, but is following certain laws or patterns which bring certitude in any field, not merely in that of religion. Daily life, in short, is based not upon inferences logically thought out, but upon concrete assents resting on countless *probabilities;* daily life is a constant act of faith. Put differently, it rests largely upon implicit or unconscious reasoning.

Before the *Grammar* was actually written, however, and while he was in the midst of plans for a new translation of the Bible, Newman wrote out the design for an elaborate *Prolegomena* (1857), which would counteract the influence of agnostic propaganda. He tried to show that, considered rationally and objectively, revelation is indeed strange. But, considering man's estate, asks Newman, which is stranger, revelation or skepticism? For him, all things considered, skepticism is impossible, "utter skepticism is false." Like Matthew Arnold, he was saying: "Do you realize that when you believe *this,* you must accept *that?*" He was saying: "Do you wish to continue a skeptic, once you know all of the implications of skepticism for your existence?" Three years later at the urging of W. G. Ward he sketched out a memorandum, "The Fluctuations of Human Opinion." Here he set down in five paragraphs the questions which any intelligent non-Catholic might ask, as militating against taking the claims of Catholicism seriously. No one could better express agnostic or atheistic reasons against Christian beliefs than could Newman. Small wonder Huxley declared that merely from the 1843 *Essay on Miracles* and the *Essay on Development* he could "compile a Primer of 'Infidelity.'" Looked at properly, Huxley's statement simply means that Newman was, more than most Victorians, superbly equipped to meet skeptics on their own ground, to show the limits of reason and logic in matters of faith, to admit candidly just where the act of faith must be the proper resource, to set forth the plausible reasons for approaching belief and the true principles on which that belief is actually held. Newman was convinced that modern infidelity must be met with intellectual weapons as strong as its own, so that religious knowledge could be seen to be as "objective" and "rational" and "ordered" as secular knowledge. He wanted the world to know that there was as much "common sense" in religious faith as there is in modern man's "science and progress." How far Newman succeeded in his courageous enterprise will be judged differently by different readers. Surely no one can deny that he made a gallant effort, and that in so doing he wrote some of his most splendid prose.

In reading the *Grammar of Assent*, one should always bear in mind Newman's aims and methods. We have already noted that his aim was *not* to convert; his book is directed at a chosen body of readers: those who accept Newman's postulates—the existence of a God, the immortality of the soul, the freedom of the will, the existence of sin and virtue, the possibility of a revelation and of a mediator between God and man. His aim is to supply a "rhetoric" of belief as well as the logical cogency for believing. His method is easy and informal, personal and

empirical and inductive. He avoids the terminology of the
schools, and, though his own terminology is sometimes confusing and (to the uninitiated) rather recondite, his vocabulary and his illustrations are remarkable for their naturalness.
So far as its structure is concerned, the *Grammar of Assent*
strikes many readers as somewhat arbitrary. To grasp his
argument entire, one has to reread the book and note how the
various parts contribute to make an artistic whole. Newman
loved the music of Beethoven; and in some ways the structure
of the *Grammar* is remarkably like that of a Beethoven quartet
—both require an experience of the whole before its parts and
their relations may be appreciated. Even Newman's language
must be understood before his method is clearly compre-
hended. His language is in fact sometimes quite loose, often
arbitrary and personal, and very frequently old-fashioned even
for a Victorian writing in the late 1860's. He has his own use
for "presumption," "speculation," "opinion," "inquire," and
"investigate." Some of these words (and others we might point
out) are used in the denotations accepted and employed by
Addison and Dr. Johnson. Critics have observed that in a
decade when Darwin's *Origin of Species* had given rise to a
new idiom, Newman chose to cling to that of the "evidential"
school of theologians of the days of Paley; he aimed in 1870,
in the vocabulary of Locke, Butler, and Whately, to meet the
deistic arguments of the Oxford common room of the 1830's.
In spite of this handicap, however, Newman succeeded in
throwing some fresh light on the way we arrive at any belief.

It has been said that the key to the *Grammar of Assent* is
the psychological treatment of the difference between inference and assent.[1] All of Part II is devoted to "Assent and
Inference." Throughout the entire volume, however, Newman
regards assent as being in its nature unconditional, in contrast
to inference, which is always conditional. Everywhere, too, he
insists on the importance of the real and the concrete, as

[1] Wilfrid Ward, *Life of Newman,* II, 245-46.

against the notional and the abstract. He holds that the act of assent to a new conclusion, whether ostensibly from an act of conscious inference or not, is always a definite step in response to many rational and non-rational influences, unconscious as well as conscious—not the mere mechanical, passive, logical recognition then and there of an inference from premises. This is possibly his subtlest and most original contribution to the problem of assent. By means of it he managed to view the unbeliever's attitude in a new and creative way. The conventional way had been to regard the believer and unbeliever as living in separate worlds, the unbeliever failing to believe simply because he was dishonest, stubborn, and perverse. Newman's acquaintance with such candid and sincere doubters as William Froude, the brother of Hurrell Froude, made him feel that the case for Christianity could not be drawn up with the completeness of a barrister's brief, and stated in such a way as to make it quickly conclusive to any honest man. In the *Grammar of Assent* unbelief appears, not as due to conscious dishonesty, but as resulting from an attitude and a background different from those of the believer. Newman thus tries to analyze the mind of believer and unbeliever, and to clarify the difference between them. He draws attention to all those subtle personal intangibles which contribute to one's final assent to any new conclusion, religious or otherwise: memories, prejudices, fears, desires, unconscious drives, impressions, ideas—in short, the background of the whole inner man. "The religious mind," says Newman, "sees much [in the evidence] which is invisible to the irreligious mind. They have not [in fact] the same evidence before them." Moreover, the degree to which the individual has developed a *conscience* will help to determine for him the validity of religious evidence. Since the cause of Christianity cannot be drawn up with any neat and compelling completeness for the mind, much will therefore depend on how far a good or a bad man will commit himself to the "probabilities" that make up so much of the antecedent reasonings resulting in faith. As Ward says, "Moral defect must in the long run lead the mind to miss the deepest grounds for belief." [1] Newman had already written, years before, that "a good and a bad man will think very different things probable." [2] Thus we see Newman analyzing the intellectual, moral, and psychological elements which go into the making of any assent. But it was not this analysis that became by general consent the most striking lesson taught by the *Grammar;* it was Newman's doctrine of the "illative sense," which seemed to many readers an admirable solution to the old problem of reason, faith, and certitude.

The "illative sense" may be defined as the spontaneous divination by the mind in concrete matters that a conclusion is inevitable if it is felt to be "as good as proved," even though not determined by a process of reasoning logically complete. The "illative sense" works with probabilities as well as with certitudes. As I have elsewhere pointed out, "it is the mind in its perfection, judging and correlating at the highest point of any given individual; it concerns itself with principles, doctrines, facts, memories, experiences, testimonies in order to attain insights too delicate and subtle for logical analysis." [3] With all these elements making for an assent, the "illative sense" works with "a cumulation of *probabilities,* independent of each other, arising out of the nature and circumstances of the particular case . . . ; probabilities too fine to avail separately, too subtle and circuitous to be convertible into syllogisms, too numerous and various for such conversion, even were they convertible." The "illative sense," working with convergent probabilities, arrives at a certitude comparable with that of the schoolboy who knows that a regular polygon inscribed in a circle, its sides being continually diminished, will tend ever to become that circle, though never quite reaching it. Religious faith, so far as its "logical cogency" is concerned, is thus a matter of handling "probabilities" with as great a scrupulous-

---

[1] Ward, *Life of Newman,* II, 247.
[2] Newman, *Oxford University Sermons,* p. 191.
[3] C. F. Harrold, *John Henry Newman,* p. 157.

ness as that of a scientist handling mathematical fact. On the other hand, says Newman, although we are obliged, in matters of science, to withhold our assent from a conclusion of which we have not yet a strict logical demonstration, we are obliged, in matters of religion, to follow conscience and to look for certainties by modes of proof which, if reduced to formal propositions, would fail to satisfy the severe requirements of science. We cannot wait until complete, logical demonstration is ours. This is because we are dealing not with some matter of only a relative importance—a theory, a merely secular problem—but with the eternal and infinite nature of man's destiny, which demands action. Thirty years earlier,[1] Newman had said bluntly and aphoristically, "Religion is for practice, and that immediate."

This is not the place to enter fully into Newman's complex and subtle argument. It is enough to say that the *Grammar of Assent*, seeking empirically to show how men do actually arrive at assents, is an elaborate study of the mental operations underlying apprehension, inference (whether "formal," "informal," or "natural"), assent, certitude; also of the contrast between inference and assent, and the difference between "real" and "notional" assent or apprehension. All this is skillfully illustrated by numerous examples, drawn from literature and life, and touched with poetic beauty, or delicate humor, or Newman's own peculiar quiet irony. Sometimes the illustrations become fascinating digressions which make the book worth reading aside from its intellectual, argumentative content. In fact there are two ways in which readers may approach the *Grammar*, though both ways may be employed simultaneously, with, of course, the most satisfying results. One way is to begin with the first chapter and read doggedly through the book, following Newman's sinuous argument as well as one can, and enjoying the illustrations both for their function in the argument and for their own sakes. This is the way of the scholar or special student, who will *read* the book as a book,

[1] In "Private Judgment," *Essays Critical and Historical* (1872), II, 353.

rethinking Newman's thoughts as they appear on the page. The other way is to skim through the various chapters, catching a general view of his argument, but lingering over certain passages which, by their imaginative and literary quality, lift the book above the level of the usual treatise of its kind. I refer, for example, to the long quotation from Newman's "Tamworth Reading-Room" articles; to the definition of God in section 1 of chapter v, to the treatment of conscience in the same section; to the passage on the pleasure of research in the second section of chapter vi; to the definition of the nature of a religion in section 5 of chapter vii, and to the passage on the transmutations of three Protestants (who become, respectively, a Catholic, a Unitarian, and an atheist) in the same section; to Newman's discussion of logic, and his application of it to the textual problems of Falstaff's death in "Henry V," in subsection 1 of section 1 of chapter viii; to the discussion of the "illative sense" in chapter ix; to the superb summary of the tenets of a worldly or "civilized" religion in subsection 1 in section 2 of chapter x.

Newman composed the *Grammar of Assent* with considerable misgivings. For one thing, he was keenly conscious of his ignorance of the vast literature of metaphysics; for another, he had a "haunting fear," as Ward tells us, "of the men who knew much and understood little," and also a fear of those Catholics by whom "every word I publish will be malevolently scrutinized, and every expression which can possibly be perverted sent straight to Rome. . . . I shall be fighting *under the lash.*" [1] In spite of many a bad half-hour, when he felt that he should never have attempted so formidable a task at his advanced age, he labored on at Rednal, away from the smoke and stir of Birmingham. The book was ready in February of 1870. A specimen bound copy was sent to Newman on February 21—his sixty-ninth birthday. The *Grammar of Assent* met with prompt criticism. Both Leslie Stephen and Fitz-James

[1] Ward, *Life,* II, 252.

Stephen attacked it in *Fraser's Magazine;* and by the end of
the year, Father Harper published an elaborate attack in the
Month. Yet the book had a wide circulation and made Newman deeply happy. He could look back over the hard labor it
had been for him, and say: "Oh! what a toil it has been to me
—for three years—how many times I have written it...for I
never was so ignorant before, of the practical good and use
of anything I have written....I have at times been quite
frightened lest the labor of thought might inflict on me some
terrible retribution at my age. It is my last work." [1] He was in
fact mistaken in these latter remarks. After bringing out six
volumes of his various essays, sketches, and arguments (pre-
viously printed in periodicals), he was destined in 1875 to
write indeed his "last work," the *Letter to the Duke of Norfolk,*
in which he was to show that almost to the very end he remained an agile and formidable controversialist.

[1] *Op. cit.,* II, 266.

—C. F. H.

A SELECT BIBLIOGRAPHY

BIOGRAPHY:

Newman, Bertram. *Cardinal Newman: a Biographical and Literary Study.* New York: Century, 1925. Chap. ix.

Ross, J. E. *John Henry Newman: Anglican Minister, Catholic Priest, Roman Cardinal.* New York: Norton, 1933. Chap. vii.

Ward, Wilfrid. *Life of John Henry Cardinal Newman.* 2 vols. London: Longmans, Green, 1912. Vol. II, chap. xxviii.

CRITICISM:

Bonnegent, C. *La théorie de la certitude dans Newman.* Paris, 1920.

Bremond, Henri, *The Mystery of Newman,* translated from the French by H. C. Corrance. London: Williams & Norgate, 1907. Conclusion.

Cronin, J. F. *Cardinal Newman: His Theory of Knowledge.* Washington, D. C.: Catholic University of America, 1935.

D'Arcy, M. C. *The Nature of Belief.* London: Sheed and Ward, 1931. Chaps. iv, v, vi.

Harrold, C. F. *John Henry Newman: an Expository and Critical Study of His Mind, Thought and Art.* New York: Longmans, Green, 1945. Chap. vi.

Juergens, S. P. *Newman on the Psychology of Faith in the Individual.* New York: Macmillan, 1928.

SHORT CRITICAL WORKS:

Bacchus, F. "How To Read the Grammar of Assent." *The Month,* February 1924, pp. 106-15.

Barry, W. "Catholicism and Reason," *Contemporary Review,* XLVIII (1885), 656-75. (See A. M. Fairbairn's *Catholicism: Roman and Anglican,* New York, Scribner's, 1899.)

Baudin, E. "La philosophie de la foi chez Newman," *La revue de philosophie,* VIII (1906), 571-98; IX (1906), 20-55, 253-85, 373-90.

Brickel, A. G. "Newman's Theory of Knowledge," *American Catholic Quarterly Review,* XLIII (1918), 507-18.

Farges, A. *La crise de la certitude.* Paris: 1907. Pages on *Newmanisme.*

Harper, T. "Dr. Newman's Essay in Aid of a Grammar of Assent," *The Month,* XII (1870), 599-611, 667-92.

MacRae, A. *Die religiöse Gewissheit bei J. H. Newman.* Jena: 1898.

Stephen, Leslie. "Newman's Theory of Belief," *An Agnostic's Apology.* London: Smith and Elder, 1893.

Toohey, J. J. "The Grammar of Assent and the Old Philosophy," *Irish Theological Quarterly,* October 1907, pp. 466-84.

Ward, Wilfrid. "Newman's Philosophy," *Last Lectures.* London: Longmans, Green, 1918.

PART I

ASSENT AND APPREHENSION

CHAPTER I

MODES OF HOLDING AND APPREHENDING PROPOSITIONS

I

MODES OF HOLDING PROPOSITIONS

1. PROPOSITIONS (consisting of a subject and predicate united by the copula) may take a categorical, conditional, or interrogative form.

(1) An interrogative, when they ask a Question, (e.g. Does Free-trade benefit the poorer classes?) and imply. the possibility of an affirmative or negative resolution of it.

(2) A conditional, when they express a Conclusion (e.g. Free-trade therefore benefits the poorer classes), and at once imply, and imply their dependence on, other propositions.

(3) A categorical, when they simply make an Assertion (e.g. Free-trade does benefit), and imply the absence of any condition or reservation of any kind, looking neither before nor behind, as resting in themselves and being intrinsically complete.

These three modes of shaping a proposition, distinct as they are from each other, follow each other in natural sequence. A proposition, which starts with being a Question, may become a Conclusion, and then be changed into an Assertion; but it has of course ceased to be a question, so far forth as it has become a conclusion, and has rid itself of its argumentative form—that is, has ceased to be a conclusion,—so far forth as it has become an assertion. A question has not yet got so far as to be a conclusion, though it is the necessary preliminary of a conclusion;

and an assertion has got beyond being a mere conclusion, though it is the natural issue of a conclusion. Their correlation is the measure of their distinction one from another.

No one is likely to deny that a question is distinct both from a conclusion and from an assertion; and an assertion will be found to be equally distinct from a conclusion. For, if we rest our affirmation on arguments, this shows that we are not asserting; and, when we assert, we do not argue. An assertion is as distinct from a conclusion, as a word of command is from a persuasion or recommendation. Command and assertion, as such, both of them, in their different ways, dispense with, discard, ignore antecedents of any kind, though antecedents may have been a *sine qua non* condition of their being elicited. They both carry with them the pretension of being personal acts.

In insisting on the intrinsic distinctness of these three modes of putting a proposition, I am not maintaining that they may not co-exist as regards one and the same subject. For what we have already concluded, we may, if we will, make a question of; and what we are asserting, we may of course conclude over again. We may assert to one man, and conclude to another, and ask of a third; still, when we assert, we do not conclude, and, when we assert or conclude, we do not question.

2. The internal act of holding propositions is for the most part analogous to the external act of enunciating them; as there are three ways of enunciating, so are there three ways of holding them, each corresponding to each. These three mental acts are Doubt, Inference, and Assent. A question is the expression of a doubt; a conclusion is the expression of an act of inference; and an assertion is the expression of an act of assent. To doubt, for instance, is not to see one's way to hold that Free-trade is or that it is not a benefit; to infer, is to hold on sufficient grounds that Free-trade may, must, or should be a

benefit; to assent to the proposition, is to hold that Free-trade is a benefit.

Moreover, propositions, while they are the material of these three enunciations, are also the objects of the three corresponding mental acts; and as without a proposition there cannot be a question, conclusion, or assertion, so without a proposition there is nothing to doubt about, nothing to infer, nothing to assent to. Mental acts of whatever kind presuppose their objects.

And, since the three enunciations are distinct from each other, therefore the three mental acts also, Doubt, Inference, and Assent, are, with reference to one and the same proposition, distinct from each other; else, why should their several enunciations be distinct? And indeed it is very evident, that, so far forth as we infer, we do not doubt, and that, when we assent, we are not inferring, and, when we doubt, we cannot assent.

And in fact, these three modes of entertaining propositions, —doubting them, inferring them, assenting to them, are so distinct in their action, that, when they are severally carried out into the intellectual habits of an individual, they become the principles and notes of three distinct states or characters of mind. For instance, in the case of Revealed Religion, according as one or other of these is paramount within him, a man is a sceptic as regards it; or a philosopher, thinking it more or less probable considered as a conclusion of reason; or he has an unhesitating faith in it, and is recognized as a believer. If he simply disbelieves, or dissents, then he is assenting to the contradictory of the thesis, viz. to the proposition that there is no Revelation.

Many minds of course there are, which are not under the predominant influence of any one of the three. Thus men are to be found of irreflective, impulsive, unsettled, or again of acute minds, who do not know what they believe and what they do not, and who may be by turns sceptics, inquirers, or believers; who doubt, assent, infer, and doubt again, according to the circumstances of the season. Nay further, in all minds there is a certain co-existence of these distinct acts; that is, of two of them, for we can at once infer and assent, though we cannot at once either assent or infer and also doubt. Indeed, in a multitude of cases we infer truths, or apparent truths, before, and while, and after we assent to them.

Lastly, it cannot be denied that these three acts are all natural to the mind; I mean, that, in exercising them, we are not violating the laws of our nature, as if they were in themselves an extravagance or weakness, but are acting according to it, according to its legitimate constitution. Undoubtedly, it is possible, it is common, in the particular case, to err in the exercise of Doubt, of Inference, and of Assent; that is, we may be withholding a judgment about propositions on which we have the means of coming to some conclusion; or we may be assenting to propositions which we ought to receive only on the credit of their premisses, or again to keep ourselves in suspense about; but such errors of the individual belong to the individual, not to his nature, and cannot avail to forfeit for him his natural right, under proper circumstances, to doubt, or to infer, or to assent. We do but fulfil our nature in doubting, inferring, and assenting; and our duty is, not to abstain from the exercise of any function of our nature, but to do what is in itself right rightly.

3. So far in general:—in this Essay I treat of propositions only in their bearing upon concrete matter, and I am mainly concerned with Assent; with Inference, in its relation to Assent, and only such inference as is not demonstration; with Doubt hardly at all. I dismiss Doubt with one observation. I have here spoken of it simply as a suspense of mind, in which sense of the word, to have "no doubt" about a thesis is equivalent to one or other of the two remaining acts, either to inferring it or else assenting to it. However, the word is often taken to

mean the deliberate recognition of a thesis as being uncertain; in this sense Doubt is nothing else than an assent, viz. an assent to a proposition inconsistent with the thesis, as I have already noticed in the case of Disbelief.

Confining myself to the subject of Assent and Inference, I observe two points of contrast between them.

The first I have already noted. Assent is unconditional; else, it is not really represented by assertion. Inference is conditional, because a conclusion at least implies the assumption of premisses, and still more, because in concrete matter, on which I am engaged, demonstration is impossible.

The second has regard to the apprehension necessary for holding a proposition. We cannot assent to a proposition, without some intelligent apprehension of it; whereas we need not understand it at all in order to infer it. We cannot give our assent to the proposition that "x is z," till we are told something about one or other of the terms; but we can infer, if "x is y, and y is z, that x is z," whether we know the meaning of x and z or no.

These points of contrast and their results will come before us in due course: here, for a time leaving the consideration of the modes of holding propositions, I proceed to inquire into what is to be understood by apprehending them.

2

MODES OF APPREHENDING PROPOSITIONS

BY OUR APPREHENSION of propositions I mean our imposition of a sense on the terms of which they are composed. Now what do the terms of a proposition, the subject and predicate, stand for? Sometimes they stand for certain ideas existing in our own minds, and for nothing outside of them; sometimes for things simply external to us, brought home to us through the experiences and informations we have of them. All things in the exterior world are unit and individual, and are nothing else; but the mind not only contemplates those unit realities, as they exist, but has the gift, by an act of creation, of bringing before it abstractions and generalizations, which have no existence, no counterpart, out of it.

Now there are propositions, in which one or both of the terms are common nouns, as standing for what is abstract, general, and non-existing, such as "Man is an animal, some men are learned, an Apostle is a creation of Christianity, a line is length without breadth, to err is human, to forgive divine." These I shall call notional propositions, and the apprehension with which we infer or assent to them, notional.

And there are other propositions, which are composed of singular nouns, and of which the terms stand for things external to us, unit and individual, as "Philip was the father of Alexander," "the earth goes round the sun," "the Apostles first preached to the Jews;" and these I shall call real propositions, and their apprehension real.

There are then two kinds of apprehension or interpretation to which propositions may be subjected, notional and real.

Next I observe, that the same proposition may admit of both of these interpretations at once, having a notional sense as used by one man, and a real as used by another. Thus a schoolboy may perfectly apprehend, and construe with spirit, the poet's words, "Dum Capitolium scandet cum tacitâ Virgine Pontifex;" he has seen steep hills, flights of steps and processions; he knows what enforced silence is; also he knows all about the Pontifex Maximus, and the Vestal Virgins; he has an abstract hold upon every word of the description, yet without the words therefore bringing before him at all the living image which they would light up in the mind of a contemporary of the poet, who had seen the fact described, or of a modern historian who had duly informed himself in the religious phenomena, and by meditation had realized the Roman ceremonial, of the age of Augustus. Again, "Dulce et decorum est pro patriâ mori," is a mere commonplace, a terse expression of abstractions in the mind of the poet himself, if Philippi is to be the index of his patriotism, whereas it would be the record of experiences, a sovereign dogma, a grand aspiration, inflaming the imagination, piercing the heart, of a Wallace or a Tell.

As the multitude of common nouns have originally been singular, it is not surprising that many of them should so remain still in the apprehension of particular individuals. In the proposition "Sugar is sweet," the predicate is a common noun as used by those who have compared sugar in their thoughts with honey or glycerine; but it may be the only distinctively sweet thing in the experience of a child, and may be used by him as a noun singular. The first time that he tastes sugar, if his nurse says, "Sugar is sweet" in a notional sense, meaning by sugar, lump-sugar, powdered, brown, and candied, and by sweet, a specific flavour or scent which is found in many articles of food and many flowers, he may answer in a real sense, and in an individual proposition, "Sugar is sweet," meaning "this sugar is this sweet thing."

Thirdly, in the same mind and at the same time, the same proposition may express both what is notional and what is real. When a lecturer in mechanics or chemistry shows to his class by experiment some physical fact, he and his hearers at once enunciate it as an individual thing before their eyes, and also as generalized by their minds into a law of nature. When Virgil says, "Varium et mutabile semper fœmina," he both sets before his readers what he means to be a general truth, and at the same time applies it individually to the instance of Dido. He expresses at once a notion and a fact.

Of these two modes of apprehending propositions, notional and real, real is the stronger; I mean by stronger the more vivid and forcible. It is so to be accounted for the very reason that it is concerned with what is either real or is taken for real; for intellectual ideas cannot compete in effectiveness with the experience of concrete facts. Various proverbs and maxims sanction me in so speaking, such as "Facts are stubborn things," "Experientia docet," "Seeing is believing;" and the popular contrast between theory and practice, reason and sight, philosophy and faith. Not that real apprehension, as such, impels to action, any more than notional; but it excites and stimulates the affections and passions, by bringing facts home to them as motive causes. Thus it indirectly brings about what the apprehension of large principles, of general laws, or of moral obligations, never could effect.

Reverting to the two modes of holding propositions, conditional and unconditional, which was the subject of the former Section, that is, inferences and assents, I observe that inferences, which are conditional acts, are especially cognate to notional apprehension, and assents, which are unconditional, to real. This distinction, too, will come before us in the course of the following chapters.

And now I have stated the main subjects of which I propose to treat; viz. the distinctions in the use of propositions, which I have been drawing out, and the questions which those distinctions involve.

CHAPTER II

ASSENT CONSIDERED AS APPREHENSIVE

I HAVE ALREADY SAID of an act of Assent, first, that it is in itself the absolute acceptance of a proposition without any condition; and next that in order to its being made, it presupposes the condition, not only of some previous inference in favour of the proposition, but especially of some concomitant apprehension of its terms. I proceed to the latter of these two subjects; that is, of Assent considered as apprehensive, leaving the discussion of Assent as unconditional for a later place in this Essay.

By apprehension of a proposition, I mean, as I have already said, the interpretation of the terms of which it is composed. When we infer, we consider a proposition in relation to other propositions; when we assent to it, we consider it for its own sake and in its intrinsic sense. That sense must be in some degree known to us; else, we do but assert the proposition, we in no wise assent to it. Assent I have described to be a mental assertion; in its very nature then it is of the mind, and not of the lips. We can assert without assenting; assent is more than assertion just by this much, that it is accompanied by some apprehension of the matter asserted. This is plain; and the only question is, what measure of apprehension is sufficient.

And the answer to this question is equally plain:—it is the predicate of the proposition which must be apprehended. In a proposition one term is predicated of another; the subject is referred to the predicate, and the predicate gives us information about the subject;—therefore to apprehend the proposition is to have that information, and to assent to it is to acquiesce in it as true. Therefore I apprehend a proposition, when I apprehend its predicate. The subject itself need not be apprehended *per se* in order to a genuine assent: for it is the very thing which the predicate has to elucidate, and therefore by its formal place in the proposition, so far as it is the subject, it is something unknown, something which the predicate makes known; but the predicate cannot make it known, unless it is known itself. Let the question be, "What is Trade?" here is a distinct profession of ignorance about "Trade;" and let the answer be, "Trade is the interchange of goods;"—trade then need not be known, as a condition of assent to the proposition, except so far as the account of it which is given in answer, "the interchange of goods," makes it known; and that must be apprehended in order to make it known. The very drift of the proposition is to tell us something about the subject; but there is no reason why our knowledge of the subject, whatever it is, should go beyond what the predicate tells us about it. Further than this the subject need not be apprehended: as far as this it must; it will not be apprehended thus far, unless we apprehend the predicate.

If a child asks, "What is lucern?" and is answered, "Lucern is medicago sativa, of the class Diadelphia and order Decandria;" and henceforth says obediently, "Lucern is medicago sativa," &c., he makes no act of assent to the proposition which he enunciates, but speaks like a parrot. But if he is told, "Lucern is food for cattle," and is shown cows grazing in a meadow, then, though he never saw lucern, and knows nothing at all about it, besides what he has learned from the predicate, he is in a position to make as genuine an assent to the proposition "Lucern is food for cattle," on the word of his informant, as if he knew ever so much more about lucern. And as soon as he has got as far as this, he may go further. He now knows enough about lucern, to enable him to apprehend propositions which have lucern for their predicate, should they come before him for assent, as, "That field is sown with lucern," or "Clover is not lucern."

Yet there is a way, in which the child can give an indirect assent even to a proposition, in which he understood neither subject nor predicate. He cannot indeed in that case assent to the proposition itself, but he can assent to its truth. He cannot do more than assert that "Lucern is medicago sativa," but he can assent to the proposition, "That lucern is medicago sativa is true." For here is a predicate which he sufficiently apprehends, what is inapprehensible in the proposition being confined to the subject. Thus the child's mother might teach him to repeat a passage of Shakespeare, and when he asked the meaning of a particular line, such as "The quality of mercy is not strained," or "Virtue itself turns vice, being misapplied," she might answer him, that he was too young to understand it yet, but that it had a beautiful meaning, as he would one day know: and he, in faith on her word, might give his assent to such a proposition,—not, that is, to the line itself which he had got by heart, and which would be beyond him, but to its being true, beautiful, and good.

Of course I am speaking of assent itself, and its intrinsic conditions, not of the ground or motive of it. Whether there is an obligation upon the child to trust his mother, or whether there are cases where such trust is impossible, are irrelevent questions, and I notice them in order to put them aside. I am examining the act of assent itself, not its preliminaries, and I have specified three directions, which among others the assent may take, viz. assent immediately to a proposition itself, assent to its truth, and assent both to its truth and to the ground of its being true,—"Lucern is food for cattle,"—"That lucern is medicago sativa is true,"—"My mother's word, that lucern is medicago sativa, and is food for cattle, is the truth." Now in each of these there is one and the same absolute adhesion of the mind to the proposition, on the part of the child;

he assents to the apprehensible proposition, and to the truth of the inapprehensible, and to the veracity of his mother in her assertion of the inapprehensible. I say the same absolute adhesion, because, unless he did assent without any reserve to the proposition that lucern was food for cattle, or to the accuracy of the botanical name and description of it, he would not be giving an unreserved assent to his mother's word: yet, though these assents are all unreserved, still they certainly differ in strength, and this is the next point to which I wish to draw attention. It is indeed plain, that, though the child assents to his mother's veracity, without perhaps being conscious of his own act, nevertheless that particular assent of his has a force and life in it which the other assents have not, insomuch as he apprehends the proposition, which is the subject of it, with greater keenness and energy than belongs to his apprehension of the others. Her veracity and authority is to him no abstract truth or item of general knowledge, but is bound up with that image and love of her person which is part of himself, and makes a direct claim on him for his summary assent to her general teachings.

Accordingly, by reason of this circumstance of his apprehension, he would not hesitate to say, did his years admit of it, that he would lay down his life in defence of his mother's veracity. On the other hand, he would not make such a profession in the case of the propositions, "Lucern is food for cattle," or "That lucern is medicago sativa is true;" and yet it is clear too, that, if he did in truth assent to these propositions, he would have to die for them also, rather than deny them, when it came to the point, unless he made up his mind to tell a falsehood. That he would have to die for all three propositions severally rather than deny them, shows the completeness and absoluteness of assent in its very nature; that he would not spontaneously challenge so severe a trial in the case of two out of the three particular acts of assent, illustrates in what sense one assent may be stronger than another.

It appears then, that, in assenting to proposition, an apprehension in some sense of their terms is not only necessary to assent, as such, but also gives a distinct character to its acts. If therefore we would know more about Assent, we must know more about the apprehension which accompanies it. Accordingly, to the subject of Apprehension I proceed.

CHAPTER III

THE APPREHENSION OF PROPOSITIONS

I HAVE SAID in these Introductory Chapters that there can be no assent to a proposition, without some sort of apprehension of its terms; next that there are two modes of apprehension, notional and real; thirdly, that, while assent may be given to a proposition on either apprehension of it, still its acts are elicited more heartily and forcibly, when they are made upon real apprehension which has things for its objects, than when they are made in favour of notions and with a notional apprehension. The first of these three points I have just been discussing; now I will proceed to the second, viz. the two modes of apprehending propositions, leaving the third for the Chapters which follow.

I have used the word *apprehension,* and not *understanding,* because the latter word is of uncertain meaning, standing sometimes for the faculty or act of conceiving a proposition, sometimes for that of comprehending it, neither of which come into the sense of *apprehension.* It is possible to apprehend without understanding. I apprehend what is meant by saying that John is Richard's wife's father's aunt's husband, but, if I am unable so to take in these successive relationships as to understand the upshot of the whole, viz. that John is great-uncle-in-law to Richard, I cannot be said to understand the proposition. In like manner, I may take a just view of a man's conduct, and therefore apprehend it, and yet may profess that I cannot understand it; that is, I have not the key to it, and do not see its consistency in detail: I have no just conception of it. Apprehension then is simply an intelligent acceptance of the idea or of the fact which a proposition enunciates. "Pride will have a fall;" "Napoleon died at St. Helena;" I have no difficulty in entering into the sentiment contained in the former of these, or into the fact declared in the latter; that is, I apprehend them both.

Now apprehension, as I have said, has two subject matters: according as language expresses things external to us, or our own thoughts, so is apprehension real or notional. It is notional in the grammarian, it is real in the experimentalist. The grammarian has to determine the force of words and phrases; he has to master the structure of sentences and the composition of paragraphs; he has to compare language with language, to ascertain the common ideas expressed under different idiomatic forms, and to achieve the difficult work of recasting the mind of the original author in the mould of a translation. On the other hand, the philosopher or experimentalist aims at investigating, questioning, ascertaining facts, causes, effects, actions, qualities: these are things, and he makes his words distinctly subordinate to these, as means to an end. The primary duty of a literary man is to have clear conceptions, and to be exact and intelligible in expressing them; but in a philosopher it is a merit even to be not altogether vague, inchoate, and obscure in his teaching, and if he fails even of this low standard of language, we remind ourselves that his obscurity perhaps is owing to his depth. No power of words in a lecturer would be sufficient to make psychology easy to his hearers; if they are to profit by him, they must throw their minds into the matters in discussion, must accompany his treatment of them with an active, personal concurrence, and interpret for themselves, as he proceeds, the dim suggestions and adumbrations of objects, which he has a right to presuppose, while he uses them, as images existing in their apprehension as well as in his own.

In something of a parallel way it is the least pardonable fault in an Orator to fail in clearness of style, and the most pardonable fault of a Poet.

So again, an Economist is dealing with facts; whatever there is of theory in his work professes to be founded on facts, by facts alone must his sense be interpreted, and to those only who are well furnished with the necessary facts does he address himself; yet a clever schoolboy, from a thorough grammatical knowledge of both languages, might turn into English a French treatise on national wealth, produce, consumption, labour, profits, measures of value, public debt, and the circulating medium, with an apprehension of what it was that his author was stating sufficient for making it clear to an English reader, while he had not the faintest conception himself what the treatise, which he was translating, really determined. The man uses language as the vehicle of things, and the boy of abstractions.

Hence in literary examinations, it is a test of good scholarship to be able to construe aright, without the aid of understanding the sentiment, action, or historical occurrence conveyed in the passage thus accurately rendered, let it be a battle in Livy, or some subtle train of thought in Virgil or Pindar. And those who have acquitted themselves best in the trial, will often be disposed to think they have most notably failed, for the very reason that they have been too busy with the grammar of each sentence, as it came, to have been able, as they construed on, to enter into the facts or the feelings, which, unknown to themselves, they were bringing out of it.

To take a very different instance of this contrast between notions and facts;—pathology and medicine, in the interests of science, and as a protection to the practitioner, veil the shocking realities of disease and physical suffering under a notional phraseology, under the abstract terms of debility, distress, irritability, paroxysm, and a host of Greek and Latin words. The arts of medicine and surgery are necessarily experimental; but for writing and conversing on these subjects they require to be stripped of the association of the facts from which they are derived.

Such are the two modes of apprehension. The terms of a proposition do or do not stand for things. If they do, then they are singular terms, for all things that are, are units. But if they do not stand for things they must stand for notions, and are common terms. Singular nouns come from experience, common from abstraction. The apprehension of the former I call real, and of the latter notional. Now let us look at this difference between them more narrowly.

1. Real Apprehension is, as I have said, in the first instance an experience or information about the concrete. Now, when these informations are in fact presented to us, (that is, when they are directly subjected to our bodily senses or our mental sensations, as when we say, "The sun shines," or "The prospect is charming," or indirectly by means of a picture or even a narrative,) then there is no difficulty in determining what is meant by saying that our enunciation of a proposition concerning them implies an apprehension of things, because we can actually point out the objects which they indicate. But supposing those things are no longer before us, supposing they have passed beyond our field of view, or the book is closed in which the description of them occurs, how can an apprehension of things be said to remain to us? Yes, it remains on our minds by means of the faculty of memory. Memory consists in a present imagination of things that are past; memory retains the impressions and likenesses of what they were when before us; and when we make use of the proposition which refers to them, it supplies us with objects by which to interpret it. They are things still, as being the reflections of things in a mental mirror.

Hence the poet calls memory "the mind's eye." I am in a foreign country among unfamiliar sights; at will I am able to conjure up before me the vision of my home, and all that belongs to it, its rooms and their furniture, its books, its inmates, their countenances, looks, and movements. I see those who once were there and are no more; past scenes, and the very expression of the features, and the tones of the voices, of those who took part in them, in a time of trial or difficulty. I create nothing; I see the facsimiles of facts; and of these facsimiles the words and propositions which I use concerning them are from habitual association the proper or the sole expression.

And so again, I may have seen a celebrated painting, or some great pageant, or some public man; and I have on my memory stored up and ready at hand, but latent, an impress more or less distinct of that experience. The words "the Madonna di S. Sisto," or "the last Coronation," or "the Duke of Welling-ton," have power to revive that impress of it. Memory has to do with individual things and nothing that is not individual. And my apprehension of its notices is conveyed in a collection of singular and real propositions.

I have hitherto been adducing instances from (for the most part) objects of sight; but the memory preserves the impress, though not so vivid, of the experiences which come to us through our other senses also. The memory of a beautiful air, or the scent of a particular flower, as far as any remembrance remains of it, is the continued presence in our minds of a like-ness of it, which its actual presence has left there. I can bring before me the music of the *Adeste Fideles*, as if I were actually hearing it; and the scent of a clematis as if I were in my garden; and the flavour of a peach as if it were in season; and the thought I have of all these is as of something indivi-dual and from without,—as much as the things themselves, the tune, the scent, and the flavour, are from without,—though, compared with the things themselves, these images (as they may be called) are faint and intermitting.

Nor need such an image be in any sense an abstraction; though I may have eaten a hundred peaches in times past, the impression, which remains on my memory of the flavour, may be of any of them, of the ten, twenty, thirty units, as the case may be, not a general notion, distinct from every one of them, and formed from all of them by a fabrication of my mind.

And so again the apprehension which we have of our past

mental acts of any kind, of hope, inquiry, effort, triumph, disappointment, suspicion, hatred, and a hundred others, is an apprehension of the memory of those definite acts, and therefore an apprehension of things; not to say that many of them do not need memory, but are such as admit of being actually summoned and repeated at our will. Such an apprehension again is elicited by propositions embodying the notices of our history, of our pursuits and their results, of our friends, of our bereavements, of our illnesses, of our fortunes, which remain imprinted upon our memory as sharply and deeply as is any recollection of sight. Nay, and such recollections may have in them an individuality and completeness which outlives the impressions made by sensible objects. The memory of countenances and of places in times past may fade away from the mind; but the vivid image of certain anxieties or deliverances never.

And by means of these particular and personal experiences, thus impressed upon us, we attain an apprehension of what such things are at other times when we have not experience of them; an apprehension of sights and sounds, of colours and forms, of places and persons, of mental acts and states, parallel to our actual experiences, such, that, when we meet with definite propositions expressive of them, our apprehension cannot be called abstract and notional. If I am told "there is a raging fire in London," or "London is on fire," "fire" need not be a common noun in my apprehension more than "London." The word may recall to my memory the experience of a fire which I have known elsewhere, or of some vivid description which I have read. It is of course difficult to draw the line and to say where the office of memory ends, and where abstraction takes its place; and again, as I said in my first pages, the same proposition is to one man an image, to another a notion; but still there is a host of predicates, of the most various kinds, "lovely," "vulgar," "a conceited man," "a manufacturing town," "a catastrophe," and any number of others, which, though as predicates they would be accounted common nouns, are in fact in the mouths of particular persons singular, as conveying images of things individual, as the rustic in Virgil says,—

> Urbem, quam dicunt Romam, Meliboee, putavi,
> Stultus ego, huic nostrae similem.

And so the child's idea of a king, as derived from his picture-book, will be that of a fierce or stern or venerable man, seated above a flight of steps, with a crown on his head and a sceptre in his hand. In these two instances indeed the experience does but mislead, when applied to the unknown; but it often happens on the contrary, that it is a serviceable help, especially when a man has large experiences and has learned to distinguish between them and apply them duly, as in the instance of the hero "who knew many cities of men and many minds."

Further, we are able by an inventive faculty, or, as I may call it, the faculty of composition, to follow the descriptions of things which have never come before us, and to form, out of such passive impressions as experience has heretofor left on our minds, new images, which, though mental creations, are in no sense abstractions, and though ideal, are not notional. They are concrete units in the minds both of the party describing and the party informed of them. Thus I may never have seen a palm or a banana, but I have conversed with those who have, or I have read graphic accounts of it, and, from my own previous knowledge of other trees, have been able with so ready an intelligence to interpret their language, and to light up such an image of it in my thoughts, that, were it not that I never was in the countries where the tree is found, I should fancy that I had actually seen it. Hence again it is the very praise we give to the characters of some great poet or historian that he is so individual. I am able as it were to gaze on Tiberius, as Tacitus draws him, and to figure to myself our James the First, as he is painted in Scott's Romance. The assassination of Cæsar, his "Et tu, Brute?" his collecting his robes about him, and his fall under Pompey's statue, all this becomes a fact to me and an object of real apprehension. Thus it is that we live in the past and in the distant; by means of our capacity of interpreting the statements of others about former ages or foreign climes by the lights of our own experience. The picture, which historians are able to bring before us, of Cæsar's death, derives its vividness and effect from its virtual appeal to the various images of our memory.

This faculty of composition is of course a step beyond experience, but we have now reached its furthest point; it is mainly limited as regards its materials, by the sense of sight. As regards the other senses, new images cannot well be elicited and shaped out of old experiences. No description, however complete, could convey to my mind an exact likeness of a tune or an harmony, which I have never heard; and still less of a scent, which I have never smelt. Generic resemblances and metaphorical substitutes are indeed producible; but I should not acquire any real knowledge of the Scotch air "There's nae luck" by being told it was like "Auld lang syne," or "Robin Gray;" and if I said that Mozart's melodies were as a summer's sky or as the breath of Zephyr, I should be better understood by those who knew Mozart than by those who did not. Such vague illustrations suggest intellectual notions, not images.

And quite as difficult is it to create or to apprehend by description images of mental facts, of which we have no direct experience. I may indeed, as I have already said, bring home to my mind so complex a fact as an historical character, by composition out of my experiences about character generally; Tiberius, James the First, Louis the Eleventh, or Napoleon; but who is able to infuse into me, or how shall I imbibe, a sense of the peculiarities of the style of Cicero or Virgil, if I have not read their writings? or how shall I gain a shadow of a perception of the wit or the grace ascribed to the conversation of the French salons, being myself an untravelled John Bull? And so again, as regards the affections and passions of our nature, they are *sui generis* respectively, and incommensurable, and must be severally experienced in order to be apprehended really. I can understand the *rabbia* of a native of Southern Europe, if I am of a passionate temper myself; and the taste for speculation or betting found in great traders or on the turf, if I am fond of enterprise or games of chance; but on the other hand, not all the possible descriptions of head-long love will make me comprehend the *delirium,* if I never have had a fit of it; nor will ever so many sermons about the inward satisfaction of strict conscientiousness create in my mind the image of a virtuous action and its attendant senti-ments, if I have been brought up to lie, thieve, and indulge my appetites. Thus we meet with men of the world who can-not enter into the very idea of devotion, and think, for instance, that, from the nature of the case, a life of religious seclusion must be either one of unutterable dreariness or abandoned sensuality, because they know of no exercise of the affections but what is merely human; and with others again, who, living in the home of their own selfishness, ridicule as something fanatical and pitiable the self-sacrifices of generous high-mindedness and chivalrous honour. They cannot create images of these things, any more than children on the contrary can of vice, when they ask whereabouts and who the bad men are; for they have no personal memories, and have to content themselves with notions drawn from books or from what others tell them.

So much on the apprehension of things and on the real in our use of language; now let us pass on to the notional sense.

2. Experience tells us only of individual things, and these things are innumerable. Our minds might have been so con-structed as to be able to receive and retain an exact image of each of these various objects, one by one, as it came before us, but only in and for itself, without the power of comparing it with any of the others. But this is not our case: on the con-trary, to compare and to contrast are among the most promi-nent and busy of our intellectual functions. Instinctively, even

though unconsciously, we are ever instituting comparisons between the manifold phenomena of the external world, as we meet with them, criticizing, referring to a standard, collecting, analyzing them. Nay, as if by one and the same action, as soon as we perceive them, we also perceive that they are like each other or unlike, or rather both like and unlike at once. We apprehend spontaneously, even before we set about apprehending, that man is like man, yet unlike; and unlike a horse, a tree, a mountain, or a monument, yet in some, though not the same respects, like each of them. And in consequence, as I have said, we are ever grouping and discriminating, measuring and sounding, framing cross classes and cross divisions, and thereby rising from particulars to generals, that is from images to notions.

In processes of this kind we regard things, not as they are in themselves, but mainly as they stand in relation to each other. We look at nothing simply for its own sake; we cannot look at any one thing without keeping our eyes on a multitude of other things besides. "Man" is no longer what he really is, an individual presented to us by our senses, but as we read him in the light of those comparisons and contrasts which we have made him suggest to us. He is attenuated into an aspect, or relegated to his place in a classification. Thus his appellation is made to suggest, not the real being which he is in this or that specimen of himself, but a definition. If I might use a harsh metaphor, I should say he is made the logarithm of his true self, and in that shape is worked with the ease and satisfaction of logarithms.

It is plain what a different sense language will bear in this system of intellectual notions from what it has when it is the representative of things: and such a use of it is not only the very foundation of all science, but may be, and is, carried out in literature and in the ordinary intercourse of man with man. And thus it comes to pass that individual propositions about the concrete almost cease to be, and are diluted or starved into abstract notions. The events of history and the characters who figure in it lose their individuality. States and governments, society and its component parts, cities, nations, even the physical face of the country, things past, and things contemporary, all that fulness of meaning which I have described as accruing to language from experience, now that experience is absent, necessarily becomes to the multitude of men nothing but a heap of notions, little more intelligible than the beauties of a prospect to the short-sighted, or the music of a great master to a listener who has no ear.

I suppose most men will recollect in their past years how many mistakes they have made about persons, parties, local occurrences, nations, and the like, of which at the time they had no actual knowledge of their own: how ashamed or how amused they have since been at their own gratuitous idealism when they came into possession of the real facts concerning them. They were accustomed to treat the definite Titus or Sempronius as the *quidam homo,* the *individuum vagum* of the logician. They spoke of his opinions, his motives, his practices, as their traditional rule for the *species* Titus or Sempronius enjoined. In order to find out what individual men in flesh and blood were, they fancied that they had nothing to do but to refer to commonplaces, alphabetically arranged. Thus they were well up with the character of a Whig statesman or Tory magnate, a Wesleyan, a Congregationalist, a parson, a priest, a philanthropist, a writer of controversy, a sceptic; and found themselves prepared, without the trouble of direct inquiry, to draw the individual after the peculiarities of his type. And so with national character; the late Duke of Wellington must have been impulsive, quarrelsome, witty, clever at repartee, for he was an Irishman; in like manner, we must have cold and selfish Scots, crafty Italians, vulgar Americans, and Frenchmen, half tiger, half monkey. As to the French, those who are old enough to recollect the wars with Napoleon, know what eccentric notions were popularly entertained about them in England; how it was even a surprise to find some military man, who was a prisoner of war, to be tall and stout, because it was a received idea that all Frenchmen were under-sized and lived on frogs.

Such again are the ideal personages who figure in romances and dramas of the old school; tyrants, monks, crusaders, princes in disguise, and captive damsels; or benevolent or angry fathers, and spendthrift heirs; like the symbolical characters in some of Shakespeare's plays, "a Tapster," or "a Lord Mayor," or in the stage direction "Enter two murderers."

What I have been illustrating in the case of persons, might be instanced in regard to places, transactions, physical calamities, events in history. Words which are used by an eye-witness to express things, unless he be especially eloquent or graphic, may only convey general notions. Such is, and ever must be, the popular and ordinary mode of apprehending language. On only few subjects have any of us the opportunity of realizing in our minds what we speak and hear about; and we fancy that we are doing justice to individual men and things by making them a mere *synthesis* of qualities, as if any number whatever of abstractions would, by being fused together, be equivalent to one concrete.

Here then we have two modes of thought, both using the same words, both having one origin, yet with nothing in common in their results. The informations of sense and sensation are the initial basis of both of them; but in the one we take hold of objects from within them, and in the other we view them outside of them; we perpetuate them as images in the one case, we transform them into notions in the other. And natural to us as are both processes in their first elements and in their growth, however divergent and independent in their direction, they cannot really be inconsistent with each other; yet no one from the sight of a horse or a dog would be able to anticipate its zoological definition, nor from a knowledge of its definition to draw such a picture as would direct the eye to the living specimen.

Each use of propositions has its own excellence and serviceableness, and each has its own imperfection. To apprehend notionally is to have breadth of mind, but to be shallow; to apprehend really is to be deep, but to be narrow-minded. The latter is the conservative principle of knowledge, and the former the principle of its advancement. Without the apprehension of notions we should for ever pace round one small circle of knowledge; without a firm hold upon things, we shall waste ourselves in vague speculations. However, real apprehension has the precedence, as being the scope and end and the test of notional; and the fuller is the mind's hold upon things or what it considers such, the more fertile is it in its aspect of them, and the more practical in its definitions.

Of course, as these two are not inconsistent with each other, they may co-exist in the same mind. Indeed there is no one who does not to a certain extent exercise both the one and the other. Viewed in relation to Assent, which has led to my speaking of them, they do not in any way affect the nature of Assent itself, which is in all cases absolute and unconditional; but they give it an external character corresponding respectively to their own: so much so, that at first sight it might seem as if Assent admitted of degrees, on account of the variation of vividness in these different apprehensions. As notions come of abstractions, so images come of experiences; the more fully the mind is occupied by an experience, the keener will be its assent to it, if it assents, and on the other hand, the duller will be its assent and the less operative, the more it is engaged with an abstraction; and thus a scale of assents is conceivable, either in the instance of one mind upon different subjects. or of many minds upon one subject, varying from an assent which looks like mere inference up to a belief both intense and practical,—from the acceptance which we accord to some accidental news of the day to the supernatural dogmatic faith of the Christian.

It follows to treat of Assent under this double aspect of its subject-matter,—assent to notions, and assent to things.

CHAPTER IV

NOTIONAL AND REAL ASSENT

1. I HAVE SAID that our apprehension of a proposition varies
in strength, and that it is stronger when it is concerned
with a proposition expressive to us of things than when concerned with a proposition expressive of notions; and I have
given this reason for it, viz. that what is concrete exerts a force
and makes an impression on the mind which nothing abstract
can rival. That is, I have argued that, because the object is
more powerful, therefore so is the apprehension of it.

I do not think it unfair reasoning thus to take the apprehension for its object. The mind is ever stimulated in proportion
to the cause stimulating it. Sights, for instance, sway us, as
scents do not; whether this be owing to a greater power in the
thing seen, or to a greater receptivity and expansiveness in the
sense of seeing, is a superfluous question. The strong object
would make the apprehension strong. Our sense of seeing is
able to open to its object, as our sense of smell cannot open
to its own. Its objects are able to awaken the mind, take possession of it, inspire it, act through it, with an energy and
variousness which is not found in the case of scents and their
apprehension. Since we cannot draw the line between the
object and the act, I am at liberty to say, as I have said, that,
as is the thing apprehended, so is the apprehension.

And so in like manner as regards apprehension of mental
objects. If an image derived from experience or information
is stronger than an abstraction, conception, or conclusion—if
I am more arrested by our Lord's bearing before Pilate and
Herod than by the "Justum et tenacem" &c. of the poet, more

29

arrested by His Voice saying to us "Give to him that asketh thee," than by the best arguments of the Economist against indiscriminate almsgiving, it does not matter for my present purpose whether the objects give strength to the apprehension or the apprehension gives large admittance into the mind to the object. It is in human nature to be more affected by the concrete than by the abstract; it may be the reverse with other beings. The apprehension, then, may be as fairly said to possess the force which acts upon us, as the object apprehended.

2. Real apprehension, then, may be pronounced stronger than notional, because things, which are its objects, are confessedly more impressive and effective than notions, which are the subjects of notional. Experiences and their images strike and occupy the mind, as abstractions and their combinations do not. Next, passing on to Assent, I observe that it is this variation in the mind's apprehension of an object to which it assents, and not any incompleteness in the assent itself, that leads us to speak of strong and weak assents, as if Assent itself admitted of degrees. In either mode of apprehension, be it real or be it notional, the assent preserves its essential characteristic of being unconditional. The assent of a Stoic to the "Justum et tenacem" &c. may be as genuine an assent, as absolute and entire, as little admitting of degree or variation, as distinct from an act of inference, as the assent of a Christian to the history of our Lord's Passion in the Gospel.

3. However, characteristic as it is of Assent, to be thus in its nature simply one and indivisible, and thereby essentially different from Inference, which is ever varying in strength, never quite at the same pitch in any two of its acts, still it is at the same time true that it may be difficult in fact, by external tokens, to distinguish given acts of assent from given acts of inference. Thus, whereas no one could possibly confuse the real assent of a Christian to the fact of our Lord's crucifixion, with the notional acceptance of it, as a point of history, on the part of a philosophical heathen (so removed from each

other, *toto coelo*, are the respective modes of apprehending it in the two cases, though in both the assent is in its nature one and the same), nevertheless it would be easy to mistake the Stoic's notional assent, genuine though it might be, to the moral nobleness of the just man "struggling in the storms of fate," for a mere act of inference resulting from the principles of his Stoical profession, or again for an assent merely to the inferential necessity of the nobleness of that struggle. Nothing, indeed, is more common than to praise men for their consistency to their principles, whatever those principles are, that is, to praise them on an inference, without thereby implying any assent to the principles themselves.

The cause of this resemblance between acts so distinct is obvious. Resemblance exists only in cases of notional assents; when the assent is given to notions, then indeed it is possible to hesitate in deciding whether it is assent or inference, whether the mind is merely without doubt or whether it is actually certain. And the reason is this: notional Assent seems like Inference, because the apprehension which accompanies acts of inference is notional also,—because Inference is engaged for the most part on notional propositions, both premiss and conclusion. This point, which I have implied throughout, I here distinctly record, and shall enlarge upon hereafter. Only propositions about individuals are not notional, and these are seldom the matter of inference. Thus, did the Stoic infer the fact of our Lord's death instead of assenting to it, that proposition as inferred would have been as much an abstraction to him as the "Justum et tenacem," &c.; nay further, the "Justus et tenax" was at least a notion in his mind, but "Jesus Christ" would in the schools of Athens or of Rome have stood for less, for an unknown being, the x or y of a formula. Except then in some of the cases of singular conclusions, inferences are employed on notions, unless, I say, they are employed on mere symbols; and, indeed, when they are symbolical, then are they clearest and most cogent, as I shall hereafter show. The next clearest are such as carry out the necessary results of previous classifications, and therefore may be called definitions or conclusions, as we please. For instance, having divided beings into their classes, the definition of man is inevitable.

4. We may call it then the normal state of Inference to apprehend propositions as notions:—and we may call it the normal state of Assent to apprehend propositions as things. If notional apprehension is most congenial to Inference, real apprehension will be the most natural concomitant on Assent. An act of Inference includes in its object the dependence of its thesis upon its premisses, that is, upon a relation which is an abstraction; but an act of Assent rests wholly on the thesis as its object, and the reality of the thesis is almost a condition of its unconditionality.

5. I am led on to make one remark more, and it shall be my last.

An act of assent, it seems, is the most perfect and highest of its kind, when it is exercised on propositions, which are apprehended as experiences and images, that is, which stand for things; and, on the other hand, an act of inference is the most perfect and highest of its kind, when it is exercised on propositions which are apprehended as notions, that is, which are creations of the mind. An act of Inference indeed may be made with either of these modes of apprehension; so may an act of assent; but, when inferences are exercised on things, they tend to be conjectures or presentiments, without logical force; and when assents are exercised on notions, they tend to be mere assertions without any personal hold on them on the part of those who make them. If this be so, the paradox is true, that, when Inference is clearest, Assent may be least forcible, and, when Assent is most intense, Inference may be least distinct;—for, though acts of assent require previous acts of inference, they require them, not as adequate causes, but as *sine quâ non* conditions: and, while the apprehension strengthens Assent, Inference often weakens the apprehension.

I

NOTIONAL ASSENTS

I SHALL CONSIDER ASSENT made to propositions which express abstractions or notions under five heads; which I shall call Profession, Credence, Opinion, Presumption, and Speculation.

1. *Profession*

There are assents so feeble and superficial, as to be little more than assertions. I class them all together under the head of Profession. Such are the assents made upon habit and without reflection; as when a man calls himself a Tory or a Liberal, as having been brought up as such; or again, when he adopts as a matter of course the literary or other fashions of the day, admiring the poems, or the novels, or the music, or the personages, or the costume, or the wines, or the manners, which happen to be popular, or are patronized in the higher circles. Such again are the assents of men of wavering restless minds, who take up and then abandon beliefs so readily, so suddenly, as to make it appear that they had no view (as it is called) on the matter they professed, and did not know to what they assented or why.

Then, again, when men say they have no doubt of a thing, this is a case, in which it is difficult to determine whether they assent to it, infer it, or consider it highly probable. There are many cases, indeed, in which it is impossible to discriminate between assent, inference, and assertion, on account of the otiose, passive, inchoate character of the act in question. If I say that tomorrow will be fine, what does this enunciation mean? Perhaps it means that it ought to be fine, if the glass tells truly; then it is the inference of a probability. Perhaps it means no more than a surmise, because it is fine to-day, or has been so for the week past. And perhaps it is a compliance with the word of another, in which case it is sometimes a real assent, sometimes a polite assertion or a wish.

Many a disciple of a philosophical school, who talks fluently, does but assert, when he seems to assent to the *dicta* of his master, little as he may be aware of it. Nor is he secured against this self-deception by knowing the arguments on which those *dicta* rest, for he may learn the arguments by heart, as a careless schoolboy gets up his Euclid. This practice of asserting simply on authority, with the pretence and without the reality of assent, is what is meant by formalism. To say "I do not understand a proposition, but I accept it on authority," is not formalism, but faith; it is not a direct assent to the proposition, still it *is* an assent to the authority which enunciates it; but what I here speak of is professing to understand without understanding. It is thus that political and religious watchwords are created; first one man of name and then another adopts them, till their use becomes popular, and then every one professes them, because every one else does. Such words are "liberality," "progress," "light," "civilization;" such are "justification by faith only," "vital religion," "private judgment," "the Bible and nothing but the Bible." Such again are "Rationalism," "Gallicanism," "Jesuitism," "Ultramontanism"—all of which, in the mouths of conscientious thinkers, have a definite meaning, but are used by the multitude as war-cries, nicknames, and shibboleths, with scarcely enough of the scantiest grammatical apprehension of them to allow of their being considered in truth more than assertions.

Thus, instances occur now and then, when, in consequence of the urgency of some fashionable superstition or popular delusion, some eminent scientific authority is provoked to come forward and to set the world right by his "ipse dixit." He, indeed, himself knows very well what he is about; he has a right to speak, and his reasonings and conclusions are sufficient, not only for his own, but for general assent, and, it may be, are as simply true and impregnable, as they are authoritative; but an intelligent hold on the matter in dispute, such as he has himself, cannot be expected in the case of men in general. They, nevertheless, one and all, repeat and retail his arguments, as suddenly as if they had not to study them, as heartily as if they understood them, changing round and becoming as strong antagonists of the error which their master has exposed, as if they had never been its advocates. If their word is to be taken, it is not simply his authority that moves them, which would be sensible enough and suitable in them, both apprehension and assent being in that case grounded on the maxim "Cuique in arte suâ credendum;" but so far forth as they disown this motive, and claim to judge in a scientific question of the worth of arguments which require some real knowledge, they are little better, not of course in a very serious matter, than pretenders and formalists.

Not only Authority, but Inference also may impose on us assents which in themselves are little better than assertions, and which, so far as they are assents, can only be notional assents, as being assents, not to the propositions inferred, but to the truth of those propositions. For instance, it can be proved by irrefragable calculations, that the stars are not less than billions of miles distant from the earth; and the process of calculation, upon which such statements are made, is not so difficult as to require authority to secure our acceptance of both it and of them; yet who can say that he has any real, nay, any notional apprehension of a billion or a trillion? We can, indeed, have some notion of it, if we analyze it into its factors, if we compare it with other numbers, or if we illustrate it by analogies or by its implications; but I am speaking of the vast number in itself. We cannot assent to a proposition of which it is the predicate; we can but assent to the truth of it.

This leads me to the question, whether belief in a mystery can be more than an assertion. I consider it can be an assent, and my reasons for saying so are as follows:—A mystery is a proposition conveying incompatible notions, or is a statement of the inconceivable. Now we can assent to propositions (and a mystery is a proposition), provided we can apprehend them; therefore we can assent to a mystery, for, unless we in some sense apprehend it, we should not recognize it to be a mystery, that is, a statement uniting incompatible notions. The same act, then, which enables us to discern that the words of the proposition express a mystery, capacitates us for assenting to it. Words which make nonsense, do not make a mystery. No one would call Warton's line—"Revolving swans proclaim the welkin near"—an inconceivable assertion. It is equally plain, that the assent which we give to mysteries, as such, is notional assent; for, by the supposition, it is assent to propositions which we cannot conceive, whereas, if we had had experience of them, we should be able to conceive them, and without experience assent is not real.

But the question follows, Can processes of inference end in a mystery? that is, not only in what is incomprehensible, that the stars are billions of miles from each other, but in what is inconceivable, in the co-existence of (seeming) incompatibilities? For how, it may be asked, can reason carry out notions into their contradictories? since all the developments of a truth must from the nature of the case be consistent both with it and with each other. I answer, certainly processes of inference, however accurate, can end in mystery; and I solve the objection to such a doctrine thus:—our notion of a thing may be only partially faithful to the original; it may be in excess of the thing, or it may represent it incompletely, and, in consequence, it may serve for it, it may stand for it, only to a certain point, in certain cases, but no further. After that point is reached, the notion and the thing part company; and then the notion, if still used as the representative of the thing, will work out conclusions, not inconsistent with itself, but with the thing to which it no longer corresponds.

This is seen most familiarly in the use of metaphors. Thus, in an Oxford satire, which deservedly made a sensation in its day, it is said that Vice "from its hardness takes a polish too." [1] Whence we might argue, that, whereas Caliban was vicious, he was therefore polished; but politeness and Caliban are incompatible notions. Or again, when some one said, perhaps

[1] "The Oxford Spy," 1818; by J. S. Boone, p. 107.

to Dr. Johnson, that a certain writer (say Hume) was a clear thinker, he made answer, "All shallows are clear." But supposing Hume to be in fact both a clear and a deep thinker, yet supposing clearness and depth are incompatible in their literal sense, which the objection seems to imply, and still in their full literal sense were to be ascribed to Hume, then our reasoning about his intellect has ended in the mystery, "Deep Hume is shallow;" whereas the contradiction lies, not in the reasoning, but in the fancying that inadequate notions can be taken as the exact representations of things.

Hence in science we sometimes use a definition or a *formula*, not as exact, but as being sufficient for our purpose, for working out certain conclusions, for a practical approximation, the error being small, till a certain point is reached. This is what in theological investigations I should call an economy.

A like contrast between notions and the things which they represent is the principle of suspense and curiosity in those enigmatical sayings which were frequent in the early stage of human society. In them the problem proposed to the acuteness of the hearers, is to find some real thing which may unite in itself certain conflicting notions which in the question are attributed to it: "Out of the eater came forth meat, and out of the strong came forth sweetness;" or, "What creature is that, which in the morning goes on four legs, at noon on two, and on three in the evening?" The answer, which names the thing, interprets and thereby limits the notions under which it has been represented.

Let us take an example in algebra. Its calculus is commonly used to investigate, not only the relations of quantity generally, but geometrical facts in particular. Now it is at once too wide and too narrow for such a purpose, fitting on to the doctrine of lines and angles with a bad fit, as the coat of a short and stout man might serve the needs of one who was tall and slim. Certainly it works well for geometrical purposes up to a certain point, as when it enables us to dispense with the cumbrous method of proof in questions of ratio and proportion which is adopted in the fifth book of Euclid; but what are we to make of the fourth power of *a*, when it is to be translated into geometrical language? If from this algebraical expression we determined that space admitted of four dimensions, we should be enunciating a mystery, because we should be applying to space a notion which belongs to quantity. In this case algebra is in excess of geometrical truth. Now let us take an instance in which it falls short of geometry,—What is the meaning of the square root of *minus a*? Here the mystery is on the side of algebra; and, in accordance with the principle which I am illustrating, it has sometimes been considered as an abortive effort to express, what is really beyond the capacity of algebraical notation, the direction and position of lines in the third dimension of space, as well as their length upon a plane. When the calculus is urged on by the inevitable course of the working to do what it cannot do, it stops short as if in resistance, and protests by an absurdity.

Our notions of things are never simply commensurate with the things themselves; they are aspects of them, more or less exact, and sometimes a mistake *ab initio*. Take an instance from arithmetic:—We are accustomed to subject all that exists to numeration; but, to be correct, we are bound first to reduce to some level of possible comparison the things which we wish to number. We must be able to say, not only that they are ten, twenty, or a hundred, but so many definite somethings. For instance, we could not without extravagance throw together Napoleon's brain, ambition, hand, soul, smile, height, and age at Marengo, and say that there were seven of them, though there are seven words; nor will it even be enough to content ourselves with what may be called a negative level, viz. that these seven are a non-existing or a departed seven. Unless numeration is to issue in nonsense, it must be conducted on conditions. This being the case, there are, for what we know, collections of beings, to whom the notion of number cannot be attached, except *catachrestically*, because, taken individually, no positive point of real agreement can be found between them, by which to call them. If indeed we can denote them by a plural noun, then we can measure that plurality; but if they agree in nothing, they cannot agree in bearing a common name, and to say that they amount to a thousand these or those, is not to number them, but to count up a certain number of names or words which we have written down.

Thus, the Angels have been considered by divines to have each of them a species to himself; and we may fancy each of them so absolutely *sui similis* as to be like nothing else, so that it would be as untrue to speak of a thousand Angels as of a thousand Hannibals or Ciceros. It will be said, indeed, that all beings but One at least will come under the notion of creatures, and are dependent upon that One; but that is true of the brain, smile, and height of Napoleon, which no one would call three creatures. But, if all this be so, much more does it apply to our speculations concerning the Supreme Being, whom it may be unmeaning, not only to number with other beings, but to subject to number in regard to His own intrinsic characteristics. That is, to apply arithmetical notions to Him may be as unphilosophical as it is profane. Though He is at once Father, Son, and Holy Ghost, the word "Trinity" belongs to those notions of Him which are forced on us by the necessity of our finite conceptions, the real and immutable distinction which exists between Person and Person implying in itself no infringement of His real and numerical Unity. And if it be asked how, if we cannot speak of Him as Three, we can speak of Him as One, I reply that He is not One in the way in which created things are severally units; for one, as applied to ourselves, is used in contrast to two or three and a whole series of numbers; but of the Supreme Being it is safer to use the word "nomad" than unit, for He has not even such relation to His creatures as to allow, philosophically speaking, of our contrasting Him with them.

Coming back to the main subject, which I have illustrated at the risk of digression, I observe, that an alleged fact is not therefore impossible because it is inconceivable, for the incompatible notions, in which consists its inconceivableness, need not each of them really belong to it in that fulness which would involve their being incompatible with each other. It is true indeed that I deny indeed the possibility of two straight lines enclosing a space, on the ground of its being inconceivable; but I do so because a straight line is a notion and nothing more, not a thing, to which I may have attached a notion more or less unfaithful. I have defined a straight line in my own way at my own pleasure; the question is not one of facts at all, but of the consistency with each other of definitions and their logical consequences.

"Space is not infinite, for nothing but the Creator is such:"—starting from this thesis as a theological information, to be assumed as a fact, though not one of experience, we arrive at once at an insoluble mystery; for, if space be not infinite, it is finite, and finite space is a contradiction in notions, space, as such, implying the absence of boundaries. Here again it is our notion that carries us beyond the fact, and in opposition to it, showing that from the first what we apprehend of space does not in all respects correspond to the thing, of which indeed we have no image.

This, then, is another instance in which the juxtaposition of notions by the logical faculty lands us in what are commonly called mysteries. Notions are but aspects of things; the free deductions from one of these aspects necessarily contradict the free deductions from another. After proceeding in our investigations a certain way, suddenly a blank or a maze presents itself before the mental vision, as when the eye is confused by the varying slides of a telescope. Thus, we believe in the infinitude of the Divine Attributes, but we can have no experience of infinitude as a fact; the word stands for a definition or a notion. Hence, when we try how to reconcile in the moral world the fulness of mercy with exactitude in sanctity and justice, or to explain that the physical tokens of creative skill need not suggest any want of creative power, we feel we are not masters of our subject. We apprehend sufficiently to be able to assent to these theological truths as mysteries; did we not apprehend them at all, we should be merely asserting; though even then we might convert that assertion into an assent, if we wished to do so, as I have already shown, by making it the subject of a proposition, and predicating of it that it is true.

2. *Credence*

What I mean by giving credence to propositions is pretty much the same as having "no doubt" about them. It is the sort of assent which we give to those opinions and professed facts which are ever presenting themselves to us without any effort of ours, and which we commonly take for granted, thereby obtaining a broad foundation of thought for ourselves, and a medium of intercourse between ourselves and others. This form of notional assent comprises a great variety of subject-matters; and is, as I have implied, of an otiose and passive character, accepting whatever comes to hand, from whatever quarter, warranted or not, so that it convey nothing on the face of it to its own disadvantage. From the time that we begin to observe, think, and reason, to the final failure of our powers, we are ever acquiring fresh and fresh informations by means of our senses, and still more from others and from books. The friends or strangers whom we fall in with in the course of the day, the conversations or discussions to which we are parties, the newspapers, the light reading of the season, our recreations, our rambles in the country, our foreign tours, all pour their contributions of intellectual matter into the storehouses of our memory; and, though much may be lost, much is retained. These informations, thus received with a spontaneous assent, constitute the furniture of the mind, and make the difference between its civilized condition and a state of nature. They are its education, as far as general knowledge can so be called; and, though education is discipline as well as learning, still, unless the mind implicitly welcomes the truths, real or ostensible, which these informations supply, it will gain neither formation nor a stimulus for its activity and progress. Besides, to believe frankly what it is told, is in the young an exercise of teachableness and humility.

Credence is the means by which, in high and low, in the man of the world and in the recluse, our bare and barren nature is overrun and diversified from without with a rich and living clothing. It is by such ungrudging, prompt assents to what is offered to us so lavishly, that we become possessed of the principles, doctrines, sentiments, facts, which constitute useful, and especially liberal knowledge. These various teachings, shallow though they be, are of a breadth which secures us against those *lacunae* of knowledge which are apt to befall the professed student, and keep us up to the mark in literature, in the arts, in history, and in public matters. They give us in great measure our morality, our politics, our social code, our art of life. They supply the elements of public opinion, the watchwords of patriotism, the standards of thought and action; they are our mutual understandings, our channels of sympathy, our means of co-operation, and the bond of our civil union. They become our moral language; we learn them as we learn our mother tongue; they distinguish us from foreigners; they are, in each of us, not indeed personal, but national characteristics.

This account of them implies that they are received with a notional, not a real assent; they are too manifold to be received in any other way. Even the most practised and earnest minds must needs be superficial in the greater part of their attainments. They know just enough on all subjects, in literature, history, politics, philosophy, and art, to be able to converse sensibly on them, and to understand those who are really deep in one or other of them. This is what is called, with a special appositeness, a gentleman's knowledge, as contrasted with that of a professional man, and is neither worthless nor despicable, if used for its proper ends; but it is never more than the furniture of the mind, as I have called it; it never is thoroughly assimilated with it. Yet of course there is nothing to hinder those who have even the largest stock of such notions from devoting themselves to one or other of the subjects to which those notions belong, and mastering it with a real apprehension; and then their general knowledge of all subjects may be made variously useful in the direction of that particular study or pursuit which they have selected.

I have been speaking of secular knowledge; but religion may be made a subject of notional assent also, and is especially so made in our own country. Theology, as such, always is notional, as being scientific: religion, as being personal, should be real; but, except within a small range of subjects, it commonly is not real in England. As to Catholic populations, such as those of mediæval Europe, or the Spain of this day, or quasi-Catholic as those of Russia, among them assent to religious objects is real, not notional. To them the Supreme Being, our Lord, the Blessed Virgin, Angels and Saints, heaven and hell, are as present as if they were objects of sight; but such a faith does not suit the genius of modern England. There is in the literary world just now an affectation of calling religion a "sentiment;" and it must be confessed that usually it is nothing more with our own people, educated or rude. Objects are barely necessary to it. I do not say so of old Calvinism or Evangelical Religion; I do not call the religion of Leighton, Beveridge, Wesley, Thomas Scott, or Cecil a mere sentiment; nor do I so term the high Anglicanism of the present generation. But these are only denominations, parties, schools, compared with the national religion of England in its length and breadth. "Bible Religion" is both the recognized title and the best description of English religion.

It consists, not in rites or creeds, but mainly in having the Bible read in Church, in the family, and in private. Now I am far indeed from undervaluing that mere knowledge of Scripture which is imparted to the population thus promiscuously. At least in England, it has to a certain point made up for great and grievous losses in its Christianity. The reiteration again and again in fixed course in the public service of the words of inspired teachers under both Covenants, and that in grave majestic English, has in matter of fact been to our people a vast benefit. It has attuned their minds to religious thoughts; it has given them a high moral standard; it has served them in associating religion with compositions which, even humanly considered, are among the most sublime and beautiful ever written; especially, it has impressed upon them the series of Divine Providences in behalf of man from his creation to his end, and, above all, the words, deeds, and sacred sufferings of Him in whom all the Providences of God centre.

So far the indiscriminate reading of Scripture has been of service; still, much more is necessary than the benefits which I have enumerated, to answer to the idea of a Religion; whereas our national form professes to be little more than thus reading the Bible and living a correct life. It is not a religion of persons and things, of acts of faith and of direct devotion; but of sacred scenes and pious sentiments. It has been comparatively careless of creed and catechism; and has in consequence shown little sense of the need of consistency in the matter of its teaching. Its doctrines are not so much facts, as stereotyped aspects of facts; and it is afraid, so to say, of walking round them. It induces its followers to be content with this meagre view of revealed truth; or, rather, it is suspicious and protests, or is frightened, as if it saw a figure in a picture move out of its frame, when our Lord, the Blessed Virgin, or the Holy Apostles, are spoken of as real beings, and really such as Scripture implies them to be. I am not denying that the assent which it inculcates and elicits is genuine as regards its contracted range of doctrine, but it is at best notional. What Scripture especially illustrates from its first page to its last, is God's Providence; and that is nearly the only doctrine held with a real assent by the mass of religious Englishmen. Hence the Bible is so great a solace and refuge to them in trouble. I repeat, I am not speaking of particular schools and parties in England, whether of the High Church or the Low, but of the mass of piously-minded and well-living people in all ranks of the community.

3. *Opinion*

That class of assents which I have called Credence, being a spontaneous acceptance of the various informations, which are by whatever means conveyed to our minds, sometimes goes by the name of Opinion. When we speak of a man's opinions, what do we mean, but the collection of notions which he happens to have, and does not easily part with, though he has neither sufficient proof nor firm grasp of them? This is true; however, Opinion is a word of various significations, and I prefer to use it in my own. Besides standing for Credence, it is sometimes taken to mean Conviction, as when we speak of the "variety of religious opinions," or of being "persecuted for religious opinions," or of our having "no opinion on a particular point," or of another having "no religious opinions." And sometimes it is used in contrast with Conviction, as synonymous with a light and casual, though genuine assent; thus, if a man was every day changing his mind, that is, his assents, we might say, that he was very changeable in his opinions.

I shall here use the word to denote an assent, but an assent to a proposition, not as true, but as probably true, that is, to the probability of that which the proposition enunciates; and, as that probability may vary in strength without limit, so may the cogency and moment of the opinion. This account of opinion may seem to confuse it with Inference; for the strength of an inference varies with its premises, and is a probability; but the two acts of mind are really distinct. Opinion, as being an assent, is independent of premises. We have opinions which we never think of defending by argument, though, of course, we think they can be so defended. We are even obstinate in them, or what is called "opinionated," and may say that we have a right to think just as we please, reason or no reason; whereas Inference is in its nature and by its profession conditional and uncertain. To say that "we shall have a fine hay-harvest if the present weather lasts," does not come of the same state of mind as, "I am of opinion that we shall have a fine hay-harvest this year."

Opinion, thus explained, has more connexion with Credence than with Inference. It differs from Credence in these two points, viz. that, while Opinion explicitly assents to the probability of a given proposition, Credence is an implicit assent to its truth. It differs from Credence in a third respect, viz. in being a reflex act;—when we take a thing for granted, we have credence in it; when we begin to reflect upon our credence, and to measure, estimate, and modify it, then we are forming an opinion.

It is in this sense that Catholics speak of theological opinion, in contrast with faith in dogma. It is much more than an inferential act, but it is distinct from an act of certitude. And this is really the sense which Protestants give to the word, when they interpret it by Conviction; for their highest opinion in religion is, generally speaking, an assent to a probability—as even Butler has been understood or misunderstood to teach, —and therefore consistent with toleration of its contradictory.

Opinion, being such as I have described, is a notional assent, for the predicate of the proposition, on which it is exercised, is the abstract word "probable."

4. *Presumption*

By Presumption I mean an assent to first principles; and by first principles I mean the propositions with which we start in reasoning on any given subject matter. They are in consequence very numerous, and vary in great measure with the persons who reason, according to their judgment and power of assent, being received by some minds, not by others, and only a few of them received universally. They are all of them notions, not images, because they express what is abstract, not what is individual and from direct experience.

1. Sometimes our trust in our powers of reasoning and

memory, that is, our implicit assent to their telling truly, is treated as a first principle; but we cannot properly be said to have any trust in them as faculties. At most we trust in particular acts of memory and reasoning. We are sure there was a yesterday, and that we did this or that in it; we are sure that three times six is eighteen, and that the diagonal of a square is longer than the side. So far as this we may be said to trust the mental act, by which the object of our assent is verified; but, in doing so, we imply no recognition of a general power or faculty, or of any capability or affection of our minds, over and above the particular act. We know indeed that we have a faculty by which we remember, as we know we have a faculty by which we breathe; but we gain this knowledge by abstraction or inference from its particular acts, not by direct experience. Nor do we trust in the faculty of memory or reasoning as such, even after that we have inferred its existence; for its acts are often inaccurate, nor do we invariably assent to them.

However, if I must speak my mind, I have another ground for reluctance to speak of our trusting memory or reasoning, except indeed by a figure of speech. It seems to me unphilosophical to speak of trusting ourselves. We are what we are, and we use, not trust our faculties. To debate about trusting in a case like this, is parallel to the confusion implied in wishing I had had a choice if I would be created or no, or speculating what I should be like, if I were born of other parents. "Proximus sum egomet mihi." Our consciousness of self is prior to all questions of trust or assent. We act according to our nature, by means of ourselves, when we remember or reason. We are as little able to accept or reject our mental constitution, as our being. We have not the option; we can but misuse or mar its functions. We do not confront or bargain with ourselves; and therefore I cannot call the trustworthiness of the faculties of memory and reasoning one of our first principles.

2. Next, as to the proposition, that there are things existing external to ourselves, this I do consider a first principle, and

one of universal reception. It is founded on an instinct; I so call it, because the brute creation possesses it. This instinct is directed towards individual phenomena, one by one, and has nothing of the character of a generalization; and, since it exists in brutes, the gift of reason is not a condition of its existence, and it may justly be considered an instinct in man also. What the human mind does is what brutes cannot do, viz. to draw from our ever-recurring experiences of its testimony in particulars a general proposition, and, because this instinct or intuition acts whenever the phenomena of sense present themselves, to lay down in broad terms, by an inductive process, the great aphorism, that there is an external world, and that all the phenomena of sense proceed from it. This general proposition, to which we go on to assent, goes (*extensivè*, though not *intensivè*) far beyond our experience, illimitable as that experience may be, and represents a notion.

3. I have spoken, and I think rightly spoken, of instinct as a force which spontaneously impels us, not only to bodily movements, but to mental acts. It is instinct which leads the quasi-intelligent principle (whatever it is) in brutes to perceive in the phenomena of sense a something distinct from and beyond those phenomena. It is instinct which impels the child to recognize in the smiles or the frowns of a countenance which meets his eyes, not only a being external to himself, but one whose looks elicit in him confidence or fear. And, as he instinctively interprets these physical phenomena, as tokens of things beyond themselves, so from the sensations attendant upon certain classes of his thoughts and actions he gains a perception of an external being, who reads his mind, to whom he is responsible, who praises and blames, who promises and threatens. As I am only illustrating a general view by examples, I shall take this analogy for granted here. As then we have our initial knowledge of the universe through sense, so do we in the first instance begin to learn about its Lord and God from conscience; and, as from particular acts of that instinct, which makes experiences, mere images (as they ultimately are) upon

the retina, the means of our perceiving something real beyond them, we go on to draw the general conclusion that there is a vast external world, so from the recurring instances in which conscience acts, forcing upon us importunately the mandate of a Superior, we have fresh and fresh evidence of the existence of a Sovereign Ruler, from whom those particular dictates which we experience proceed; so that, with limitations which cannot here be made without digressing from my main subject, we may, by means of that induction from particular experiences of conscience, have as good a warrant for concluding the Ubiquitous Presence of One Supreme Master, as we have, from parallel experience of sense, for assenting to the fact of a multiform and vast world, material and mental.

However, this assent is notional, because we generalize a consistent, methodical form of Divine Unity and Personality with Its attributes, from particular experiences of the religious instinct, which are themselves, only *intensivè* not *extensivè*, and in the imagination, not intellectually, notices of Its Presence; though at the same time that assent may become real of course, as may the assent to the external world, viz. when we apply our general knowledge to a particular instance of that knowledge, as, according to a former remark, the general "varium et mutabile" was realized in Dido. And in thus treating the origin of these great notions, I am not forgetting the aid which from our earliest years we receive from teachers, nor am I denying the influence of certain original forms of thinking or formative ideas, connatural with our minds, without which we could not reason at all. I am only contemplating the mind as it moves in fact, by whatever hidden mechanism; as a locomotive engine could not move without steam, but still, under whatever number of forces, it certainly does start from Birmingham and does arrive in London.

4. And so again, as regards the first principles expressed in such propositions as "There is a right and a wrong," "a true and a false," "a just and an unjust," "a beautiful and a deformed;" they are abstractions to which we give a notional

assent in consequence of our particular experiences of qualities in the concrete, to which we give a real assent. As we
form our notion of whiteness from the actual sight of snow,
milk, a lily, or a cloud, so, after experiencing the sentiment
of approbation which arises in us on the sight of certain acts
one by one, we go on to assign to that sentiment a cause, and
to those acts a quality, and we give to this notional cause or
quality the name of virtue, which is an abstraction, not a thing.
And in like manner, when we have been affected by a certain
specific admiring pleasure at the sight of this or that concrete
object, we proceed by an arbitrary act of the mind to give a
name to the hypothetical cause or quality in the abstract, which
excites it. We speak of it as beautifulness, and henceforth,
when we call a thing beautiful, we mean by the word a certain
quality of things which creates in us this special sensation.

These so-called first principles, I say, are really conclusions
or abstractions from particular experiences; and an assent to
their existence is not an assent to things or their images, but
to notions, real assent being confined to the propositions
directly embodying those experiences. Such notions indeed
are an evidence of the reality of the special sentiments in
particular instances, without which they would not have been
formed; but in themselves they are abstractions from facts,
not elementary truths prior to reasoning.

I am not of course dreaming of denying the objective existence of the Moral Law, nor our instinctive recognition of the
immutable difference in the moral quality of acts, as elicited
in us by one instance of them. Even one act of cruelty, ingratitude, generosity, or justice, reveals to us at once *intensivè*
the immutable distinction between those qualities and their
contraries; that is, in that particular instance and *pro hac vice*.
From such experience—an experience which is ever recurring—
we proceed to abstract and generalize; and thus the abstract
proposition "There is a right and a wrong," as representing an
act of inference, is received by the mind with a notional, not
a real assent. However, in proportion as we obey the particular

dictates which are its tokens, so are we led on more and more to view it in the association of those particulars, which are real, and virtually to change our notion of it into the image of that objective fact, which in each particular case it undeniably is.

5. Another of these presumptions is the belief in causation. It is to me a perplexity that grave authors seem to enunciate as an intuitive truth, that every thing must have a cause. If this were so, the voice of nature would tell false; for why in that case stop short at One, who is Himself without cause? The assent which we give to the proposition, as a first principle, that nothing happens without a cause, is derived, in the first instance, from what we know of ourselves; and we argue analogically from what it is within us to what is external to us. One of the first experiences of an infant is that of his willing and doing; and, as time goes on, one of the first temptations of the boy is to bring home to himself the fact of his sovereign arbitrary power, though it be at the price of waywardness, mischievousness, and disobedience. And when his parents, as antagonists of this wilfulness, begin to restrain him, and to bring his mind and conduct into shape, then he has a second series of experiences of cause and effect, and that upon a principle or rule. Thus the notion of causation is one of the first lessons which he learns from experience, that experience limiting it to agents possessed of intelligence and will. It is the notion of power combined with a purpose and an end. Physical phenomena, as such, are without sense; and experience teaches us nothing about physical phenomena as causes. Accordingly, wherever the world is young, the movements and changes of physical nature have been and are spontaneously ascribed by its people to the presence and will of hidden agents, who haunt every part of it, the woods, the mountains and the streams, the air and the stars, for good or for evil;—just as children again, by beating the ground after falling, imply that what has bruised them has intelligence;—nor is there any thing illogical in such a belief. It rests on the argument from analogy.

As time goes on, and society is formed, and the idea of

science is mastered, a different aspect of the physical universe presents itself to the mind. Since causation implies a sequence of acts in our own case, and our doing is always posterior, never contemporaneous or prior, to our willing, therefore, when we witness invariable antecedents and consequents, we call the former the cause of the latter, though intelligence is absent, from the analogy of external appearances. At length we go on to confuse causation with order; and, because we happen to have made a successful analysis of some complicated assemblage of phenomena, which experience has brought before us in the visible scene of things, and have reduced them to a tolerable dependence on each other, we call the ultimate points of this analysis, and the hypothetical facts in which the whole mass of phenomena is gathered up, by the name of causes, whereas they are really only the formula under which those phenomena are conveniently represented. Thus the constitutional formula, "The king can do no wrong," is not a fact, or a cause of the Constitution, but a happy mode of bringing out its genius, of determining the correlations of its elements, and of grouping or regulating political rules and proceedings in a particular direction and in a particular form. And in like manner, that all the particles of matter throughout the universe are attracted to each other with a force varying inversely with the square of their respective distances, is a profound idea, harmonizing the physical works of the Creator; but even could it be proved to be a universal fact, and also to be the actual cause of the movements of all bodies in the universe, still it would not be an experience, any more than is the mythological doctrine of the presence of innumerable spirits in those same physical phenomena.

Of these two senses of the word "cause," viz. that which brings a thing to be, and that on which a thing under given circumstances follows, the former is that of which our experience is the earlier and more intimate, being suggested to us by our consciousness of willing and doing. The latter of the two requires a discrimination and exactness of thought for its apprehension, which implies special mental training; else, how do we learn to call food the cause of refreshment, but day never the cause of night, though night follows day more surely than refreshment follows food? Starting, then, from experience, I consider a cause to be an effective will; and, by the doctrine of causation, I mean the notion, or first principle, that all things come of effective will; and the reception or presumption of this notion is a notional assent.

6. As to causation in the second sense, viz. an ordinary succession of antecedents and consequents, or what is called the Order of Nature, when so explained, it falls under the doctrine of general laws; and of this I proceed to make mention, as another first principle or notion, derived by us from experience, and accepted with what I have called a presumption. By natural law I mean the fact that things happen uniformly according to fixed circumstances, and not without them and at random: that is, that they happen in an order; and, as all things in the universe are unit and individual, order implies a certain repetition, whether of things or like things, or of their affections and relations. Thus we have experience, for instance, of the regularity of our physical functions, such as the beating of the pulse and the heaving of the breath; of the recurring sensations of hunger and thirst; of the alternation of waking and sleeping, and the succession of youth and age. In like manner we have experience of the great recurring phenomena of the heavens and earth, of day and night, summer and winter. Also, we have experience of a like uniform succession in the instance of fire burning, water choking, stones falling down and not up, iron moving towards a magnet, friction followed by sparks and crackling, an oar looking bent in the stream, and compressed steam bursting its vessel. Also, by scientific analysis, we are led to the conclusion that phenomena, which seem very different from each other, admit of being grouped together as modes of the operation of one hypothetical law, acting under varied circumstances. For instance, the motion of a stone falling freely, of a projectile, and of a planet, may

be generalized as one and the same property, in each of them, of the particles of matter; and this generalization loses its character of hypothesis, and becomes a probability, in proportion as we have reason for thinking on other grounds that the particles of all matter really move and act towards each other in one certain way in relation to space and time, and not in half a dozen ways; that is, that nature acts by uniform laws. And thus we advance to the general notion or first principle of the sovereignty of law throughout the universe.

There are philosophers who go farther, and teach, not only a general, but an invariable, and inviolable, and necessary uniformity in the action of the laws of nature, holding that everything is the result of some law or laws, and that exceptions are impossible; but I do not see on what ground of experience or reason they take up this position. Our experience, rather, is adverse to such a doctrine, for what concrete fact or phenomenon exactly repeats itself? Some abstract conception of it, more perfect than the recurrent phenomenon itself, is necessary before we are able to say that it has happened even twice, and the variations which accompany the repetition are of the nature of exceptions. The earth, for instance, never moves exactly in the same orbit year by year, but is in perpetual vacillation. It will, indeed, be replied that this arises from the interaction of one law with another, of which the actual orbit is only the accidental issue, that the earth is under the influence of a variety of attractions from cosmical bodies, and that, if it is subject to continual aberrations in its course, these are accounted for accurately or sufficiently by the presence of those extraordinary and variable attractions:—science, then, by its analytical processes sets right the *primâ facie* confusion. Of course; still let us not by our words imply that we are appealing to experience, when really we are only accounting, and that by hypothesis, for the absence of experience. The confusion is a fact, the reasoning processes are not facts. The extraordinary attractions assigned to account for our experience of that confusion are not themselves experienced phenomenal facts, but more or less probable hypotheses, argued out by means of an assumed analogy between the cosmical bodies to which those attractions are referred, and falling bodies on the earth. I say "assumed," because that analogy (in other words, the unfailing uniformity of nature) is the very point which has to be proved. It is true, that we can make experiment of the law of attraction in the case of bodies on the earth; but, I repeat, to assume from analogy that, as stones do fall to the earth, so Jupiter, if let alone, would fall upon the earth and the earth upon Jupiter, and with certain peculiarities of velocity on either side, is to have recourse to an explanation which is not necesarily valid, unless nature is necessarily uniform. Nor, indeed, has it yet been proved, nor ought it to be assumed, even that the law of velocity of falling bodies on the earth is invariable in its operation; for that again is only an instance of the general proposition, which is the very thesis in debate. It seems safer, then, to hold that the order of nature is not necesary, but general in its manifestations.

But, it may be urged, if a thing happens once, it must happen always; for what is to hinder it? Nay, on the contrary, why, because one particle of matter has a certain property, should all particles have the same? Why, because particles have instanced the property a thousand times, should the thousand and first instance it also? It is *primâ facie* unaccountable that an accident should happen twice, not to speak of its happening always. If we expect a thing to happen twice, it is because we think it is not an accident, but has a cause. What has brought about a thing once, may bring it about twice. *What* is to hinder its happening? rather, What is to make it happen? Here we are thrown back from the question of Order to that of Causation. A law is not a cause, but a fact; but when we come to the question of cause, then, as I have said, we have no experience of any cause but Will. If, then, I must answer the question, What is to alter the order of nature? I reply, That which willed it;—That which willed it, can unwill it; and the invariableness of law depends on the unchangeableness of that Will.

And here I am led to observe that, as a cause implies a will, so order implies a purpose. Did we see flint celts, in their various receptacles all over Europe, scored always with certain special and characteristic marks, even though those marks had no assignable meaning or final cause whatever, we should take that very repetition, which indeed is the principle of order, to be a proof of intelligence. The agency then which has kept up and keeps up the general laws of nature, energizing at once in Sirius and on the earth, and on the earth in its primary period as well as in the nineteenth century, must be Mind, and nothing else, and Mind at least as wide and as enduring in its living action, as the immeasurable ages and spaces of the universe on which that agency has left its traces.

In these remarks I have digressed from my immediate subject, but they have some bearing on points which will subsequently come into discussion.

5. *Speculation*

Speculation is one of those words which, in the vernacular, have so different a sense from what they bear in philosophy. It is commonly taken to mean a conjecture, or a venture on chances; but its proper meaning is mental sight, or the contemplation of mental operations and their results as opposed to experience, experiment, or sense, analogous to its meaning in Shakespeare's line, "Thou hast no speculation in those eyes." In this sense I use it here.

And I use it in this sense to denote those notional assents which are the most direct, explicit, and perfect of their kind, viz. those which are the firm, conscious acceptance of propositions as true. This kind of assent includes the assent to all reasoning and its conclusions, to all general propositions, to all rules of conduct, to all proverbs, aphorisms, sayings, and reflections on men and society. Of course mathematical investigations and truths are the subjects of this speculative assent.

So are legal judgments, and constitutional maxims, as far as they appeal to us for assent. So are the determinations of science; so are the principles, disputations, and doctrines of theology. That there is a God, that He has certain attributes, and in what sense He can be said to have attributes, that He has done certain works, that He has made certain revelations of Himself and of His will, and what they are, and the multiplied bearings of the parts of the teaching, thus developed and formed, upon each other, all this is the subject of notional assent, and of that particular department of it which I have called Speculation. As far as these particular subjects can be viewed in the concrete and represent experiences, they can be received by real assent also; but as expressed in general propositions they belong to notional apprehension and assent.

2

REAL ASSENTS

I HAVE IN A MEASURE anticipated the subject of Real Assent by what I have been saying about Notional. In comparison of the directness and force of the apprehension, which we have of an object, when our assent is to be called real, Notional Assent and Inference seem to be thrown back into one and the same class of intellectual acts, though the former of the two is always an unconditional acceptance of a proposition, and the latter is an acceptance on the condition of an acceptance of its premises. In its Notional Assents as well as in its inferences, the mind contemplates its own creations instead of things; in Real, it is directed towards things, represented by the impressions which they have left on the imagination. These images, when assented to, have an influence both on the individual and on society, which mere notions cannot exert.

I have already given various illustrations of Real Assent; I will follow them up here by some instances of the change of Notional Assent into Real.

1. For instance: boys at school look like each other, and pursue the same studies, some of them with greater success than others; but it will sometimes happen, that those who acquitted themselves but poorly in class, when they come into the action of life, and engage in some particular work, which they have already been learning in its theory and with little promise of proficiency, are suddenly found to have what is called an eye for that work—an eye for trade matters, or for engineering, or a special taste for literature—which no one expected from them at school, while they were engaged on notions. Minds of this stamp not only know the received rules of their profession, but enter into them, and even anticipate them, or dispense with them, or substitute other rules instead. And when new questions are opened, and arguments are drawn up on one side and the other in long array, they with a natural ease and promptness form their views and give their decision, as if they have no need to reason, from their clear apprehension of the lie and issue of the whole matter in dispute, as if it were drawn out in a map before them. These are the reformers, systematizers, inventors, in various departments of thought, speculative and practical; in education, in administration, in social and political matters, in science. Such men indeed are far from infallible; however great their powers, they sometimes fall into great errors, in their own special department, while second-rate men who go by rule come to sound and safe conclusions. Images need not be true; but I am illustrating what vividness of apprehension is, and what is the strength of belief consequent upon it.

2. Again:—twenty years ago, the Duke of Wellington wrote his celebrated letter on the subject of the national defences. His authority gave it an immediate circulation among all classes of the community; none questioned what he said, nor as if taking his words on faith merely, but as intellectually recognizing their truth; yet few could be said to see or feel that truth. His letter lay, so to say, upon the pure intellect of the national mind, and nothing for a time came of it. But eleven

years afterwards, after his death, the anger of the French colonels with us, after the attempt upon Louis Napoleon's life, transferred its facts to the charge of the imagination. Then forthwith the national assent became in various ways an operative principle, especially in its promotion of the volunteer movement. The Duke, having a special eye for military matters, had realized the state of things from the first; but it took a course of years to impress upon the public mind an assent to his warning deeper and more energetic than the reception it is accustomed to give to a clever article in a newspaper or a review.

3. And so generally: great truths, practical or ethical, float on the surface of society, admitted by all, valued by few, exemplifying the poet's adage, "Probitas laudatur et alget," until changed circumstances, accident, or the continual pressure of their advocates, force them upon its attention. The iniquity, for instance, of the slave-trade ought to have been acknowledged by all men from the first; it was acknowledged by many, but it needed an organized agitation, with tracts and speeches innumerable, so to affect the imagination of men as to make their acknowledgment of that iniquitousness operative.

In like manner, when Mr. Wilberforce, after succeeding in the slave question, urged the Duke of Wellington to use his great influence in discountenancing duelling, he could only get from him in answer, "A relic of barbarism, Mr. Wilberforce;" as if he accepted a notion without realizing a fact: at length, the growing intelligence of the community, and the shock inflicted upon it by the tragical circumstances of a particular duel, were fatal to that barbarism. The governing classes were roused from their dreamy acquiescence in an abstract truth, and recognized the duty of giving it practical expression.

4. Let us consider, too, how differently young and old are affected by the words of some classic author, such as Homer or Horace. Passages, which to a boy are but rhetorical commonplaces, neither better nor worse than a hundred others which any clever writer might supply, which he gets by heart and

thinks very fine, and imitates, as he thinks, successfully, in his own flowing versification, at length come home to him, when long years have passed, and he has had experience of life, and pierce him, as if he had never before known them, with their sad earnestness and vivid exactness. Then he comes to understand how it is that lines, the birth of some chance morning or evening at an Ionian festival, or among the Sabine hills, have lasted generation after generation, for thousands of years, with a power over the mind, and a charm, which the current literature of his own day, with all its obvious advantages, is utterly unable to rival. Perhaps this is the reason of the medieval opinion about Virgil, as if a prophet or magician; his single words and phrases, his pathetic half lines, giving utterance, as the voice of Nature herself, to that pain and weariness, yet hope of better things, which is the experience of her children in every time.

5. And what the experience of the world effects for the illustration of classical authors, that office the religious sense, carefully cultivated, fulfils towards Holy Scripture. To the devout and spiritual, the Divine Word speaks of things, not merely of notions. And, again, to the disconsolate, the tempted, the perplexed, the suffering, there comes, by means of their very trials, an enlargement of thought, which enables them to see in it what they never saw before. Henceforth there is to them a reality in its teachings, which they recognize as an argument, and the best of arguments, for its divine origin. Hence the practice of meditation on the Sacred Text, so highly thought of by Catholics. Reading, as we do, the gospels from our youth up, we are in danger of becoming so familiar with them as to be dead to their force, and to view them as a mere history. The purpose, then, of meditation is to realize them; to make the facts which they relate stand out before our minds as objects, such as may be appropriated by a faith as living as the imagination which apprehends them.

It is obvious to refer to the unworthy use made of the more solemn parts of the sacred volume by the mere popular preacher. His very mode of reading, whether warnings or prayers, is as if he thought them to be little more than fine writing, poetical in sense, musical in sound, and worthy of inspiration. The most awful truths are to him but sublime or beautiful conceptions, and are adduced and used by him, in season and out of season, for his own purposes, for embellishing his style or rounding his periods. But let his heart at length be ploughed by some keen grief or deep anxiety, and Scripture is a new book to him. This is the change which so often takes place in what is called religious conversion, and it is a change so far simply for the better, by whatever infirmity or error it is in the particular case acompanied. And it is strikingly suggested to us, to take a saintly example, in the confession of the patriarch Job, when he contrasts his apprehension of the Almighty before and after his afflictions. He says he had indeed a true apprehension of the Divine Attributes before as well as after; but with the trial came a great change in the character of that apprehension:—"With the hearing of the ear," he says, "I have heard Thee, but now mine eye seeth Thee; therefore I reprehend myself, and do penance in dust and ashes."

Let these instances suffice of Real Assent in its relation to Notional; they lead me to make three remarks in further illustration of its character.

1. The fact of the distinctness of the images which are required for real assent, is no warrant for the existence of the objects which those images represent. A proposition, be it ever so keenly apprehended, may be true or may be false. If we simply put aside all inferential information, such as is derived from testimony, from general belief, from the concurrence of the senses, from common sense, or otherwise, we have no right to consider that we have apprehended a truth, merely because of the strength of our mental impression of it. Hence the proverb, "Fronti nulla fides." An image, with the characters of perfect veracity and faithfulness, may be ever so distinct

and eloquent an object presented before the mind (or, as it is sometimes called, an "objectum internum," or a "subject-object"); but, nevertheless, there may be no external reality in the case, corresponding to it, in spite of its impressiveness. One of the most remarkable instances of this fallacious impressiveness is the illusion which possesses the minds of able men, those especially who are exercised in physical investigations, in favour of the inviolability of the laws of nature. Philosophers of the school of Hume discard the very supposition of miracles, and scornfully refuse to hear evidence in their behalf in given instances, from their intimate experience of physical order and of the ever-recurring connexion of antecedent and consequent. Their imagination usurps the functions of reason; and they cannot bring themselves even to entertain as a hypothesis (and this is all that they are asked to do) a thought contrary to that vivid impression of which they are the victims, that the uniformity of nature which they witness hour by hour, is equivalent to a necessary, inviolable law.

Yet it is plain, and I shall take it for granted here, that when I assent to a proposition, I ought to have some more legitimate reason for doing so, than the brilliancy of the image of which that proposition is the expression. That I have no experience of a thing happening except in one way, is a cause of the intensity of my assent, if I assent, but not a reason for my assenting. In saying this, I am not disposed to deny the presence in some men of an idiosyncratic sagacity, which really and rightly sees reasons in impressions which common men cannot see, and is secured from the peril of confusing truth with make-belief; but this is genius, and beyond rule. I grant too, of course, that accidentally impressiveness does in matter of fact, as in the instance which I have been giving, constitute the motive principle of belief; for the mind is ever exposed to the danger of being carried away by the liveliness of its conceptions, to the sacrifice of good sense and conscientious caution, and the greater and the more rare are its gifts, the greater is the risk of swerving from the line of reason and duty; but here I am not speaking of transgressions of rule any more than of exceptions to it, but of the normal constitution of our minds, and of the natural and rightful effect of acts of the imagination upon us, and this is, not to create assent, but to intensify it.

2. Next, Assent, however strong, and accorded to images however vivid, is not therefore necessarily practical. Strictly speaking, it is not imagination that causes action; but hope and fear, likes and dislikes, appetite, passion, affection, the stirrings of selfishness and self-love. What imagination does for us is to find a means of stimulating those motive powers; and it does so by providing a supply of objects strong enough to stimulate them. The thought of honour, glory, duty, self-aggrandisement, gain, or on the other hand of Divine Goodness, future reward, eternal life, perseveringly dwelt upon, leads us along a course of action corresponding to itself, but only in case there be that in our minds which is congenial to it. However, when there is that preparation of mind, the thought does lead to the act. Hence it is that the fact of a proposition being accepted with a real assent is accidentally an earnest of that proposition being carried out in conduct, and the imagination may be said in some sense to be of a practical nature, inasmuch as it leads to practice indirectly by the action of its object upon the affections.

3. There is a third remark suggested by the view which I have been taking of real assents, viz. that they are of a personal character, each individual having his own, and being known by them. It is otherwise with notions; notional apprehension is in itself an ordinary act of our common nature. All of us have the power of abstraction, and can be taught either to make or to enter into the same abstractions; and thus to co-operate in the establishment of a common measure between mind and mind. And, though for one and all of us to assent to the notions which we thus apprehend in common, is a further step, as requiring the adoption of a common stand-point of principle and judgment, yet this too depends in good measure on certain

logical processes of thought, with which we are all familiar,
and on facts which we all take for granted. But we cannot
make sure, for ourselves or others, of real apprehension and
assent, because we have to secure first the images which are
their objects, and these are often peculiar and special. They
depend on personal experience; and the experience of one
man is not the experience of another. Real assent, then, as the
experience which it presupposes, is proper to the individual,
and as such, thwarts rather than promotes the intercourse of
man with man. It shuts itself up, as it were, in its own home,
or at least it is its own witness and its own standard; and, as
in the instances above given, it cannot be reckoned on, anticipated, accounted for, inasmuch as it is the accident of this
man or that.

I call the characteristics of an individual accidents, in spite
of the universal reign of law, because they are severally the
co-incidents of many laws, and there are no laws as yet discovered of such coincidence. A man who is run over in the
street and killed, in one sense suffers according to rule or law;
he was crossing, he was short-sighted or pre-occupied in mind,
or he was looking another way; he was deaf, lame, or flurried;
and the cab came up at a great pace. If all this was so, it was
by a necessity that he was run over; it would have been a
miracle if he had escaped. So far is clear; but what is not clear
is how all these various conditions met together in the particular case, how it was that a man, shortsighted, hard of hearing,
deficient in presence of mind, happened to get in the way of
a cab hurrying along to catch a train. This concrete fact does
not come under any law of sudden deaths, but, like the earth's
yearly path which I spoke of above, is the accident of the
individual.

It does not meet the case to refer to the law of averages, for
such laws deal with percentages, not with individuals, and it
is about individuals that I am speaking. That this particular
man out of the three millions congregated in the metropolis,

was to have the experience of this catastrophe, and to be the select victim to appease that law of averages, no statistical tables could foretell, even though they could determine that it was in the fates that in that week or day some four persons in the length and breadth of London should be run over. And in like manner that this or that person should have the particular experiences necessary for real assent on any point, that the Deist should become a Theist, the Erastian a Catholic, the Protectionist a Free-trader, the Conservative a Legitimist, the high Tory an out-and-out Democrat, are facts, each of which may be the result of a multitude of coincidences in one and the same individual, coincidences which we have no means of determining, and which, therefore, we may call accidents. For—

> There's a Divinity that shapes our ends,
> Rough hew them how we will.

Such accidents are the characteristics of persons, as *differentiae* and properties are the characteristics of species or natures.

That a man dies when deprived of air, is not an accident of his person, but a law of his nature; that he cannot live without quinine or opium, or out of the climate of Madeira, is his own peculiarity. If all men every where usually had the yellow fever once in their lives, we should call it (speaking according to our knowledge) a law of the human constitution; if the inhabitants of a particular country commonly had it, we should call it a law of the climate; if a healthy man has a fever in a healthy place, in a healthy season, we call it an accident, though it be reducible to the coincidence of laws, because there is no known law of their coincidence. To be rational, to have speech, to pass through successive changes of mind and body from infancy to death, belong to man's nature; to have a particular history, to be married or single, to have children or to be childless, to live a given number of years, to have a certain constitution, moral temperament, intellectual outfit, mental formation, these and the like, taken all together, are the accidents which make up our notion of a man's person, and are the ground-work or condition of his particular experiences.

Moreover, various of the experiences which befall this man may be the same as those which befall that, although those experiences result each from the combination of its own accidents, and are ultimately traceable each to its own special condition or history. That is, images which are possessed in common, with their apprehensions and assents, may nevertheless be personal characteristics. If two or three hundred men are to be found, who cannot live out of Madeira, that inability would still be an accident and a peculiarity of each of them. Even if in each case it implied delicacy of lungs, still that delicacy is a vague notion, comprehending under it a great variety of cases in detail. If "five hundred brethren at once" saw our risen Lord, that common experience would not be a law, but a personal accident which was the prerogative of each. And so again in this day the belief of so many thousands in His Divinity, is not therefore notional, because it is common, but may be a real and personal belief, being produced in different individual minds by various experiences and disposing causes, variously combined; such as a warm or strong imagination, great sensibility, compunction and horror at sin, frequenting the Mass and other rites of the Church, meditating on the contents of the Gospels, familiarity with hymns and religious poems, dwelling on the Evidences, parental example and instruction, religious friends, strange providences, powerful preaching. In each case the image in the mind, with the experiences out of which it is formed, would be a personal result; and, though the same in all, would in each case be so idiosyncratic in its circumstances, that it would stand by itself, a special formation, unconnected with any law; though at the same time it would necessarily be a principle of sympathy and a bond of intercourse between those whose minds had been thus variously wrought into a common assent, far stronger than could follow upon any multitude of mere notions which they unanimously held. And even when that assent is not the result of concurrent causes, if such a case is possible, but has one single origin, as the study of Scripture, careful teaching, or a religious temper, still its presence argues a special history, and a personal formation, which an abstraction does not. For an abstraction can be made at will, and may be the work of a moment; but the moral experiences which perpetuate themselves in images, must be sought after in order to be found, and encouraged and cultivated in order to be appropriated.

I have now said all that occurs to me on the subject of Real Assents, perhaps not without some risk of subtlety and minuteness. They are sometimes called beliefs, convictions, certitudes; and, as given to moral objects, they are perhaps as rare as they are powerful. Till we have them, in spite of a full apprehension and assent in the field of notions, we have no intellectual moorings, and are at the mercy of impulses, fancies, and wandering lights, whether as regards personal conduct, social and political action, or religion. These beliefs, be they true or false in the particular case, form the mind out of which they grow, and impart to it a seriousness and manliness which inspires in other minds a confidence in its views, and is one secret of persuasiveness and influence in the public stage of the world. They create, as the case may be, heroes and saints, great leaders, statesmen, preachers, and reformers, the pioneers of discovery in science, visionaries, fanatics, knight-errants, demagogues, and adventurers. They have given to the world men of one idea, of immense energy, of adamantine will, of revolutionary power. They kindle sympathies between man and man, and knit together the innumerable units which constitute a race and a nation. They become the principle of its political existence; they impart to it homogeneity of thought and fellowship of purpose. They have given form to the medieval theocracy and to the Mahometan superstition; they are now the life both of "Holy Russia," and of that freedom of speech and action which is the special boast of Englishmen.

3

NOTIONAL AND REAL ASSENTS CONTRASTED

IT APPEARS from what has been said, that, though Real Assent is not intrinsically operative, it accidentally and indirectly affects practice. It is in itself an intellectual act, of which the object is presented to it by the imagination; and though the pure intellect does not lead to action, nor the imagination either, yet the imagination has the means, which pure intellect has not, of stimulating those powers of the mind from which action proceeds. Real Assent then, or Belief, as it may be called, viewed in itself, that is, simply as Assent, does not lead to action; but the images in which it lives, representing as they do the concrete, have the power of the concrete upon the affections and passions, and by means of these indirectly become operative. Still this practical influence is not invariable, nor to be relied on; for, given images may have no tendency to affect given minds, or to excite them to action. Thus, a philosopher or a poet may vividly realize the brilliant rewards of military genius or of eloquence, without wishing either to be a commander or an orator. However, on the whole, broadly contrasting Belief with Notional Assent and with Inference, we shall not, with this explanation, be very wrong in pronouncing that acts of Notional Assent and of Inference do not affect our conduct, and acts of Belief, that is, of Real Assent, do (not necessarily, but do) affect it.

I have scarcely spoken of Inference since my Introductory Chapter, though I intend, before I conclude, to consider it fully; but I have said enough to admit of my introducing it here in contrast with Real Assent or Belief, and that contrast is necessary in order to complete what I have been saying about the latter. Let me then, for the sake of the latter, be allowed here to say, that, while Assent, or Belief, presupposes some apprehension of the things believed, Inference requires no apprehension of the things inferred; that in consequence,

Inference is necessarily concerned with surfaces and aspects; that it begins with itself, and ends with itself; that it does not reach as far as facts; that it is employed upon formulas; that, as far as it takes real objects of whatever kind into account, such as motives and actions, character and conduct, art, science, taste, morals, religion, it deals with them, not as they are, but simply in its own line, as materials of argument or inquiry, that they are to it nothing more than major and minor premises and conclusions. Belief, on the other hand, being concerned with things concrete, not abstract, which variously excite the mind from their moral and imaginative properties, has for its objects, not only directly what is true, but inclusively what is beautiful, useful, admirable, heroic; objects which kindle devotion, rouse the passions, and attach the affections; and thus it leads the way to actions of every kind, to the establishment of principles, and the formation of character, and is thus again intimately connected with what is individual and personal.

I insisted on this marked distinction between Beliefs on the one hand, and Notional Assents and Inferences on the other, many years ago in words which it will be to my purpose to use now.[1] I quote them, because, over and above their appositeness in this place, they present the doctrine which I have been insisting, from a second point of view, and with a freshness and force which I cannot now command, and, moreover, (though they are my own, nevertheless, from the length of time which has elapsed since their publication,) almost with the cogency of an independent testimony.

They occur in a protest which I had occasion to write in February, 1841, against a dangerous doctrine maintained, as I considered, by two very eminent men of that day, now no more—Lord Brougham and Sir Robert Peel. That doctrine was

[1] *Vide* "The Tamworth Reading Room," in *Essays and Sketches,* Vol. II, of the present edition of Newman's *Works.* [—Ed.]

to the effect that the claims of religion could be secured and sustained in the mass of men, and in particular in the lower classes of society, by acquaintance with literature and physical science, and through the instrumentality of Mechanics' Institutes and Reading Rooms, to the serious disparagement, as it seemed to me, of direct Christian instruction. In the course of my remarks is found the passage which I shall here quote and which, with whatever differences in terminology, and hardihood of assertion, befitting the circumstances of its publication, nay, as far as words go, inaccuracy of theological statement, suitably illustrates the subject here under discussion. It runs thus:—

"People say to me, that it is but a dream to suppose that Christianity should regain the organic power in human society which once it possessed. I cannot help that; I never said it could. I am not a politician; I am proposing no measures, but exposing a fallacy and resisting a pretence. Let Benthamism reign, if men have no aspirations; but do not tell them to be romantic and then solace them with 'glory:' do not attempt by philosophy what once was done by religion. The ascendency of faith may be impracticable, but the reign of knowledge is incomprehensible. The problem for statesmen of this age is how to educate the masses, and literature and science cannot give the solution.

"Science gives us the grounds or premises from which religious truths are to be inferred; but it does not set about inferring them, much less does it reach the inference—that is not its province. It brings before us phenomena, and it leaves us, if we will, to call them works of design, wisdom, or benevolence; and further still, if we will, to proceed to confess an Intelligent Creator. We have to take its facts, and to give them a meaning, and to draw our own conclusions from them. First comes knowledge, then a view, then reasoning, and then belief. This is why science has so little of a religious tendency; deductions have no power of persuasion. The heart is commonly reached, not through the reason, but through the imagination, by means of direct impressions, by the testimony of facts and events, by history, by description. Persons influence us, voices melt us, looks subdue us, deeds inflame us. Many a man will live and die upon a dogma: no man will be a martyr for a conclusion. A conclusion is but an opinion; it is not a thing which *is*, but which *we are 'quite sure about'*; and it has often been observed, that we never say we are sure and certain without implying that we doubt. To say that a thing *must* be, is to admit that it *may not* be. No one, I say, will die for his own calculations: he dies for realities. This is why a literary religion is so little to be depended upon; it looks well in fair weather; but its doctrines are opinions, and when called to suffer for them it slips them between its folios, or burns them at its hearth. And this again is the secret of the distrust and raillery with which moralists have been so commonly visited. They say and do not. Why? Because they are contemplating the fitness of things, and they live by the square, when they should be realizing their high maxims in the concrete. Now Sir Robert Peel thinks better of natural history, chemistry, and astronomy than of such ethics; but these too, what are they more than divinity *in posse*? He protests against *'controversial* divinity:' is *inferential* much better?

"I have no confidence, then, in philosophers who *cannot help* being religious, and are Christians by *implication*. They sit at home, and reach forward to distances which astonish us; but they hit without grasping, and are sometimes as confident about shadows as about realities. They have worked out by a calculation the lie of a country which they never saw, and mapped it by means of a gazetteer; and, like blind men, though they can put a stranger on his way, they cannot walk straight themselves, and do not feel it quite their business to walk at all.

"Logic makes but a sorry rhetoric with the multitude; first shoot round corners, and you may not despair of converting by a syllogism. Tell men to gain notions of a Creator from His works, and, if they were to set about it (which nobody does) they would be jaded and wearied by the labyrinth they were tracing. Their minds would be gorged and surfeited by the logical operation. Logicians are more set upon concluding rightly, than on right conclusions. They cannot see the end for the process. Few men have that power of mind which may hold fast and firmly a variety of thoughts. We ridicule 'men of one idea;' but a great many of us are born to be such, and we should be happier if we knew it. To most men argument makes the point in hand only more doubtful, and considerably less impressive. After all, man is *not* a reasoning animal; he is a seeing, feeling, contemplating, acting animal. He is influenced by what is direct and precise. It is very well to freshen our impressions and convictions from physics, but to create them we must go elsewhere. Sir Robert Peel 'never can think it possible that a mind can be so constituted, that, after being familiarized with the wonderful discoveries which have been made in every part of experimental science, it can retire from such contemplations without more enlarged conceptions of God's providence, and a higher reverence for His name!' If he speaks of religious minds, he perpetrates a truism; if of irreligious, he insinuates a paradox.

"Life is not long enough for a religion of inferences; we shall never have done beginning, if we determine to begin with proof. We shall ever be laying our foundations; we shall turn theology into evidences, and divines into textuaries. We shall never get at our first principles. Resolve to believe nothing, and you must prove your proofs and analyze your elements, sinking farther and farther, and finding 'in the lowest depth a lower deep,' till you come to the broad bosom of scepticism. I would rather be bound to defend the reasonableness of assuming that Christianity is true, than demonstrate a moral governance from the physical world. Life is for action. If we insist on proofs for everything, we shall never come to action: to act you must assume, and that assumption is faith.

"Let no one suppose, that in saying this I am maintaining that all proofs are equally difficult, and all propositions equally debatable. Some assumptions are greater than others, and some doctrines involve postulates larger than others, and more numerous. I only say, that impressions lead to action, and that reasonings lead from it. Knowledge of premisses, and inferences upon them,—this is not to *live*. It is very well as a matter of liberal curiosity and of philosophy to analyze our modes of thought: but let this come second, and when there is leisure for it, and then our examinations will in many ways even be subservient to action. But if we commence with scientific knowledge and argumentative proof, or lay any great stress upon it as the basis of personal Christianity, or attempt to make man moral and religious by libraries and museums, let us in consistency take chemists for our cooks, and mineralogists for our masons.

"Now I wish to state all this as matter of fact, to be judged by the candid testimony of any persons whatever. Why we are so constituted that faith, not knowledge or argument, is our principle of action, is a question with which I have nothing to do; but I think it is a fact, and, if it be such, we must resign ourselves to it as best we may, unless we take refuge in the intolerable paradox, that the mass of men are created for nothing, and are meant to leave life as they entered it.

"So well has this practically been understood in all ages of the world, that no religion yet has been a religion of physics or of philosophy. It has ever been synonymous with revelation. It never has been a deduction from what we know; it has ever been an assertion of what we are to believe. It has never lived in a conclusion; it has ever been a message, a history, or a vision. No legislator or priest ever dreamed of educating our moral nature by science or by argument. There is no difference here between true religions and pretended. Moses was instructed not to reason from the creation, but to work miracles. Christianity is a history supernatural, and almost scenic: it tells us what its Author is, by telling us what He has done.

"Lord Brougham himself has recognized the force of this principle. He has not left his philosophical religion to argument; he has committed it to the keeping of the imagination. Why should he depict a great republic of letters, and an intellectual pantheon, except that he feels that instances and patterns, not logical reasonings, are the living conclusions which alone have a hold over the affections or can form the character?"

CHAPTER V

APPREHENSION AND ASSENT IN THE MATTER OF RELIGION

WE ARE NOW ABLE to determine what a dogma of faith is, and what it is to believe it. A dogma is a proposition; it stands for a notion or for a thing; and to believe it is to give the assent of the mind to it, as it stands for one or for the other. To give a real assent to it is an act of religion; to give a notional, is a theological act. It is discerned, rested in, and appropriated as a reality, by the religious imagination; it is held as a truth, by the theological intellect.

Not as if there were in fact, or could be, any line of demarcation or party-wall between these two modes of assent, the religious and theological. As intellect is common to all men as well as imagination, every religious man is to a certain extent a theologian, and no theology can start or thrive without the initiative and abiding presence of religion. As in matters of this world, sense, sensation, instinct, intuition, supply us with facts, and the intellect uses them; so, as regards our relations with the Supreme Being, we get our facts from the witness, first of nature, then of revelation, and our doctrines, in which they issue, through the exercise of abstraction and inference. This is obvious; but it does not interfere with holding that there is a theological habit of mind, and a religious, each distinct from each, religion using theology, and theology using religion. This being understood, I propose to consider the dogmas of the Being of a God, and of the Divine Trinity in Unity, in their relation to assent, both notional and real, and principally to real assent;—however, I have not yet finished all I have to say by way of introduction.

Now first, my subject is assent, and not inference. I am not proposing to set forth the arguments which issue in the belief of these doctrines, but to investigate what it is to believe in them, what the mind does, what it contemplates, when it makes an act of faith. It is true that the same elementary facts which create an object for an assent, also furnish matter for an inference: and in showing what we believe, I shall unavoidably be in a measure showing why we believe; but this is the very reason that makes it necessary for me at the outset to insist on the real distinction between these two concurring and coincident courses of thought, and to premise by way of caution, lest I should be misunderstood, that I am not considering the question that there is a God, but rather what God is.

And secondly, I mean by belief, not precisely faith, because faith, in its theological sense, includes a belief, not only in the thing believed, but also in the ground of believing; that is, not only belief in certain doctrines, but belief in them expressly because God has revealed them; but here I am engaged only with what is called the material object of faith, with the thing believed, not with the formal. The Almighty witnesses to Himself in Revelation; we believe that He is One and that He is Three, because He says so. We believe also what He tells us about His Attributes, His providences and dispensations, His determinations and acts, what He has done and what He will do. And if all this is too much for us, whether to bring at one time before our minds from its variety, or even to apprehend at all or enunciate from our narrowness of intellect or want of learning, then at least we believe *in globo* all that He has revealed to us about Himself, and that, because He has revealed it. However, this "because He says it" does not enter into the scope of the present inquiry, but only the truths themselves, and these particular truths, "He is One," "He is Three;" and of these two, both of which are in Revelation, I shall consider "He is One," not as a revealed truth, but as, what it is also, a natural truth, the foundation of all religion. And with it I begin.

1

BELIEF IN ONE GOD

THERE IS ONE GOD, such and such in Nature and Attributes. I say "such and such," for, unless I explain what I mean by "one God," I use words which may mean any thing or nothing. I may mean a mere *anima mundi;* or an initial principle which once was in action and now is not; or collective humanity. I speak then of the God of the Theist and of the Christian: a God who is numerically One, who is Personal; the Author, Sustainer, and Finisher of all things, the Life of Law and Order, the Moral Governor; One who is Supreme and Sole; like Himself, unlike all things besides Himself, which all are but His creatures; distinct from, independent of them all; One who is self-existing, absolutely infinite, who has ever been and ever will be, to whom nothing is past or future; who is all perfection, and the fulness and archetype of every possible excellence, the Truth Itself, Wisdom, Love, Justice, Holiness; One who is All-powerful, All-knowing, Omnipresent, Incomprehensible. These are some of the distinctive prerogatives which I ascribe unconditionally and unreservedly to the great Being whom I call God.

This being what Theists mean when they speak of God, their assent to this truth admits without difficulty of being what I have called a notional assent. It is an assent following upon acts of inference, and other purely intellectual exercises; and it is an assent to a large development of predicates, correlative to each other, or at least intimately connected together, drawn out as if on paper, as we might map a country which we had never seen, or construct mathematical tables, or master the methods of discovery of Newton or Davy, without being geographers, mathematicians, or chemists ourselves.

So far is clear; but the question follows, Can I attain to any more vivid assent to the Being of a God, than that which is given merely to notions of the intellect? Can I enter with a personal knowledge into the circle of truths which make up that great thought? Can I rise to what I have called an imaginative apprehension of it? Can I believe as if I saw? Since such a high assent requires a present experience or memory of the fact, at first sight it would seem as if the answer must be in the negative; for how can I assent as if I saw, unless I have seen? but no one in this life can see God. Yet I conceive a real assent is possible, and I proceed to show how.

When it is said that we cannot see God, this is undeniable; but still in what sense have we a discernment of His creatures, of the individual beings which surround us? The evidence which we have of their presence lies in the phenomena which address our senses, and our warrant for taking these for evidence is our instinctive certitude that they are evidence. By the law of our nature we associate those sensible phenomena or impressions with certain units, individuals, substances, whatever they are to be called, which are outside and out of the reach of sense, and we picture them to ourselves in those phenomena. The phenomena are as if pictures; but at the same time they give us no exact measure or character of the unknown things beyond them;—for who will say there is any uniformity between the impressions which two of us would respectively have of some third thing, supposing one of us had only the sense of touch, and the other only the sense of hearing? Therefore, when we speak of our having a picture of the things which are perceived through the senses, we mean a certain representation, true as far as it goes, but not adequate.

And so of those intellectual and moral objects which are brought home to us through our senses:—that they exist, we know by instinct; that they are such and such, we apprehend from the impressions which they leave upon our minds. Thus the life and writings of Cicero or Dr. Johnson, of St. Jerome or St. Chrysostom, leave upon us certain impressions of the intellectual and moral character of each of them, *sui generis,* and unmistakable. We take up a passage of Chrysostom or a passage of Jerome; there is no possibility of confusing the one with the other; in each case we see the man in his language. And so of any great man whom we may have known: that he is not a mere impression on our senses, but a real being, we know by instinct; that he is such and such, we know by the matter or quality of that impression.

Now certainly the thought of God, as Theists entertain it, is not gained by an instinctive association of His presence with any sensible phenomena; but the office which the senses directly fulfil as regards creation, that devolves indirectly on certain of our mental phenomena as regards the Creator. Those phenomena are found in the sense of moral obligation. As from a multitude of instinctive perceptions, acting in particular instances, of something beyond the senses, we generalize the notion of an external world, and then picture that world in and according to those particular phenomena from which we started, so from the perceptive power which identifies the intimations of conscience with the reverberations or echoes (so to say) of an external admonition, we proceed on to the notion of a Supreme Ruler and Judge, and then again we image Him and His attributes in those recurring intimations, out of which, as mental phenomena, our recognition of His existence was originally gained. And, if the impressions which His creatures make on us through our senses oblige us to regard those creatures as *sui generis* respectively, it is not wonderful that the notices which He indirectly gives us, through our conscience, of His own nature are such as to make us understand that He is like Himself and like nothing else.

I have already said I am not proposing here to prove the Being of a God; yet I have found it impossible to avoid saying where I look for the proof of it. For I am looking for that proof in the same quarter as that from which I would commence a proof of His attributes and character,—by the same means as those by which I show how we apprehend Him, not merely as a notion, but as a reality. The last indeed of these three investigations alone concerns me here, but I cannot altogether exclude the two former from my consideration. However, I repeat, what I am directly aiming at, is to explain how we gain an image of God and give a real assent to the proposition that He exists. And next, in order to do this, of course I must start from some first principle;—and that first principle, which I assume and shall not attempt to prove, is that which I should also use as a foundation in those other two inquiries, viz. that we have by nature a conscience.

I assume, then, that Conscience has a legitimate place among our mental acts; as really so, as the action of memory, of reasoning, of imagination, or as the sense of the beautiful; that, as there are objects which, when presented to the mind, cause it to feel grief, regret, joy, or desire, so there are things which excite in us approbation or blame, and which we in consequence call right or wrong; and which, experienced in ourselves, kindle in us that specific sense of pleasure or pain, which goes by the name of a good or bad conscience. This being taken for granted, I shall attempt to show that in this special feeling, which follows on the commission of what we call right or wrong, lie the materials for the real apprehension of a Divine Sovereign and Judge.

The feeling of conscience being, I repeat, a certain keen sensibility, pleasant or painful,—self-approval and hope, or compunction and fear,—attendant on certain of our actions, which in consequence we call right or wrong, is twofold:—it is a moral sense, and a sense of duty; a judgment of the reason and a magisterial dictate. Of course its act is indivisible; still it has these two aspects, distinct from each other, and admitting of a separate consideration. Though I lost my sense of the obligation which I lie under to abstain from acts of dishonesty, I should not in consequence lose my sense that such actions were an outrage offered to my moral nature. Again; though I lost my sense of their moral deformity, I should not therefore lose my sense that they were forbidden to me. Thus conscience has both a critical and a judicial office, and though its promptings, in the breasts of the millions of human beings to whom it is given, are not in all cases correct, that does not necessarily interfere with the force of its testimony and of its sanction: its testimony that there is a right and a wrong, and its sanction to that testimony conveyed in the feelings which attend on right or wrong conduct. Here I have to speak of conscience in the latter point of view, not as supplying us, by means of its various acts, with the elements of morals, such as may be developed by the intellect into an ethical code, but simply as the dictate of an authoritative monitor bearing upon the details of conduct as they come before us, and complete in its several acts, one by one.

Let us then thus consider conscience, not as a rule of right conduct, but as a sanction of right conduct. This is its primary and most authoritative aspect; it is the ordinary sense of the word. Half the world would be puzzled to know what was meant by the moral sense; but every one knows what is meant by a good or bad conscience. Conscience is ever forcing on us by threats and by promises that we must follow the right and avoid the wrong; so far it is one and the same in the mind of every one, whatever be its particular errors in particular minds as to the acts which it orders to be done or to be avoided; and in this respect it corresponds to our perception of the beautiful and deformed. As we have naturally a sense of the beautiful and graceful in nature and art, though tastes proverbially differ, so we have a sense of duty and obligation, whether we all associate it with the same certain actions in particular or not. Here, however, Taste and Conscience part company: for the sense of beautifulness, as indeed the Moral Sense, has no special relations to persons, but contemplates objects in themselves; conscience, on the other hand, is concerned with persons primarily, and with actions mainly as viewed in their doers, or rather with self alone and one's own actions, and with others only indirectly and as if in association with self. And further, taste is its own evidence, appealing to nothing beyond its own sense of the beautiful or the ugly, and enjoying the specimens of the beautiful simply for their own sake; but conscience does not repose on itself, but vaguely reaches forward to something beyond self, and dimly discerns a sanction higher than self for its decisions, as is evidenced in that keen sense of obligation and responsibility which informs them. And hence it is that we are accustomed to speak of conscience as a voice,—a term which we should never think of applying to the sense of the beautiful; and moreover a voice, or the echo of a voice, imperative and constraining, like no other dictate in the whole of our experience.

And again, in consequence of this prerogative of dictating and commanding, which is of its essence, Conscience has an intimate bearing on our affections and emotions, leading us to reverence and awe, hope and fear, especially fear, a feeling which is foreign for the most part, not only to Taste, but even to the Moral Sense, except in consequence of accidental associations. No fear is felt by any one who recognizes that his conduct has not been beautiful, though he may be mortified at himself, if perhaps he has thereby forfeited some advantage; but, if he has been betrayed into any kind of immorality, he has a lively sense of responsibility and guilt, though the act be no offence against society,—of distress and apprehension, even though it may be of present service to him,—of compunction and regret, though in itself it be most pleasurable,—of confusion of face, though it may have no witnesses. These various perturbations of mind, which are characteristic of a bad conscience, and may be very considerable,—self-reproach, poignant shame, haunting remorse, chill dismay at the prospect of the future,—and their contraries, when the conscience is good, as real though less forcible, self-approval, inward peace, lightness of heart, and the like,—these emotions constitute a specific difference between conscience and our other intellectual senses,—common sense, good sense, sense of expedience, taste, sense of honour, and the like,—as indeed they would also constitute between conscience and the moral sense, supposing these two were not aspects of one and the same feeling, exercised upon one and the same subject-matter.

So much for the characteristic phenomena, which conscience presents, nor is it difficult to determine what they imply. I refer once more to our sense of the beautiful. This sense is attended by an intellectual enjoyment, and is free from whatever is of the nature of emotion, except in one case, viz. when it is excited by personal objects; then it is that the tranquil feeling of admiration is exchanged for the excitement of affection and passion. Conscience too, considered as a moral sense, an intellectual sentiment, is a sense of admiration and disgust, of approbation and blame: but it is something more than a moral sense, it is always, what the sense of the beautiful is only in certain cases; it is always emotional. No wonder then that it always implies what that sense only sometimes implies; that it always involves the recognition of a living object, towards which it is directed. Inanimate things cannot stir our affections; these are correlative with persons. If, as is the case, we feel responsibility, are ashamed, are frightened, at transgressing the voice of conscience, this implies that there is One to whom we are responsible, before whom we are ashamed, whose claims upon us we fear. If, on doing wrong, we feel the same tearful, broken-hearted sorrow which overwhelms us on hurting a mother; if, on doing right, we enjoy the same sunny serenity of mind, the same soothing, satisfactory delight which follows on our receiving praise from a father, we certainly have within us the image of some person, to whom our love and veneration look, in whose smile we find our happiness, for whom we yearn, towards whom we direct our pleadings, in whose anger we are troubled and waste away. These feelings in us are such as require for their exciting cause an intelligent being: we are not affectionate towards a stone, nor do we feel shame before a horse or a dog; we have no remorse or compunction on breaking mere human law: yet, so it is, conscience excites all these painful emotions, confusion, foreboding, self-condemnation; and on the other hand it sheds upon us a deep peace, a sense of security, a resignation, and a hope, which there is no sensible, no earthly object to elicit. "The wicked flees, when no one pursueth;" then why does he flee? whence his terror? Who is it that he sees in solitude, in darkness, in the hidden chambers of his heart? If the cause of these emotions does not belong to this visible world, the Object to which his perception is directed must be Supernatural and Divine; and thus the phenomena of Conscience, as a dictate, avail to impress the imagination with the picture [1] of a Supreme Governor, a Judge, holy, just, powerful, all-seeing, retributive, and is the creative principle of religion, as the Moral Sense is the principle of ethics.

And let me here refer again to the fact, to which I have already drawn attention, that this instinct of the mind recognizing an external Master in the dictate of conscience, and imaging the thought of Him in the definite impressions which conscience creates, is parallel to that other law of, not only human, but of brute nature, by which the presence of unseen individual beings is discerned under the shifting shapes and colours of the visible world. Is it by sense, or by reason, that brutes understand the real unities, material and spiritual, which are signified by the lights and shadows, the brilliant ever-changing calidoscope, as it may be called, which plays upon their *retina?* Not by reason, for they have not reason; not by sense, because they are transcending sense; therefore it is an instinct. This faculty on the part of brutes, unless we were used to it, would strike us as a great mystery. It is one peculiarity of animal natures to be susceptible of phenomena through the channels of sense; it is another to have in those sensible phenomena a perception of the individuals to which this or that group of them belongs. This perception of individual things amid the maze of shapes and colours which meets their sight, is given to brutes in large measures, and that, apparently from the moment of their birth. It is by no mere physical

[1] On the Formation of Images, *vide supra*, ch. iii, 1, pp. 22, 23.

instinct, such as that which leads him to his mother for milk, that the new-dropped lamb recognizes each of his fellow lambkins as a whole, consisting of many parts bound up in one, and, before he is an hour old, makes experience of his and their rival individualities. And much more distinctly do the horse and dog recognize even the personality of their masters. How are we to explain this apprehension of things, which are one and individual, in the midst of a world of pluralities and transmutations, whether in the instance of brutes or again of children? But until we account for the knowledge which an infant has of his mother or his nurse, what reason have we to take exception at the doctrine, as strange and difficult, that in the dictate of conscience, without previous experiences or analogical reasoning, he is able gradually to perceive the voice, or the echoes of the voice, of a Master, living, personal, and sovereign?

I grant, of course, that we cannot assign a date, ever so early, before which he had learned nothing at all, and formed no mental associations, from the words and conduct of those who have the care of him. But still, if a child of five or six years old, when reason is at length fully awake, has already mastered and appropriated thoughts and beliefs, in consequence of their teaching, in such sort as to be able to handle and apply them familiarly, according to the occasion, as principles of intellectual action, those beliefs at the very least must be singularly congenial to his mind, if not connatural with its initial action. And that such a spontaneous reception of religious truths is common with children, I shall take for granted, till I am convinced that I am wrong in so doing. The child keenly understands that there is a difference between right and wrong; and when he has done what he believes to be wrong, he is conscious that he is offending One to whom he is amenable, whom he does not see, who sees him. His mind reaches forward with a strong presentiment to the thought of a Moral Governor, sovereign over him, mindful, and just. It comes to him like an impulse of nature to entertain it.

It is my wish to take an ordinary child, but still one who is safe from influences destructive of his religious instincts. Supposing he has offended his parents, he will all alone and without effort, as if it were the most natural of acts, place himself in the presence of God, and beg of Him to set him right with them. Let us consider how much is contained in this simple act. First, it involves the impression on his mind of an unseen Being with whom he is in immediate relation, and that relation so familiar that he can address Him whenever he himself chooses; next, of One whose goodwill towards him he is assured of, and can take for granted—nay, who loves him better, and is nearer to him, than his parents; further, of One who can hear him, wherever he happens to be, and who can read his thoughts, for his prayer need not be vocal; lastly, of One who can effect a critical change in the state of feeling of others towards him. That is, we shall not be wrong in holding that this child has in his mind the image of an Invisible Being, who exercises a particular providence among us, who is present every where, who is heart-reading, heart-changing, ever-accessible, open to impetration. What a strong and intimate vision of God must he have already attained, if, as I have supposed, an ordinary trouble of mind has the spontaneous effect of leading him for consolation and aid to an Invisible Personal Power!

Moreover, this image brought before his mental vision is the image of One who by implicit threat and promise commands certain things which he, the same child, coincidently, by the same act of his mind, approves; which receive the adhesion of his moral sense and judgment, as right and good. It is the image of One who is good, inasmuch as enjoining and enforcing what is right and good, and who, in consequence, not only excites in the child hope and fear,—nay (it may be added), gratitude towards Him, as giving a law and maintaining it by reward and punishment,—but kindles in him love towards Him, as giving him a good law, and therefore as being good Himself, for it is the property of goodness to kindle love, or rather the very object of love is goodness; and all those distinct elements of the moral law, which the typical child, whom I am supposing, more or less consciously loves and approves,—truth, purity, justice, kindness, and the like,—are but shapes and aspects of goodness. And having in his degree a sensibility towards them all, for the sake of them all he is moved to love the Lawgiver, who enjoins them upon him. And, as he can contemplate these qualities and their manifestations under the common name of goodness, he is prepared to think of them as indivisible, correlative, supplementary of each other in one and the same Personality, so that there is no aspect of goodness which God is not; and that the more, because the notion of a perfection embracing all possible excellences, both moral and intellectual, is especially congenial to the mind, and there are in fact intellectual attributes, as well as moral, included in the child's image of God, as above represented.

Such is the apprehension which even a child may have of his Sovereign, Lawgiver, and Judge; which is possible in the case of children, because, at least, some children possess it, whether others possess it or no; and which, when it is found in children, is found to act promptly and keenly, by reason of the paucity of their ideas. It is an image of the good God, good in Himself, good relatively to the child, with whatever incompleteness; an image before it has been reflected on, and before it is recognized by him as a notion. Though he cannot explain or define the word "God," when told to use it, his acts show that to him it is far more than a word. He listens, indeed, with wonder and interest to fables or tales; he has a dim, shadowy sense of what he hears about persons and matters of this world; but he has that within him which actually vibrates, responds, and gives a deep meaning to the lessons of his first teachers about the will and the providence of God.

How far this initial religious knowledge comes from without, and how far from within, how much is natural, how much implies a special divine aid which is above nature, we have no means of determining, nor is it necessary for my present purpose to determine. I am not engaged in tracing the image of God in the mind of a child or a man to its first origins, but showing that he can become possessed of such an image, over and above all mere notions of God, and in what that image consists. Whether its elements, latent in the mind, would ever be elicited without extrinsic help is very doubtful; but whatever be the actual history of the first formation of the divine image within us, so far at least is certain, that, by informations external to ourselves, as time goes on, it admits of being strengthened and improved. It is certain too, that, whether it grows brighter and stronger, or, on the other hand, is dimmed, distorted, or obliterated, depends on each of us individually, and on his circumstances. It is more than probable that, in the event, from neglect, from the temptations of life, from bad companions, or from the urgency of secular occupations, the light of the soul will fade away and die out. Men transgress their sense of duty, and gradually lose those sentiments of shame and fear, the natural supplements of transgression, which, as I have said, are the witnesses of the Unseen Judge. And, even were it deemed impossible that those who had in their first youth a genuine apprehension of Him, could ever utterly lose it, yet that apprehension may become almost undistinguishable from an inferential acceptance of the great truth, or may dwindle into a mere notion of their intellect. On the contrary, the image of God, if duly cherished, may expand, deepen, and be completed, with the growth of their powers and in the course of life, under the varied lessons, within and without them, which are brought home to them concerning that same God, One and Personal, by means of education, social intercourse, experience, and literature.

To a mind thus carefully formed upon the basis of its natural conscience, the world, both of nature and of man, does but give back a reflection of those truths about the One Living God, which have been familiar to it from childhood. Good and evil meet us daily as we pass through life, and there are those who think it philosophical to act towards the manifestations of each with some sort of impartiality, as if evil had as much right to be there as good, or even a better, as having more striking triumphs and a broader jurisdiction. And because the course of things is determined by fixed laws, they consider that those laws preclude the present agency of the Creator in the carrying out of particular issues. It is otherwise with the theology of a religious imagination. It has a living hold on truths which are really to be found in the world, though they are not upon the surface. It is able to pronounce by anticipation, what it takes a long argument to prove—that good is the rule, and evil the exception. It is able to assume that, uniform as are the laws of nature, they are consistent with a particular Providence. It interprets what it sees around it by this previous inward teaching, as the true key of that maze of vast complicated disorder; and thus it gains a more and more consistent and luminous vision of God from the most unpromising materials. Thus conscience is a connecting principle between the creature and his Creator; and the firmest hold of theological truths is gained by habits of personal religion. When men begin all their works with the thought of God, acting for His sake and to fulfil His will, when they ask His blessing on themselves and their life, pray to Him for the objects they desire, and see Him in the event, whether it be according to their prayers or not, they will find everything that happens tend to confirm them in the truths about Him which live in their imagination, varied and unearthly as those truths may be. Then they are brought into His presence as that of a Living Person, and are able to hold converse with Him, and that with a directness and simplicity, with a confidence and intimacy, *mutatis mutandis,* which we use towards an earthly superior; so that it is doubtful whether we realize the company of our fellow-men with greater keenness than these favoured minds are able to contemplate and adore the Unseen, Incomprehensible Creator.

This vivid apprehension of religious objects, on which I have been enlarging, is independent of the written records of

Revelation; it does not require any knowledge of Scripture, nor of the history or the teaching of the Catholic Church. It is independent of books. But if so much may be traced out in the twilight of Natural Religion, it is obvious how great an addition in fulness and exactness is made to our mental image of the Divine Personality and Attributes, by the light of Christianity. And, indeed, to give us a clear and sufficient object for our faith, is one main purpose of the Supernatural Dispensations of Religion. This purpose is carried out in the written Word, with an effectiveness which inspiration alone could secure, first, by the histories which form so large a portion of the Old Testament; and scarcely less impressively in the prophetical system, as it is gradually unfolded and perfected in the writings of those who were its ministers and spokesmen. And as the exercise of the affections strengthens our apprehension of the object of them, it is impossible to exaggerate the influence exerted on the religious imagination by a book of devotions so sublime, so penetrating, so full of deep instruction as the Psalter, to say nothing of other portions of the Hagiographa. And then as regards the New Testament, the Gospels, from their subject, contain a manifestation of the Divine Nature, so special, as to make it appear from the contrast as if nothing were known of God, when they are unknown. Lastly, the Apostolic Epistles, the long history of the Church, with its fresh and fresh exhibitions of Divine Agency, the Lives of the Saints, and the reasonings, internal collisions, and decisions of the Theological School, form an extended comment on the words and works of our Lord.

I think I need not say more in illustration of the subject which I proposed for consideration in this Section. I have wished to trace the process by which the mind arrives, not only at a notional, but at an imaginative or real assent to the doctrine that there is One God, that is, an assent made with an apprehension, not only of what the words of the proposition mean, but of the object denoted by them. Without a proposition or thesis there can be no assent, no belief, at all; any more than there can be an inference without a conclusion. The proposition that there is One Personal and Present God may be held in either way; either as a theological truth, or as a religious fact or reality. The notion and the reality assented to are represented by one and the same proposition, but serve as distinct interpretations of it. When the proposition is apprehended for the purposes of proof, analysis, comparison, and the like intellectual exercises, it is used as the expression of a notion; when for the purposes of devotion, it is the image of a reality. Theology, properly and directly, deals with notional apprehension; religion with imaginative.

Here we have the solution of the common mistake of supposing that there is a contrariety and antagonism between a dogmatic creed and vital religion. People urge that salvation consists, not in believing the propositions that there is a God, that there is a Saviour, that our Lord is God, that there is a Trinity, but in believing in God, in a Saviour, in a Sanctifier; and they object that such propositions are but a formal and human medium destroying all true reception of the Gospel, and making religion a matter of words or of logic, instead of its having its seat in the heart. They are right so far as this, that men can and sometimes do rest in the propositions themselves as expressing intellectual notions; they are wrong, when they maintain that men need do so or always do so. The propositions may and must be used, and can easily be used, as the expression of facts, not notions, and they are necessary to the mind in the same way that language is ever necessary for denoting facts, both for ourselves as individuals, and for our intercourse with others. Again, they are useful in their dogmatic aspect as ascertaining and making clear for us the truths on which the religious imagination has to rest. Knowledge must ever precede the exercise of the affections. We feel gratitude and love, we feel indignation and dislike, when we have the informations actually put before us which are to kindle those several emotions. We love our parents, as our parents, when we know them to be our parents; we must know concerning

God, before we can feel love, fear, hope, or trust towards Him. Devotion must have its objects; those objects, as being supernatural, when not represented to our senses by material symbols, must be set before the mind in propositions. The formula, which embodies a dogma for the theologian, readily suggests an object for the worshipper. It seems a truism to say, yet it is all that I have been saying, that in religion the imagination and affections should always be under the control of reason. Theology may stand as a substantive science, though it be without the life of religion; but religion cannot maintain its ground at all without theology. Sentiment, whether imaginative or emotional, falls back upon the intellect for its stay, when sense cannot be called into exercise; and it is in this way that devotion falls back upon dogma.

2

BELIEF IN THE HOLY TRINITY

OF COURSE I CANNOT HOPE to carry all inquiring minds with me in what I have been laying down in the foregoing Section. I have appealed to the testimony given implicitly by our conscience to the Divine Being and His Attributes, and there are those, I know, whose experience will not respond to the appeal:—doubtless; but are there any truths which have reality, whether of experience or of reason, which are not disputed by some schools of philosophy or some bodies of men? If we assume nothing but what has universal reception, the field of our possible discussions will suffer much contraction; so that it must be considered sufficient in any inquiry, if the principles or facts assumed have a large following. This condition is abundantly fulfilled as regards the authority and religious meaning of conscience;—that conscience is the voice of God has almost grown into a proverb. This solemn dogma is recognized as such by the great mass both of the young and of the uneducated, by the religious few and the irreligious many. It is proclaimed in the history and literature of nations; it has had supporters in all ages, places, creeds, forms of social life, professions, and classes. It has held its ground under great intellectual and moral disadvantages; it has recovered its supremacy, and ultimately triumphed in the minds of those who had rebelled against it. Even philosophers, who have been antagonists on other points, agree in recognizing the inward voice of that solemn Monitor, personal, peremptory, unargumentative, irresponsible, minatory, definitive. This I consider enough to relieve me of the necessity of arguing with those who would resolve our sense of right and wrong into a sense of the Expedient, of the Beautiful, or would refer its authoritative suggestions to the effect of teaching or of association. There are those who can see and hear for all the common purposes of life, yet have no eye for colours or their shades, or no ear for music; moreover, there are degrees of sensibility to colours and to sounds, in the comparison of man with man, while some men are stone-blind or stone-deaf. Again, all men, as time goes on, have the prospect of losing that keenness of sight and hearing which they possessed in their youth; and so, in like manner, we may lose in manhood and in age that sense of a Supreme Teacher and Judge which was the gift of our first years; and that the more, because in most men the imagination suffers from the lapse of time and the experience of life, long before the bodily senses fail. And this accords with the advice of the sacred writer to "remember our Creator in the days of our youth," while our moral sensibilities are fresh, "before the sun and the light and the moon and the stars be darkened, and the clouds return after the rain." Accordingly, if there be those who deny that the dictate of conscience is ever more than a taste, or an association, it is a less difficulty to me to believe that they are deficient either in the religious sense or in their memory of early years, than that they never had at all what those around them without hesitation profess, in their own case, to have received from nature.

So much on the doctrine of the Being and Attributes of God, and of the real apprehension with which we can contemplate and assent to it:—now I turn to the doctrine of the Holy Trinity, with the purpose of investigating in like manner how far it belongs to theology, how far to the faith and devotion of the individual; how far the propositions enunciating it are confined to the expression of intellectual notions, and how far they stand for things also, and admit of that assent which we give to objects presented to us by the imagination. And first I have to state what our doctrine is.

No one is to be called a Theist, who does not believe in a Personal God, whatever difficulty there may be in defining the word "Personal." Now it is the belief of Catholics about the Supreme Being, that this essential characteristic of His Nature is reiterated in three distinct ways or modes; so that the Almighty God, instead of being One Person only, which is the teaching of Natural Religion, has Three Personalities, and is at once, according as we view Him in the one or the other of them, the Father, the Son, and the Spirit—a Divine Three, who bear towards Each Other the several relations which those names indicate, and are in that respect distinct from Each Other, and in that alone.

This is the teaching of the Athanasian Creed; viz. that the One Personal God, who is not a logical or physical unity, but a Living *Monas,* more really one even than an individual man is one—He ("unus," not "unum," because of the inseparability of His Nature and Personality),—He at once is Father, is Son, is Holy Ghost, Each of whom is that One Personal God in the fulness of His Being and Attributes; so that the Father is all that is meant by the word "God," as if we knew nothing of Son, or of Spirit; and in like manner the Son and the Spirit are Each by Himself all that is meant by the word, as if the Other Two were unknown; moreover, that by the word "God" is meant nothing over and above what is meant by the "Father," or by "the Son," or by "the Holy Ghost;" and that the Father is in no sense the Son, nor the Son the Holy Ghost, nor the Holy Ghost the Father. Such is the prerogative of the Divine Infinitude, that that One and Single Personal Being, the Almighty God, is really Three, while He is absolutely One.

Indeed, the Catholic dogma may be said to be summed up in this very formula on which St. Augustine lays so much stress, "Tres et Unus," not merely "Unum;" hence that formula is the key-note, as it may be called, of the Athanasian Creed. In that Creed we testify to the Unus Increatus, to the Unus Immensus, Omnipotens, Deus, and Dominus; yet Each of the Three also is by Himself Increatus, Immensus, Omnipotens, for Each is that One God, though Each is not the Other; Each, as is intimated by Unus Increatus, is the One Personal God of Natural Religion.

That this doctrine, thus drawn out, is of a notional character, is plain; the question before me is whether in any sense it can become the object of real apprehension, that is, whether any portion of it may be considered as addressed to the imagination, and is able to exert that living mastery over the mind, which is instanced as I have shown above, as regards the proposition, "There is a God."

"There is a God," when really apprehended, is the object of a strong energetic adhesion, which works a revolution in the mind; but when held merely as a notion, it requires but a cold and ineffective acceptance, though it be held ever so unconditionally. Such in its character is the assent of thousands, whose imaginations are not at all kindled, nor their hearts inflamed, nor their conduct affected, by the most august of all conceivable truths. I ask, then, as concerns the doctrine of the Holy Trinity, such as I have drawn it out to be, is it capable of being apprehended otherwise than notionally? Is it a theory, undeniable indeed, but addressed to the student, and to no one else? Is it the elaborate, subtle, triumphant exhibition of a truth, completely developed, and happily adjusted, and accurately balanced on its centre, and impregnable on every side, as a scientific view, "totus, teres, atque rotundus," challenging all assailants, or, on the other hand, does it come to the unlearned, the young, the busy, and the afflicted, as a fact which is to arrest them, penetrate them, and to support and animate them in their passage through life? That is, does it admit of being held in the imagination, and being embraced with a real assent? I maintain it does, and that it is the normal faith which every Christian has, on which he is stayed, which is his spiritual life, there being nothing in the exposition of the dogma, as I have given it above, which does not address the imagination, as well as the intellect.

Now let us observe what is not in that exposition;—there are no scientific terms in it. I will not allow that "Personal" is such, because it is a word in common use, and though it cannot mean precisely the same when used of God as when it is used of man, yet it is sufficiently explained by that common use, to allow of its being intelligibly applied to the Divine Nature. The other words, which occur in the above account of the doctrine,—Three, One, He, God, Father, Son, Spirit,—are none of them words peculiar to theology, have all a popular meaning, and are used according to that obvious and popular meaning, when introduced into the Catholic dogma. No human words indeed are worthy of the Supreme Being, none are adequate; but we have no other words to use but human, and those in question are among the simplest and most intelligible that are to be found in language.

There are then no terms in the foregoing exposition which do not admit of a plain sense, and they are there used in that sense; and, moreover, that sense is what I have called real, for the words in their ordinary use stand for things. The words, Father, Son, Spirit, He, One, and the rest, are not abstract terms, but concrete, and adapted to excite images. And these words thus simple and clear, are embodied in simple, clear, brief, categorical propositions. There is nothing abstruse either in the terms themselves, or in their setting. It is otherwise of course with formal theological treatises on the subject of the dogma. There we find such words as substance, essence, existence, form, subsistence, notion, circumincession; and, though these are far easier to understand than might at first sight be thought, still they are doubtless addressed to the intellect, and can only command a notional assent.

It will be observed also that not even the words "mysteriousness" and "mystery" occur in the exposition which I have given of the doctrine; I omitted them, because they are not parts of the Divine Verity as such, but in relation to creatures and to the human intellect; and because they are of a notional character. It is plain of course even at first sight that the doctrine is an inscrutable mystery, or has an inscrutable mysteriousness; few minds indeed but have theology enough to see this; and if an educated man, to whom it is presented, does not perceive that mysteriousness at once, that is a sure token that he does not rightly apprehend the propositions which contain the doctrine. Hence it follows that the thesis "the doctrine of the Holy Trinity in unity is mysterious" is indirectly an article of faith. But such an article, being a reflection made upon a revealed truth in an inference, expresses a notion, not a thing. It does not relate to the direct apprehension of the object, but to a judgment of our reason upon the object. Accordingly the mysteriousness of the doctrine is not, strictly speaking, intrinsical to it, as it is proposed to the religious apprehension, though in matter of fact a devotional mind on perceiving that mysteriousness, will lovingly appropriate it, as involved in the divine revelation; and, as such a mind turns all thoughts which come before it to a sacred use, so will it dwell upon the mystery of the Trinity with awe and veneration, as a truth befitting, so to say, the Immensity and Incomprehensibility of the Supreme Being.

However, I do not put forward the mystery as the direct object of real or religious apprehension; nor again, the complex doctrine (when it is viewed *per modum unius,* as one whole), in which the mystery lies. Let it be observed, it is possible for the mind to hold a number of propositions either in their combination, as one whole, or one by one; one by one, with an intelligent perception indeed of all, and of the general direction of each towards the rest, yet of each separately from the rest, for its own sake only, and not in connexion and one with the rest. Thus I may know London quite well, and find my way from street to street in any part of it without difficulty, yet be quite unable to draw a map of it. Comparison, calculation, cataloguing, arranging, classifying, are intellectual acts subsequent upon, and not necessary for, a real apprehension of the things on which they are exercised. Strictly speaking then, the dogma of the Holy Trinity, as a complex whole, or as a mystery, is not the formal object of religious apprehension and assent; but as it is a number of propositions, taken one by one. That complex whole also, is the object of assent, but it is the notional object; and when presented to religious minds, it is received by them notionally; and again implicitly, viz. in the real assent which they give to the word of God as conveyed to them through the instrumentality of His Church. On these points it may be right to enlarge.

Of course, as I have been saying, a man of ordinary intelligence will be at once struck with the apparent contrariety between the propositions one with another which constitute the Heavenly Dogma, and, by reason of his spontaneous activity of mind and by an habitual association, he will be compelled to view the Dogma in the light of that contrariety,—so much so that to hold one and all of these separate propositions will be to such a man all one with holding the mystery, as a mystery; and in consequence he will so hold it;—but still, I say, so far he will hold it only with a notional apprehension. He will accurately take in the meaning of each of the dogmatic propositions in its relation to the rest of them, combining them into one whole and embracing what he cannot realize, with an assent, notional indeed, but as genuine and thorough as any real assent can be. But the question is whether a real assent to the mystery, as such, is possible; and I say it is not possible, because, though we can image the separate propositions, we cannot image them all together. We cannot, because the mystery transcends all our experience; we have no experiences in our memory which we can put together, compare, contrast, unite, and thereby transmute into an image of the Ineffable Verity;—certainly; but what *is* in some degree a matter of experience, what *is* presented for the imagination, the affections, the devotion, the spiritual life of the Christian to repose upon with a real assent, what stands for things, not for notions only, is each of those propositions taken one by one, and that, not in the case of intellectual and thoughtful minds only, but of all religious minds whatever, in the case of a child or a peasant, as well as of a philosopher.

This is only one instance of a general principle which holds good in all such real apprehension as is possible to us, of God and His Attributes. Not only do we see Him at best only in shadows, but we cannot bring even those shadows together, for they flit to and fro, and are never present to us at once. We can indeed combine the various matters which we know of Him by an act of the intellect, and treat them theologically, but such theological combinations are no objects for the imagination to gaze upon. Our image of Him never is one, but broken into numberless partial aspects, independent each of each. As we cannot see the whole starry firmament at once, but have to turn ourselves from east to west, and then round to east again, sighting first one constellation and then another, and losing these in order to gain those, so it is, and much more, with such real apprehensions as we can secure of the Divine Nature. We know one truth about Him and another truth,— but we cannot image both of them together; we cannot bring them before us by one act of the mind; we drop the one while we turn to take up the other. None of them are fully dwelt on and enjoyed, when they are viewed in combination. Moreover, our devotion is tried and confused by the long list of propositions which theology is obliged to draw up, by the limitations, explanations, definitions, adjustments, balancings, cautions, arbitrary prohibitions, which are imperatively required by the weakness of human thought and the imperfections of human languages. Such exercises of reasoning indeed do but increase and harmonize our notional apprehension of the dogma, but they add little to the luminousness and vital force with which its separate propositions come home to our imagination, and if they are necessary, as they certainly are, they are necessary not so much for faith, as against unbelief.

Break a ray of light into its constituent colours, each is beautiful, each may be enjoyed; attempt to unite them, and perhaps you produce only a dirty white. The pure and indivisible Light is seen only by the blessed inhabitants of heaven; here we have but such faint reflections of It as its diffraction supplies; but they are sufficient for faith and devotion. Attempt to combine them into one, and you gain nothing but a mystery, which you can describe as a notion, but cannot depict as an imagination. And this, which holds of the Divine Attributes, holds also of the Holy Trinity in Unity. And hence, perhaps, it is that the latter doctrine is never spoken of as a Mystery in the sacred book, which is addressed far more to the imagination and affections than to the intellect. Hence, too, what is more remarkable, in the Creeds the dogma is not called a mystery; not in the Apostles' nor the Nicene, nor even in the Athanasian. The reason seems to be, that the Creeds have a place in the Ritual; they are devotional acts, and of the nature of prayers, addressed to God; and, in such addresses, to speak of intellectual difficulties would be out of place. It must be recollected especially that the Athanasian Creed has sometimes been called the "Psalmus *Quicunque.*" It is not a mere collection of notions, however momentous. It is a psalm or hymn of praise, of confession, and of profound, self-prostrating homage, parallel to the canticles of the elect in the Apocalypse. It appeals to the imagination quite as much as to the intellect. It is the war-song of faith, with which we warn first ourselves, then each other, and then all those who are within its hearing, and the hearing of the Truth, who our God is, and how we must worship Him, and how vast our responsibility will be if we know what to believe, and yet believe not. It is

The Psalm that gathers in one glorious lay
All chants that o'er from heaven to earth found way;
Creed of the Saints, and Anthem of the Blest,
And calm-breathed warning of the kindliest love
That ever heaved a wakeful mother's breast.

For myself, I have ever felt it as the most simple and sublime, the most devotional formulary to which Christianity has given birth, more so even than the *Veni Creator* and the *Te Deum*. Even the antithetical form of its sentences, which is a stumbling-block to so many, as seeming to force, and to exult in forcing a mystery upon recalcitrating minds, has to my apprehension, even notionally considered, a very different drift. It is intended as a check upon our reasonings, lest they rush on in one direction beyond the limits of the truth, and it turns them back into the opposite direction. Certainly it implies a glorying in the Mystery; but it is not simply a statement of the Mystery for the sake of its mysteriousness.

What is more remarkable still, a like silence as to the mysteriousness of the doctrine is observed in the successive definitions of the Church concerning it. Confession after confession, canon after canon is drawn up in the course of centuries; Popes and Councils have found it their duty to insist afresh upon the dogma; they have enunciated it in new or additional propositions; but not even in their most elaborate formularies do they use the word "mystery," as far as I know. The great Council of Toledo pursues the scientific ramifications of the doctrine, with the exact diligence of theology, at a length four times that of the Athanasian Creed; the fourth Lateran completes, by a final enunciation, the development of the sacred doctrine after the mind of St. Augustine; the Creed of Pope Pius IV. prescribes the general rule of faith against the heresies of these latter times; but in none of them do we find either the word "mystery," or any suggestion of mysteriousness.

Such is the usage of the Church in its dogmatic statements concerning the Holy Trinity, as if fulfilling the maxim, "Lex orandi, lex credendi." I suppose it is founded on a tradition, because the custom is otherwise as regards catechisms and theological treatises. These belong to particular ages and places, and are addressed to the intellect. In them, certainly, the mysteriousness of the doctrine is almost uniformly insisted on. But, however this contrast of usage is to be explained, the creeds are enough to show that the dogma may be taught in its fulness for the purposes of popular faith and devotion without directly insisting on that mysteriousness, which is necessarily contained in the combined view of its separate propositions. That systematized whole is the object of notional assent, and its propositions, one by one, are the objects of real.

To show this in fact, I will enumerate the separate propositions of which the dogma consists. They are nine, and stand as follows:—

1. There are Three who give testimony in heaven, the Father, the Word or Son, and the Holy Spirit. 2. From the Father is, and ever has been, the Son. 3. From the Father and Son is, and ever has been, the Spirit.

4. The Father is the One Eternal Personal God. 5. The Son is the One Eternal Personal God. 6. The Spirit is the One Eternal Personal God.

7. The Father is not the Son. 8. The Son is not the Holy Ghost. 9. The Holy Ghost is not the Father.

Now I think it is a fact, that, whereas these nine propositions contain the Mystery, yet, taken, not as a whole, but separately, each by itself, they are not only apprehensible, but admit of a real apprehension.

Thus, for instance, if the proposition "There is One who bears witness of Himself," or "reveals Himself," would admit of a real assent, why does not also the proposition "There are Three who bear witness"?

Again, if the word "God" may create an image in our minds, why may not the proposition "The Father is God"? or again, "The Son," or "The Holy Ghost is God"?

Again, to say that "the Son is other than the Holy Ghost," or "neither Son nor Holy Ghost is the Father," is not a simple negative, but also a declaration that Each of the Divine Three by Himself is complete in Himself, and simply and absolutely God as though the other Two were not revealed to us.

Again, from our experience of the works of man, we accept with a real apprehension the proposition "The Angels are made by God," correcting the word "made," as is required in the case of a creating Power, and a spiritual work:—why then may we not in like manner refine and elevate the human analogy, yet keep the image, when a Divine Birth is set before us in terms which properly belong to what is human and earthly? If our experience enables us to apprehend the essential fact of sonship, as being a communication of, being and of nature from one to another, why should we not thereby in a certain measure realize the proposition "The Word is the Son of God"?

Again, we have abundant instances in nature of the general law of one thing coming from another or from others:—as the child issues in the man as his quasi-successor, and the child and the man issue in the old man, like them both, but not the same, so different as almost to have a fresh personality distinct from each, so we may form some image, however vague, of the procession of the Holy Spirit from Father and Son. This is what I should say of the propositions which I have numbered two and three, which are the least susceptible of a real assent out of the nine.

So much at first sight; but the force of what I have been saying will be best understood, by considering what Scripture and the Ritual of the Church witness in accordance with it. In referring to these two great storehouses of faith and devotion, I must premise, as when I spoke of the Being of a God, that I am not proving by means of them the dogma of the Holy Trinity, but using the one and the other in illustration of the action of the separate articles of that dogma upon the imagination, though the complex truth, in which, when combined, they issue, is not in sympathy or correspondence with it, but altogether beyond it; and next of the action and influence of those separate articles by means of the imagination, upon the affections and obedience of Christians, high and low.

This being understood, I ask what chapter of St. John or St. Paul is not full of the Three Divine Names, introduced in one or other of the above nine propositions, expressed or implied, or in their parallels, or in parts or equivalents of them? What lesson is there given us by these two chief writers of the New Testament, which does not grow out of Their Persons and Their Offices? At one time we read of the grace of the Second Person, the love of the First, and the communication of the Third; at another we are told by the Son, "I will pray the Father, and He will send you another Paraclete;" and then, "All that the Father hath are Mine; the Paraclete shall receive of Mine." Then again we read of "the foreknowledge of the Father, the sanctification of the Spirit, the Blood of Jesus Christ;" and again we are to "pray in the Holy Ghost, abide in the love of God, and look for the mercy of Jesus." And so, in like manner, to Each, in one passage or another, are ascribed the same titles and works: Each is acknowledged as Lord; Each is eternal; Each is Truth; Each is holiness; Each is all in all; Each is Creator; Each wills with a Supreme Will; Each is the Author of the new birth; Each speaks in His ministers; Each is the Revealer; Each is the Lawgiver; Each is the teacher of the elect; in Each the elect have fellowship; Each leads them on; Each raises them from the dead. What is all this, but "the Father Eternal, the Son Eternal, and the Holy Ghost Eternal, the Father, Son, and Holy Ghost Omnipotent; the Father, Son, and Holy Ghost God," of the Athanasian Creed? And if the New Testament be, as it confessedly is, so real in its teaching, so luminous, so impressive, so constraining, so full of images, so sparing in mere notions, whence is this but because, in its references to the Objects of our supreme worship, it is ever ringing the changes (so to say) on the nine propositions which I have set down, and on the particular statements into which they may be severally resolved?

Take one of them, as an instance, viz. the dogmatic sentence

"The Son is God." What an illustration of the real assent which can be given to this proposition, and its power over our affections and emotions, is the first half of the first chapter of St. John's Gospel! or again the vision of our Lord in the first chapter of the Apocalypse! or the first chapter of St. John's first Epistle! Again, how burning are St. Paul's words when he speaks of our Lord's crucifixion and death! what is the secret of that flame, but this same dogmatic sentence, "The Son is God"? why should the death of the Son be more awful than any other death, except that He, though man, was God? And so, again, all through the Old Testament, what is it which gives an interpretation and a persuasive power to so many passages and portions, especially in the Psalms and the Prophets, but this same theological formula, "The Messias is God," a proposition which never could thus vivify in the religious mind the letter of the sacred text, unless it appealed to the imagination, and could be held with a much stronger assent than any that is merely notional.

This same power of the dogma may be illustrated from the Ritual. Consider the services for Christmas or Epiphany; for Easter, Ascension, and (I may say) preeminently Corpus Christi; what are these great Festivals but comments on the words, "The Son is God"? Yet who will say that they have the subtlety, the ardity, the coldness of mere scholastic science? Are they addressed to the pure intellect, or to the imagination? do they interest our logical faculty, or excite our devotion? Why is it that personally we often find ourselves so ill-fitted to take part in them, except that we are not good enough, that in our case the dogma is far too much a theological notion, far too little an image living within us? And so again, as to the Divinity of The Holy Ghost: consider the breviary offices for Pentecost and its Octave, the grandest perhaps in the whole year; are they created out of mere abstractions and inferences, or what are sometimes called metaphysical distinctions, or has not the categorical proposition of St. Athanasius, "The Holy Ghost is God," such a place in the imagination and the heart, as suffices to give birth to the noble Hymns, *Veni Creator*, and *Veni Sancte Spiritus?*

I sum up then to the same effect as in the preceding Section. Religion has to do with the real, and the real is the particular; theology has to do with what is notional, and the notional is the general and systematic. Hence theology has to do with the dogma of the Holy Trinity as a whole made up of many propositions; but Religion has to do with each of those separate propositions which compose it, and lives and thrives in the contemplation of them. In them it finds the motives for devotion and faithful obedience; while theology on the other hand forms and protects them by virtue of its function of regarding them, not merely one by one, but as a system of truth.

One other remark is in place here. If the separate articles of the Athanasian Creed are so closely connected with vital and personal religion as I have shown them to be, if they supply motives on which a man may act, if they determine the state of mind, the special thoughts, affections, and habits, which he carries with him from this world to the next, is there cause to wonder, that the Creed should proclaim aloud, that those who are not internally such as Christ, by means of it, came to make them, are not capable of the heaven to which He died to bring them? Is not the importance of accepting the dogma the very explanation of that careful minuteness with which the few simple truths which compose it are inculcated, are reiterated, in the Creed? And shall the Church of God, to whom "the dispensation" of the Gospel is committed, forget the concomitant obligation, "Woe is unto me if I preach not the Gospel"? Are her ministers by their silence to bring upon themselves the Prophet's anathema, "Cursed is he that doth the work of the Lord deceitfully"? Can they ever forget the lesson conveyed to them in the Apostle's protestation, "God is faithful, as our preaching which was among you was not Yea and Nay.... For we are a good odour of Christ unto God in them that are in the way of salvation, and in them that are perishing. For we are not as the many, who adulterate the word of God; but with sincerity, but as from God, in the presence of God, so speak we in Christ"? [1]

3

BELIEF IN DOGMATIC THEOLOGY

IT IS A FAMILIAR CHARGE against the Catholic Church in the mouths of her opponents, that she imposes on her children as matters of faith, not only such dogmas as have an intimate bearing on moral conduct and character, but a great number of doctrines which none but professed theologians can understand, and which in consequence do but oppress the mind, and are the perpetual fuel of controversy. The first who made this complaint was no less a man than the great Constantine, and on no less an occasion than the rise of the Arian heresy, which he, as yet a catechumen, was pleased to consider a trifling and tolerable error. So, deciding the matter, he wrote at once a letter to Alexander, Bishop of Alexandria, and to Arius, who was a presbyter in the same city, exhorting them to drop the matter in dispute, and to live in peace with one another. He was answered by the meeting of the Council of Nicæa, and by the insertion of the word "Consubstantial" into the Creed of the Church.

What the Emperor thought of the controversy itself, that Bishop Jeremy Taylor thought of the insertion of the "Consubstantial," viz. that it was a mischievous affair, and ought never to have taken place. He thus quotes and comments on the Emperor's letter: "The Epistle of Constantine to Alexander and Arius tells the truth, and chides them both for commencing the question, Alexander for broaching it, Arius for taking it up. And although this be true, that it had been better for the

[1] *Vide* Note II at the end of the volume.

Church it had never begun, yet, being begun, what is to be done with it? Of this also, in that admirable epistle, we have the Emperor's judgment (I suppose not without the advice and privity of Hosius), . . . for first he calls it a certain vain piece of a question, ill begun, and more unadvisedly published,—a question which no law or ecclesiastical canon defineth; a fruitless contention; the product of idle brains; a matter so nice, so obscure, so intricate, that it was neither to be explicated by the clergy nor understood by the people; a dispute of words, a doctrine inexplicable, but most dangerous when taught, lest it introduce discord or blasphemy; and, therefore, the objector was rash, and the answer unadvised, for it concerned not the substance of faith or the worship of God, nor the chief commandment of Scripture; and, therefore, why should it be the matter of discord? for though the matter be grave, yet, because neither necessary nor explicable, the contention is trifling and toyish. . . . So that the matter being of no great importance, but vain and a toy in respect of the excellent blessings of peace and charity, it were good that Alexander and Arius should leave contending, keep their opinions to themselves, ask each other forgiveness, and give mutual toleration." [1]

Moreover, Taylor is of opinion that "they both did believe One God, and the Holy Trinity;" an opinion in the teeth of historical fact. Also he is of opinion, that "that faith is best which hath greatest simplicity, and that it is better in all cases humbly to submit, than curiously to inquire and pry into the mystery under the cloud, and to hazard our faith by improving knowledge." He is, further, of opinion, that "if the Nicene Fathers had done so too, possibly the Church would never have repented it." He also thinks that their insertion of the "Consubstantial" into the Creed was a bad precedent.

Whether it was likely to act as a precedent or not, it has not been so in fact, for fifteen hundred years have passed since the Nicene Council, and it is the one instance of a scientific

[1] Liberty of Prophesying, § 2.

word having been introduced into the Creed from that day to this. And after all, the word in question has a plain meaning, as the Council used it, easily stated and intelligible to all; for "consubstantial with the Father," is nothing more than "really one with the Father," being adopted to meet the evasion of the Arians. The Creed then remains now what it was in the beginning, a popular form of faith, suited to every age, class, and condition. Its declarations are categorical, brief, clear, elementary, of the first importance, expressive of the concrete, the objects of real apprehension, and the basis and rule of devotion. As to the proper Nicene formula itself, excepting the one term "Consubstantial," it has not a word which does not relate to the rudimental facts of Christianity. The Niceno-Constantinopolitan and the various ante-Nicene Symbols, of which the Apostles' is one, add summarily one or two notional articles, such as "the communion of Saints," and "the forgiveness of sins," which, however, may be readily converted into real propositions. On the other hand, one chief dogma, which is easy to popular apprehension, is necessarily absent from all of them, the Real Presence; but the omission is owing to the ancient "Disciplina Arcani," which withheld the Sacred Mystery from catechumens and heathen, to whom the Creed was known.

So far the charge which Taylor brings forward has no great plausibility; but it is not the whole of his case. I cannot deny that a large and ever-increasing collection of propositions, abstract notions, not concrete truths, become, by the successive definitions of Councils, a portion of the *credenda,* and have an imperative claim upon the faith of every Catholic; and this being the case, it will be asked me how I am borne out by facts in enlarging, as I have done, on the simplicity and directness, on the tangible reality, of the Church's dogmatic teaching.

I will suppose the objection urged thus:—why has not the Catholic Church limited her *credenda* to propositions such as those in her Creed, concrete and practical, easy of apprehension, and of a character to win assent? such as "Christ is God;"

"This is My Body;" "Baptism gives life to the soul;" "The Saints intercede for us;" "Death, judgment, heaven, hell, the four last things;" "There are seven gifts of the Holy Ghost," "three theological virtues," "seven capital sins," and the like, as they are found in her catechisms. On the contrary, she makes it imperative on every one, priest and layman, to profess as revealed truth all the canons of the Councils, and innumerable decisions of Popes, propositions so various, so notional, that but few can know them, and fewer can understand them. What sense, for instance, can a child or a peasant, nay, or any ordinary Catholic, put upon the Tridentine Canons, even in translation? such as, "Siquis dixerit homines sine Christi justitiâ, per quam nobis meruit, justificari, aut per eam ipsam formaliter justos esse, anathema sit;" or "Siquis dixerit justificatum peccare, dum intuitu æternæ mercedis bene operatur, anathema sit." Or again, consider the very anathematism annexed by the Nicene Council to its Creed, the language of which is so obscure, that even theologians differ about its meaning. It runs as follows:—"Those who say that once the Son was not, and before He was begotten He was not, and that He was made out of that which was not, or who pretend that He was of other hypostasis or substance, or that the Son of God is created, mutable, or alterable, the Holy Catholic and Apostolic Church anathematizes." These doctrinal enunciations are *de fide;* peasants are bound to believe them as well as controversialists, and to believe them as truly as they believe that our Lord is God. How then are the Catholic *credenda* easy and within reach of all men?

I begin my answer to this objection by recurring to what has already been said concerning the relation of theology with its notional propositions to religious and devotional assent. Devotion is excited doubtless by the plain, categorical truths of revelation, such as the articles of the Creed; on these it depends; with these it is satisfied. It accepts them one by one; it is careless about intellectual consistency; it draws from each of them the spiritual nourishment which it was intended to supply. Far different, certainly, is the nature and duty of the intellect. It is ever active, inquisitive, penetrating; it examines doctrine and doctrine; it compares, contrasts, and forms them into a science; that science is theology. Now theological science, being thus the exercise of the intellect upon the *credenda* of revelation, is, though not directly devotional, at once natural, excellent, and necessary. It is natural, because the intellect is one of our highest faculties; excellent, because it is our duty to use our faculties to the full; necessary, because, unless we apply our intellect to revealed truth rightly, others will exercise their minds upon it wrongly. Accordingly, the Catholic intellect makes a survey and a catalogue of the doctrines contained in the *depositum* of revelation, as committed to the Church's keeping; it locates, adjusts, defines them each, and brings them together into a whole. Moreover, it takes particular aspects or portions of them; it analyzes them, whether into first principles really such, or into hypotheses of an illustrative character. It forms generalizations, and gives names to them. All these deductions are true, if rightly deduced, because they are deduced from what is true; and therefore in one sense they are a portion of the *depositum* of faith or *credenda*, while in another sense they are additions to it: however, additions or not, they have, I readily grant, the characteristic disadvantage of being abstract and notional statements.

Nor is this all: the disavowal of error is far more fruitful in additions than the enforcement of truth. There is another set of deductions, inevitable also, and also part or not part of the revealed *credenda*, according as we please to view them. If a proposition is true, its contradictory is false. If then a man believes that Christ is God, he believes also, and that necessarily, that to say He is not God is false, and that those who so say are in error. Here then again the prospect opens upon us of a countless multitude of propositions, which in their first elements are close upon devotional truth, of groups of propositions, and those groups divergent, independent, ever springing into life with an inexhaustible fecundity, according to the ever-germinating forms of heresy, of which they are the antagonists. These too have their place in theological science.

Such is theology in contrast to religion; and as follows from the circumstances of its formation, though some of its statements easily find equivalents in the language of devotion, the greater number of them are more or less unintelligible to the ordinary Catholic, as law-books to the private citizen. And especially those portions of theology which are the indirect creation, not of orthodox, but of heretical thought, such as the repudiations of error contained in the Canons of Councils, of which specimens have been given above, will ever be foreign, strange, and hard to the pious but uncontroversial mind; for what have good Christians to do, in the ordinary course of things, with the subtle hallucinations of the intellect? This is manifest from the nature of the case; but then the question recurs, why should the refutations of heresy be our objects of faith? if no mind, theological or not, can believe what it cannot understand, in what sense can the Canons of Councils and other ecclesiastical determinations be included in those *credenda* which the Church presents to every Catholic as if apprehensible, and to which every Catholic gives his firm interior assent?

In solving this difficulty I wish it first observed, that, if it is the duty of the Church to act as "the pillar and ground of the Truth," she is manifestly obliged from time to time, and to the end of time, to denounce opinions incompatible with that truth, whenever able and subtle minds in her communion venture to publish such opinions. Suppose certain Bishops and priests at this day began to teach that Islamism or Buddhism was a direct and immediate revelation from God, she would be bound to use the authority which God has given her to declare that such a proposition will not stand with Christianity, and that those who hold it are none of hers; and she would be bound to impose such a declaration on that very knot of persons who had committed themselves to the novel proposition, in order that, if they would not recant, they might be separated from her communion, as they were separate from her faith. In such a case, her masses of population would either not hear of the controversy, or they would at once take part with her, and without effort take any test, which secured the exclusion of the innovators; and she on the other hand would feel that what is a rule for some Catholics must be a rule for all. Who is to draw the line between who are to acknowledge that rule, and who are not? It is plain, there cannot be two rules of faith in the same communion, or rather, as the case really would be, an endless variety of rules, coming into force according to the multiplication of heretical theories, and to the degrees of knowledge and varieties of sentiment in individual Catholics. There is but one rule of faith for all; and it would be a greater difficulty to allow of an uncertain rule of faith, than (if that was the alternative, as it is not), to impose upon uneducated minds a profession which they cannot understand.

But it is not the necessary result of unity of profession, nor is it the fact, that the Church imposes dogmatic statements on the interior assent of those who cannot apprehend them. The difficulty is removed by the dogma of the Church's infallibility, and of the consequent duty of "implicit faith" in her word. The "One Holy Catholic and Apostolic Church" is an article of the Creed, and an article, which, inclusive of her infallibility, all men, high and low, can easily master and accept with a real and operative assent. It stands in the place of all abstruse propositions in a Catholic's mind, for to believe in her word is virtually to believe in them all. Even what he cannot understand, at least he can believe to be true; and he believes it to be true because he believes in the Church.

The *rationale* of this provision for unlearned devotion is as follows:—It stands to reason that all of us, learned and unlearned, are bound to believe the whole revealed doctrine in all its parts and in all that it implies, according as portion after portion is brought home to our conscience as belonging to it; and it also stands to reason, that a doctrine, so deep and so various, as the revealed *depositum* of faith, cannot be brought home to us and made our own all at once. No mind, however large, however penetrating, can directly and fully by one act understand any one truth, however simple. What can be more intelligible than that "Alexander conquered Asia," or that "Veracity is a duty"? but what a multitude of propositions is included under either of these theses! still, if we profess either, we profess all that it includes. Thus, as regards the Catholic Creed, if we really believe that our Lord is God, we believe all that is meant by such a belief; or, else, we are not in earnest, when we profess to believe the proposition. In the act of believing it at all, we forthwith commit ourselves by anticipation to believe truths which at present we do not believe, because they have never come before us;—we limit henceforth the range of our private judgment in prospect by the conditions, whatever they are, of that dogma. Thus the Arians said that they believed in our Lord's divinity, but when they were pressed to confess His eternity, they denied it: thereby showing in fact that they never had believed in His divinity at all. In other words, a man who really believes in our Lord's proper divinity, believes *implicitè* in His eternity.

And so, in like manner, of the whole *depositum* of faith, or the revealed word:—if we believe in the revelation, we believe in what is revealed, in all that is revealed, however it may be brought home to us, by reasoning or in any other way. He who believes that Christ is the Truth, and that the Evangelists are truthful, believes all that He has said through them, though he has only read St. Matthew and has not read St. John. He who believes in the *depositum* of Revelation, believes in all the doctrines of the *depositum;* and since he cannot know them all at once, he knows some doctrines, and does not know others; he may know only the Creed, nay, perhaps only the chief portions of the Creed; but, whether he knows little or much, he has the intention of believing all that there is to believe, whenever and as soon as it is brought home to him, if he believes in Revelation at all. All that he knows now as revealed, and all that he shall know, and all that there is to know, he embraces it all in his intention by one act of faith; otherwise, it is but an accident that he believes this or that, not because it is a revelation. This virtual, interpretative, or prospective belief is called a believing *implicitè;* and it follows from this, that, granting that the Canons of Councils and the other ecclesiastical documents and confessions, to which I have referred, are really involved in the *depositum* or revealed word, every Catholic, in accepting the *depositum,* does *implicitè* accept those dogmatic decisions.

I say, "granting these various propositions are virtually contained in the revealed word," for this is the only question left; and that it is to be answered in the affirmative, is clear at once to the Catholic, from the fact that the Church declares that they really belong to it. To her is committed the care and the interpretation of the revelation. The word of the Church is the word of the revelation. That the Church is the infallible oracle of truth is the fundamental dogma of the Catholic religion; and "I believe what the Church proposes to be believed" is an act of real assent, including all particular assents, notional and real; and, while it is possible for unlearned as well as learned, it is imperative on learned as well as unlearned. And thus it is, that by believing the word of the Church *implicitè,* that is, by believing all that that word does or shall declare itself to contain, every Catholic, according to his intellectual capacity, supplements the shortcomings of his knowledge without blunting his real assent to what is elementary, and takes upon himself from the first the whole truth of revelation, progressing from one apprehension of it to another according to his opportunities of doing so.

PART II

ASSENT AND INFERENCE

CHAPTER VI

ASSENT CONSIDERED AS UNCONDITIONAL

I HAVE NOW SAID as much as need be said about the relation of Assent to Apprehension, and shall turn to the consideration of the relation existing between Assent and Inference. As apprehension is a concomitant, so inference is ordinarily the antecedent of assent;—on this surely I need not enlarge;—but neither apprehension nor inference interferes with the unconditional character of the assent, viewed in itself. The circumstances of an act, however necessary to it, do not enter into the act; assent is in its nature absolute and unconditional, though it cannot be given except under certain conditions.

This is obvious; but what presents some difficulty is this, how it is that a conditional acceptance of a proposition,—such as is an act of inference,—is able to lead, as it does, to an unconditional acceptance of it,—such as is assent; how it is that a proposition which is not, and cannot be, demonstrated, which at the highest can only be proved to be truth-like, not true, such as "I shall die," nevertheless claims and receives our unqualified adhesion. To the consideration of this paradox, as it may be called, I shall now proceed; that is, to the consideration, first, of the act of assent to a proposition, which act is unconditional; next, of the act of inference, which goes before the assent and is conditional; and, thirdly, of the solution of the apparent inconsistency which is involved in holding that an unconditional acceptance of a proposition can be the result of its conditional verification.

119

1

SIMPLE ASSENT

THE DOCTRINE which I have been enunciating requires such careful explanation, that it is not wonderful that writers of great ability and name are to be found who have put it aside for a doctrine of their own; but no doctrine on the subject is without its difficulties, and certainly not theirs, though it carries with it a show of common sense. The authors to whom I refer wish to maintain that there are degrees of assent, and that, as the reasons for a proposition are strong or weak, so is the assent. It follows from this that absolute assent has no legitimate exercise, except as ratifying acts of intuition or demonstration. What is thus brought home to us is indeed to be accepted unconditionally; but as to reasonings in concrete matters, they are never more than probabilities, and the probability in each conclusion which we draw is the measure of our assent to that conclusion. Thus assent becomes a sort of necessary shadow, following upon inference, which is the substance; and is never without some alloy of doubt, because inference in the concrete never reaches more than probability.

Such is what may be called the *à priori* method of regarding assent in its relation to inference. It condemns an unconditional assent in concrete matters on what may be called the nature of the case. Assent cannot rise higher than its source; inference in such matters is at best conditional, therefore assent is conditional also.

Abstract argument is always dangerous, and this instance is no exception to the rule; I prefer to go by facts. The theory to which I have referred cannot be carried out in practice. It may be rightly said to prove too much; for it debars us from unconditional assent in cases in which the common voice of mankind, the advocates of this theory included, would protest against the prohibition. There are many truths in concrete matter, which no one can demonstrate, yet every one unconditionally accepts; and though of course there are innumerable propositions to which it would be absurd to give an absolute assent, still the absurdity lies in the circumstances of each particular case, as it is taken by itself, not in their common violation of the pretentious axiom that probable reasoning can never lead to certitude.

Locke's remarks on the subject are an illustration of what I have been saying. This celebrated writer, after the manner of his school, speaks freely of degrees of assent, and considers that the strength of assent given to each proposition varies with the strength of the inference on which the assent follows; yet he is obliged to make exceptions to his general principle,— exceptions, unintelligible on his abstract doctrine, but demanded by the logic of facts. The practice of mankind is too strong or the antecedent theorem, to which he is desirous to subject it.

First he says, in his chapter "On Probability," "Most of the propositions we think, reason, discourse, nay, act upon, are such as we cannot have undoubted knowledge of their truth; yet some of them *border so near* upon certainty, that we *make* no doubt at all about them, but *assent* to them *as firmly,* and act according to that assent as resolutely, *as if they were infallibly demonstrated,* and that our knowledge of them was perfect and certain." Here he allows that inferences, which are only "near upon certainty," are so near, that we legitimately accept them with "no doubt at all," and "assent to them as firmly as if they were infallibly demonstrated." That is, he affirms and sanctions the very paradox to which I am committed myself.

Again; he says, in his chapter on "The Degrees of Assent," that "when any particular thing, consonant to the constant observation of ourselves and others in the like case, comes attested by the concurrent reports of all that mention it, we receive it as easily, and build as firmly upon it, as if it were certain knowledge, and we reason and act thereupon, *with as little doubt as if it were perfect demonstration.*" And he repeats, "These *probabilities* rise so near to certainty, that they *govern our thoughts as absolutely,* and influence all our actions as fully, as *the most evident demonstration;* and in what concerns us, we make little or no difference between them and certain knowledge. *Our belief thus grounded, rises to assurance.*" Here again, "probabilities" may be so strong as to "govern our thoughts as absolutely" as sheer demonstration, so strong that belief, grounded on them, "rises to assurance," that is, to certitude.

I have so high a respect both for the character and the ability of Locke, for his manly simplicity of mind and his outspoken candour, and there is so much in his remarks upon reasoning and proof in which I fully concur, that I feel no pleasure in considering him in the light of an opponent to views which I myself have ever cherished as true, with an obstinate devotion; and I would willingly think that in the passage which follows in his chapter on "Enthusiasm," he is aiming at superstitious extravagances which I should repudiate myself as much as he can do; but, if so, his words go beyond the occasion, and contradict what I have quoted from him above.

"He that would seriously set upon the search of truth, ought, in the first place, to prepare his mind with a love of it. For he that loves it not will not take much pains to get it, nor be much concerned when he misses it. There is nobody, in the commonwealth of learning, who does not profess himself a lover of truth,—and there is not a rational creature, that would not take it amiss, to be thought otherwise of. And yet, for all this, one may truly say, there are very few lovers of truth, for truth-sake, even amongst those who persuade themselves that they are so. How a man may know, whether he be so, in earnest, is worth inquiry; and I think, there is this one unerring mark of it, viz. *the not entertaining any proposition with greater assurance than the proofs it is built on will warrant.* Whoever goes beyond this measure of assent, it is plain, receives not truth in the love of it, loves not truth for truth-sake, but for some other by-end. For the evidence that any proposition is true (*except such as are self-evident*) lying only in the proofs a man has of it, whatsoever degrees of assent he affords it *beyond the degrees of that* evidence, it is plain *all that surplusage of assurance* is owing to some other affection, and not to the love of truth; it being as *impossible* that the love of truth should carry *my assent above the evidence* there is to me that it is true, as that the love of truth should make me assent to any proposition for the sake of that evidence which it has not that it is true; which is in effect to love it as a truth, because it is possible or probable that it may not be true." [1]

Here he says that it is not only illogical, but immoral to "carry our *assent above* the *evidence* that a proposition is true," to have "a surplusage of *assurance beyond* the degrees of that evidence." And he excepts from this rule only self-evident propositions. How then is it not consistent with right reason, with the love of truth for its own sake, to allow in his words quoted above, certain strong "probabilities" to "govern our thoughts as absolutely as the most evident demonstration"? how is there no "surplusage of assurance beyond the degrees of evidence" when in the case of those strong probabilities, we permit "our belief, thus grounded, to rise to assurance," as he pronounces we are rational in doing? Of course he had in view one set of instances, when he implied that demonstration was the condition of absolute assent, and another set when he said that it was no such condition; but he surely cannot be acquitted of slovenly thinking in thus treating a cardinal subject. A philosopher should so anticipate the application, and guard the enunciation of his principles, as to secure them against the risk of their being made to change places with each other, to defend what he is eager to denounce, and to condemn what he finds it necessary to sanction. However, whatever is to be thought of his *à priori* method and his logical consistency, his *animus*, I fear, must be understood as hostile

[1] Reference is made to Locke's statements in "Essay on Development of Doctrine," ch. vii § 2.

to the doctrine which I am going to maintain. He takes a view of the human mind, in relation to inference and assent, which to me seems theoretical and unreal. Reasonings and convictions which I deem natural and legitimate, he apparently would call irrational, enthusiastic, perverse, and immoral; and that, as I think, because he consults his own ideal of how the mind ought to act, instead of interrogating human nature, as an existing thing, as it is found in the world. Instead of going by the testimony of psychological facts, and thereby determining our constitutive faculties and our proper condition, and being content with the mind as God has made it, he would form men as he thinks they ought to be formed, into something better and higher, and calls them irrational and indefensible, if (so to speak) they take to the water, instead of remaining under the narrow wings of his own arbitrary theory.

1. Now the first question which this theory leads me to consider is, whether there is such an act of the mind as assent at all. If there is, it is plain it ought to show itself unequivocally as such, as distinct from other acts. For if a professed act can only be viewed as the necessary and immediate repetition of another act, if assent is a sort of reproduction and double of an act of inference, if when inference determines that a proposition is somewhat, or not a little, or a good deal, or very like truth, assent as its natural and normal counterpart says that it *is* somewhat, or not a little, or a good deal, or very like truth, then I do not see what we mean by saying, or why we say at all, that there is any such act. It is simply superfluous, in a psychological point of view, and a curiosity for subtle minds, and the sooner it is got out of the way the better. When I assent, I am supposed, it seems, to do precisely what I do when I infer, or rather not quite so much, but something which is included in inferring; for, while the disposition of my mind towards a given proposition is identical in assent and in inference, I merely drop the thought of the premises when I assent, though not of their influence on the proposition inferred. This then, and no more after all, is what nature prescribes, and

this, and no more than this, is the conscientious use of our faculties, so to assent forsooth as to do nothing else than infer. Then, I say, if this be really the state of the case, if assent in no real way differs from inference, it is one and the same thing with it. It is another name for inference, and to speak of it at all does but mislead. Nor can it fairly be urged as a parallel case that an act of conscious recognition, though distinct from an act of knowledge, is after all only its repetition. On the contrary, such a recognition is a reflex act with its own object, viz. the act of knowledge itself. As well might it be said that the hearing of the notes of my voice is a repetition of the act of singing:—it gives no plausibility then to the anomaly I am combating.

I lay it down, then, as a principle that either assent is intrinsically distinct from inference, or the sooner we get rid of the word in philosophy the better. If it be only the echo of an inference, do not treat it as a substantive act; but, on the other hand, supposing it be not such an idle repetition, as I am sure it is not, supposing the word "assent" does hold a rightful place in language and in thought, if it does not admit of being confused with concluding and inferring, if the two words are used for two operations of the intellect which cannot change their character, if in matter of fact they are not always found together, if they do not vary with each other, if one is sometimes found without the other, if one is strong when the other is weak, if sometimes they seem even in conflict with each other, then, since we know perfectly well what an inference is, it comes upon us to consider what, as distinct from inference, an assent is, and we are, by the very fact of its being distinct, advanced one step towards that account of it which I think is the true one. The first step then towards deciding the point, will be to inquire what the experience of human life, as it is daily brought before us, teaches us of the relation to each other of inference and assent.

(1) First, we know from experience that assents may endure without the presence of the inferential acts upon which they

were originally elicited. It is plain, that, as life goes on, we are not only inwardly formed and changed by the accession of habits, but we are also enriched by a great multitude of beliefs and opinions, and that, on a variety of subjects. These beliefs and opinions, held, as some of them are, almost as first principles, are assents, and they constitute, as it were, the clothing and furniture of the mind. I have already spoken of them under the head of "Credence" and "Opinion." Sometimes we are fully conscious of them; sometimes they are implicit, or only now and then come directly before our reflective faculty. Still they are assents; and, when we first admitted them, we had some kind of reason, slight or strong, recognized or not, for doing so. However, whatever those reasons were, even if we ever realized them, we have long forgotten them. Whether it was the authority of others, or our own observation, or our reading, or our reflections, which became the warrant of our assent, any how we received the matters in question into our minds as true, and gave them a place there. We assented to them, and we still assent, though we have forgotten what the warrant was. At present they are self-sustained in our minds, and have been so for long years; they are in no sense conclusions; they imply no process of thought. Here then is a case in which assent stands out as distinct from inference.

(2) Again; sometimes assent fails, while the reasons for it and the inferential act which is the recognition of those reasons, are still present, and in force. Our reasons may seem to us as strong as ever, yet they do not secure our assent. Our beliefs, founded on them, were and are not; we cannot perhaps tell when they went; we may have thought that we still held them, till something happened to call our attention to the state of our minds, and then we found that our assent had become an assertion. Sometimes, of course, a cause may be found why they went; there may have been some vague feeling that a fault lay at the ultimate basis, or in the underlying conditions, of our reasonings; or some misgiving that the subject-matter of them was beyond the reach of the human mind; or

a consciousness that we had gained a broader view of things in general than when we first gave our assent; or that there were strong objections to our first convictions, which we had never taken into account. But this is not always so; sometimes our mind changes so quickly, so unaccountably, so disproportionately to any tangible arguments to which the change can be referred, and with such abiding recognition of the force of the old arguments, as to suggest the suspicion that moral causes, arising out of our condition, age, company, occupations, fortunes, are at the bottom. However, what once was assent is gone; yet the perception of the old arguments remains, showing that inference is one thing, and assent another.

(3) And as assent sometimes dies out without tangible reasons, sufficient to account for its failure, so sometimes, in spite of strong and convincing arguments, it is never given. We sometimes find men loud in their admiration of truths which they never profess. As, by the law of our mental constitution, obedience is quite distinct from faith, and men may believe without practising, so is assent also independent of our acts of inference. Again, prejudice hinders assent to the most incontrovertible proofs. Again, it not unfrequently happens, that while the keenness of the ratiocinative faculty enables a man to see the ultimate result of a complicated problem in a moment, it takes years for him to embrace it as a truth, and to recognize it as an item in the circle of his knowledge. Yet he does at last so accept it, and then we say that he assents.

(4) Again; very numerous are the cases, in which good arguments, and really good as far as they go, and confessed by us to be good, nevertheless are not strong enough to incline our minds ever so little to the conclusion at which they point. But why is it that we do not assent a little, in proportion to those arguments? On the contrary, we throw the full *onus probandi* on the side of the conclusion, and we refuse to assent to it at all, until we can assent to it altogether. The proof is capable of growth; but the assent either exists or does not exist.

(5) I have already alluded to the influence of moral motives in hindering assent to conclusions which are logically unimpeachable. According to the couplet,

> A man convinced against his will
> Is of the same opinion still;—

assent then is not the same as inference.

(6) Strange as it may seem, this contrast between inference and assent is exemplified even in the province of mathematics. Argument is not always able to command our assent, even though it be demonstrative. Sometimes of course it forces its way, that is, when the steps of the reasoning are few, and admit of being viewed by the mind altogether. Certainly, one cannot conceive a man having before him the series of conditions and truths on which it depends that the three angles of a triangle are together equal to two right angles, and yet not assenting to that proposition. Were all propositions as plain, though assent would not in consequence be the same acts as inference, yet it would certainly follow immediately upon it. I allow then as much as this, that, when an argument is in itself and by itself conclusive of a truth, it has by a law of our nature the same command over our assent, or rather the truth which it has reached has the same command, as our senses have. Certainly our intellectual nature is under laws, and the correlative of ascertained truth is unreserved assent.

But I am not speaking of short and lucid demonstrations; but of long and intricate mathematical investigations; and in that case, though every step may be indisputable, it still requires a specially sustained attention and an effort of memory to have in the mind all at once all the steps of the proof, with their bearings on each other, and the antecedents which they severally involve; and these conditions of the inference may interfere with the promptness of our assent.

Hence it is that party spirit or national feeling or religious prepossessions have before now had power to retard the reception of truths of a mathematical character; which never could have been, if demonstrations were *ipso facto* assents. Nor indeed would any mathematician, even in questions of pure science, assent to his own conclusions, on new and difficult ground, and in the case of abstruse calculations, however often he went over his work, till he had the corroboration of other judgments besides his own. He would have carefully revised his inference, and would assent to the probability of his accuracy in inferring, but still he would abstain from an immediate assent to the truth of his conclusion. Yet the corroboration of others cannot add to his perception of the proof; he would still perceive the proof, even though he failed in gaining their corroboration. And yet again he might arbitrarily make it his rule, never to assent to his conclusions without such corroboration, or at least before the lapse of a sufficient interval. Here again inference is distinct from assent.

I have been showing that inference and assent are distinct acts of the mind, and that they may be made apart from each other. Of course I cannot be taken to mean that there is no legitimate or actual connexion between them, as if arguments adverse to a conclusion did not naturally hinder assent; or as if the inclination to give assent were not greater or less according as the particular act of inference expressed a stronger or weaker probability; or as if assent did not always imply grounds in reason, implicit, if not explicit, or could be rightly given without sufficient grounds. So much is it commonly felt that assent must be preceded by inferential acts, that obstinate men give their own will as their very reason for assenting, if they can think of nothing better; "stat pro ratione voluntas." Indeed, I doubt whether assent is ever given without some preliminary, which stands for a reason; but it does not follow from this, that it may not be withheld in cases when there are good reasons for giving it to a proposition, or may not be withdrawn after it has been given, the reasons remaining, or may not remain when the reasons are forgotten, or must always vary in strength, as the reasons vary; and this substantiveness, as I may call it, of the act of assent is the very point which I have wished to establish.

2. And in showing that assent is distinct from an act of inference, I have gone a good way towards showing in what it differs from it. If assent and inference are each of them the acceptance of a proposition, but the special characteristic of inference is that it is conditional, it is natural to suppose that assent is unconditional. Again, if assent is the acceptance of truth, and truth is the proper object of the intellect, and no one can hold conditionally what by the same act he holds to be true, here too is a reason for saying that assent is an adhesion without reserve or doubt to the proposition to which it is given. And again, it is to be presumed that the word has not two meanings: what it has at one time, it has at another. Inference is always inference; even if demonstrative, it is still conditional; it establishes an introvertible conclusion on the condition of incontrovertible premises. To the conclusion thus drawn, assent gives its absolute recognition. In the case of all demonstration, assent, when given, is unconditionally given. In one class of subjects, then, assent certainly is always unconditional; but if the word stands for an undoubting and unhesitating act of the mind once, why does it not denote the same always? what evidence is there that it ever means any thing else than that which the whole world will unite in witnessing that it means in certain cases? why are we not to interpret what is controverted by what is known? This is what is suggested on the first view of the question; but to continue:—

In demonstrative matters assent excludes the presence of doubt: now are instances producible, on the other hand, of its ever co-existing with doubt in cases of the concrete? As the above instances have shown, on very many questions we do not give an assent at all. What commonly happens is this, that, after hearing and entering into what may be said for a proposition, we pronounce neither for nor against it. We may accept the conclusion as a conclusion, dependent on premises, abstract, and tending to the concrete; but we do not follow up our inference of a proposition by giving an assent to it. That there are concrete propositions to which we give unconditional assents, I shall presently show; but I am now asking for instances of conditional, for instances in which we assent a little and not much. Usually, we do not assent at all. Every day, as it comes, brings with it opportunities for us to enlarge our circle of assents. We read the newspapers; we look through debates in Parliament, pleadings in the law courts, leading articles, letters of correspondents, reviews of books, criticisms in the fine arts, and we either form no opinion at all upon the subjects discussed, as lying out of our line, or at most we have only an opinion about them. At the utmost we say that we are inclined to believe this proposition or that, that we are not sure it is not true, that much may be said for it, that we have been much struck by it; but we never say that we give it a degree of assent. We might as well talk of degrees of truth as of degrees of assent.

Yet Locke heads one of his chapters with the title "Degrees of Assent;" and a writer, of this century, who claims our respect from the tone and drift of his work, thus expresses himself after Locke's manner: "Moral evidence," he says, "may produce a variety of degrees of assents, from suspicion to moral certainty. For, here, the degree of assent depends upon the degree in which the evidence on one side preponderates, or exceeds that on the other. And as this preponderancy may vary almost infinitely, so likewise may the degrees of assent. For a few of these degrees, though but for a few, names have been invented. Thus, when the evidence on one side preponderates a very little, there is ground for suspicion, or conjecture. Presumption, persuasion, belief, conclusion, conviction, moral certainty,—doubt, wavering, distrust, disbelief,—are words which imply an increase or decrease of this preponderancy. Some of these words also admit of epithets which denote a further increase or diminution of the assent." [1]

[1] Gambier on Moral Evidence, p. 6.

Can there be a better illustration than this passage supplies of what I have been insisting on above, viz. that, in teaching various degrees of assent, we tend to destroy assent, as an act of the mind, altogether? This author makes the degrees of assent "infinite," as the degrees of probability are infinite. His assents are really only inferences, and assent is a name without a meaning, the needless repetition of an inference. But in truth "suspicion, conjecture, presumption, persuasion, belief, conclusion, conviction, moral certainty," are not, "assents" at all; they are simply more or less strong inferences of a proposition; and "doubt, wavering, distrust, disbelief," are recognitions, more or less strong, of the probability of its contradictory.

There is only one sense in which we are allowed to call such acts or states of mind assents. They are opinions; and, as being such, they are, as I have already observed, when speaking of Opinion, assents to the plausibility, probability, doubtfulness, or untrustworthiness, of a proposition; that is, not variations of assent to an inference, but assents to a variation in inferences. When I assent to a doubtfulness, or to a probability, my assent, as such, is as complete as if I assented to a truth; it is not a certain degree of assent. And, in like manner, I may be certain of an uncertainty; that does not destroy the specific notion conveyed in the word "certain."

I do not know then when it is that we ever deliberately profess assent to a proposition without meaning to convey to others the impression that we accept it unreservedly, and that because it is true. Certainly, we familiarly use such phrases as a half-assent, as we also speak of half-truths; but a half-assent is not a kind of assent any more than a half-truth is a kind of truth. As the object is indivisible, so is the act. A half-truth is a proposition which in one aspect is a truth, and in another is not; to give a half-assent is to feel drawn towards assent, or to assent one moment and not the next, or to be in the way to assent to it. It means that the proposition in question deserves a hearing, that it is probable or attractive, that it opens important views, that it is a key to perplexing difficulties, or the like.

3. Treating the subject then, not according to *à priori* fitness, but according to the facts of human nature, as they are found in the concrete action of life, I find numberless cases in which we do not assent at all, none in which assent is evidently conditional;—and many, as I shall now proceed to show, in which it is unconditional, and these in subject-matters which admit of nothing higher than probable reasoning. If human nature is to be its own witness, there is no medium between assenting and not assenting. Locke's theory of the duty of assenting more or less according to degrees of evidence, is invalidated by the testimony of high and low, young and old, ancient and modern, as continually given in their ordinary sayings and doings. Indeed, as I have shown, he does not strictly maintain it himself; yet, though he feels the claims of nature and fact to be too strong for him in certain cases, he gives no reason why he should violate his theory in these, and yet not in many more.

Now let us review some of those assents, which men give on evidence short of intuition and demonstration, yet which are as unconditional as if they had that highest evidence.

First of all, starting from intuition, of course we all believe, without any doubt, that we exist; that we have an individuality and identity all our own; that we think, feel and act, in the home of our own minds; that we have a present sense of good and evil, of a right and a wrong, of a true and a false, of a beautiful and a hideous, however we analyze our ideas of them. We have an absolute vision before us of what happened yesterday or last year, so as to be able without any chance of mistake to give evidence upon it in a court of justice, let the consequences be ever so serious. We are sure that of many things we are ignorant, that of many things we are in doubt, and that of many things we are not in doubt.

Nor is the assent which we give to facts limited to the range of self-consciousness. We are sure beyond all hazard of a mistake, that our own self is not the only being existing; that there is an external world; that it is a system with parts and a whole, a universe carried on by laws; and that the future is affected by the past. We accept and hold with an unqualified assent, that the earth, considered as a phenomenon, is a globe; that all its regions see the sun by turns; that there are vast tracts on it of land and water; that there are really existing cities on definite sites, which go by the names of London, Paris, Florence, and Madrid. We are sure that Paris or London, unless suddenly swallowed up by an earthquake or burned to the ground, is to-day just what it was yesterday, when we left it.

We laugh to scorn the idea that we had no parents, though we have no memory of our birth; that we shall never depart this life, though we can have no experience of the future; that we are able to live without food, though we have never tried; that a world of men did not live before our time, or that that world has had no history; that there has been no rise and fall of states, no great men, no wars, no revolutions, no art, no science, no literature, no religion.

We should be either indignant or amused at the report of our intimate friend being false to us; and we are able sometimes, without any hesitation, to accuse certain parties of hostility and injustice to us. We may have a deep consciousness, which we never can lose, that we on our part have been cruel to others, and that they have felt us to be so, or that we have been, and have been felt to be, ungenerous to those who love us. We may have an overpowering sense of our moral weakness, of the precariousness of our life, health, wealth, position, and good fortune. We may have a clear view of the weak points of our physical constitution, of what food or medicine is good for us, and what does us harm. We may be able to master, at least in part, the course of our past history; its turning-points, our hits, and our great mistakes. We may have a sense of the presence of a Supreme Being, which never has been dimmed by even a passing shadow, which has inhabited us ever since we can recollect any thing, and which we cannot imagine our losing. We may be able, for others have been able, so to realize the precepts and truths of Christianity, as deliberately to surrender our life, rather than transgress the one or to deny the other.

On all these truths we have an immediate and an unhesitating hold, nor do we think ourselves guilty of not loving truth for truth's sake, because we cannot reach them through a series of intuitive propositions. Assent on reasonings not demonstrative is too widely recognized an act to be irrational, unless man's nature is irrational, too familiar to the prudent and clear-minded to be an infirmity or an extravagance. None of us can think or act without the acceptance of truths, not intuitive, not demonstrated, yet sovereign. If our nature has any constitution, any laws, one of them is this absolute reception of propositions as true, which lie outside the narrow range of conclusions to which logic, formal or virtual, is tethered; nor has any philosophical theory the power to force on us a rule which will not work for a day.

When, then, philosophers lay down principles, on which it follows that our assent, except when given to objects of intuition or demonstration, is conditional, that the assent given to propositions by well-ordered minds necessarily varies with the proof producible for them, and that it does not and cannot remain one and the same while the proof is strengthened or weakened,—are they not to be considered as confusing together two things very distinct from each other, a mental act or state and a scientific rule, an interior assent and a set of logical formulas? When they speak of degrees of assent, surely they have no intention at all of defining the position of the mind itself relative to the adoption of a given conclusion, but they are recording their perception of the relation of that conclusion towards its premisses. They are contemplating how representative symbols work, not how the intellect is affected towards the thing which those symbols represent. In real truth they as little mean to assert the principle of measuring our assents by our logic, as they would fancy they could record the refresh-

ment which we receive from the open air by the readings of
the graduated scale of a thermometer. There is a connexion
doubtless between a logical conclusion and an assent, as there
is between the variation of the mercury and our sensations;
but the mercury is not the cause of life and health, nor is
verbal argumentation the principle of inward belief. If we feel
hot or chilly, no one will convince us to the contrary by insisting that the glass is at 60°. It is the mind that reasons and
assents, not a diagram on paper. I may have difficulty in the
management of a proof, while I remain unshaken in my
adherence to the conclusion. Supposing a boy cannot make his
answer to some arithmetical or algebraical question tally with
the book, need he at once distrust the book? Does his trust in
it fall down a certain number of degrees, according to the
force of his difficulty? On the contrary, he keeps to the principle, implicit but present to his mind, with which he took up
the book, that the book is more likely to be right than he is;
and this mere preponderance of probability is sufficient to
make him faithful to his belief in its correctness, till its in-
correctness is actually proved.

My own opinion is, that the class of writers of whom I have
been speaking, have themselves as little misgiving about the
truths which they pretend to weigh out and measure as their
unsophisticated neighbours; but they think it a duty to remind
us, that since the full etiquette of logical requirements has not
been satisfied, we must believe those truths at our peril. They
warn us, that an issue which can never come to pass, in matter
of fact, is nevertheless in theory a possible supposition. They
do not, for instance, intend for a moment to imply that there
is even the shadow of a doubt that Great Britain is an island,
but they think we ought to know, if we do not know, that there
is no proof of the fact, in mode and figure, equal to the proof
of a proposition of Euclid; and that in consequence they and
we are all bound to suspend our judgment about such a fact,
though it be in an infinitesimal degree, lest we should seem
not to love truth for truth's sake. Having made their protest,

they subside without scruple into that same absolute assurance
of only partially-proved truths, which is natural to the illogical
imagination of the multitude.

4. It remains to explain some conversational expressions, at
first sight favourable to that doctrine of degrees in assent,
which I have been combating.

(1) We often speak of giving a modified and qualified, or
a presumptive and *primâ facie* assent, or (as I have already
said) a half-assent to opinions or facts; but these expressions
admit of an easy explanation. Assent, upon the authority of
others is often, as I have noticed, when speaking of notional
assents, little more than a profession or acquiescence or inference, not a real acceptance of a proposition. I report, for instance, that there was a serious fire in the town in the past
night; and then perhaps I add, that at least the morning papers
say so;—that is, I have perhaps no positive doubt of the fact;
still, by referring to the newspapers I imply that I do not take
on myself the responsibility of the statement. In thus qualify-
ing my apparent assent, I show that it was not a genuine assent
at all. In like manner a *primâ facie* assent is an assent to an
antecedent probability of a fact, not to the fact itself; as I
might give a *primâ facie* assent to the Plurality of worlds or
to the personality of Homer, without pledging myself to either
absolutely. "Half-assent," of which I spoke above, is an inclination to assent, or again, an intention of assenting, when certain
difficulties are surmounted. When we speak without thought,
assent has as vague a meaning as half-assent; but when we
deliberately say, "I assent," we signify an act of the mind so
definite as to admit of no change but that of its ceasing to be.

(2) And so, too, though we sometimes use the phrase "conditional assent," yet we only mean thereby to say that we will
assent under certain contingencies. Of course we may, if we
please, include a condition in the proposition to which our
assent is given; and then, that condition enters into the matter
of the assent, but not into the assent itself. To assent to "If
this man is in a consumption, his days are numbered," is as

little a conditional assent, as to assent to "Of this consumptive patient the days are numbered," which (though without the conditional form), is an equivalent proposition. In such cases strictly speaking, the assent is given neither to antecedent nor consequent of the conditional proposition, but to their connexion, that is, to the enthymematic *inferentia*. If we place the condition external to the proposition, then the assent will be given to "That 'his days are numbered' is conditionally true;" and of course we can assent to the conditionality of a proposition as well as to its probability. Or again, if so be, we may give our assent not only to the *inferentia* in a complex conditional proposition, but to each of the simple propositions, of which it is made up, besides. "There will be a storm soon, for the mercury falls;"—here, besides assenting to the connexion of the propositions, we may assent also to "The mercury falls," and to "There will be a storm." This is assenting to the premiss, *inferentia*, and thing inferred, all at once;—we assent to the whole syllogism, and to its component parts.

(3) In like manner are to be explained the phrases, "deliberate assent," a "rational assent;" "a sudden," "impulsive," or "hesitating" assent. These expressions denote, not kinds or qualities, but the circumstances of assenting. A deliberate assent is an assent following upon deliberation. It is sometimes called a conviction, a word which commonly includes in its meaning two acts, both the act of inference, and the act of assent consequent upon the inference. This subject will be considered in the next Section. On the other hand, a hesitating assent is an assent to which we have been slow and intermittent in coming; or an assent which, when given, is thwarted and obscured by external and flitting misgivings, though not such as to enter into the act itself, or essentially to damage it.

There is another sense in which we speak of a hesitating or uncertain assent; viz. when we assent in act, but not in the habit of our minds. Till assent to a doctrine or fact is my habit, I am at the mercy of inferences contrary to it; I assent to-day, and give up my belief, or incline to disbelief, to-morrow. I may find it my duty, for instance, after the opportunity of careful inquiry and inference, to assent to another's innocence, whom I have for years considered guilty; but from long prejudice I may be unable to carry my new assent well about me, and may every now and then relapse into momentary thoughts injurious to him.

(4) A more plausible objection to the absolute absence of all doubt or misgiving in an act of assent is found in the use of the terms firm and weak assent, or in the growth of belief and trust. Thus, we assent to the events of history, but not with that fulness and force of adherence to the received account of them with which we realize a record of occurrences which are within our own memory. And again, we assent to the praise bestowed on a friend's good qualities with an energy which we do not feel, when we are speaking of virtue in the abstract: and if we are political partisans, our assent is very cold, when we cannot refuse it, to representations made in favour of the wisdom or patriotism of statesmen whom we dislike. And then as to religious subjects, we speak of strong faith and feeble faith; of the faith which would move mountains, and of the ordinary faith "without which it is impossible to please God." And as we can grow in graces, so surely can we inclusively in faith. Again we rise from one work on Christian evidences with our faith enlivened and invigorated; from another perhaps with the distracted father's words in our mouth, "I believe, help my unbelief."

Now it is evident, first of all, that habits of mind may grow, as being a something permanent and continuous; and by assent growing, it is often only meant that the habit grows and has greater hold upon the mind.

But again, when we carefully consider the matter, it will be found that this increase or decrease of strength does not lie in the assent itself, but in its circumstances and concomitants; for instance, in the emotions, in the ratiocinative faculty, or in the imagination.

For instance, as to the emotions, this strength of assent may be nothing more than the strength of love, hatred, interest, desire, or fear, which the object of the assent elicits, and this is especially the case when that object is of a religious nature. Such strength is adventitious and accidental; it may come, it may go; it is found in one man, not in another; it does not interfere with the genuineness and perfection of the act of assent. Balaam assented to the fact of his own intercourse with the supernatural, as well as Moses; but, to use religious language, he had light without love; his intellect was clear, his heart was cold. Hence his faith would popularly be considered wanting in strength. On the other hand, prejudice implies strong assents to the disadvantage of its object; that is, it encourages such assents, and guards them from the chance of being lost.

Again, when a conclusion is recommended to us by the number and force of the arguments in proof of it, our recognition of them invests it with a luminousness, which in one sense adds strength to our assent to it, as it certainly does protect and embolden that assent. Thus we assent to a review of recent events, which we have studied from original documents, with a triumphant peremptoriness which it neither occurs to us, nor is possible for us, to exercise, when we make an act of assent to the assassination of Julius Cæsar, or to the existence of the Abipones, though we are as securely certain of these latter facts as of the doings and occurrences of yesterday.

And further, all that I have said about the apprehension of propositions is in point here. We may speak of assent to our Lord's divinity as strong or feeble, according as it is given to the reality as impressed upon the imagination, or to the notion of it as entertained by the intellect.

(5) Nor, lastly, does this doctrine of the intrinsic integrity and indivisibility (if I may so speak) of assent interfere with the teaching of Catholic theology as to the pre-eminence of strength in divine faith, which has a supernatural origin, when compared with all belief which is merely human and natural. For first, that pre-eminence consists, not in its differing from

human faith, merely in degree of assent, but in its being superior in nature and kind,[1] so that the one does not admit of a comparison with the other; and next, its intrinsic superiority is not a matter of experience, but is above experience.[2] Assent is ever assent;[3] but in the assent which follows on a divine announcement, and is vivified by a divine grace, there is, from the nature of the case, a transcendent adhesion of mind, intellectual and moral, and a special self-protection,[4] beyond the operation of those ordinary laws of thought, which alone have a place in my discussion.

[1] "Supernaturalis mentis assensus, rebus fidei exhibitus, cùm præcipuè dependeat à gratiâ Dei intrinsecus mentem illuminante et commovente, potest esse, et est, major quocunque assensu certitudini naturali præstito, seu ex motivis naturalibus orto," &c.—Dmouski, Instit. t. i. p. 28.

[2] "Hoc [viz. multo certior est homo de eo quod audit à Deo qui falli non potest, quàm de eo quod videt propriâ ratione quâ falli potest] intelligendum est de certitudine fidei secundum appretiationem, non secundum intentionem; nam sæpe contingit, ut scientia clariùs percipiatur ab intellectu, atque ut connexio scientiæ cum veritate magis appareat, quàm connexio fidei cum eâdem; cognitiones enim naturales, utpote captui nostro accommodatæ, magis animum quietant, delectant, et veluti satiant."—Scavini, Theol. Moral. t. ii. p. 428.

[3] "Suppono enim, veritatem fidei non esse certiorem veritate metaphysicâ aut geometricâ quoad modum assensionis, sed tantum quoad modum adhæsionis; quia utrinque intellectus absolutè sine modo limitante assentitur. Sola autem adhæsio voluntatis diversa est; quia in actu fidei gratia seu habitus infusus roborat intellectum et voluntatem, ne tam facilè mutentur aut perturbentur."—Amort, Theol. t. i. p. 312.

"Hæc distinctio certitudinis [ex diversitate motivorum] extrinsecam tantum differentiam importat, cùm omnis naturalis certitudo, formaliter spectata, sit æqualis; debet enim essentialiter erroris periculum amovere, exclusio autem periculi erroris in indivisibili consistit; aut enim habetur aut non habetur."—Dmouski, ibid. p. 27.

[4] Fides est certior omni veritate naturali, etiam geometricè aut metaphysicè certâ; idque non solum certitudine adhæsionis sed etiam assentionis.... Intellectus sentit se in multis veritatibus etiam metaphysicè certis posse per objectiones perturbari, e. g. si legat scepticos.... E contrà circa ea, quæ constat esse revelata à Deo, nullus potest perturbari."—Amort, ibid. p. 367.

2

COMPLEX ASSENT

I HAVE BEEN CONSIDERING ASSENT as the mental assertion of an intelligible proposition, as an act of the intellect direct, absolute, complete in itself, unconditional, arbitrary, yet not incompatible with an appeal to argument, and at least in many cases exercised unconsciously. On this last characteristic of assent I have not insisted, as it has not come in my way; nor is it more than an accident of acts of assent, though an ordinary accident. That it is of ordinary occurrence cannot be doubted. A great many of our assents are merely expressions of our personal likings, tastes, principles, motives, and opinions, as dictated by nature, or resulting from habit; in other words, they are acts and manifestations of self: now what is more rare than self-knowledge? In proportion then to our ignorance of self, is our consciousness of those innumerable acts of assent, which we are incessantly making. And so again in what may be almost called the mechanical operation of our minds, in our continual acts of apprehension and inference, speculation and resolve, propositions pass before us and receive our assent without our consciousness. Hence it is that we are so apt to confuse together acts of assent and acts of inference. Indeed, I may fairly say, that those assents which we give with a direct knowledge of what we are doing, are few compared with the multitude of like acts which pass through our minds in long succession without our observing them.

That mode of assent which is exercised thus unconsciously, I may call simple assent, and of it I have treated in the foregoing Section; but now I am going to speak of such assents as must be made consciously and deliberately, and which I shall call complex or reflex assents. And I begin by recalling what I have already stated about the relation in which Assent and Inference stand to each other,—inference, which holds propositions conditionally, and assent, which unconditionally accepts them; the relation is this:—

Acts of inference are both the antecedents of assent before assenting, and its usual concomitants after assenting. For instance, I hold absolutely that the country which we call India exists, upon trustworthy testimony; and next, I may continue to believe it on the same testimony. In like manner, I have ever believed that Great Britain is an island, for certain sufficient reasons; and on the same reasons I may persist in the belief. But it may happen that I forget my reasons for what I believe to be so absolutely true; or I may never have asked myself about them, or formally marshalled them in order, and have been accustomed to assent without a recognition of my assent or of its grounds, and then perhaps something occurs which leads to my reviewing and completing those grounds, analyzing and arranging them, yet without on that account implying of necessity any suspense, ever so slight, of assent, to the proposition that India is in a certain part of the earth, and that Great Britain is an island. With no suspense of assent at all; any more than the boy in my former illustration had any doubt about the answer set down in his arithmetic book, when he began working out the question; any more than he would be doubting his eyes and his common sense, that the two sides of a triangle are together greater than the third, because he drew out the geometrical proof of it. He does but repeat, after his formal demonstration, that assent which he made before it, and assents to his previous assenting. This is what I call a reflex or complex assent.

I say, there is no necessary incompatility between thus assenting and yet proving,—for the conclusiveness of a proposition is not synonymous with its truth. A proposition may be true, yet not admit of being concluded;—it may be a conclusion and yet not a truth. To contemplate it under one aspect, is not to contemplate it under another; and the two aspects may be consistent, from the very fact that they are two *aspects*. There-

fore to set about concluding a proposition is not *ipso facto* to
doubt its truth; we may aim at inferring a proposition, while
all the time we assent to it. We have to do this as a common
occurrence, when we take on ourselves to convince another
on any point in which he differs from us. We do not deny our
own faith, because we become controversialists; and in like
manner we may employ ourselves in proving what we already
believe to be true, simply in order to ascertain the producible
evidence in its favour, and in order to fulfil what is due to
ourselves and to the claims of responsibilities of our education
and social position.

I have been speaking of investigation, not of inquiry; it is
quite true that inquiry is inconsistent with assent, but inquiry
is something more than the mere exercise of inference. He
who inquires has not found; he is in doubt where the truth
lies, and wishes his present profession either proved or disproved. We cannot without absurdity call ourselves at once
believers and inquirers also. Thus it is sometimes spoken of as
a hardship that a Catholic is not allowed to inquire into the
truth of his creed;—of course he cannot, if he would retain the
name of believer. He cannot be both inside and outside of the
Church at once. It is merely common sense to tell him that, if
he is seeking, he has not found. If seeking includes doubting,
and doubting excludes believing, then the Catholic who sets
about inquiring, thereby declares that he is not a Catholic.
He has already lost faith. And this is his best defence to himself for inquiring, viz. that he is no longer a Catholic, and
wishes to become one. They who would forbid him to inquire,
would in that case be shutting the stable-door after the steed
is stolen. What can he do better than inquire, if he is in doubt?
how else can he become a Catholic again? Not to inquire is
in his case to be satisfied with disbelief.

However, in thus speaking, I am viewing the matter in the
abstract, and without allowing for the manifold inconsistencies
of individuals, as they are found in the world, who attempt
to unite incompatibilities; who do not doubt, but who act as

if they did; who, though they believe, are weak in faith, and put themselves in the way of losing it by unnecessarily listening to objections. Moreover, there are minds, undoubtedly, with whom at all times to question a truth is to make it questionable, and to investigate is equivalent to inquiring; and again, there may be beliefs so sacred or so delicate, that, if I may use the metaphor, they will not wash without shrinking and losing colour. I grant all this; but here I am discussing broad principles, not individual cases; and these principles are, that inquiry implies doubt, and that investigation does not imply it, and that those who assent to a doctrine or fact may without inconsistency investigate its credibility, though they cannot literally inquire about its truth.

Next, I consider that, in the case of educated minds, investigations into the argumentative proof of the things to which they have given their assent, is an obligation, or rather a necessity. Such a trial of their intellects is a law of their nature, like the growth of childhood into manhood, and analogous to the moral ordeal which is the instrument of their spiritual life. The lessons of right and wrong, which are taught them at school, are to be carried out into action amid the good and evil of the world; and so again the intellectual assents, in which they have in like manner been instructed from the first, have also to be tested, realized, and developed by the exercise of their mature judgment.

Certainly, such processes of investigation, whether in religious subjects or secular, often issue in the reversal of the assents which they were originally intended to confirm; as the boy who works out an arithmetical problem from his book may end in detecting, or thinking he detects, a false print in the answer. But the question before us is whether acts of assent and of inference are compatible; and my vague consciousness of the possibility of a reversal of my belief in the course of my researches, as little interferes with the honesty and firmness of that belief while those researches proceed, as the recognition of the possibility of my train's oversetting is an evidence of an intention on my part of undergoing so great a calamity. My mind is not moved by a scientific computation of chances, nor can any law of averages affect my particular case. To incur a risk is not to expect reverse; and if my opinions are true, I have a right to think that they will bear examining. Nor, on the other hand, does belief, viewed in its idea, imply a positive resolution in the party believing never to abandon that belief. What belief, as such, does imply is, not an intention never to change, but the utter absence of all thought, or expectation, or fear of changing. A spontaneous resolution never to change is inconsistent with the idea of belief; for the very force and absoluteness of the act of assent precludes any such resolution. We do not commonly determine not to do what we cannot fancy ourselves ever doing. We should readily indeed make such a formal promise if we were called upon to do so; for, since we have the truth, and truth cannot change, how can we possibly change in our belief, except indeed through our own weakness or fickleness? We have no intention whatever of being weak or fickle; so our promise is but the natural guarantee of our sincerity. It is possible then, without disloyalty to our convictions, to examine their grounds, even though in the event they are to fail under the examination, for we have no suspicion of this failure.

And such examination, as I have said, does but fulfil a law of our nature. Our first assents, right or wrong, are often little more than prejudices. The reasonings, which precede and accompany them, though sufficient for their purpose, do not rise up to the importance and energy of the assents themselves. As time goes on, by degrees and without set purpose, by reflection and experience, we begin to confirm or to correct the notions and the images to which those assents are given. At times it is a necessity formally to undertake a survey and revision of this or that class of them, of those which relate to religion, or to social duty, or to politics, or to the conduct of life. Sometimes this review begins in doubt as to the matters which we propose to consider, that is, in a suspension of the assents hitherto familiar to us; sometimes those assents are too strong to allow of being lost on the first stirring of the inquisitive intellect, and if, as time goes on, they give way, our change of mind, be it for good or for evil, is owing to the accumulating force of the arguments, sound or unsound, which bear down upon the propositions which we have hitherto received. Objections, indeed, as such, have no direct force to weaken assent; but, when they multiply, they tell against the implicit reasonings or the formal inferences which are its warrant, and suspend its acts and gradually undermine its habit. Then the assent goes; but whether slowly or suddenly, noticeably or imperceptibly, is a matter of circumstance or accident. However, whether the original assent is continued on or not, the new assent differs from the old in this, that it has the strength of explicitness and deliberation, that it is not a mere prejudice, and its strength the strength of prejudice. It is an assent, not only to a given proposition, but to the claim of that proposition on our assent as true; it is an assent to an assent, or what is commonly called a conviction.

Of course these reflex acts may be repeated in a series. As I pronounce that "Great Britain is an island," and then pronounce "That 'Great Britain is an island' has a claim on my assent," or is to "be assented to," or to be "accepted as true," or to be "believed," or simply "is true" (these predicates being equivalent), so I may proceed, "The proposition 'that *Great-Britain-is-an-island* is to be believed,' is to be believed," &c., &c., and so on to *ad infinitum*. But this would be trifling. The mind is like a double mirror, in which reflections of self within self multiply themselves till they are undistinguishable, and the first reflection contains all the rest. At the same time, it is worth while to notice two other reflex propositions:—"That 'Great Britain is an island' is probable" is true;—and "That 'Great Britain is an island' is uncertain" is true:—for the former of these is the expression of Opinion, and the latter of formal or theological Doubt, as I have already determined.

I have one step farther to make:—let the proposition to which the assent is given be as absolutely true as the reflex act pronounces it to be, that is, objectively true as well as subjectively, then the assent may be called a *perception,* the conviction a *certitude,* the proposition or truth a *certainty,* or thing known, or a matter of *knowledge,* and to assent to it is to *know.*

Of course, in thus speaking, I open the all-important question, what is truth, and what apparent truth? what is genuine knowledge, and what is its counterfeit? what are the tests for discriminating certitude from mere persuasion or delusion? Whatever a man holds to be true, he will say he holds for certain; and for the present I must allow him in his assumption, hoping in one way or another, as I proceed, to lessen the difficulties which lie in the way of calling him to account for so doing. And I have the less scruple in taking this course, as believing that, among fairly prudent and circumspect men, there are far fewer instances of false certitude than at first sight might be supposed. Men are often doubtful about propositions which are really true; they are not commonly certain of such as are simply false. What they judge to be a certainty is in matter of fact for the most part a truth. Not that there is not a great deal of rash talking even among the educated portion of the community, and many a man makes professions of certitude, for which he has no warrant; but that such off-hand, confident language is no token how these persons will express themselves when brought to book. No one will with justice consider himself certain of any matter, unless he has sufficient reasons for so considering; and it is rare that what is not true should be so free from every circumstance and token of falsity as to create no suspicion in his mind to its disadvantage, no reason for suspense of judgment. However, I shall have to remark on this difficulty by and by; here I will mention two conditions of certitude, in close connexion with that necessary preliminary of investigation and proof of which I have been speaking, which will throw some light upon it.

The one, which is *à priori*, or from the nature of the case, will tell us what is not certitude; the other, which is *à posteriori*, or from experience, will tell us in a measure what certitude is.

Certitude, as I have said, is the perception of a truth with the perception that it is a truth, or the consciousness of knowing, as expressed in the phrase, "I know that I know," or "I know that I know that I know," or simply "I know;" for one reflex assertion of the mind about self sums up the series of self-consciousnesses without the need of any actual evolution of them.

1. But if so, if by certitude about a thing is to be understood the knowledge of its truth, let it be considered that what is once true is always true, and cannot fail, whereas what is once known need not always be known, and is capable of failing. It follows, that if I am certain of a thing, I believe it will remain what I now hold it to be, even though my mind should have the bad fortune to let it drop. Since mere argument is not the measure of assent, no one can be called certain of a proposition, whose mind does not spontaneously and promptly reject, on their first suggestion, as idle, as impertinent, as sophistical, any objections which are directed against its truth. No man is certain of a truth, who can endure the thought of the fact of its contradictory existing or occurring; and that not from any set purpose or effort to reject that thought, but, as I have said, by the spontaneous action of the intellect. What is contradictory to the truth, with its apparatus of argument, fades out of the mind as fast as it enters it; and though it be brought back to the mind ever so often by the pertinacity of an opponent, or by a voluntary or involuntary act of imagination, still that contradictory proposition and its arguments are mere phantoms and dreams, in the light of our certitude, and their very entering into the mind is the first step of their going out of it. Such is the position of our minds towards the heathen fancy that Enceladus lies under Etna; or, not to take so extreme a case, that Joanna Southcote was a messenger from heaven, or the Emperor Napoleon really had a star. Equal to

this peremptory assertion of negative propositions is the revolt of the mind from suppositions incompatible with positive statements of which we are certain, whether abstract truths or facts; as that a straight line is the longest possible distance between its two extreme points, that Great Britain is in shape an exact square or circle, that I shall escape dying, or that my intimate friend is false to me.

We may indeed, say, if we please, that a man ought not to have so supreme a conviction in a given case, or in any case whatever; and that he is therefore wrong in treating opinions which he does not himself hold, with this even involuntary contempt;—certainly, we have a right to say so, if we will; but if, in matter of fact, a man has such a conviction, if he is sure that Ireland is to the West of England, or that the Pope is the Vicar of Christ, nothing is left to him, if he would be consistent, but to carry his conviction out into this magisterial intolerance of any contrary assertion; and if he were in his own mind tolerant, I do not say patient (for patience and gentleness are moral duties, but I mean intellectually tolerant), of objections as objections, he would virtually be giving countenance to the views which those objections represented. I say I certainly should be very intolerant of such a notion as that I shall one day be Emperor of the French; I should think it too absurd even to be ridiculous, and that I must be mad before I could entertain it. And did a man try to persuade me that treachery, cruelty, or ingratitude was as praiseworthy as honesty and temperance, and that a man who lived the life of a knave and died the death of a brute had nothing to fear from future retribution, I should think there was no call on me to listen to his arguments, except with the hope of converting him, though he called me a bigot and a coward for refusing to inquire into his speculations. And if, in a matter in which my temporal interests were concerned, he attempted to reconcile me to fraudulent acts by what he called philosophical views, I should say to him, "Retro Satana," and that, not from any suspicion of his ability to reverse immutable principles, but from a consciousness of my own moral changeableness, and a fear, on that account, that I might not be intellectually true to the truth. This, then, from the nature of the case, is a main characteristic of certitude in any matter, to be confident indeed that that certitude will last, but to be confident of this also, that, if it did fail, nevertheless, the thing itself, whatever it is, of which we are certain, will remain just as it is, true and irreversible. If this be so, it is easy to instance cases of an adherence to propositions, which does not fulfil the conditions of certitude; for instance:—

(1) How positive and circumstantial disputants may be on two sides of a question of fact, on which they give their evidence, till they are called to swear to it, and then how guarded and conditional their testimony becomes! Again, how confident are they in their rival accounts of a transaction at which they were present, till a third person makes his appearance, whose word will be decisive about it! Then they suddenly drop their tone, and trim their statements, and by provisos and explanations leave themselves loopholes for escape, in case his testimony should turn out to their disadvantage. At first no language could be too bold or absolute to express the distinctness of their knowledge on this side or that; but second thoughts are best, and their giving way shows that their belief does not come up to the mark of certitude.

(2) Again, can we doubt that many a confident expounder of Scripture, who is so sure that St. Paul meant this, and that St. John and St. James did not mean that, would be seriously disconcerted at the presence of those Apostles, if their presence were possible, and that they have now an especial "boldness of speech" in treating their subject, because there is no one authoritatively to set them right, if they are wrong?

(3) Take another instance, in which the absence of certitude is professed from the first. Though it is a matter of faith with Catholics that miracles never cease in the Church, still that this or that professed miracle really took place, is for the most part only a matter of opinion, and when it is believed,

whether on testimony or tradition, it is not believed to the exclusion of all doubt, whether about the fact or its miraculousness. Thus I may believe in the liquefaction of St. Pantaleon's blood, and believe it to the best of my judgment to be a miracle, yet, supposing a chemist offered to produce exactly the same phenomena under exactly similar circumstances by the materials put at his command by his science, so as to reduce what seemed beyond nature within natural laws, I should watch with some suspense of mind and misgiving the course of his experiment, as having no Divine Word to fall back upon as a ground of certainty that the liquefaction was miraculous.

(4) Take another virtual exhibition of fear; I mean irritation and impatience of contradiction, vehemence of assertion, determination to silence others,—these are the tokens of a mind which has not yet attained the tranquil enjoyment of certitude. No one, I suppose, would say that he was certain of the Plurality of worlds: that uncertitude on the subject is just the explanation, and the only explanation satisfactory to my mind, of the strange violence of language which has before now dishonoured the philosophical controversy upon it. Those who are certain of a fact are indolent disputants; it is enough for them that they have the truth; and they have little disposition, except at the call of duty, to criticize the hallucinations of others, and much less are they angry at their positiveness or ingenuity in argument; but to call names, to impute motives, to accuse of sophistry, to be impetuous and overbearing, is the part of men who are alarmed for their own position, and fear to have it approached too nearly. And in like manner the intemperance of language and of thought, which is sometimes found in converts to a religious creed, is often attributed, not without plausibility (even though erroneously in the particular case), to some flaw in the completeness of their certitude, which interferes with the harmony and repose of their convictions.

(5) Again, this intellectual anxiety, which is incompatible

with certitude, shows itself in our running back in our minds
to the arguments on which we came to believe, in not letting
our conclusions alone, in going over and strengthening the
evidence, and, as it were, getting it by heart, as if our highest
assent were only an inference. And such too is our unnecessarily declaring that we are certain, as if to reassure ourselves,
and our appealing to others for their suffrage in behalf of the
truths of which we are so sure; which is like our asking another
whether we are weary and hungry, or have eaten and drunk
to our satisfaction.

All laws are general; none are invariable; I am not writing as
a moralist or casuist. It must ever be recollected that these
various phenomena of mind, though signs, are not infallible
signs of uncertitude; they may proceed, in the particular case,
from other circumstances. Such anxieties and alarms may be
merely emotional and from the imagination, not intellectual;
parallel to that beating of the heart, nay, as I have been told,
that trembling of the limbs of even the bravest men, before a
battle, when standing still to receive the first attack of the
enemy. Such too is that palpitating self-interrogation, that
trouble of the mind lest it should not believe strongly enough,
which, and not doubt, underlies the sensitiveness described
in the well-known lines,—

> With eyes too tremblingly awake,
> To bear with dimness for His sake.

And so again, a man's over-earnestness in argument may
arise from zeal or charity; his impatience from loyalty to the
truth; his extravagance from want of taste, from enthusiasm,
or from youthful ardour; and his restless recurrence to argument, not from personal disquiet, but from a vivid appreciation
of the controversial talent of an opponent, or of his own, or of
the mere philosophical difficulties of the subject in dispute.
These are points for the consideration of those who are concerned in registering and explaining what may be called the
meteorological phenomena of the human mind, and do not

interfere with the broad principle which I would lay down, that to fear argument is to doubt the conclusion, and to be certain of a truth is to be careless of objections to it;—nor with the practical rule, that mere assent is not certitude, and must not be confused with it.

2. Now to consider what Certitude is, not simply as it must be, but in our actual experience of it.

It is accompanied, as a state of mind, by a specific feeling, proper to it, and discriminating it from other states, intellectual and moral, I do not say, as its practical test or as its *differentia*, but as its token, and in a certain sense its form. When a man says he is certain, he means he is conscious to himself of having this specific feeling. It is a feeling of satisfaction and self-gratulation, of intellectual security, arising out of a sense of success, attainment, possession, finality, as regards the matter which has been in question. As a conscientious deed is attended by a self-approval which nothing but itself can create, so certitude is united to a sentiment *sui generis* in which it lives and is manifested. These two parallel sentiments indeed have no relationship with each other, the enjoyable self-repose of certitude being as foreign to a good deed, as the self-approving glow of conscience is to the perception of a truth; yet knowledge, as well as virtue, is an end, and both knowledge and virtue, when reflected on, carry with them respectively their own reward in the characteristic sentiment, which, as I have said, is proper to each. And, as the performance of what is right is distinguished by this religious peace, so the attainment of what is true is attested by this intellectual security.

And, as the feeling of self-approbation, which is proper to good conduct, does not belong to the sense or to the possession of the beautiful or of the becoming, of the pleasant or of the useful, so neither is the special relaxation and repose of mind, which is the token of Certitude, ever found to attend upon simple Assent, on processes of Inference, or on Doubt; nor on investigation, conjecture, opinion, as such, or on any other

state or action of mind, besides certitude. On the contrary,
those acts and states of mind have gratifications proper to
themselves, and unlike that of certitude, as will sufficiently
appear on considering them separately.

(1) Philosophers are fond of enlarging on the pleasures of
Knowledge, (that is, Knowledge as such,) nor need I here
prove that such pleasures exist; but the repose in self and in
its object, as connected with self, which I attribute to certitude,
does not attach to mere knowing, that is, to the perception of
things, but to the consciousness of having that knowledge.
The simple and direct perception of things has its own great
satisfaction; but it must recognize them as realities, and recognize them as known, before it becomes the perception and has
the satisfaction which belong to certitude. Indeed, as far as I
see, the pleasure of perceiving truth without reflecting on it as
truth, is not very different, except in intensity and in dignity,
from the pleasure, as such, of assent or belief given to what is
not true, nay, from the pleasure of the mere passive reception
of recitals or narratives, which neither profess to be true nor
claim to be believed. Representations of any kind are in their
own nature pleasurable, whether they be true or not, whether
they come to us, or do not come, as true. We read a history,
or a biographical notice, with pleasure; and we read a romance
with pleasure; and a pleasure which is quite apart from the
question of fact or fiction. Indeed, when we would persuade
young people to read history, we tell them that it is as interesting as a romance or a novel. The mere acquisition of new
images, and those images striking, great, various, unexpected,
beautiful, with mutual relations and bearings, as being parts
of a whole, with continuity, succession, evolution, with recurring complications and corresponding solutions, with a crisis
and a catastrophe, is highly pleasurable, quite independently
of the question whether there is any truth in them. I am not
denying that we should be balked and disappointed to be told
they were all untrue, but this seems to arise from the reflection
that we have been taken in; not as if the fact of their truth

were a distinct element of pleasure, though it would increase the pleasure, as investing them with a character of marvellousness, and as associating them with known or ascertained places. But even if the pleasure of knowledge is not thus founded on the imagination, at least it does not consist in that triumphant repose of the mind after a struggle, which is the characteristic of certitude.

And so too as to such statements as gain from us a half-assent, as superstitious tales, stories of magic, of romantic crime, of ghosts, or such as we follow for the moment with a faint and languid assent,—contemporary history, political occurrences, the news of the day,—the pleasure resulting from these is that of novelty or curiosity, and is like the pleasure arising from the excitement of chance and from variety; it has in it no sense of possession: it is simply external to us, and has nothing akin to the thought of a battle and a victory.

(2) Again, the pursuit of knowledge has its own pleasure, distinct from the pleasures of knowledge, as it is distinct from that of consciously possessing it. This will be evident at once, if we consider what a vacuity and depression of mind sometimes comes upon us on the termination of an inquiry, however successfully terminated, compared with the interest and spirit with which we carried it on. The pleasure of a search, like that of a hunt, lies in the searching, and ends at the point at which the pleasure of certitude begins. Its elements are altogether foreign to those which go to compose the serene satisfaction of certitude. First, the successive steps of discovery, which attend on an investigation, are continual and ever-extending informations, and pleasurable, not only as such, but also as the evidence of past efforts, and the earnest of success at the last. Next, there is the interest which attaches to a mystery, not yet removed, but tending to removal,—the complex pleasure of wonder, expectation, sudden surprises, suspense, and hope, of advances fitful, yet sure, to the unknown. And there is the pleasure which attaches to the toil and conflict of the strong, the consciousness and successive evidences of power, moral

and intellectual, the pride of ingenuity and skill, of industry, patience, vigilance, and perseverance.

Such are the pleasures of investigation and discovery; and to these we must add, what I have suggested in the last sentence, the logical satisfaction, as it may be called, which accompanies these efforts of mind. There is great pleasure, as is plain, at least to certain minds, in proceeding from particular facts to principles, in generalizing, discriminating, reducing into order and meaning the maze of phenomena which nature presents to us. This is the kind of pleasure attendant on the treatment of probabilities which point at conclusions without reaching them, or of objections which must be weighed and measured, and adjusted for what they are worth, over and against propositions which are antecedently evident. It is the special pleasure belonging to Inference as contrasted with Assent, a pleasure almost poetical, as twilight has more poetry in it than noon-day. Such is the joy of the pleader, with a good case in hand, and expecting the separate attacks of half a dozen acute intellects, each advancing from a point of his own. I suppose this was the pleasure which the Academics had in mind, when they propounded that happiness lay, not in finding the truth, but in seeking it. To seek, indeed, with the certainty of not finding what we seek, cannot in any serious matter, be pleasurable, any more than the labour of Sisyphus or the Danaides; but when the result does not concern us very much, clever arguments and rival ones have the attraction of a game of chance or skill, whether or not they lead to any definite conclusion.

(3) Are there pleasures of Doubt, as well as of Inference and of Assent? In one sense, there are. Not indeed, if doubt simply means ignorance, uncertainty, or hopeless suspense; but there is a certain grave acquiescence in ignorance, a recognition of our impotence to solve momentous and urgent questions, which has a satisfaction of its own. After high aspirations, after renewed endeavours, after bootless toil, after long wanderings, after hope, effort, weariness, failure, painfully

alternating and recurring, it is an immense relief to the ex-hausted mind to be able to say, "At length I know that I can know nothing about any thing,"—that is, while it can maintain itself in a posture of thought which has no promise of perma-nence, because it is unnatural. But here the satisfaction does not lie in not knowing, but in knowing there is nothing to know. It is a positive act of assent or conviction, given to what in the particular case is an untruth. It is the assent and the false certitude which are the cause of the tranquillity of mind. Ignorance remains the evil which it ever was, but something of the peace of certitude is gained in knowing the worst, and in having reconciled the mind to the endurance of it.

I may seem to have been needlessly diffuse in thus dwelling on the pleasurable affections severally attending on these various conditions of the intellect, but I have had a purpose in doing so. That Certitude is a natural and normal state of mind, and not (as is sometimes objected) one of its extravagances or infirmities, is proved indeed by the remarks which I have made above on the same objection, as directed against assent; for certitude is only one of its forms. But I have thought it well in addition to suggest, even at the expense of a digression, that as no one would refuse to Inquiry, Doubt, and Knowledge a legitimate place among our mental constituents, so no one can reasonably ignore a state of mind which not only is shown to be substantive by possessing a sentiment *sui generis,* and characteristic, but is analogical to Inquiry, Doubt, and Knowl-edge, in the fact of its thus having such a sentiment of its own.

CHAPTER VII

CERTITUDE

1

ASSENT AND CERTITUDE CONTRASTED

IN PROCEEDING TO COMPARE together simple assent and complex, that is, assent and certitude, I begin by observing, that popularly no distinction is made between the two; or rather, that in religious teaching that is called certitude to which I have given the name of assent. I have no difficulty in adopting such a use of the words, though the course of my investigation has led me to another. Perhaps religious assent may be fitly called, to use a theological term, "material certitude;" and the first point of comparison which I shall make between the two states of mind, will serve to set me right with the common way of speaking.

1. It certainly follows then, from the distinctions which I have made, that great numbers of men must be considered to pass through life with neither doubt nor, on the other hand, certitude (as I have used the words) on the most important propositions which can occupy their minds, but with only a simple assent, that is, an assent which they barely recognize, or bring home to their consciousness or reflect upon, as being assent. Such an assent is all that religious Protestants commonly have to show, who believe nevertheless with their whole hearts the contents of Holy Scripture. Such too is the state of mind of multitudes of good Catholics, perhaps the majority, who live and die in a simple, full, firm belief in all that the Church teaches, because she teaches it,—in the belief of the irreversible truth of whatever she defines and declares,—

but who, as being far removed from Protestant and other dis-
sentients, and having but little intellectual training, have never
had the temptation to doubt, and never the opportunity to be
certain. There were whole nations in the middle ages thus
steeped in the Catholic Faith, who never used its doctrines
as matter for argument or research, or changed the original
belief of their childhood into the more scientific convictions
of philosophy. As there is a condition of mind which is characterized by invincible ignorance, so there is another which
may be said to be possessed of invincible knowledge; and it
would be paradoxical in me to deny to such a mental state
the highest quality of religious faith,—I mean certitude.

I allow this, and therefore I will call simple assent *material*
certitude; or, to use a still more apposite term for it, *interpreta-*
tive certitude. I call it interpretative, signifying thereby that,
though the assent in the individuals here contemplated is not a
reflex act, still the question only has to be started about the truth
of the objects of their assent, in order to elicit from them an
act of faith in response which will fulfil the conditions of
certitude, as I have drawn them out. As to the argumentative
process necessary for such an act, it is valid and sufficient, if
it be carried out seriously, and proportionate to their several
capacities. "The Catholic Religion is true, because its objects,
as present to my mind, control and influence my conduct as
nothing else does;" or "because it has about it an odour of
truth and sanctity *sui generis,* as perceptible to my moral
nature as flowers to my sense, such as can only come from
heaven;" or "because it has never been to me any thing but
peace, joy, consolation, and strength, all through my troubled
life." And if the particular argument used in some instances
needs strengthening, then let it be observed, that the keenness
of the real apprehension with which the assent is made, though
it cannot be the legitimate basis of the assent, may still legitimately act, and strongly act, in confirmation. Such, I say, would
be the promptitude and effectiveness of the reasoning, and
the facility of the change from assent to certitude proper, in

the case of the multitudes in question, did the occasion for reflection occur; but it does not occur; and accordingly, most genuine and thorough as is the assent, it can only be called virtual, material, or interpretative certitude, if I have above explained certitude rightly.

Of course these remarks hold good in secular subjects as well as religious:—I believe, for instance, that I am living in an island, that Julius Cæsar once invaded it, that it has been conquered by successive races, that it has had great political and social changes, and that at this time it has colonies, establishments, and imperial dominion all over the earth. All this I am accustomed to take for granted without a thought; but, were the need to arise, I should not find much difficulty in drawing out from my own mental resources reasons sufficient to justify me in these beliefs.

It is true indeed that, among the multitudes who are thus implicitly certain, there may be those who would change their assents, did they seek to place them upon an argumentative footing; for instance, some believers in Christianity, did they examine into its claims, might end in renouncing it. But this is only saying that there are genuine assents, and assents that ultimately become not genuine; and again, that there is an assent which is not a virtual certitude, and is lost in the attempt to make it certitude. And of course we are not gifted with that insight into the minds of individuals, which enables us to determine before the event, when it is that an assent is really such, and when not, or not a deeply rooted assent. Men may assent lightly, or from mere prejudice, or without understanding what it is to which they assent. They may be genuine believers in Revelation up to the time when they begin formally to examine,—nay, and really have implicit reasons for their belief,—and then, being overcome by the number of views which they have to confront, and swayed by the urgency of special objections, or biassed by their imaginations, or frightened by a deeper insight into the claims of religion upon the soul, may, in spite of their habitual and latent grounds for believing, shrink back and withdraw their assent. Or again, they may once have believed, but their assent has gradually become a mere profession, without their knowing it; then, when by accident they interrogate themselves, they find no assent within them at all, to turn into certitude. The event, I say, alone determines whether what is outwardly an assent is really such an act of the mind as admits of being developed into certitude, or is a mere self-delusion or a cloak for unbelief.

2. Next, I observe, that, of the two modes of apprehending propositions, notional and real, assent, as I have already said, has closer relations with real than with notional. Now a simple assent need not be notional; but the reflex or confirmatory assent of certitude always is given to a notional proposition, viz. to the truth, necessity, duty, &c., of our assent to the simple assent and to its proposition. Its predicate is a general term, and cannot stand for a fact, whereas the original proposition, included in it, may, and often does, express a fact. Thus, "The cholera is in the midst of us" is a real proposition; but "That 'the cholera is in the midst of us' is beyond all doubt" is a notional. Now assent to a real proposition is assent to an imagination, and an imagination, as supplying objects to our emotional and moral nature, is adapted to be a principle of action: accordingly, the simple assent to "The cholera is among us," is more emphatic and operative, than the confirmatory assent, "It is beyond reasonable doubt that 'the cholera is among us.'" The confirmation gives momentum to the complex act of the mind, but the simple assent gives it its edge. The simple assent would still be operative in its measure, though the reflex assent was, not "It is undeniable," but "It is probable" that "the cholera is among us;" whereas there would be no operative force in the mental act at all, though the reflex assent was to the truth, not to the probability of the fact, if the fact which was the object of the simple assent was nothing more than "The cholera is in China." The reflex assent then, which is the

characteristic of certitude, does not immediately touch us; it is purely intellectual, and, taken by itself, has scarcely more force than the recording of a conclusion.

I have taken an instance, in which the matter which is submitted for examination and for assent, can hardly fail of being interesting to the minds employed upon it; but in many cases, even though the fact assented to has a bearing upon action, it is not directly of a nature to influence the feelings or conduct, except of particular persons. And in such instances of certitude, the previous labour of coming to a conclusion, and that repose of mind which I have above described as attendant on an assent to its truth, often counteracts whatever of lively sensation the fact thus concluded is in itself adapted to excite; so that what is gained in depth and exactness of belief is lost as regards freshness and vigour. Hence it is that literary or scientific men, who may have investigated some difficult point of history, philosophy, or physics, and have come to their own settled conclusion about it, having had a perfect right to form one, are far more disposed to be silent as to their convictions, and to let others alone, than partisans on either side of the question, who take it up with less thought and seriousness. And so again, in the religious world, no one seems to look for any great devotion or fervour in controversialists, writers on Christian Evidences, theologians, and the like, it being taken for granted, rightly or wrongly, that such men are too intellectual to be spiritual, and are more occupied with the truth of doctrine than with its reality. If, on the other hand, we would see what the force of simple assent can be, viewed apart from its reflex confirmation, we have but to look at the generous and uncalculating energy of faith as exemplified in the primitive Martyrs, in the youths who defied the pagan tyrant, or the maidens who were silent under his tortures. It is assent, pure and simple, which is the motive cause of great achievements; it is a confidence, growing out of instincts rather than arguments, stayed upon a vivid apprehension, and animated by a transcendent logic, more concentrated in will and in deed for the very reason that it has not been subjected to any intellectual development.

It must be borne in mind, that, in thus speaking, I am contrasting with each other the simple and the reflex assent, which together make up the complex act of certitude. In its complete exhibition keenness in believing is united with repose and persistence.

3. We must take the constitution of the human mind as we find it, and not as we may judge it ought to be;—thus I am led on to another remark, which is at first sight disadvantageous to certitude. Introspection of our intellectual operations is not the best of means for preserving us from intellectual hesitations. To meddle with the springs of thought and action is really to weaken them; and, as to that argumentation which is the preliminary to certitude, it may indeed be unavoidable, but, as in the case of other serviceable allies, it is not so easy to discard it, after it has done its work, as it was in the first instance to obtain its assistance. Questioning, when encouraged on any subject-matter, readily becomes a habit, and leads the mind to substitute exercises of inference for assent, whether simple or complex. Reasons for assenting suggest reasons for not assenting, and what were realities to our imagination, while our assent was simple, may become little more than notions, when we have attained to certitude. Objections and difficulties tell upon the mind; it may lose its elasticity, and be unable to throw them off. And thus, even as regards things which it may be absurd to doubt, we may, in consequence of some past suggestion of the possibility of error, or of some chance association to their disadvantage, be teazed from time to time and hampered by involuntary questionings, as if we were not certain, when we are. Nay, there are those, who are visited with these even permanently, as a sort of *muscæ volitantes* of their mental vision, ever flitting to and fro, and dimming its clearness and completeness—visitants, for which they are not responsible, and which they know to be unreal, still so

seriously interfering with their comfort and even with their energy, that they may be tempted to complain that even blind prejudice has more of quiet and of durability than certitude.

As even saints may suffer from imaginations in which they have no part, so the shreds and tatters of former controversies, and the litter of an argumentative habit, may beset and obstruct the intellect,—questions which have been solved without their solutions, chains of reasoning with missing links, difficulties which have their roots in the nature of things, and which are necessarily left behind in a philosophical inquiry because they cannot be removed, and which call for the exercise of good sense and for strength of will to put them down with a high hand, as irrational or preposterous. Whence comes evil? why are we created without our consent? how can the Supreme Being have no beginning? how can He need skill, if He is omnipotent? if He is omnipotent, why does He permit suffering? if He permits suffering, how is He all-loving? if He is all-loving, how can He be just? if He is infinite, what has He to do with the finite? how can the temporary be decisive of the eternal?—these, and a host of like questions, must arise in every thoughtful mind, and, after the best use of reason, must be deliberately put aside, as beyond reason, as (so to speak) no-thoroughfares, which, having no outlet themselves, have no legitimate power to divert us from the King's highway, and to hinder the direct course of religious inquiry from reaching its destination. A serious obstruction, however, they will be now and then to particular minds, enfeebling the faith which they cannot destroy,—being parallel to the uncomfortable associations with which we regard one whom we have fallen-in with, acquaintance or stranger, arising from some chance word, look, or action of his which we have witnessed, and which prejudices him in our imagination, though we are angry with ourselves that it should do so.

Again, when, in confidence of our own certitude, and with a view to philosophical fairness, we have attempted successfully to throw ourselves out of our habits of belief into a simply

dispassionate frame of mind, then vague antecedent improb-
abilities, or what seem to us as such,—merely what is strange
or marvellous in certain truths, merely the fact that things
happen in one way and not in another, when they must happen
in some way,—may disturb us, as suggesting to us, "Is it possible? who would have thought it! what a coincidence!" without really touching the deep assent of our whole intellectual
being to the object, whatever it be, thus irrationally assailed.
Thus we may wonder at the Divine Mercy of the Incarnation,
till we grow startled at it, and ask why the earth has so special
a theological history, or why we are Christians and others not,
or how God can really exert a particular governance, since He
does not punish such sinners as we are, thus seeming to doubt
His power or His equity, though in truth we are not doubting
at all.

The occasion of this intellectual waywardness may be
slighter still. I gaze on the Palatine Hill, or on the Parthenon,
or on the Pyramids, which I have read of from a boy, or upon
the matter-of-fact reality of the sacred places in the Holy Land,
and I have to force my imagination to follow the guidance of
sight and of reason. It is to me so strange that a life-long belief
should be changed into sight, and things should be so near me,
which hitherto had been visions. And so in times, first of suspense, then of joy; "When the Lord turned the captivity of
Sion, then" (according to the Hebrew text) "we were like unto
them that dream." Yet it was a dream which they were certain
was a truth, while they seemed to doubt it. So, too, was it in
some sense with the Apostles after our Lord's resurrection.

Such vague thoughts, haunting or evanescent, are in no
sense akin to that struggle between faith and unbelief, which
made the poor father cry out, "I believe, help Thou mine unbelief!" Nay, even what in some minds seems like an under-
current of scepticism, or a faith founded on a perilous sub-
stratum of doubt, need not be more than a temptation, though
robbing certitude of its normal peacefulness. In such a case,
faith may still express the steady conviction of the intellect;

it may still be the grave, deep, calm, prudent assurance of mature experience, though it is not the ready and impetuous assent of the young, the generous, or the unreflecting.

4. There is another characteristic of certitude, in contrast with assent, which it is important to insist upon, and that is, its persistence. Assents may and do change; certitudes endure. This is why religion demands more than an assent to its truth; it requires a certitude, or at least an assent which is convertible into certitude on demand. Without certitude in religious faith there may be much decency of profession and of observance, but there can be no habit of prayer, no directness of devotion, no intercourse with the unseen, no generosity of self-sacrifice. Certitude then is essential to the Christian; and if he is to persevere to the end, his certitude must include in it a principle of persistence. This it has, as I shall explain in the next Section.

2

INDEFECTIBILITY OF CERTITUDE

IT IS THE CHARACTERISTIC of certitude that its object is a truth, a truth as such, a proposition as true. There are right and wrong convictions, and certitude is a right conviction; if it is not right with a consciousness of being right, it is not certitude. Now truth cannot change; what is once truth is always truth; and the human mind is made for truth, and so rests in truth, as it cannot rest in falsehood. When then it once becomes possessed of a truth, what is to dispossess it? but this is to be certain; therefore once certitude, always certitude. If certitude in any matter be the termination of all doubt or fear about its truth, and an unconditional conscious adherence to it, it carries with it an inward assurance, strong though implicit, that it shall never fail. Indefectibility almost enters into its very idea, enters into it at least so far as this, that its failure, if of frequent occurrence, would prove that certitude was after all and in fact an impossible act, and that what looked like it was a mere extravagance of the intellect. Truth would still be truth, but the knowledge of it would be beyond us and unattainable. It is of great importance then to show, that, as a general rule, certitude does not fail; that failures of what was taken for certitude are the exception; that the intellect, which is made for truth, can attain truth, and, having attained it, can keep it, can recognize it, and preserve the recognition.

This is on the whole reasonable; yet are the stipulations, thus obviously necessary for an act or state of certitude, ever fulfilled? We know what conjecture is, and what opinion, and what assent is, can we point out any specific state or habit of thought, of which the distinguishing mark is unchangeableness? On the contrary, any conviction, false as well as true, may last; and any conviction, true as well as false, may be lost. A conviction in favour of a proposition may be exchanged for a conviction of its contradictory; and each of them may be attended, while they last, by that sense of security and repose, which a true object alone can legitimately impart. No line can be drawn between such real certitudes as have truth for their object, and apparent certitudes. No distinct test can be named, sufficient to discriminate between what may be called the false prophet and the true. What looks like certitude always is exposed to the chance of turning out to be a mistake. If our intimate, deliberate conviction may be counterfeit in the case of one proposition, why not in the case of another? if in the case of one man, why not in the case of a hundred? Is certitude then ever possible without the attendant gift of infallibility? can we know what is right in one case, unless we are secured against error in any? Further, if one man is infallible, why is he different from his brethren? unless indeed he is distinctly marked out for the prerogative. Must not all men be infallible by consequence, if any man is to be considered as certain?

The difficulty, thus stated argumentatively, has only too accurate a response in what actually goes on in the world. It is a fact of daily occurrence that men change their certitudes, that is, what they consider to be such, and are as confident

and well-established in their new opinions as they were once
in their old. They take up forms of religion only to leave them
for their contradictories. They risk their fortunes and their
lives on impossible adventures. They commit themselves by
word and deed, in reputation and position, to schemes which
in the event they bitterly repent of and renounce; they set out
in youth with intemperate confidence in prospects which fail
them, and in friends who betray them, ere they come to middle
age; and they end their days in cynical disbelief of truth and
virtue any where;—and often, the more absurd are their means
and their ends, so much the longer do they cling to them, and
then again so much the more passionate is their eventual
disgust and contempt of them. How then can certitude be
theirs, how is certitude possible at all, considering it is so often
misplaced, so often fickle and inconsistent, so deficient in
available criteria? And, as to the feeling of finality and security, ought it ever to be indulged? Is it not a mere weakness
or extravagance, a deceit, to be eschewed by every clear and
prudent mind? With the countless instances, on all sides of us,
of human fallibility, with the constant exhibitions of antagonist certitudes, who can so sin against modesty and sobriety
of mind, as not to be content with probability, as the true
guide of life, renouncing ambitious thoughts, which are sure
either to delude him, or to disappoint?

This is what may be objected: now let us see what can be
said in answer, particularly as regards religious certitude.

1

First, as to fallibility and infallibility. It is very common,
doubtless, especially in religious controversy, to confuse infallibility with certitude, and to argue that, since we have not
the one we have not the other, for that no one can claim to
be certain on any point, who is not infallible about all; but the
two words stand for things quite distinct from each other. For
example, I remember for certain what I did yesterday, but still
my memory is not infallible; I am quite clear that two and

two makes four, but I often make mistakes in long addition sums. I have no doubt whatever that John or Richard is my true friend, but I have before now trusted those who failed me, and I may do so again before I die. A certitude is directed to this or that particular proposition; it is not a faculty or gift, but a disposition of mind relatively to a definite case which is before me. Infallibility, on the contrary, is just that which certitude is not; it *is* a faculty or gift, and relates, not to some one truth in particular, but to all possible propositions in a given subject-matter. We ought, in strict propriety, to speak, not of infallible acts, but of acts of infallibility. A belief or opinion as little admits of being called infallible, as a deed can correctly be called immortal. A deed is done and over; it may be great, momentous, effective, any thing but immortal; it is its fame, it is the work which it brings to pass, which is immortal, not the deed itself. And as a deed is good or bad, but never immortal, so a belief, opinion, or certitude is true or false, but never infallible. We cannot speak of things which exist or things which once were, as if they were something *in posse*. It is persons and rules that are infallible, not what is brought out into act, or committed to paper. A man is infallible, whose words are always true; a rule is infallible, if it is unerring in all its possible applications. An infallible authority is certain in every particular case that may arise; but a man who is certain in some one definite case, is not on that account infallible.

I am quite certain that Victoria is our Sovereign, and not her father, the late Duke of Kent, without laying any claim to the gift of infallibility; as I may do a virtuous action, without being impeccable. I may be certain that the Church is infallible, while I am myself a fallible mortal; otherwise, I cannot be certain that the Supreme Being is infallible, until I am infallible myself. It is a strange objection, then, which is sometimes urged against Catholics, that they cannot prove and assent to the Church's infallibility, unless they first believe in their own. Certitude, as I have said, is directed to one or other definite concrete proposition. I am certain of proposition one, two, three, four, or five, one by one, each by itself. I may be certain of one of them, without being certain of the rest; that I am certain of the first makes it neither likely nor unlikely that I am certain of the second; but were I infallible, then I should be certain, not only of one of them, but of all, and of many more besides, which have never come before me as yet. Therefore we may be certain of the infallibility of the Church, while we admit that in many things we are not, and cannot be, certain at all.

It is wonderful that a clear-headed man, like Chillingworth, sees this as little as the run of every-day objectors to the Catholic religion; for in his celebrated *Religion of Protestants* he writes as follows:—"You tell me they cannot be saved, unless they believe in your proposals with an infallible faith. To which end they must believe also your propounder, the Church, to be simply infallible. Now how is it possible for them to give a rational assent to the Church's infallibility, *unless they have some infallible means to know that she is infallible?* Neither can they infallibly know the infallibility of this means, but by some other; and so on for ever, unless they can dig so deep, as to come at length to the Rock, that is, to settle all upon something evident of itself, which is not so much as pretended." [1]

Now what is an "infallible means"? It is a means of coming at a fact without the chance of mistake. It is a proof which is sufficient for certitude in the particular case, or a proof that is certain. When then Chillingworth says that there can be no "rational assent to the Church's infallibility" without "some infallible means of knowing that she is infallible," he means nothing else than some means which is certain; he says that for a rational assent to infallibility there must be an absolutely valid or certain proof. This is intelligible; but observe how his argument will run, if worded according to this interpretation: "The doctrine of the Church's infallibility requires a proof

[1] ii. n. 154. *Vide* Note I at the end of the volume.

that is certain; and that certain proof requires another previous certain proof, and that again another, and so on *ad infinitum,* unless indeed we dig so deep as to settle all upon something evident of itself." What is this but to say that nothing in this world is certain but what is self-evident? that nothing can be absolutely proved? Can he really mean this? What then becomes of physical truth? of the discoveries in optics, chemistry, and electricity, or of the science of motion? Intuition by itself will carry us but a little way into that circle of knowledge which is the boast of the present age.

I can believe then in the infallible Church without my own personal infallibility. Certitude is at most nothing more than infallibility *pro hac vice,* and promises nothing as to the truth of any proposition beside its own. That I am certain of this proposition to-day, is no ground for thinking that I shall have a right to be certain of that proposition to-morrow; and that I am wrong in my convictions about to-day's proposition, does not hinder my having a true conviction, a genuine certitude, about to-morrow's proposition. If indeed I claimed to be infallible, one failure would shiver my claim to pieces; but I may claim to be certain of the truth to which I have already attained, though I should arrive at no new truths in addition as long as I live.

2

Let us put aside the word "infallibility;" let us understand by certitude, as I have explained it, nothing more than the relation of the mind toward given propositions:—still, it may be urged, it involves a sense of security and of repose, at least as regards these in particlar. Now how can this security be mine, without which certitude is not, if I know, as I know too well, that before now I have thought myself certain, when I was certain after all of an untruth? Is not the very possibility of certitude lost to me for ever by that one mistake? What happened once, may happen again. All my certitudes before and after are henceforth destroyed by the introduction of a reasonable doubt, underlying them all. *Ipso facto* they cease to be certitudes,—they come short of unconditional assents by the measure of that counterfeit assurance. They are nothing more to me than opinions or anticipations, judgments on the verisimilitude of intellectual views, not the possession and enjoyment of truths. And who has not thus been balked by false certitudes a hundred times in the course of his experience? and how can certitude have a legitimate place in our mental constitution, when it thus manifestly ministers to error and to scepticism?

This is what may be objected, and it is not, as I think, difficult to answer. Certainly, the experience of mistakes in the assents which we have made is to the prejudice of subsequent ones. There is an antecedent difficulty in our allowing ourselves to be certain of something to-day, if yesterday we had to give up our belief of something else, of which we had up to that time professed ourselves to be certain. This is true; but antecedent objections to an act are not sufficient of themselves to prohibit its exercise; they may demand of us an increased circumspection before committing ourselves to it, but may be met with reasons more than sufficient to overcome them.

It must be recollected that certitude is a deliberate assent given expressly after reasoning. If then my certitude is unfounded, it is the reasoning that is in fault, not my assent to it. It is the law of my mind to seal up the conclusions to which ratiocination has brought me, by that formal assent which I have called a certitude. I could indeed have withheld my assent, but I should have acted against my nature, had I done so when there was what I considered a proof; and I did only what was fitting, what was incumbent on me, upon those existing conditions, in giving it. This is the process by which knowledge accumulates and is stored up both in the individual and in the world. It has sometimes been remarked, when men have boasted of the knowledge of modern times, that no wonder we see more than the ancients, because we are mounted upon their shoulders. The conclusions of one generation are the truths of the next. We are able, it is our duty, deliberately to take things for granted which our forefathers had a duty to doubt about; and unless we summarily put down disputation on points which have been already proved and ruled, we shall waste our time, and make no advances. Circumstances indeed may arise, when a question may legitimately be revived, which has already been definitely determined; but a re-consideration of such a question need not abruptly unsettle the existing certitude of those who engage in it, or throw them into a scepticism about things in general, even though eventually they find they have been wrong in a particular matter. It would have been absurd to prohibit the controversy which has lately been held concerning the obligations of Newton to Pascal; and supposing it had issued in their being established, the partisans of Newton would not have thought it necessary to renounce their certitude of the law of gravitation itself, on the ground that they had been mistaken in their certitude that Newton discovered it.

If we are never to be certain, after having been once certain wrongly, then we ought never to attempt a proof because we have once made a bad one. Errors in reasoning are lessons and warnings, not to give up reasoning, but to reason with greater caution. It is absurd to break up the whole structure of our knowledge, which is the glory of the human intellect, because the intellect is not infallible in its conclusions. If in any particular case we have been mistaken in our inferences and the certitudes which followed upon them, we are bound of course to take the fact of this mistake into account, in making up our minds on any new question, before we proceed to decide upon it. But if while weighing the arguments on one side and the other and drawing our conclusion, that old mistake has been allowed for, or has been, to use a familiar mode of speaking, discounted, then it has no outstanding claim against our acceptance of that conclusion, after it has actually been drawn. Whatever be the legitimate weight of the fact of that mistake in our inquiry, justice has been done to it, before we have allowed ourselves to be certain again. Suppose I am walking out in the moonlight, and see dimly the outlines of some figure among the trees;—it is a man. I draw nearer,—it is still a man; nearer still, and all hesitation is at an end,—I am certain it is a man. But he neither moves, nor speaks when I address him; and then I ask myself what can be his purpose in hiding among the trees at such an hour. I come quite close to him, and put out my arm. Then I find for certain that what I took for a man is but a singular shadow, formed by the falling of the moonlight on the interstices of some branches or their foliage. Am I not to indulge my second certitude, because I was wrong in my first? does not any objection, which lies against my second from the failure of my first, fade away before the evidence on which my second is founded?

Or again: I depose on my oath in a court of justice, to the best of my knowledge and belief, that I was robbed by the prisoner at the bar. Then, when the real offender is brought before me, I am obliged, to my great confusion, to retract. Because I have been mistaken in my certitude, may I not at least be certain that I have been mistaken? And further, in spite of the shock which that mistake gives me, is it impossible that the sight of the real culprit may give me so luminous a conviction that at length I have got the right man, that, were it decent towards the court, or consistent with self-respect, I may find myself prepared to swear to the identity of the second, as I have already solemnly committed myself to the identity of the first? It is manifest that the two certitudes stand each on its own basis, and the antecedent objection to my admission of a truth which was brought home to me second, drawn from a hallucination which came first, is a mere abstract argument, impotent when directed against good evidence lying in the concrete.

3

If in the criminal case which I have been supposing, the second certitude, felt by a witness, was a legitimate state of mind, so was the first. An act, viewed in itself, in itself is not wrong, because it is done wrongly. False certitudes are faults because they are false, not because they are supposed certitudes. They are, or may be, the attempts and the failures of an intellect insufficiently trained, or off its guard. Assent is an act of the mind, congenial to its nature; and it, as other acts, may be made both when it ought to be made, and when it ought not. It is a free act, a personal act for which the doer is responsible, and the actual mistakes in making it, be they ever so numerous or serious, have no force whatever to prohibit the act itself. We are accustomed in such cases, to appeal to the maxim, "Usum non tollit abusus;" and it is plain that, if what may be called functional disarrangements of the intellect are to be considered fatal to the recognition of the functions themselves, then the mind has no laws whatever and no normal constitution. I just now spoke of the growth of knowledge; there is also a growth in the use of those faculties by which knowledge is acquired. The intellect admits of an education; man is a being of progress; he has to learn how to fulfil his end, and to be what facts show that he is intended to be. His mind is in the first instance in disorder, and runs wild; his faculties have their rudimental and inchoate state, and are gradually carried on by practice and experience to their perfection. No instances then whatever of mistaken certitude are sufficient to constitute a proof, that certitude itself is a perversion or extravagance of his nature.

We do not dispense with clocks, because from time to time they go wrong, and tell untruly. A clock, organically considered, may be perfect, yet it may require regulating. Till that needful work is done, the moment-hand perhaps marks the half-minute, when the minute-hand is at the quarter-past, and the hour-hand is just at noon, and the quarter-bell strikes the three quarters, and the hour-bell strikes four, while the sun-dial precisely tells two o'clock. The sense of certitude may be called the bell of the intellect; and that it strikes when it should not is a proof that the clock is out of order, no proof that the bell will be untrustworthy and useless, when it comes to us adjusted and regulated from the hands of the clock-maker.

Our conscience too may be said to strike the hours, and will strike them wrongly, unless it be duly regulated for the per-formance of its proper function. It is the loud announcement of the principle of right in the details of conduct, as the sense of certitude is the clear witness to what is true. Both certitude and conscience have a place in the normal condition of the mind. As a human being, I am unable, if I were to try, to live without some kind of conscience; and I am as little able to live without those landmarks of thought which certitude se-cures for me; still, as the hammer of a clock may tell untruly, so may my conscience and my sense of certitude be attached to mental acts, whether of consent or of assent, which have no claim to be thus sanctioned. Both the moral and the intellectual sanction are liable to be biassed by personal inclinations and motives; both require and admit of discipline; and as it is no disproof of the authority of conscience that false consciences abound, neither does it destroy the importance and the uses of certitude, because even educated minds, who are earnest in their inquiries after the truth, in many cases remain under the power of prejudice or delusion.

To this deficiency in mental training a wider error is to be attributed,—the mistaking for conviction and certitude states and frames of mind which make no pretence to the funda-mental condition on which conviction rests as distinct from assent. The multitude of men confuse together the probable, the possible, and the certain, and apply these terms to doc-trines and statements almost at random. They have no clear view what it is they know, what they presume, what they suppose, and what they only assert. They make little distinction between credence, opinion, and profession; at various times they give them all perhaps the name of certitude, and accordingly, when they change their minds, they fancy they have given up points of which they had a true conviction. Or at least bystanders thus speak of them, and the very idea of certitude falls into disrepute.

In this day the subject-matter of thought and belief has so increased upon us, that a far higher mental formation is required than was necessary in times past, and higher than we have actually reached. The whole world is brought to our doors every morning, and our judgment is required upon social concerns, books, persons, parties, creeds, national acts, political principles and measures. We have to form our opinion, make our profession, take our side on a hundred matters on which we have but little right to speak at all. But we do speak, and must speak, upon them, though neither we nor those who hear us are well able to determine what is the real position of our intellect relatively to those many questions, one by one, on which we commit ourselves; and then, since many of these questions change their complexion with the passing hour, and many require elaborate consideration, and many are simply beyond us, it is not wonderful, if, at the end of a few years, we have to revise or to repudiate our conclusions; and then we shall be unfairly said to have changed our certitudes, and shall confirm the doctrine, that, except in abstract truth, no judgment rises higher than probability.

Such are the mistakes about certitude among educated men; and after referring to them, it is scarcely worth while to dwell upon the absurdities and excesses of the rude intellect, as seen in the world at large; as if any one could dream of treating as deliberate assents, as assents upon assents, as convictions or certitudes, the prejudices, credulities, infatuations, superstitions, fanaticisms, the whims and fancies, the sudden irrevocable plunges into the unknown, the obstinate determinations, —the offspring, as they are, of ignorance, wilfulness, cupidity, and pride,—which go so far to make up the history of mankind; yet these are often set down as instances of certitude and of its failure.

4

I have spoken of certitude as being assigned a definite and fixed place among our mental acts;—it follows upon examination and proof, as the bell sounds the hour when the hands reach it,—so that no act or state of the intellect is certitude, however it may resemble it, which does not observe this appointed law. This proviso greatly diminishes the catalogue of genuine certitudes. Another restriction is this:—the occasions or subject matter of certitude are under law also. Putting aside the daily exercise of the senses, the principal subjects in secular knowledge, about which we can be certain, are the truths or facts which are its basis. As to this world, we are certain of the elements of knowledge, whether general, scientific, historical, or such as bear on our daily needs and habits, and relate to ourselves, our homes and families, our friends, neighbourhood, country, and civil state. Beyond these elementary points of knowledge lies a vast subject-matter of opinion, credence, and belief, viz. the field of public affairs, of social and professional life, of business, of duty, of literature, of taste, nay, of the experimental sciences. On subjects such as these the reasonings and conclusions of mankind vary,—"mundum tradidit disputationi eorum;"—and prudent men in consequence seldom speak confidently, unless they are warranted to do so by genius, great experience, or some special qualification. They determine their judgments by what is probable, what is safe, what promises best, what has verisimilitude, what impresses and sways them. They neither can possess, nor need certitude, nor do they look out for it.

Hence it is that—the province of certitude being so contracted, and that of opinion so large—it is common to call probability the guide of life. This saying, when properly explained, is true; however, we must not suffer ourselves to carry a true maxim to an extreme; it is far from true, if we so hold it as to forget that without first principles there can be no conclusions at all, and that thus probability does in some sense presuppose and require the existence of truths which are certain. Especially is the maxim untrue, in respect to the other great department of knowledge, the spiritual, if taken to support the doctrine, that the first principles and elements of religion, which are universally received, are mere matter of opinion; though in this day, it is too often taken for granted that religion is one of those subjects on which truth cannot be discovered, and on which one conclusion is pretty much on a level with another. But on the contrary the initial truths of divine knowledge ought to be viewed as parallel to the initial truths of secular: as the latter are certain, so too are the former. I cannot indeed deny that a decent reverence for the Supreme Being, an acquiescence in the claims of Revelation, a general profession of Christian doctrine, and some sort of attendance on sacred ordinances, is in fact all the religion that is usual with even the better sort of men, and that for all this a sufficient basis may certainly be found in probabilities; but if religion is to be devotion, and not a mere matter of sentiment, if it is to be made the ruling principle of our lives, if our actions, one by one, and our daily conduct, are to be consistently directed towards an Invisible Being, we need something higher than a mere balance of arguments to fix and to control our minds. Sacrifice of wealth, name, or position, faith and hope, self-conquest, communion with the spiritual world, presuppose a real hold and habitual intuition of the objects of Revelation, which is certitude under another name.

To this issue indeed we may bring the main difference, viewed philosophically between nominal Christianity on the one hand, and vital Christianity on the other. Rational, sensible men, as they consider themselves, men who do not comprehend the very notion of loving God above all things, are content with such a measure of probability for the truths of religion, as serves them in their secular transactions; but those who are deliberately staking their all upon the hopes of the next world, think it reasonable, and find it necessary, before starting on their new course, to have some points, clear and immutable, to start from; otherwise, they will not start at all. They ask, as a preliminary condition, to have the ground sure under their feet; they look for more than human reasonings and inferences, for nothing less than the "strong consolation," as the Apostle speaks, of "those immutable things in which it is impossible for God to lie," His counsel and His oath. Christian earnestness may be ruled by the world to be a perverseness or a delusion; but as long as it exists it will pre-suppose certitude as the very life which is to animate it.

This is the true parallel between human and divine knowledge; each of them opens into a large field of mere opinion, but in both the one and the other the primary principles, the general, fundamental, cardinal truths are immutable. In human matters we are guided by probabilities, but, I repeat, they are probabilities founded on certainties. It is on no probability that we are constantly receiving the informations and dictates of sense and memory, of our intellectual instincts, of the moral sense, and of the logical faculty. It is on no probability that we receive the generalizations of science, and the great outlines of history. These are certain truths; and from them each of us forms his own judgments and directs his own course, according to the probabilities which they suggest to him, as the navigator applies his observations and his charts for the determination of his course. Such is the main view to be taken of the separate provinces of probability and certainty in matters of this world; and so, as regards the world invisible and future, we have a direct and conscious knowledge of our Maker, His attributes, His providences, acts, works, and will, from nature, and revelation; and beyond this knowledge lies the large domain of theology, metaphysics, and ethics, on which it is not allowed to us to advance beyond probabilities, or to attain to more than an opinion.

Such on the whole is the analogy between our knowledge of matters of this world and matters of the world unseen;— indefectible certitude in primary truths, manifold variations of opinion in their application and disposition.

5

I have said that certitude, whether in human or divine knowledge, is attainable as regards general and cardinal truths; and that in neither department of knowledge, on the whole, is certitude discredited, lost, or reversed; for, in matter of fact, whether in human or divine, those primary truths have ever kept their place from the time when they first took possession of it. However, there is one obvious objection, which may be made to this representation, and I proceed to take notice of it.

It may be urged then that time was when the primary truths of science were unknown, and when in consequence various theories were held, contrary to each other. The first element of all things was said to be water, to be air, to be fire; the framework of the universe was eternal; or it was the ever-new combination of innumerable atoms: the planets were fixed in solid crystal revolving spheres; or they moved round the earth in epicycles mounted upon circular orbits; or they were carried whirling round about the sun, while the sun was whirling round the earth. About such doctrines there was no certitude, no more than there is now certitude about the origin of languages, the age of man, or the evolution of species, considered as philosophical questions. Now theology is at present in the very same state in which natural science was five hundred years ago; and this is the proof of it,—that, instead of there being one received theological science in the world, there are a multitude of hypotheses. We have a professed science of Atheism, another of Deism, a Pantheistic, ever so many Christian theologies, to say nothing of Judaism, Islamism, and the Oriental religions. Each of these creeds has its own upholders, and these upholders all certain that it is the very and the only truth, and these same upholders, it may happen, presently giving it up, and then taking up some other creed, and being certain again, as they profess, that it and it only is the truth, these various so-called truths being incompatible with each other. Are not Jews certain about their interpretation of their law? yet they become Christians: are not Catholics certain about the new law? yet they become Protestants. At present then, and as yet, there is no clear certainty any where about religious truth at all; it has still to be discovered; and therefore for Catholics to claim the right to lay down the first principles of theological science in their own way, is to assume the very matter in dispute. First let their doctrines be universally received, and then they will have a right to place them on a level with the certainty which belongs to the laws of motion or of refraction. This is the objection which I propose to consider.

Now first as to the want of universal reception which is urged against the Catholic dogmas, this part of the objection will not require many words. Surely a truth or a fact may be certain, though it is not generally received;—we are each of us ever gaining through our senses various certainties, which no one shares with us; again, the certainties of the sciences are in the possession of a few countries only, and for the most part only of the educated classes in those countries; yet the philosophers of Europe and America would feel certain that the earth rolled round the sun, in spite of the Indian belief of its being supported by an elephant with a tortoise under it. The Catholic Church then, though not universally acknowledged, may without inconsistency claim to teach the primary truths of religion, just as modern science, though but partially received, claims to teach the great principles and laws which are the foundation of secular knowledge, and that with a significance to which no other religious system can pretend, because it is its very profession to speak to all mankind, and its very badge to be ever making converts all over the earth, whereas other religions are more or less variable in their teaching, tolerant of each other, and vocal, and professedly local, in their *habitat* and character.

This, however, is not the main point of the objection; the real difficulty lies not in the variety of religions, but in the contradiction, conflict, and change of religious certitudes.

Truth need not be universal, but it must of necessity be certain; and certainty, in order to be certainty, must endure; yet how is this reasonable expectation fulfilled in the case of religion? On the contrary, those who have been the most certain in their beliefs are sometimes found to lose them, Catholics as well as others; and then to take up new beliefs, perhaps contrary ones, of which they become as certain as if they had never been certain of the old.

In answering this representation, I begin with recurring to the remark which I have already made, that assent and certitude have reference to propositions, one by one. We may of course assent to a number of propositions all together, that is, we may make a number of assents all at once; but in doing so we run the risk of putting upon one level, and treating as if of the same value, acts of the mind which are very different from each other in character and circumstance. An assent, indeed, is ever an assent; but given assents may be strong or weak, deliberate or impulsive, lasting or ephemeral. Now a religion is not a proposition, but a system; it is a rite, a creed, a philosophy, a rule of duty, all at once; and to accept a religion is neither a simple assent to it nor a complex, neither a conviction nor a prejudice, neither a notional assent nor a real, not a mere act of profession, nor of credence, nor of opinion, nor of speculation, but it is a collection of all these various kinds of assents at once and together, some of one description, some of another; but, out of all these different assents, how many are of that kind which I have called certitude? Certitudes indeed do not change, but who shall pretend that assents are indefectible?

For instance: the fundamental dogma of Protestantism is the exclusive authority of Holy Scripture; but in holding this a Protestant holds a host of propositions, explicitly or implicitly, and holds them with assents of various character. Among these propositions, he holds that Scripture is the Divine Revelation itself, that it is inspired, that nothing is known in doctrine but what is there, that the Church had no authority in matters of doctrine, that, as claiming it, it was condemned long ago in the Apocalypse, that St. John wrote the Apocalypse, that justification is by faith only, that our Lord is God, that there are seventy-two generations between Adam and our Lord. Now of which, out of all these propositions, is he certain? and to how many of them is his assent of one and the same description? His belief, that Scripture is commensurate with the Divine Revelation, is perhaps implicit, not conscious; as to inspiration, he does not well know what the word means, and his assent is scarcely more than a profession; that no doctrine is true but what can be proved from Scripture he understands, and his assent to it is what I have called speculative; that the Church has no authority he holds with a real assent or belief; that the Church is condemned in the Apocalypse is a standing prejudice; that St. John wrote the Apocalypse is his opinion; that justification is by faith only, he accepts, but scarcely can be said to apprehend; that our Lord is God perhaps he is certain; that there are seventy-two generations between Adam and Christ he accepts on credence. Yet, if he were asked the question, he would most probably answer that he was certain of the truth of "Protestantism," though "Protestantism" means these things and a hundred more all at once, and though he believes with actual certitude only one of them all,—that indeed a dogma of most sacred importance, but not the discovery of Luther or Calvin. He would think it enough to say that he was a foe to "Romanism" and "Socinianism," and to avow that he gloried in the Reformation. He looks upon each of these religious professions, Protestantism, Romanism, Socinianism and Theism, merely as units, as if they were not each made up of many elements, as if they had nothing in common, as if a transition from the one to the other involved a simple obliteration of all that had been as yet written on his mind, and would be the reception of a new faith.

When, then, we are told that a man has changed from one religion to another, the first question which we have to ask, is, have the first and the second religions nothing in common?

If they have common doctrines, he has changed only a portion of his creed, not the whole: and the next question is, has he ever made much of any doctrines but such as are if otherwise common to his new creed and his old? what doctrines was he certain of among the old, and what among the new?

Thus, of three Protestants, one becomes a Catholic, a second a Unitarian, and a third an unbeliever: how is this? The first becomes a Catholic, because he assented, as a Protestant, to the doctrine of our Lord's divinity, with a real assent and a genuine conviction, and because this certitude, taking possession of his mind, led him on to welcome the Catholic doctrines of the Real Presence and of the Theotocos, till his Protestantism fell off from him, and he submitted himself to the Church. The second became a Unitarian, because, proceeding on the principle that Scripture was the rule of faith and that a man's private judgment was its rule of interpretation, and finding that the doctrine of the Nicene and Athanasian Creeds did not follow by logical necessity from the text of Scripture, he said to himself, "The word of God has been made of none effect by the traditions of men," and therefore nothing was left for him but to profess what he considered primitive Christianity, and to become a Humanitarian. The third gradually subsided into infidelity, because he started with the Protestant dogma, cherished in the depths of his nature, that a priesthood was a corruption of the simplicity of the Gospel. First, then, he would protest against the sacrifice of the Mass; next he gave up baptismal regeneration, and the sacramental principle; then he asked himself whether dogmas were not a restraint on Christian liberty as well as sacraments; then came the question, what after all was the use of teachers of religion? why should any one stand between him and his Maker? After a time it struck him, that this obvious question had to be answered by the Apostles, as well as by the Anglican clergy; so he came to the conclusion that the true and only revelation of God to man is that which is written on the heart. This did for a time, and he remained a Deist. But then it occurred to him, that this inward moral law was there within the breast, whether there was a God or not, and that it was a roundabout way of enforcing that law, to say that it came from God, and simply unnecessary, considering it carried with it its own sacred and sovereign authority, as our feelings instinctively testified; and when he turned to look at the physical world around him, he really did not see what scientific proof there was there of the Being of God at all, and it seemed to him as if all things would go on quite as well as at present, without that hypothesis as with it; so he dropped it, and became a *purus, putus* Atheist.

Now the world will say, that in these three cases old certitudes were lost, and new were gained; but it is not so: each of the three men started with just one certitude, as he would have himself professed, had he examined himself narrowly; and he carried it out and carried it with him into a new system of belief. He was true to that one conviction from first to last; and on looking back on the past, would perhaps insist upon this, and say he had really been consistent all through, when others made much of his great changes in religious opinion. He has indeed made serious additions to his initial ruling principle, but he has lost no conviction of which he was originally possessed.

I will take one more instance. A man is converted to the Catholic Church from his admiration of its religious system, and his disgust with Protestantism. That admiration remains; but, after a time, he leaves his new faith, perhaps returns to his old. The reason, if we may conjecture, may sometimes be this: he has never believed in the Church's infallibility; in her doctrinal truth he has believed, but in her infallibility, no. He was asked, before he was received, whether he held all that the Church taught, he replied he did; but he understood the question to mean, whether he held those particular doctrines "which at that time the Church in matter of fact formally taught," whereas it really meant "whatever the Church then or at any future time should teach." Thus, he never had the indispensable and elementary faith of a Catholic, and was simply no subject for reception into the fold of the Church. This being the case, when the Immaculate Conception is defined, he feels that it is something more than he bargained for when he became a Catholic, and accordingly he gives up his religious profession. The world will say that he has lost his certitude of the divinity of the Catholic Faith, but he never had it.

The first point to be ascertained, then, when we hear of a change of religious certitude in another, is, what the doctrines are on which his so-called certitude before now and at present has respectively fallen. All doctrines besides these were the accidents of his profession, and the indefectibility of certitude would not be disproved, though he changed them every year. There are few religions which have no points in common; and these, whether true or false, when embraced with an absolute conviction, are the pivots on which changes take place in that collection of credences, opinions, prejudices, and other assents, which make up what is called a man's selection and adoption of a form of religion, a denomination, or a Church. There have been Protestants whose idea of enlightened Christianity has been a strenuous antagonism to what they consider the unmanliness and unreasonableness of Catholic morality, an antipathy to the precepts of patience, meekness, forgiveness of injuries, and chastity. All this they have considered a woman's religion, the ornament of monks, of the sick, the feeble, and the old. Lust, revenge, ambition, courage, pride, these, they have fancied, made the man, and want of them the slave. No one could fairly accuse such men of any great change of their convictions, or refer to them in proof of the defectibility of certitude, if they were one day found to have taken up the profession of Islam.

And if this intercommunion of religions holds good, even when the common points between them are but errors held in common, much more natural will be the transition from one religion to another, without injury to existing certitudes, when the common points, the objects of those certitudes, are truths; and still stronger in that case and more constraining will be the sympathy, with which minds that love truth, even when they have surrounded it with error, will yearn towards the Catholic faith, which contains within itself, and claims as its own, all truth that is elsewhere to be found, and more than all, and nothing but truth. This is the secret of the influence, by which the Church draws to herself converts from such various and conflicting religions. They come, not so much to lose what they have, but to gain what they have not; and in order that, by means of what they have, more may be given to them. St. Augustine tells us that there is no false teaching without an intermixture of truth; and it is by the light of those particular truths, contained respectively in the various religions of men, and by our certitudes about them, which are possible wherever those truths are found, that we pick our way, slowly perhaps, but surely, into the One Religion which God has given, taking our certitudes with us, not to lose, but to keep them more securely, and to understand and love their objects more perfectly.

Not even are idolaters and heathen out of the range of some of these religious truths and their correlative certitudes. The old Greek and Roman polytheists had, as they show in their literature, clear and strong notions, nay, vivid mental images, of a Particular Providence, of the power of prayer, of the rule of Divine Governance, of the law of conscience, of sin and guilt, of expiation by means of sacrifices, and of future retribution: I will even add, of the Unity and Personality of the Supreme Being. This it is that throws such a magnificent light over the Homeric poems, the tragic choruses, and the Odes of Pindar; and it has its counterpart in the philosophy of Socrates and of the Stoics, and in such historians as Herodotus. It would be out of place to speak confidently of a state of society which has passed away, but at first sight it does not appear why the truths which I have enumerated should not have received as genuine and deliberate an assent on the part of

Socrates or Cleanthes, (of course with divine aids, but they do not enter into this discussion), as was given to them by St. John or St. Paul, nay, an assent which rose to certitude. Much more safely may it be pronounced of a Mahometan, that he may have a certitude of the Divine Unity, as well as a Christian; and of a Jew, that he may believe as truly as a Christian in the resurrection of the body; and of a Unitarian, that he can give a deliberate and real assent to the fact of a supernatural revelation, to the Christian miracles, to the eternal moral law, and to the immortality of the soul. And so, again, a Protestant may, not only in words, but in mind and heart, hold, as if he were a Catholic, with simple certitude, the doctrines of the Holy Trinity, of the fall of man, of the need of regeneration, of the efficacy of Divine Grace, and of the possibility and danger of falling away. And thus it is conceivable that a man might travel in his religious profession all the way from heathenism to Catholicity, through Mahometanism, Judaism, Unitarianism, Protestantism, and Anglicanism, without any one certitude lost, but with a continual accumulation of truths, which claimed from him and elicited in his intellect fresh and fresh certitudes.

In saying all this, I do not forget that the same doctrines, as held in different religions, may be and often are held very differently, as belonging to distinct wholes or *forms*, as they are called, and exposed to the influence and the bias of the teaching, perhaps false, with which they are associated. Thus, for instance, whatever be the resemblance between St. Augustine's doctrine of Predestination and the tenet of Calvin upon it, the two really differ from each other *toto cœlo* in significance and effect, in consequence of the place they hold in the systems in which they are respectively incorporated, just as shades and tints show so differently in a painting according to the masses of colour to which they are attached. But, in spite of this, a man may so hold the doctrine of personal election as a Calvinist, as to be able still to hold it as a Catholic.

However, I have been speaking of certitudes which remain

unimpaired, or rather confirmed, by a change of religion; on the contrary there are others, whether we call them certitudes or convictions, which perish in the change, as St. Paul's conviction of the sufficiency of the Jewish Law came to an end on his becoming a Christian. Now how is such a series of facts to be reconciled with the doctrine which I have been enforcing? What conviction could be stronger than the faith of the Jews in the perpetuity of the Mosaic system? Those, then, it may be said, who abandoned Judaism for the Gospel, surely, in so doing, bore the most emphatic of testimonies to the defectibility of certitude. And, in like manner, a Mahometan may be so deeply convinced that Mahomet is the prophet of God, that it would be only by a quibble about the meaning of the word "certitude" that we could maintain, that, on his becoming a Catholic, he did not unequivocally prove that certitude is defectible. And it may be argued, perhaps, in the case of some members of the Church of England, that their faith in the validity of Anglican orders, and the invisibility of the Church's unity, is so absolute, so deliberate, that their abandonment of it, did they become Catholics or sceptics, would be tantamount to the abandonment of a certitude.

Now, in meeting this difficulty, I will not urge (lest I should be accused of quibbling), that certitude is a conviction of what is true, and that these so-called certitudes have come to nought, because, their objects being errors, not truths, they really were not certitudes at all; nor will I insist, as I might, that they ought to be proved first to be something more than mere prejudices, assents without reason and judgment, before they can fairly be taken as instances of the defectibility of certitude; but I simply ask, as regards the zeal of the Jews for the sufficiency of their law, (even though it implied genuine certitude, not a prejudice, not a mere conviction,) still was such zeal, such professed certitude, found in those who were eventually converted, or in those who were not; for, if those who had not that certitude became Christians and those who had it remained Jews, then loss of certitude in the latter is not instanced in the fact of the conversion of the former. St. Paul certainly is an exception, but his conversion, as also his after-life, was miraculous; ordinarily speaking, it was not the zealots who supplied members to the Catholic Church, but those "men of good will," who, instead of considering the law as perfect and eternal, "looked for the redemption of Israel," and for "the knowledge of salvation in the remission of sins." And, in like manner, as to those learned and devout men among the Anglicans at the present day, who come so near the Church without acknowledging her claims, I ask whether there are not two classes among them also,—those who are looking out beyond their own body for the perfect way, and those on the other hand who teach that the Anglican communion is the golden mean between men who believe too much and men who believe too little, the centre of unity to which East and West are destined to gravitate, the instrument and the mould, as the Jews might think of their own moribund institutions, through which the kingdom of Christ is to be established all over the earth. And next I would ask, which of these two classes supplies converts to the Church; for if they come from among those who never professed to be quite certain of the special strength of the Anglican position, such men cannot be quoted as instances of the defectibility of certitude.

There is indeed another class of beliefs, of which I must take notice, the failure of which may be taken at first sight as a proof that certitude may be lost. Yet they clearly deserve no other name than prejudices, as being founded upon reports of facts, or on arguments, which will not bear careful examination. Such was the disgust felt towards our predecessors in primitive times, the Christians of the first centuries, as a secret society, as a conspiracy against the civil power, as a set of mean, sordid, despicable fanatics, as monsters revelling in blood and impurity. Such also is the deep prejudice now against the Church among Protestants, who dress her up in the most hideous and loathsome images, which rightly attach, in the prophetic descriptions, to the evil spirit, his agents and instruments. And so of the numberless calumnies directed against individual Catholics, against religious bodies, and men in authority, which serve to feed and sustain the suspicion and dislike with which every thing Catholic is regarded in this country. But as a persistence in such prejudices is no evidence of their truth, so an abandonment of them is no evidence that certitude can fail.

There is yet another class of prejudices against the Catholic Religion, which is far more tolerable and intelligible than those on which I have been dwelling, but still in no sense certitudes. Indeed, I doubt whether they would be considered more than presumptive opinions by the persons who entertain them. Such is the idea which has possessed certain philosophers, ancient and modern, that miracles are an infringement and disfigurement of the beautiful order of nature. Such, too, is the persuasion, common among political and literary men, that the Catholic Church is inconsistent with the true interests of the human race, with social progress, with rational freedom, with good government. A renunciation of these imaginations is not a change in certitudes.

So much on this subject. All concrete laws are general, and persons, as such, do not fall under laws. Still, I have gone a good way, as I think, to remove the objections to the doctrine of the indefectibility of certitude in matters of religion, though I cannot assign to it an infallible token.

6

One further remark may be made. Certitude does not admit of an interior, immediate test, sufficient to discriminate it from false certitude. Such a test is rendered impossible from the circumstance that, when we make the mental act expressed by "I know," we sum up the whole series of reflex judgments which might, each in turn, successively exercise a critical function towards those of the series which precede it. But still, if it is the general rule that certitude is indefectible, will not that indefectibility itself become at least in the event a criterion of the genuiness of the certitude? or is there any rival state or habit of the intellect, which claims to be indefectible also? A few words will suffice to answer these questions.

Premising that all rules are but general, especially those which relate to the mind, I observe that indefectibility may at least serve as a negative test of certitude, or *sine quâ non* condition, so that whoever loses his conviction on a given point is thereby proved not to have been certain of it. Certitude ought to stand all trials, or it is not certitude. Its very office is to cherish and maintain its object, and its very lot and duty is to sustain rude shocks in maintenance of it without being damaged by them.

I will take an example. Let us suppose we are told on an unimpeachable authority, that a man whom we saw die is now alive again and at his work, as it was his wont to be; let us suppose we actually see him and converse with him; what will become of our certitude of his death? I do not think we should give it up; how could we, when we actually saw him die? At first, indeed, we should be thrown into an astonishment and confusion so great, that the world would seem to reel round us, and we should be ready to give up the use of our senses and of our memory, of our reflective powers, and of our reason, and even to deny our power of thinking, and our existence itself. Such confidence have we in the doctrine that when life goes it never returns. Nor would our bewilderment be less, when the first blow was over; but our reason would rally, and with our reason our certitude would come back to us. Whatever came of it, we should never cease to know and to confess to ourselves both of the contrary facts, that we saw him die, and that after dying we saw him alive again. The overpowering strangeness of our experience would have no power to shake our certitude in the facts which created it.

Again, let us suppose, for argument's sake, that ethnologists, philologists, anatomists, and antiquarians agreed together in separate demonstrations that there were half a dozen races of men, and that they were all descended from gorillas, or chimpanzees, or ourang-outangs, or baboons; moreover, that Adam was an historical personage, with a well-ascertained dwelling-place, surroundings and date, in a comparatively modern world. On the other hand, let me believe that the Word of God Himself distinctly declares that there were no men before Adam, that he was immediately made out of the slime of the earth, and that he is the first father of all men that are or ever have been. Here is a contradiction of statements more distinct than in the former instance; the two cannot stand together; one or other of them is untrue. But whatever means I might be led to take, for making, if possible, the antagonism tolerable, I conceive I should never give up my certitude in that truth which on sufficient grounds I determined to come from heaven. If I so believed, I should not pretend to argue, or to defend myself to others; I should be patient; I should look for better days; but I should still believe. If, indeed, I had hitherto only half believed, if I believed with an assent short of certitude, or with an acquiescence short of assent, or hastily or on light grounds, then the case would be altered; but if, after full consideration, and availing myself of my best lights, I did think that beyond all question God spoke as I thought He did, philosophers and experimentalists might take their course for me, —I should consider that they and I thought and reasoned in different mediums, and that my certitude was as little in collision with them or damaged by them, as if they attempted to counteract in some great matter chemical action by the force of gravity, or to weigh magnetic influence against capillary attraction. Of course, I am putting an impossible case, for philosophical discoveries cannot really contradict divine revelation.

So much on the indefectibility of certitude; as to the question whether any other assent is indefectible besides it, I think prejudice may be such; but it cannot be confused with certitude, for the one is an assent previous to rational grounds, and the other an assent given expressly after careful examination.

It seems then that on the whole there are three conditions

of certitude: that it follows on investigation and proof, that it is accompanied by a specific sense of intellectual satisfaction and repose, and that it is irreversible. If the assent is made without rational grounds, it is a rash judgment, a fancy, or a prejudice; if without the sense of finality, it is scarcely more than an inference; if without permanence, it is a mere conviction.

CHAPTER VIII

INFERENCE

1

FORMAL INFERENCE

INFERENCE IS THE CONDITIONAL ACCEPTANCE of a proposition, Assent is the unconditional; the object of Assent is a truth, the object of Inference is the truth-like or a verisimilitude. The problem which I have undertaken is that of ascertaining how it comes to pass that a conditional act leads to an unconditional; and, having now shown that assent really is unconditional, I proceed to show how inferential exercises, as such, always must be conditional.

We reason, when we hold this by virtue of that; whether we hold it as evident or as approximating or tending to be evident, in either case we so hold it because of holding something else to be evident or tending to be evident. In the next place, our reasoning ordinarily presents itself to our mind as a simple act, not a process or series of acts. We apprehend the antecedent and then apprehend the consequent, without explicit recognition of the medium connecting the two, as if by a sort of direct association of the first thought with the second. We proceed by a sort of instinctive perception, from premiss to conclusion. I call it instinctive, not as if the faculty were one and the same to all men in strength and quality (as we generally conceive of instinct), but because ordinarily, or at least often, it acts by a spontaneous impulse, as prompt and inevitable as the exercise of sense and memory. We perceive external objects, and we remember past events, without knowing how we do so; and in like manner we reason without effort

197

and intention, or any necessary consciousness of the path which the mind takes in passing from antecedent to conclusion.

Such is ratiocination, in what may be called a state of nature, as it is found in the uneducated,—nay, in all men, in its ordinary exercise; nor is there any antecedent ground for determining that it will not be as correct in its informations, as it is instinctive, as trustworthy as are sensible perception and memory, though its informations are not so immediate and have a wider range. By means of sense we gain knowledge directly; by means of reasoning we gain it indirectly, that is, by virtue of a previous knowledge. And if we may justly regard the universe, according to the meaning of the word, as one whole, we may also believe justly that to know one part of it is necessarily to know much more than that one part. This thought leads us to a further view of ratiocination. The proverb says, "Ex pede Herculem;" and we have actual experience how the practised zoologist can build up some intricate organization from the sight of its smallest bone, evoking the whole as if it were a remembrance; how, again, a philosophical antiquarian, by means of an inscription, interprets the mythical traditions of former ages, and makes the past live; and how a Columbus is led, from considerations which are common property, and fortuitous phenomena which are successively brought to his notice, to have such faith in a western world, as willingly to commit himself to the terrors of a mysterious ocean in order to arrive at it. That which the mind is able thus variously to bring together into unity, must have some real intrinsic connexion of part with part. But if this *summa rerum* is thus one whole, it must be constructed on definite principles and laws, the knowledge of which will enlarge our capacity of reasoning about it in particulars;—thus we are led on to aim at determining on a large scale and on system, what even gifted or practised intellects are only able by their own personal vigour to reach piecemeal and fitfully, that is, at substituting scientific methods, such as all may use, for the action of individual genius.

There is another reason for attempting to discover an instrument of reasoning (that is, of gaining new truths by means of old), which may be less vague and arbitrary than the talent and experience of the few or the common-sense of the many. As memory is not always accurate, and has on that account led to the adoption of writing, as being a *memoria technica,* unaffected by the failure of mental impressions,—as our senses at times deceive us, and have to be corrected by each other; so is it also with our reasoning faculty. The conclusions of one man are not the conclusions of another; those of the same man do not always agree together; those of ever so many who agree together may differ from the facts themselves, which those conclusions are intended to ascertain. In consequence it becomes a necessity, if it be possible, to analyze the process of reasoning, and to invent a method which may act as a common measure between mind and mind, as a means of joint investigation, and as a recognized intellectual standard,—a standard such as to secure us against hopeless mistakes, and to emancipate us from the capricious *ipse dixit* of authority.

As the index on the dial notes down the sun's course in the heavens, as a key, revolving through the intricate wards of the lock, opens for us a treasure-house, so let us, if we can, provide ourselves with some ready expedient to serve as a true record of the system of objective truth, and an available rule for interpreting its phenomena; or at least let us go as far as we can in providing it. One such experimental key is the science of geometry, which, in a certain department of nature, substitutes a collection of true principles, fruitful and interminable in consequences, for the guesses, *pro re natâ*, of our intellect, and saves it both the labour and the risk of guessing. Another far more subtle and effective instrument is algebraical science, which acts as a spell in unlocking for us, without merit or effort of our own individually, the *arcana* of the concrete physical universe. A more ambitious, because a more comprehensive contrivance still, for interpreting the concrete world is the method of logical inference. What we desiderate is something which may supersede the need of personal gifts by a far-reaching and infallible rule. Now, without external symbols to mark out and to steady its course, the intellect runs wild; but with the aid of symbols, as in algebra, it advances with precision and effect. Let then our symbols be words: let all thought be arrested and embodied in words. Let language have a monopoly of thought; and thought go for only so much as it can show itself to be worth in language. Let every prompting of the intellect be ignored, every *momentum* of argument be disowned, which is unprovided with an equivalent wording, as its ticket for sharing in the common search after truth. Let the authority of nature, commonsense, experience, genius, go for nothing. Ratiocination, thus restricted and put into grooves, is what I have called Inference, and the science, which is its regulating principle, is Logic.

The first step in the inferential method is to throw the question to be decided into the form of a proposition; then to throw the proof itself into propositions, the force of the proof lying in the comparison of these propositions with each other. When the analysis is carried out fully and put into form, it becomes the Aristotelic syllogism. However, an inference need not be expressed thus technically; an enthymeme fulfils the requirements of what I have called Inference. So does any other form of words with the mere grammatical expressions, "for," "therefore," "supposing," "so that," "similarly," and the like. Verbal reasoning, of whatever kind, as opposed to mental, is what I mean by inference, which differs from logic only inasmuch as logic is its scientific form. And it will be more convenient here to use the two words indiscriminately, for I shall say nothing about logic which does not in its substance also apply to inference.

Logical inference, then, being such, and its purpose such as I have described, the question follows, how far it answers the purpose for which it is used. It proposes to provide both a test and a common measure of reasoning; and I think it will be found partly to succeed and partly to fail; succeeding so far as words can in fact be found for representing the countless varieties and subtleties of human thought, failing on account of the fallacy of the original assumption, that whatever can be thought can be adequately expressed in words.

In the first place, inference, being conditional, is hampered with other propositions besides that which is especially its own, that is, with the premisses as well as the conclusion, and with the rules connecting the latter with the former. It views its own proper proposition in the medium of prior propositions, and measures it by them. It does not hold a proposition for its own sake, but as dependent upon others, and those others it entertains for the sake of the conclusion. Thus it is practically far more concerned with the comparison of propositions, than with the propositions themselves. It is obliged to regard all the propositions, with which it has to do, not so much for their own sake, as for the sake of each other, as regards the identity or likeness, independence or dissimilarity, which has to be mutually predicated of them. It follows from this, that the more simple and definite are the words of a proposition, and the narrower their meaning, and the more that meaning in each proposition is restricted to the relation which it has to the words of the other propositions compared with it,—in other words, the nearer the propositions concerned in the inference approach to being mental abstractions, and the less they have to do with the concrete reality, and the more closely they are made to express exact, intelligible, comprehensible, communicable notions, and the less they stand for objective things, that is, the more they are the subjects, not of real, but of notional apprehension,—so much the more suitable do they become for the purposes of inference.

Hence it is that no process of argument is so perfect, as that which is conducted by means of symbols. In Arithmetic 1 is 1, and just 1, and never any thing else but 1; it never is 2, it has no tendency to change its meaning, and to become 2; it has no portion, quality, admixture of 2 in its meaning. And 6 under all circumstances is 3 times 2, and the sum of 2 and 4;

nor can the whole world supply any thing to throw doubt upon these elementary positions. It is not so with language. Take, by contrast, the word "inference," which I have been using: it may stand for the act of inferring, as I have used it; or for the connecting principle, or *inferentia*, between premisses and conclusions; or for the conclusion itself. And sometimes it will be difficult, in a particular sentence, to say which it bears of these three senses. And so again in Algebra, *a* is never *x*, or any thing but *a*, wherever it is found; and *a* and *b* are always standard quantities, to which *x* and *y* are always to be referred, and by which they are always to be measured. In Geometry again, the subjects of argument, points, lines, and surfaces, are precise creations of the mind, suggested indeed by external objects, but meaning nothing but what they are defined to mean: they have no colour, no motion, no heat, no qualities which address themselves to the ear or to the palate; so that, in whatever combinations or relations the words denoting them occur, and to whomsoever they come, those words never vary in their meaning, but are just of the same measure and weight at one time and at another.

What is true of Arithmetic, Algebra, and Geometry, is true also of Aristotelic argumentation in its typical modes and figures. It compares two given words separately with a third, and then determines how they stand towards each other, in a *bonâ fide* identity of sense. In consequence, its formal process is best conducted by means of symbols, A, B, and C. While it keeps to these, it is safe; it has the cogency of mathematical reasoning, and draws its conclusions by a rule as unerring as it is blind.

Symbolical notation, then, being the perfection of the syllogistic method, it follows that, when words are substituted for symbols, it will be its aim to circumscribe and stint their import as much as possible, lest perchance A should not always exactly mean A, and B mean B; and to make them, as much as possible, the *calculi* of notions, which are in our absolute power, as meaning just what we choose them to mean, and as little as possible the tokens of real things, which are outside of us, and which mean we do not know how much, but so much certainly as, (in proportion as we enter into them,) may run away with us beyond the range of scientific management. The concrete matter of propositions is a constant source of trouble to syllogistic reasoning, as marring the simplicity and perfection of its process. Words, which denote things, have innumerable implications, but in inferential exercises it is the very triumph of that clearness and hardness of head, which is the characteristic talent for the art, to have stripped them of all these connatural senses, to have drained them of that depth and breadth of associations which constitute their poetry, their rhetoric, and their historical life, to have starved each term down till it has become the ghost of itself, and every where one and the same ghost, "omnibus umbra locis," so that it may stand for just one unreal aspect of the concrete thing to which it properly belongs, for a relation, a generalization, or other abstraction, for a notion neatly turned out of the laboratory of the mind, and sufficiently tame and subdued because existing only in a definition.

Thus it is that the logician for his own purposes, and most usefully as far as those purposes are concerned, turns rivers, full, winding, and beautiful, into navigable canals. To him dog or horse is not a thing which he sees, but a mere name suggesting ideas; and by dog or horse universal he means, not the aggregate of all individual dogs or horses brought together, but a common aspect, meagre but precise, of all existing or possible dogs or horses, which all the while does not really correspond to any one single dog or horse out of the whole aggregate. Such minute fidelity in the representation of individuals is neither necessary nor possible to his art; his business is not to ascertain facts in the concrete, but to find and to dress up middle terms; and, provided they and the extremes which they go between are not equivocal, either in themselves or in their use, and he can enable his pupils to show well in a *vivâ voce* disputation, or in a popular harangue, or in a written dissertation, he has achieved the main purpose of his profession.

Such are the characteristics of reasoning, viewed as a science, or scientific art, or inferential process, and we might anticipate, that, narrow as by necessity is its field of view, for that reason its pretensions to be demonstrative were incontrovertible. In a certain sense they really are so; while we talk logic, we are unanswerable; but then, on the other hand, this universal living scene of things is after all as little a logical world as it is a poetical; and, as it cannot without violence be exalted into poetical perfection, neither can it be attenuated into a logical formula. Abstract can only conduct to abstract; but we have need to attain by our reasonings to what is concrete; and the margin between the abstract conclusions of the science, and the concrete facts which we wish to ascertain, will be found to reduce the force of the inferential method from demonstration to the mere determination of the probable. Thus, whereas (as I have already said) inference starts with conditions, as starting with premises, here are two reasons why, when employed upon questions of fact, it can only conclude probabilities: first, because its premises are assumed, not proved; and secondly, because its conclusions are abstract, and not concrete. I will now consider these two points separately.

1

Inference comes short of proof in concrete matters, because it has not a full command over the objects to which it relates, but merely assumes its premises. In order to complete the proof, we are thrown upon some previous syllogism or syllogisms, in which the assumptions may be proved; and then, still farther back, we are thrown upon others again, to prove the new assumptions of that second order of syllogisms. Where is this process to stop? especially since it must run upon separated, divergent, and multiplied lines of argument, the farther the investigation is carried back. At length a score of propositions present themselves, all to be proved by propositions more evident than themselves, in order to enable them respectively to become premisses to that series of inferences which terminates in the conclusion which we originally drew. But even now the difficulty is not at an end; it would be something to arrive at length at premisses which are undeniable, however long we might be in arriving at them; but in this case the long retrospection lodges us at length at what are called first principles, the recondite sources of all knowledge, as to which logic provides no common measure of minds,—which are accepted by some, rejected by others,—in which, and not in the syllogistic exhibitions, lies the whole problem of attaining to truth,—and which are called self-evident by their respective advocates because they are evident in no other way. One of the two uses contemplated in reasoning by rule, or in verbal argumentation, was, as I have said, to establish a standard of truth and to supersede the *ipse dixit* of authority: how does it fulfil this end, if it only leads us back to first principles, about which there is interminable controversy? We are not able to prove by syllogism that there are any self-evident propositions at all; but supposing there are (as of course I hold there are), still who can determine these by logic? Syllogism, then, though of course it has its use, still does only the minutest and easiest part of the work, in the investigation of truth, for when there is any difficulty, that difficulty commonly lies in determining first principles, not in the arrangement of proofs.

Even when argument is the most direct and severe of its kind, there must be those assumptions in the process which resolve themselves into the conditions of human nature; but how many more assumptions does that process in ordinary concrete matters involve, subtle assumptions, not directly arising out of these primary conditions, but accompanying the course of reasoning, step by step, and traceable to the sentiments of the age, country, religion, social habits and ideas, of the particular inquirers or disputants, and passing current without detection, because admitted equally on all hands! And to these must be added the assumptions which are made from the necessity of the case, in consequence of the prolixity and elaborateness of any argument which should faithfully note down all the propositions which go to make it up. We recognize this tediousness even in the case of the theorems of Euclid, though mathematical proof is comparatively simple.

Logic then does not really prove; it enables us to join issue with others; it suggests ideas; it opens views; it maps out for us the lines of thought; it verifies negatively; it determines when differences of opinion are hopeless; and when and how far conclusions are probable; but for genuine proof in concrete matter we require an *organon* more delicate, versatile, and elastic than verbal argumentation.

I ought to give an illustration of what I have been stating in general terms; but it is difficult to do so without a digression. However, if it must be, I look round the room in which I happen to be writing, and take down the first book which catches my eye. It is an old volume of a Magazine of great name; I open it at random and fall upon a discussion about the then lately discovered emendations of the text of Shakespeare. It will do for my purpose.

In the account of Falstaff's death in "Henry V." (act ii. scene 3) we read, according to the received text, the well-known words, "His nose was as sharp as a pen, and 'a babbled of green fields." In the first authentic edition, published in 1623, some years after Shakespeare's death, the words, I believe, ran, "and a table of green fields," which has no sense. Accordingly, an anonymous critic, reported by Theobald in the last century, corrected them to "and 'a talked of green fields." Theobald himself improved the reading into "and 'a babbled of green fields," which since his time has been the received text. But just twenty years ago an annotated copy of the edition of 1632 was found, annotated perhaps by a contemporary, which, among as many as 20,000 corrections of the text, substituted for the corrupt reading of 1623, the words "on a table of green frieze," which has a sufficient sense, though far less acceptable to an admirer of Shakespeare, than Theobald's.

The genuineness of this copy with its annotations, as it is presented to us, I shall here take for granted.

Now I understand, or at least will suppose, the argument, maintained in the article of the Magazine in question, to run thus:—"Theobald's reading, as at present received, is to be retained, to the exclusion of the text of 1623 and of the emendation made on the copy of the edition of 1632;—to the exclusion of the text of 1623 because that text is corrupt; to the exclusion of the annotation of 1632 because it is anonymous." I wish it then observed how many large questions are opened in the discussion which ensues, how many recondite and untractable principles have to be settled, and how impotent is logic, or any reasonings which can be thrown into language, to deal with these indispensable first principles.

The first position is, "The authoritative reading of 1623 is not to be restored to the received text, because it is corrupt." Now are we to take it for granted, as a first principle, which needs no proof, that a text may be tampered with, because it is corrupt? However the corrupt reading arose, it is authoritative. It is found in an edition, published by known persons, only six years after Shakespeare's death, from his own manuscript, as it appears, and with his corrections of earlier faulty impressions. Authority cannot sanction nonsense, but it can forbid critics from experimentalizing upon it. If the text of Shakespeare is corrupt, it should be published as corrupt.

I believe the best editors of the Greek tragedians have given up the impertinence of introducing their conjectures into the text; and a classic like Shakespeare has a right to be treated with the same respect as Æschylus. To this it will be replied, that Shakespeare is for the general public and Æschylus for students of a dead language; that the run of men read for amusement or as a recreation, and that, if the editions of Shakespeare were made on critical principles, they would remain unsold. Here, then, we are brought to the question whether it is any advantage to read Shakespeare except with the care and pains which a classic demands, and whether he is in fact read at all by those whom such critical exactness would offend; and thus we are led on to further questions about cultivation of mind and the education of the masses. Further, the question presents itself, whether the general admiration of Shakespeare is genuine, whether it is not a mere fashion, whether the multitude of men understand him at all, whether it is not true that every one makes much of him, because every one else makes much of him. Can we possibly make Shakespeare light reading, especially in this day of cheap novels, by ever so much correction of his text?

Now supposing this point settled, and the text of 1623 put out of court, then comes the claim of the Annotator to introduce into Shakespeare's text the emendation made upon his copy of the edition of 1632; why is he not of greater authority than Theobald, the inventor of the received reading, and his emendation of more authority than Theobald's? If the corrupt reading must any how be got out of the way, why should not the Annotator, rather than Theobald, determine its substitute? For what we know, the authority of the anonymous Annotator may be very great. There is nothing to show that he was not a contemporary of the poet; and if so, the question arises, what is the character of his emendations? are they his own private and arbitrary conjectures, or are they informations from those who knew Shakespeare, traditions of the theatre, of the actors or spectators of his plays? Here, then, we are involved in intricate questions which can only be decided by a minute examination of the 20,000 emendations so industriously brought together by this anonymous critic. But it is obvious that a verbal argumentation upon 20,000 corrections is impossible: there must be first careful processes of perusal, classification, discrimination, selection, which mainly are acts of the mind without the intervention of language. There must be a cumulation of arguments on one side and on the other, of which only the heads or the results can be put upon paper. Next come in questions of criticism and taste, with their recondite and disputable premises, and the usual deductions from them, so subtle and difficult to follow. All this being considered, am I wrong in saying that, though controversy is both possible and useful at all times, yet it is not adequate to this occasion; rather that that sum-total of argument (whether for or against the Annotator) which is furnished by his numerous emendations,—or what may be called the multiform, evidential fact, in which the examination of these emendations results,— requires rather to be photographed on the individual mind as by one impression, than admits of delineation for the satisfaction of the many in any known or possible language, however rich in vocabulary and flexible in structure.

And now as to the third point which presents itself for consideration, the claim of Theobald's emendation to retain its place in the *textus receptus*. It strikes me with wonder that an argument in its defence could have been put forward to the following effect, viz. that true though it be, that the editors of 1623 are of much higher authority than Theobald, and that the Annotator's reading in the passage in question is more likely to be correct than Theobald's, nevertheless Theobald's has by this time acquired a prescriptive right to its place there, the prescription of more than a hundred years;—that usurpation has become legitimacy; that Theobald's words have sunk into the hearts of thousands; that in fact they have become Shakespeare's; that it would be a dangerous innovation and an evil precedent to touch them. If we begin an unsettlement of the popular mind, where is it to stop?

Thus it appears, in order to do justice to the question before us, we have to betake ourselves to the consideration of myths, pious frauds, and other grave matters, which introduce us into a *sylva*, dense and intricate, of first principles and elementary phenomena, belonging to the domains of archeology and theology. Nor is this all; when such views of the duty of garbling a classic are propounded, they open upon us a long vista of sceptical interrogations which go far to disparage the claims upon us, the genius, the very existence of the great poet to whose honour these views are intended to minister. For perhaps, after all, Shakespeare is really but a collection of many Theobalds, who have each of them a right to his own share of him. There was a great dramatic school in his day; he was one of a number of first-rate artists,—perhaps they wrote in common. How are we to know what is his, or how much? Are the best parts his, or the worst? It is said that the players put in what is vulgar and offensive in his writings; perhaps they inserted the beauties. I have heard it urged years ago, as an objection to Sheridan's claim of authorship to the plays which bear his name, that they were so unlike each other; is not this the very peculiarity of those imputed to Shakespeare? Were ever the writings of one man so various, so impersonal? can we form any one true idea of what he was in history or character, by means of them? is he not in short *"vox et prætera nihil"*? Then again, in corroboration, is there any author's life so deficient in biographical notices as his? We know about Hooker, Spenser, Spelman, Raleigh, Harvey, his contemporaries: what do we know of Shakespeare? Is he much more than a name? Is not the traditional object of an Englishman's idolatry after all a nebula of genius, destined, like Homer, to be resolved into its separate and independent luminaries, as soon as we have a criticism powerful enough for the purpose? I must not be supposed for a moment to countenance such scepticism myself,—though it is a subject worthy the attention of a sceptical age: here I have introduced it simply to suggest how many words go to make up a thoroughly valid argument; how short and easy a way to a true conclusion is the logic of good sense; how little syllogisms have to do with the formation of opinion; how little depends upon the inferential proofs; and how much upon those pre-existing beliefs and views, in which men either already agree with each other or hopelessly differ, before they begin to dispute, and which are hidden deep in our nature, or, it may be, in our personal peculiarities.

2

So much on the multiplicity of assumptions, which in spite of formal exactness, logical reasoning in concrete matters is forced to admit, and on the consequent uncertainty which attends its conclusions. Now I come to the second reason why its conclusions are thus wanting in precision.

In this world of sense we have to do with things, far more than with notions. We are not solitary, left to the contemplation of our own thoughts and their legitimate developments. We are surrounded by external beings, and our enunciations are directed to the concrete. We reason in order to enlarge our knowledge of matters, which do not depend on us for being what they are. But how is an exercise of mind, which is for the most part occupied with notions, not things, competent to deal with things, except partially and indirectly? This is the main reason why an inference, however fully worded, (except perhaps in some peculiar cases, which are out of place here,) never can reach so far as to ascertain a fact. As I have already said, arguments about the abstract cannot handle and determine the concrete. They may approximate to a proof, but they only reach the probable, because they cannot reach the particular.

Even in mathematical physics a margin is left for possible imperfection in the investigation. When the planet Neptune was discovered, it was deservedly considered a triumph of science, that abstract reasonings had done so much towards determining the planet and its orbit. There would have been no triumph in success, had there been no hazard of failure; it is no triumph to Euclid, in pure mathematics, that the geometrical conclusions of his second book can be worked out and verified by algebra.

The motions of the heavenly bodies are almost mathematical in their precision; but there is a multitude of matters, to which mathematical science is applied, which are in their nature intricate and obscure, and require that reasoning by rule should be completed by the living mind. Who would be satisfied with a navigator or engineer, who had no practice or experience whereby to carry on his scientific conclusions out of their native abstract into the concrete and the real? What is the meaning of the distrust, which is ordinarily felt, of speculators and theorists but this, that they are dead to the necessity of personal prudence and judgment to qualify and complete their logic? Science, working by itself, reaches truth in the abstract, and probability in the concrete; but what we aim at is truth in the concrete.

This is true of other inferences besides mathematical. They come to no definite conclusions about matters of fact, except as they are made effectual for their purpose by the living intelligence which uses them. "All men have their price; Fabricius is a man; he has his price;" but he had not his price; how is this? Because he is more than a universal; because he falls under other universals; because universals are ever at war with each other; because what is called a universal is only a general; because what is only general does not lead to a necessary conclusion. Let us judge him by another universal. "Men have a conscience; Fabricius is a man; he has a conscience." Until we have actual experience of Fabricius, we can only say, that, since he is a man, perhaps he will take a bribe, and perhaps he will not. "Latet dolus in generalibus;" they are arbitrary and fallacious, if we take them for more than broad views and aspects of things, serving as our notes and indications for judging of the particular, but not absolutely touching and determining facts.

Let units come first, and (so-called) universals second; let universals minister to units, not units be sacrificed to universals. John, Richard, and Robert are individual things, independent, incommunicable. We may find some kind of common measure between them, and we may give it the name of man, man as such, the typical man, the *auto-anthropos*. We are justified in so doing, and in investing it with general attributes, and bestowing on it what we consider a definition. But we think we may go on to impose our definition on the whole race, and to every member of it, to the thousand Johns, Richards, and Roberts who are found in it. No; each of them is what he is, in spite of it. Not any one of them is man, as such, or coincides with the *auto-anthropos*. Another John is not necessarily rational, because "all men are rational," for he may be an idiot;—nor because "man is a being of progress," does the second Richard progress, for he may be a dunce;—nor, because "man is made for society," must we therefore go on to deny that the second Robert is a gipsy or a bandit, as he is found to be. There is no such thing as stereotyped humanity; it must ever be a vague, bodiless idea, because the concrete units from which it is formed are independent realities. General laws are not inviolable truths; much less are they necessary causes. Since, as a rule, men are rational, progressive, and social, there is a high probability of this rule being true in the case of a particular person; but we must know him to be sure of it.

Each thing has its own nature and its own history. When the nature and the history of many things are similar, we say that they have the same nature; but there is no such thing as one and the same nature; they are each of them itself, not identical, but like. A law is not a fact, but a notion. "All men die; therefore Elias has died;" but he has not died, and did not die. He was an exception to the general law of humanity; so far, he did not come under that law, but under the law (so to say) of Elias. It was the peculiarity of his individuality, that he left the world without dying: what right have we to subject the person of Elias to the scientific notion of an abstract humanity, which we have formed without asking his leave? Why must the tyrant majority create a rule for his individual history? "But all men are mortal?" not so; what is really meant by this universal, is, that "man, as such, is mortal," that is, the abstract, typical *auto-anthropos;* to this major premiss the minor, if Elias is to be proved mortal, ought to be, "Elias was the abstract man;" but he was not, and could not be such, nor

could any one else, any more than the average man of an
Insurance Company is every idividual man who insures his
life with it. Such a syllogism proves nothing about the veritable
Elias, except in the way of antecedent probability. If it be
said that Elias was exempted from death, not by nature, but
by miracle, what is this to the purpose, undeniable as it is?
Still, to have this miraculous exemption was the personal prerogative of Elias. We call it miracle, because God ordinarily
acts otherwise. He who causes men in general to die, gave to
Elias not to die. This miraculous gift comes into the individuality of Elias. On this individuality we must fix our thoughts,
and not begin our notion of him by ignoring it. He was a man,
and something more than "man"; and if we do not take this
into account, we fall into an initial error in our thoughts of
him.

What is true of Elias is true of every one in his own place
and degree. We call rationality the distinction of man, when
compared with other animals. This is true in logic; but in fact
a man differs from a brute, not in rationality only, but in all
that he is, even in those respects in which he is most like a
brute; so that his whole self, his bones, limbs, make, life,
reason, moral feeling, immortality, and all that he is besides,
is his real *differentia,* in contrast to a horse or a dog. And in
like manner as regards John and Richard, when compared with
one another; each is himself, and nothing else, and, though,
regarded abstractedly, the two may fairly be said to have
something in common, viz. that abstract sameness which does
not exist at all, yet, strictly speaking, they have nothing in
common, for each of them has a vested interest in all that
he himself is; and, moreover, what seems to be common in
the two, becomes in fact so uncommon, so *sui simile,* in their
respective individualities—the bodily frame of each is so
singled out from all other bodies by its special constitution,
sound or weak, by its vitality, activity, pathological history
and changes, and, again, the mind of each is so distinct from
all other minds, in disposition, powers, and habits,—that,

instead of saying, as logicians say, that the two men differ only in number, we ought, I repeat, rather to say that they differ from each other in all that they are, in identity, in incommunicability, in personality.

Nor does any real thing admit, by any calculus of logic, of being dissected into all the possible general notions which it admits, nor, in consequence, of being recomposed out of them; though the attempt thus to treat it is more unpromising in proportion to the intricacy and completeness of its make. We cannot see through any one of the myriad beings which make up the universe, or give the full catalogue of its belongings. We are accustomed, indeed, and rightly, to speak of the Creator Himself as incomprehensible; and, indeed, He is so by an incommunicable attribute; but in a certain sense each of His creatures is incomprehensible to us also, in the sense that no one has a perfect understanding of them but He. We recognize and appropriate aspects of them, and logic is useful to us in registering these aspects and what they imply; but it does not give us to know even one individual being.

So much on logical argumentation; and in thus speaking of the syllogism, I speak of all inferential processes whatever, as expressed in language, (if they are such as to be reducible to science,) for they all require general notions, as conditions of their coming to a conclusion.

Thus, in the deductive argument, "Europe has no security for peace, till its large standing armies in its separate states are reduced; for a large standing army is in its very idea provocative of war," the conclusion is only probable, for it may so be that in no country is that pure idea realized, but in every country in concrete fact there may be circumstances, political or social, which destroy the abstract dangerousness.

So, too, as regards Induction and Analogy, as modes of Inference; for, whether I argue, "This place will have the cholera, unless it is drained; for there are a number of well-ascertained cases which point to this conclusion;" or, "The sun will rise to-morrow, for it rose to-day;" in either method of reasoning I appeal, in order to prove a particular case, to a general principle or law, which has not force enough to warrant more than a probable conclusion. As to the cholera, the place in question may have certain antagonist advantages, which anticipate or neutralize the miasma which is the principle of the poison; and as to the sun's rising to-morrow, there was a first day of the sun's rising, and therefore there may be a last.

This is what I have to say on formal Inference, when taken to represent Ratiocination. Science in all its departments has too much simplicity and exactness, from the nature of the case, to be the measure of fact. In its very perfection lies its incompetency to settle particulars and details. As to logic, its chain of conclusions hangs loose at both ends; both the point from which the proof should start, and the points at which it should arrive, are beyond its reach; it comes short both of first principles and of concrete issues. Even its most elaborate exhibitions fail to represent adequately the sum total of considerations by which an individual mind is determined in its judgment of things; even its most careful combinations made to bear on a conclusion want that steadiness of aim which is necessary for hitting it. As I said when I began, thought is too keen and manifold, its sources are too remote and hidden, its path too personal, delicate, and circuitous, its subject-matter too various and intricate, to admit of the trammels of any language, of whatever subtlety and of whatever compass.

Nor is it any disparagement of the proper value of formal reasonings thus to speak of them. That they cannot proceed beyond probabilities is most readily allowed by those who use them most. Philosophers, experimentalists, lawyers, in their several ways, have commonly the reputation of being, at least on moral and religious subjects, hard of belief; because, proceeding in the necessary investigation by the analytical method of verbal inference, they find within its limits no sufficient resources for attaining a conclusion. Nay, they do not always find it possible in their own special province severally; for, even when in their hearts they have no doubt about a conclusion, still often, from the habit of their minds, they are reluctant to own it, and dwell upon the deficiencies of the evidence, or the possibility of error, because they speak by rule and by book, though they judge and determine by common-sense.

Every exercise of nature or of art is good in its place; and the uses of this logical inference are manifold. It is the great principle of order in thinking; it reduces a chaos into harmony; it catalogues the accumulations of knowledge; it maps out for us the relations of its separate departments; it puts us in the way to correct its own mistakes. It enables the independent intellects of many, acting and re-acting on each other, to bring their collective force to bear upon one and the same subject-matter, or the same question. If language is an inestimable gift to man, the logical faculty prepares it for our use. Though it does not go so far as to ascertain truth, still it teaches us the direction in which truth lies, and how propositions lie towards each other. Nor is it a slight benefit to know what is probable, and what is not so, what is needed for the proof of a point, what is wanting in a theory, how a theory hangs together, and what will follow, if it be admitted. Though it does not itself discover the unknown, it is one principal way by which discoveries are made. Moreover, a course of argument, which is simply conditional, will point out when and where experiment and observation should be applied, or testimony sought for, as often happens both in physical and legal questions. A logical hypothesis is the means of holding facts together, explaining difficulties, and reconciling the imagination to what is strange. And, again, processes of logic are useful as enabling us to get over particular stages of an investigation speedily and surely, as on a journey we now and then gain time by travelling by night, make short cuts when the high-road winds, or adopt water-carriage to avoid fatigue.

But reasoning by rule and in words is too natural to us, to

admit of being regarded merely in the light of utility. Our inquiries spontaneously fall into scientific sequence, and we think in logic, as we talk in prose, without aiming at doing so. However sure we are of the accuracy of our instinctive conclusions, we as instinctively put them into words, as far as we can; as preferring, if possible, to have them in an objective shape which we can fall back upon,—first for our own satisfaction, then for our justification with others. Such a tangible defence of what we hold, inadequate as it necessarily is, considered as an analysis of our ratiocination in its length and breadth, nevertheless is in such sense associated with our holdings, and so fortifies and illustrates them, that it acts as a vivid apprehension acts, giving them luminousness and force. Thus inference becomes a sort of symbol of assent, and even bears upon action.

I have enlarged on these obvious considerations, lest I should seem paradoxical; but they do not impair the main position of this Section, that inference, considered in the sense of verbal argumentation, determines neither our principles, nor our ultimate judgments,—that it is neither the test of truth, nor the adequate basis of assent.[1]

---

[1] I have assumed throughout this Section that all verbal argumentation is ultimately syllogistic; and in consequence that it ever requires universal propositions and comes short of concrete fact. A friend refers me to the dispute between Des Cartes and Gassendi, the latter maintaining against the former that "Cogito ergo sum" implies the universal "All who think exist." I should deny this with Des Cartes; but I should say (as indeed he said), that his dictum was not an argument, but was the expression of a ratiocinative instinct, as I explain below under the head of "Natural Logic."

As to the instance "Brutes are not men; therefore men are not brutes," there seems to me no consequence here, neither a *præter* nor a *propter*, but a tautology. And as to "It was either Tom or Dick that did it; it was not Dick, ergo," this may be referred to the one great principle on which all logical reasoning is founded, but really it ought not to be accounted an inference any more than if I broke a biscuit, flung half away, and then said of the other half, "This is what remains." It does but state a fact. So, when the 1st, 2nd, or 3rd proposition of Euclid II. is put before

2

INFORMAL INFERENCE

IT IS PLAIN that formal logical sequence is not in fact the method by which we are enabled to become certain of what is concrete; and it is equally plain, from what has been already suggested, what the real and necessary method is. It is the cumulation of probabilities, independent of each other, arising out of the nature and circumstances of the particular case which is under review; probabilities too fine to avail separately, too subtle and circuitous to be convertible into syllogisms, too numerous and various for such conversion, even were they convertible. As a man's portrait differs from a sketch of him, in having, not merely a continuous outline, but all its details filled in, and shades and colours laid on and harmonized together, such is the multiform and intricate process of ratiocination, necessary for our reaching him as a concrete fact, compared with the rude operation of syllogistic treatment.

Let us suppose I wish to convert an educated, thoughtful Protestant, and accordingly present for his acceptance a syllogism of the following kind:—"All Protestants are bound to join the Church; you are a Protestant: ergo." He answers, we will say, by denying both premises; and he does so by means of arguments, which branch out into other arguments, and those into others, and all of them severally requiring to be considered by him on their own merits, before the syllogism reaches him, and in consequence mounting up, taken all together, into an array of inferential exercises large and various

---

the eyes in a diagram, a boy, before he yet has learned to reason, sees with his eyes the fact of the thesis, and this *seeing* it even makes it difficult for him to master the mathematical proof. Here, then, a *fact* is stated in the form of an *argument*.

However, I have inserted parentheses at pp. 211 and 215 in order to say "transeat" to the question.

beyond calculation. Moreover, he is bound to submit himself to this complicated process from the nature of the case; he would act rashly, if he did not; for he is a concrete individual unit, and being so, is under so many laws, and is the subject of so many predications all at once, that he cannot determine, offhand, his position and his duty by the law and the predication of one syllogism in particular. I mean he may fairly say, "Distinguo," to each of its premisses: he says, "Protestants are bound to join the Church,—under circumstances," and "I am a Protestant—in a certain sense;" and therefore the syllogism, at first sight, does not touch him at all.

Before, then, he grants the major, he asks whether all Protestants really are bound to join the Church—are they bound in case they do not feel themselves bound; if they are satisfied that their present religion is a safe one; if they are sure it is true; if, on the other hand, they have grave doubts as to the doctrinal fidelity and purity of the Church; if they are convinced that the Church is corrupt; if their conscience instinctively rejects certain of its doctrines; if history convinces them that the Pope's power is not *jure divino*, but merely in the order of Providence? if, again, they are in a heathen country where priests are not? or where the only priest who is to be found exacts of them, as a condition of their reception, a profession, which the Creed of Pope Pius IV. says nothing about; for instance, that the Holy See is fallible even when it teaches, or that the Temporal Power is an anti-Christian corruption? On one or other of such grounds he thinks he need not change his religion; but presently he asks himself, Can a Protestant be in such a state as to be really satisfied with his religion, as he has just now been professing? Can he possibly believe Protestantism came from above, as a whole? how much of it can he believe came from above? and, as to that portion which he feels did come from above, has it not all been derived to him from the Church, when traced to its source? Is not Protestantism in itself a negation? Did not the Church exist before it? and can he be sure, on the other hand, that any one of the Church's doctrines is not from above? Further, he finds he has to make up his mind what is a corruption, and what are the tests of it; what he means by a religion; whether it is obligatory to profess any religion in particular; what are the standards of truth and falsehood in religion; and what are the special claims of the Church.

And so, again, as to the minor premiss, perhaps he will answer, that he is not a Protestant; that he is a Catholic of the early undivided Church; that he is a Catholic, but not a Papist. Then he has to determine questions about division, schism, visible unity, what is essential, what is desirable; about provisional states as to the adjustment of the Church's claims with those of personal judgment and responsibility; as to the soul of the Church contrasted with the body; as to degrees of proof, and the degree necessary for his conversion; as to what is called his providential position, and the responsibility of change; as to the sincerity of his purpose to follow the Divine Will, whithersoever it may lead him; as to his intellectual capacity of investigating such questions at all.

None of these questions, as they come before him, admit of simple demonstration; but each carries with it a number of independent probable arguments, sufficient, when united, for a reasonable conclusion about itself. And first he determines that the questions are such as he personally, with such talents or attainments as he has, may fairly entertain; and then he goes on, after deliberation, to form a definite judgment upon them; and determines them, one way or another, in their bearing on the bald syllogism which was originally offered to his acceptance. And, we will say, he comes to the conclusion, that he ought to accept it as true in his case; that he is a Protestant in such a sense, of such a complexion, of such knowledge, under such circumstances, as to be called upon by duty to join the Church; that this is a conclusion of which he can be certain, and ought to be certain, and that he will be incurring grave responsibility, if he does not accept it as certain, and act upon the certainty of it. And to this conclusion he comes, as is plain, not by any possible verbal enumeration of all the considerations, minute but abundant, delicate but effective, which unite to bring him to it; but by a mental comprehension of the whole case, and a discernment of its upshot, sometimes after much deliberation, but, it may be, by a clear and rapid act of the intellect, always, however, by an unwritten summing-up, something like the summation of the terms *plus* and *minus* of an algebraical series.

This I conceive to be the real reasoning in concrete matters; and it has these characteristics:—First, it does not supersede the logical form of inference, but is one and the same with it; only it is no longer an abstraction, but carried out into the realities of life, its premises being instinct with the substance and the momentum of that mass of probabilities, which, acting upon each other in correction and confirmation, carry it home definitely to the individual case, which is its original scope.

Next, from what has been said it is plain, that such a process of reasoning is more or less implicit, and without the direct and full advertence of the mind exercising it. As by the use of our eyesight we recognize two brothers, yet without being able to express what it is by which we distinguish them; as at first sight we perhaps confuse them together, but on better knowledge, we see no likeness between them at all; as it requires an artist's eye to determine what lines and shades make a countenance look young or old, amiable, thoughtful, angry or conceited, the principle of discrimination being in each case real, but implicit;—so is the mind unequal to a complete analysis of the motives which carry it on to a particular conclusion, and is swayed and determined by a body of proof, which it recognizes only as a body, and not in its constituent parts.

And thirdly, it is plain, that, in this investigation of the method of concrete inference, we have not advanced one step towards depriving inference of its conditional character; for it is still as dependent on premises, as it is in its elementary idea. On the contrary, we have rather added to the obscurity of the problem; for a syllogism is at least a demonstration, when the premises are granted, but a cumulation of probabilities, over and above their implicit character, will vary both in their number and their separate estimated value, according to the particular intellect which is employed upon it. It follows that what to one intellect is a proof is not so to another, and that the certainty of a proposition, does properly consist in the certitude of the mind which contemplates it. And this of course may be said without prejudice to the objective truth or falsehood of propositions, since it does not follow that these propositions on the one hand are not true, and based on right reason, and those on the other not false, and based on false reason, because not all men discriminate them in the same way.

Having thus explained the view which I would take of reasoning in the concrete, viz. that, from the nature of the case, and from the constitution of the human mind, certitude is the result of arguments which, taken in the letter, and not in their full implicit sense, are but probabilities, I proceed to dwell on some instances and circumstances of a phenomenon which seems to me as undeniable as to many it may be perplexing.

1

Let us take three instances belonging respectively to the present, the past, and the future.

1. We are all absolutely certain, beyond the possibility of doubt, that Great Britain is an island. We give to that proposition our deliberate and unconditional adhesion. There is no security on which we should be better content to stake our interests, our property, our welfare, than on the fact that we are living in an island. We have no fear of any geographical discovery which may reverse our belief. We should be amused or angry at the assertion, as a bad jest, did any one say that we were at this time joined to the main-land in Norway or in France, though a canal was cut across the isthmus. We are

as little exposed to the misgiving, "Perhaps we are not on an island after all," as to the question, "Is it quite certain that the angle in a semi-circle is a right-angle?" It is a simple and primary truth with us, if any truth is such; to believe it is as legitimate an exercise of assent, as there are legitimate exercises of doubt or of opinion. This is the position of our minds towards our insularity; yet are the arguments producible for it (to use the common expression) in black and white commensurate with this overpowering certitude about it?

Our reasons for believing that we are circumnavigable are such as these:—first, we have been so taught in our childhood, and it is so in all the maps; next, we have never heard it contradicted or questioned; on the contrary, every one whom we have heard speak on the subject of Great Britain, every book we have read, invariably took it for granted; our whole national history, the routine transactions and current events of the country, our social and commercial system, our political relations with foreigners, imply it in one way or another. Numberless facts, or what we consider facts, rest on the truth of it; no received fact rests on its being otherwise. If there is any where a junction between us and the continent, where is it? and how do we know it? is it in the north or in the south? There is a manifest *reductio ad absurdum* attached to the notion that we can be deceived on such a point as this.

However, negative arguments and circumstantial evidence are not all, in such a matter, which we have a right to require. They are not the highest kind of proof possible. Those who have circumnavigated the island have a right to be certain: have we ever ourselves even fallen in with any one who has? And as to the common belief, what is the proof that we are not all of us believing it on the credit of each other? And then, when it is said that every one believes it, and every thing implies it, how much comes home to me personally of this "every one" and "every thing"? The question is, Why do I believe it myself? A living statesman is said to have fancied Demerara an island; his belief was an impression; have we personally more than an impression, if we view the matter argumentatively, a lifelong impression about Great Britain, like the belief, so long and so widely entertained, that the earth was immovable, and the sun careered round it? I am not at all insinuating that we are not rational in our certitude; I only mean that we cannot analyze a proof satisfactorily, the result of which good sense actually guarantees to us.

2. Father Hardouin maintained that Terence's Plays, Virgil's "Æneid," Horace's Odes, and the Histories of Livy and Tacitus, were the forgeries of the monks of the thirteenth century. That he should be able to argue in behalf of such a position, shows of course that the proof in behalf of the received opinion is not overwhelming. That is, we have no means of inferring absolutely, that Virgil's episode of Dido, or of the Sibyl, and Horace's "Te quoque mensorem" and "Quem tu Melpomene," belong to that Augustan age, which owes its celebrity mainly to those poets. Our common-sense, however, believes in their genuineness without any hesitation or reserve, as if it had been demonstrated, and not in proportion to the available evidence in its favour, or the balance of arguments.

So much at first sight;—but what are our grounds for dismissing thus summarily, as we are likely to do, a theory such as Hardouin's? For let it be observed first, that all knowledge of the Latin classics comes to us from the medieval transcriptions of them, and they who transcribed them had the opportunity of forging or garbling them. We are simply at their mercy; for neither by oral transmission, nor by monumental inscriptions, nor by contemporaneous manuscripts are the works of Virgil, Horace, and Terence, of Livy and Tacitus, brought to our knowledge. The existing copies, whenever made, are to us the autographic originals. Next, it must be considered, that the numerous religious bodies, then existing over the face of Europe, had leisure enough, in the course of a century, to compose, not only all the classics, but all the Fathers too. The question is, whether they had the ability. This is the main point on which the inquiry turns, or at least the most obvious; and it forms one of those arguments, which, from the nature of the case, are felt rather than are convertible into syllogisms. Hardouin allows that the Georgics, Horace's Satires and Epistles, and the whole of Cicero, are genuine: we have a standard then in these undisputed compositions of the Augustan age. We have a standard also, in the extant medieval works, of what the thirteenth century could do; and we see at once how widely the disputed works differ from the medieval. Now could the thirteenth century simulate Augustan writers better than the Augustan could simulate such writers as those of the thirteenth? No. Perhaps, when the subject is critically examined, the question may be brought to a more simple issue; but as to our personal reasons for receiving as genuine the whole of Virgil, Horace, Livy, Tacitus, and Terence, they are summed up in our conviction that the monks had not the ability to write them. That is, we take for granted that we are sufficiently informed abut the capabilities of the human mind, and the conditions of genius, to be quite sure that an age which was fertile in great ideas and in momentous elements of the future, robust in thought, hopeful in its anticipations, of singular intellectual curiosity and acumen, and of high genius in at least one of the fine arts, could not, for the very reason of its pre-eminence in its own line, have an equal pre-eminence in a contrary one. We do not pretend to be able to draw the line between what the medieval intellect could or could not do; but we feel sure that at least it could not write the classics. An instinctive sense of this, and a faith in testimony, are the sufficient, but the undeveloped argument on which to ground our certitude.

I will add, that, if we deal with arguments in the mere letter, the question of the authorship of works in any case has much difficulty. I have noticed it in the instance of Shakespeare, and of Newton. We are all certain that Johnson wrote the prose of Johnson, and Pope the poetry of Pope; but what is there but prescription, at least after contemporaries are dead, to connect together the author of the work and the owner of the name? Our lawyers prefer the examination of present witnesses to affidavits on paper; but the tradition of "testimonia," such as are prefixed to the classics and the Fathers, together with the absence of dissentient voices, is the adequate groundwork of our belief in the history of literature.

3. Once more: what are my grounds for thinking that I, in my own particular case, shall die? I am as certain of it in my own innermost mind, as I am that I now live; but what is the distinct evidence on which I allow myself to be certain? how would it tell in a court of justice? how should I fare under a cross-examination upon the grounds of my certitude? Demonstration of course I cannot have of a future event, unless by means of a Divine Voice; but what logical defence can I make for that undoubting, obstinate anticipation of it, of which I could not rid myself, if I tried?

First, the future cannot be proved *à posteriori;* therefore we are compelled by the nature of the case to put up with *à priori* arguments, that is, with antecedent probability, which is by itself no logical proof. Men tell me that there is a law of death, meaning by law a necessity; and I answer that they are throwing dust into my eyes, giving me words instead of things. What is a law but a generalized fact? and what power has the past over the future? and what power has the case of others over my own case? and how many deaths have I seen? how many ocular witnesses have imparted to me their experience of deaths, sufficient to establish what is called a law?

But let there be a law of death; so there is a law, we are told, that the planets, if let alone, would severally fall into the sun—it is the centrifugal law which hinders it, and so the centripetal law is never carried out. In like manner I am not under the law of death alone, I am under a thousand laws, if I am under one, and they thwart and counteract each other, and jointly determine the irregular line, along which my actual history runs, divergent from the special direction of any one of them. No law is carried out, except in cases where it acts freely: how do I know that the law of death will be allowed its free action in my particular case? We often are able to avert death by medical treatment: why should death have its effect, sooner or later, in every case conceivable?

It is true that the human frame, in all instances which come before me, first grows, and then declines, wastes, and decays, in visible preparation for dissolution. We see death seldom, but of this decline we are witnesses daily; still, it is a plain fact, that most men who die, die, not by any law of death, but by the law of disease; and some writers have questioned whether death is ever, strictly speaking, natural. Now, are diseases necessary? is there any law that every one, sooner or later, must fall under the power of disease? and what would happen on a large scale, were there no diseases? Is what we call the law of death any thing more than the chance of disease? Is the prospect of my death, in its logical evidence,— as that evidence is brought home to me—much more than a high probability?

The strongest proof I have for my inevitable mortality is the *reductio ad absurdum*. Can I point to the man, in historic times, who has lived his two hundred years? What has become of past generations of men, unless it is true that they suffered dissolution? But this is a circuitous argument to warrant a conclusion to which in matter of fact I adhere so relentlessly. Any how, there is a considerable "surplusage," as Locke calls it, of belief over proof, when I determine that I individually must die. But what logic cannot do, my own living personal reasoning, my good sense, which is the healthy condition of such personal reasoning, but which cannot adequately, express itself in words, does for me, and I am possessed with the most precise, absolute, masterful certitude of my dying some day or other.

I am led on by these reflections to make another remark. If it is difficult to explain how a man knows that he shall die, is it not more difficult for him to satisfy himself how he knows that he was born? His knowledge about himself does not rest on memory, nor on distinct testimony, nor on circumstantial evidence. Can he bring into one focus of proof the reasons which make him so sure? I am not speaking of scientific men, who have diverse channels of knowledge, but of an ordinary individual, as one of ourselves.

Answers doubtless may be given to some of these questions; but, on the whole, I think it is the fact that many of our most obstinate and most reasonable certitudes depend on proofs which are informal and personal, which baffle our powers of analysis, and cannot be brought under logical rule, because they cannot be submitted to logical statistics. If we must speak of Law, this recognition of a correlation between certitude and implicit proof seems to me a law of our minds.

2

I said just now that an object of sense presents itself to our view as one whole, and not in its separate details: we take it in, recognize it, and discriminate it from other objects, all at once. Such too is the intellectual view we take of the *momenta* of proof for a concrete truth; we grasp the full tale of premisses and the conclusion, *per modum unius,*—by a sort of instinctive perception of the legitimate conclusion in and through the premisses, not by a formal juxta-position of propositions; though of course such a juxta-position is useful and natural, both to direct and to verify, just as in objects of sight our notice of bodily peculiarities, or the remarks of others may aid us in establishing a case of disputed identity. And, as this man or that will receive his own impression of one and the same person, and judge differently from others about his countenance, its expression, its moral significance, its physical contour and complexion, so an intellectual question may strike two minds very differently, may awaken in them distinct associations, may be invested by them in contrary characteristics, and lead them to opposite conclusions;—and so, again, a body of proof, or a line of argument, may produce a distinct, nay, a dissimilar effect, as addressed to one or to the other.

Thus in concrete reasonings we are in great measure thrown

back into that condition, from which logic proposed to rescue us. We judge for ourselves, by our own lights, and on our own principles; and our criterion of truth is not so much the manipulation of propositions, as the intellectual and moral character of the person maintaining them, and the ultimate silent effect of his arguments or conclusions upon our minds.

It is this distinction between ratiocination as the exercise of a living faculty in the individual intellect, and mere skill in argumentative science, which is the true interpretation of the prejudice which exists against logic in the popular mind, and of the animadversions which are levelled against it, as that its formulas make a pedant and a *doctrinaire*, that it never makes converts, that it leads to rationalism, that Englishmen are too practical to be logical, that an ounce of common-sense goes farther than many cartloads of logic, that Laputa is the land of logicians, and the like. Such maxims mean, when analyzed, that the processes of reasoning which legitimately lead to assent, to action, to certitude are in fact too multiform, subtle, omnigenous, too implicit, to allow of being measured by rule, that they are after all personal,—verbal argumentation being useful, only in subordination to a higher logic. It is this which was meant by the Judge who, when asked for his advice by a friend, on his being called to important duties which were new to him, bade him always lay down the law boldly, but never give his reasons, for his decision was likely to be right, but his reasons sure to be unsatisfactory. This is the point which I proceed to illustrate.

1. I will take a question of the present moment. "We shall have a European war, *for* Greece is audaciously defying Turkey." How are we to test the validity of the reason, implied, not expressed, in the word "for"? Only the judgment of diplomatists, statesmen, capitalists, and the like, founded on experience, strengthened by practical and historical knowledge, controlled by self-interest, can decide the worth of that "for" in relation to accepting or not accepting to the conclusion which depends on it. The argument is from concrete fact to

concrete fact. How will mere logical inferences, which cannot proceed without general and abstract propositions, help us on to the determination of this particular case? It is not the case of Switzerland attacking Austria, or of Portugal attacking Spain, or of Belgium attacking Prussia, but a case without parallels. To draw a scientific conclusion, the argument must run somewhat in this way:—"All audacious defiances of Turkey on the part of Greece must end in a European war; these present acts of Greece are such: ergo;"—where the major premiss is more difficult to accept than the conclusion, and the proof becomes an "obscurum per obscurius." But, in truth, I should not betake myself to some one universal proposition to defend my own view of the matter; I should determine the particular case by its particular circumstances, by the combination of many uncatalogued experiences floating in my memory, of many reflections, variously produced, felt rather than capable of statement; and if I had them not, I should go to those who had. I assent in consequence of some such complex act of judgment, or from faith in those who are capable of making it, and practically syllogism has no part, even verificatory, in the action of my mind.

I take this instance at random in illustration; now let me follow it up by more serious cases.

2. Leighton says, "What a full confession do we make of our dissatisfaction with the objects of our bodily senses, that in our attempts to express what we conceive of the best of beings and the greatest of felicities to be, we describe by the exact contraries of all that we experience here,—the one as infinite, incomprehensible, immutable, &c.; the other as incorruptible, undefiled, and that passeth not away. At all events, this coincidence, say rather identity of attributes, is sufficient to apprise us that, to be inheritors of bliss, we must become the children of God." Coleridge quotes this passage, and adds, "Another and more fruitful, perhaps more solid, inference from the facts would be, that there is something in the human mind which makes it know that in all finite quantity, there is

an infinite, in all measures of time an eternal; that the latter are the basis, the substance, of the former; and that, as we truly are only as far as God is with us, so neither can we truly possess, that is, enjoy our being or any other real good, but by living in the sense of His holy presence." [1]

What is this an argument for? how few readers will enter into either premiss or conclusion! and of those who understand what it means, will not at least some confess that they understand it by fits and starts, not at all times? Can we ascertain its force by mood and figure? Is there any royal road by which we may indolently be carried along into the acceptance of it? Does not the author rightly number it among his "aids" for our "reflection," not instruments for our compulsion? It is plain that, if the passage is worth any thing, we must secure that worth for our own use by the personal action of our own minds, or else we shall be only professing and asserting its doctrine, without having any ground or right to assert it. And our preparation for understanding and making use of it will be the general state of our mental discipline and cultivation, our own experiences, our appreciation of religious ideas, the perspicacity and steadiness of our intellectual vision.

3. It is argued by Hume against the actual occurrence of the Jewish and Christian miracles, that, whereas "it is experience only which gives authority to human testimony, and it is the same experience which assures us of the laws of nature," therefore, "when these two kinds of experience are contrary" to each other, "we are bound to subtract the one from the other;" and, in consequence, since we have no experience of a violation of natural laws, and much experience of the violation of truth, "we may establish it as a maxim that no human testimony can have such force as to prove a miracle, and make it a just foundation for any such system of religion." [2]

I will accept the general proposition, but I resist its applica-

---

[1] "Aids to Reflection," p. 59, ed. 1839.
[2] Works, vol. iii. p. 178, ed. 1770.

tion. Doubtless it is abstractedly more likely that men should lie than that the order of nature should be infringed; but what is abstract reasoning to a question of concrete fact? To arrive at the fact of any matter, we must eschew generalities, and take things as they stand, with all their circumstances. *A priori*, of course the acts of men are not so trustworthy as the order of nature, and the pretence of miracles is in fact more common than the occurrence. But the question is not about miracles in general, or men in general, but definitely, whether these particular miracles, ascribed to the particular Peter, James, and John, are more likely to have been or not; whether they are unlikely, supposing that there is a Power, external to the world, who can bring them about; supposing they are the only means by which He can reveal Himself to those who need a revelation; supposing He is likely to reveal Himself; that He has a great end in doing so; that the professed miracles in question are like His natural works, and such as He is likely to work, in case He wrought miracles; that great effects, otherwise unaccountable, in the event followed upon the acts said to be miraculous; that they were from the first accepted as true by large numbers of men against their natural interests; that the reception of them as true has left its mark upon the world, as no other event ever did; that, viewed in their effects, they have—that is, the belief of them has—served to raise human nature to a high moral standard, otherwise unattainable: these and the like considerations are parts of a great complex argument, which so far can be put into propositions, but which, even between, and around, and behind these, is implicit and secret, and cannot by any ingenuity be imprisoned in a formula, and packed into a nut-shell. These various conditions may be decided in the affirmative or in the negative. That is a further point; here I only insist upon the nature of the argument, if it is to be philosophical. It must be no smart antithesis which may look well on paper, but the living action of the mind on a great problem of fact; and we must summon to our aid all our powers and resources, if we would encounter it worthily, and not as if it were a literary essay.

4. "Consider the establishment of the Christian religion," says Pascal in his "Thoughts." "Here is a religion contrary to our nature, which establishes itself in men's minds with so much mildness, as to use no external force; with so much energy, that no tortures could silence its martyrs and confessors; and consider the holiness, devotion, humility of its true disciples; its sacred books, their superhuman grandeur, their admirable simplicity. Consider the character of its Founder; His associates and disciples, unlettered men, yet possessed of wisdom sufficient to confound the ablest philosopher; the astonishing succession of prophets who heralded Him; the state at this day of the Jewish people who rejected Him and His religion; its perpetuity and its holiness; the light which its doctrines shed upon the contrarieties of our nature;—after considering these things, let any man judge if it be possible to doubt about its being the only true one." [1]

This is an argument parallel in its character to that by which we ascribe the classics to the Augustan age. We urge, that, though we cannot draw the line definitely between what the monks could do in literature, and what they could not, any how Virgil's "Æneid" and the Odes of Horace are far beyond the highest capacity of the medieval mind, which, however great, was different in the character of its endowments. And in like manner we maintain, that, granting that we cannot decide how far the human mind can advance by its own unaided powers in religious ideas and sentiments, and in religious practice, still the facts of Christianity, as they stand, are beyond what is possible to man, and betoken the presence of a higher intelligence, purpose, and might.

Many have been converted and sustained in their faith by this argument, which admits of being powerfully stated; but still such statement is after all only intended to be a vehicle

[1] Taylor's Translation, p. 131.

of thought, and to open the mind to the apprehension of the facts of the case, and to trace them and their implications in outline, not to convince by the logic of its mere wording. Do we not think and muse as we read it, try to master it as we proceed, put down the book in which we find it, fill out its details from our own resources, and then resume the study of it? And, when we have to give an account of it to others, should we make use of its language, or even of its thoughts, and not rather of its drift and spirit? Has it never struck us what different lights different minds throw upon the same theory and argument, nay, how they seem to be differing in detail when they are professing, and in reality showing, a concurrence in it? Have we never found, that, when a friend takes up the defence of what we have written or said, that at first we are unable to recognize in his statement of it what we meant it to convey? It will be our wisdom to avail ourselves of language, as far as it will go, but to aim mainly by means of it to stimulate, in those to whom we address ourselves, a mode of thinking and trains of thought similar to our own, leading them on by their own independent action, not by any syllogistic compulsion. Hence it is that an intellectual school will always have something of an esoteric character; for it is an assemblage of minds that think; their bond is unity of thought, and their words become a sort of *tessera*, not expressing thought, but symbolizing it.

Recurring to Pascal's argument, I observe that, its force depending upon the assumption that the facts of Christianity are beyond human nature, therefore, according as the powers of nature are placed at a high or low standard, that force will be greater or less; and that standard will vary according to the respective dispositions, opinions, and experiences, of those to whom the argument is addressed. Thus its value is a personal question; not as if there were not an objective truth and Christianity as a whole not supernatural, but that, when we come to consider where it is that the supernatural presence is found, there may be fair differences of opinion, both as to the fact and the proof of what is supernatural. There is a multitude of facts, which, taken separately, may perhaps be natural, but, found together, must come from a source above nature; and what these are, and how many are necessary, will be variously determined. And while every inquirer has a right to determine the question according to the best exercise of his judgment, still whether he so determine it for himself, or trust in part or altogether to the judgment of those who have the best claim to judge, in either case he is guided by the implicit processes of the reasoning faculty, not by any manufacture of arguments forcing their way to an irrefragable conclusion.

5. Pascal writes in another place, "He who doubts, but seeks not to have his doubts removed, is at once the most criminal and the most unhappy of mortals. If, together with this, he is tranquil and self-satisfied, if he be vain of his tranquillity, or makes his state a topic of mirth and self-gratulation, I have not words to describe so insane a creature. Truly it is to the honour of religion to have for its adversaries men so bereft of reason; their opposition, far from being formidable, bears testimony to its most distinguishing truths; for the great object of the Christian religion is to establish the corruption of our nature, and the redemption by Jesus Christ." [1] Elsewhere he says of Montaigne, "He involves every thing in such universal, unmingled scepticism, as to doubt of his very doubts. He was a pure Pyrrhonist. He ridicules all attempts at certainty in any thing. Delighted with exhibiting in his own person the contradictions that exist in the mind of a free-thinker, it is all one to him whether he is successful or not in his argument. The virtue he loved was simple, sociable, gay, sprightly, and playful; to use one of his own expressions, 'Ignorance and incuriousness are two charming pillows for a sound head.'" [2]

Here are two celebrated writers in direct opposition to each other in their fundamental view of truth and duty. Shall we

[1] Ibid. pp. 108—110.
[2] Ibid. pp. 429—436.

say that there is no such thing as truth and error, but that any thing is truth to a man which he troweth? and not rather, as the solution of a great mystery, that truth there is, and attainable it is, but that its rays stream in upon us through the medium of our moral as well as our intellectual being; and that in consequence that perception of its first principles which is natural to us is enfeebled, obstructed, perverted, by allurements of sense and the supremacy of self, and, on the other hand, quickened by aspirations after the supernatural; so that at length two characters of mind are brought out into shape, and two standards and systems of thought,—each logical when analyzed, yet contradictory of each other, and only not antagonistic because they have no common ground on which they can conflict?

6. Montaigne was endowed with a good estate, health, leisure, and an easy temper, literary tastes, and a sufficiency of books: he could afford thus to play with life, and the abysses into which it leads us. Let us take a case in contrast.

"I think," says the poor dying factory-girl in the tale, "if this should be the end of all, and if all I have been born for is just to work my heart and life away, and to sicken in this dree place, with those mill-stones in my ears for ever, until I could scream out for them to stop and let me have a little piece of quiet, and with the fluff filling my lungs, until I thirst to death for one long deep breath of the clear air, and my mother gone, and I never able to tell her again how I loved her, and of all my troubles,—I think, if this life is the end, and that there is no God to wipe away all tears from all eyes, I could go mad!" [1]

Here is an argument for the immortality of the soul. As to its force, be it great or small, will it make a figure in a logical disputation, carried on *secundum artem?* Can any scientific common measure compel the intellects of Dives and Lazarus to take the same estimate of it? Is there any test of the validity of it better than the *ipse dixit* of private judgment, that is, the

[1] [Mrs. Gaskell's] "North and South."

judgment of those who have a right to judge, and next, the agreement of many private judgments in one and the same view of it?

7. "In order to prove plainly and intelligibly," says Dr. Samuel Clarke, "that God is a Being, which must of necessity be endued with perfect knowledge, 'tis to be observed that knowledge is a perfection, without which the foregoing attributes are no perfections at all, and without which those which follow can have no foundation. Where there is no Knowledge, Eternity and Immensity are as nothing, and Justice, Goodness, Mercy, and Wisdom can have no place. The idea of eternity and omnipresence, devoid of knowledge, is as the notion of darkness compared with that of light. 'Tis as a notion of the world without the sun to illuminate it; 'tis as the notion of inanimate matter (which is the atheist's supreme cause) compared with that of light and spirit. And as for the following attributes of Justice, Goodness, Mercy, and Wisdom, 'tis evident that without knowledge there could not possibly be any such things as these at all." [1]

The argument here used in behalf of the Divine Attribute of Knowledge comes under the general proposition that the attributes imply each other, for the denial of one is the denial of the rest. To some minds this thesis is self-evident; others are utterly insensible to its force. Will it bear bringing out into words throughout the whole series of its argumentative links? for if it does, then either those who maintain it or those who reject it, the one or the other, will be compelled by logical necessity to confess that they are in error. "God is wise, if He is eternal; He is good, if He is wise; He is just, if He is good." What skill can so arrange these propositions, so add to them, so combine them, that they may be able, by the force of their juxta-position, to follow one from the other, and become one and the same by an inevitable correlation. That is not the method by which the argument becomes a demonstration.

[1] Serm. xi. init.

Such a method, used by a Theist in controversy against men who are unprepared personally for the question, will but issue in his retreat along a series of major propositions, farther and farther back, till he and they find themselves in a land of shadows, "where the light is as darkness."

To feel the true force of an argument like this, we must not confine ourselves to abstractions, and merely compare notion with notion, but we must contemplate the God of our conscience as a Living Being, as one Object and Reality, *under* the aspect of this or that attribute. We must patiently rest in the thought of the Eternal, Omnipresent, and All-knowing, rather than of Eternity, Omnipresence, and Omniscience; and we must not hurry on and force a series of deductions, which, if they are to be realized, must distil like dew into our minds, and form themselves spontaneously there, by a calm contemplation and gradual understanding of their premisses. Ordinarily speaking, such deductions do not flow forth, except according as the Image,[1] presented to us through conscience, on which they depend, is cherished within us with the sentiments which, supposing it be, as we know it is, the truth, it necessarily claims of us, and is seen reflected, by the habit of our intellect, in the appointments and the events of the external world. And, in their manifestation to our inward sense, they are analogous to the knowledge which we at length attain of the details of a landscape, after we have selected the right stand-point, and have learned to accommodate the pupil of our eye to the varying focus necessary for seeing them, have accustomed it to the glare of light, have mentally grouped or discriminated lines and shadows and given them their due meaning, and have mastered the perspective of the whole. Or they may be compared to a landscape as drawn by the pencil (unless the illustration seem forced), in which by the skill of the artist, amid the bold outlines of trees and rocks, when the eye has learned to take in their reverse aspects, the forms or

[1] *Vide supr.* ch. v. § 1, pp. 83, 86.

faces of historical personages are discernible, which we catch and lose again, and then recover, and which some who look on with us are never able to catch at all.

Analogous to such an exercise of sight, must be our mode of dealing with the verbal expositions of an argument such as Clarke's. His words speak to those who understand the speech. To the mere barren intellect they are but the pale ghosts of notions; but the trained imagination sees in them the representations of things. He who has once detected in his conscience the outline of a Lawgiver and Judge, needs no definition of Him, whom he dimly but surely contemplates there, and he rejects the mechanism of logic, which cannot contain in its grasp matters so real and so recondite. Such a one, according to the strength and perspicacity of his mind, the force of his presentiments, and his power of sustained attention, is able to pronounce about the great Sight which encompasses him, as about some visible object; and, in his investigation of the Divine Attributes, is not inferring abstraction from abstraction, but noting down the aspects and phases of that one thing on which he ever is gazing. Nor is it possible to limit the depth of meaning, which at length he will attach to words, which to the many are but definitions and ideas.

Here then again, as in the other instances, it seems clear, that methodical processes of inference, useful as they are, as far as they go, are only instruments of the mind, and need, in order to their due exercise, that real ratiocination and present imagination which gives them a sense beyond their letter, and which, while acting through them, reaches to conclusions beyond and above them. Such a living *organon* is a personal gift, and not a mere method or calculus.

3

That there are cases, in which evidence, not sufficient for a scientific proof, is nevertheless sufficient for assent and certitude, is the doctrine of Locke, as of most men. He tells us that belief, grounded on sufficient probabilities, "rises to assurance;" and as to the question of sufficiency, that where propositions "border near on certainty," then "we assent to them as firmly as if they were infallibly demonstrated." The only question is, what these propositions are: this he does not tell us, but he seems to think that they are few in number, and will be without any trouble recognized at once by common-sense; whereas, unless I am mistaken, they are to be found throughout the range of concrete matter, and that supra-logical judgment, which is the warrant for our certitude about them, is not mere common-sense, but the true healthy action of our ratiocinative powers, an action more subtle and more comprehensive than the mere appreciation of a syllogistic argument. It is often called the "judicium prudentis viri," a standard of certitude which holds good in all concrete matter, not only in those cases of practice and duty, in which we are more familiar with it, but in questions of truth and falsehood generally, or in what are called "speculative" questions, and that, not indeed to the exclusion, but as the supplement of logic. Thus a proof, except in abstract demonstration, has always in it, more or less, an element of the personal, because "prudence" is not a constituent part of our nature, but a personal endowment.

And the language in common use, when concrete conclusions are in question, implies the presence of this personal element in the proof of them. We are considered to feel, rather than to see, its cogency; and we decide, not that the conclusion must be, but that it cannot be otherwise. We say that we do not see our way to doubt it, that it is impossible to doubt, that we are bound to believe it, that we should be idiots, if we did not believe. We never should say, in abstract science, that we could not escape the conclusion that 25 was a mean proportional between 5 and 125; or that a man had no right to say that a tangent to a circle at the extremity of the radius makes an acute angle with it. Yet, though our certitude of the fact is quite as clear, we should not think it unnatural to say that the insularity of Great Britain is as good as demonstrated, or that none but a fool expects never to die. Phrases indeed such as these are sometimes used to express a shade of doubt, but it is enough for my purpose if they are also used when doubt is altogether absent. What, then, they signify, is, what I have so much insisted on, that we have arrived at these conclusions—not *ex opere operato,* by a scientific necessity independent of ourselves,—but by the action of our own minds, by our own individual perception of the truth in question, under a sense of duty to those conclusions and with an intellectual conscientiousness.

This certitude and this evidence are often called moral; a word which I avoid, as having a very vague meaning; but using it here for once, I observe that moral evidence and moral certitude are all that we can attain, not only in the case of ethical and spiritual subjects, such as religion, but of terrestrial and cosmical questions also. So far, physical Astronomy and Revelation stand on the same footing. Vince, in his treatise on Astronomy, does but use the language of philsophical sobriety, when, after speaking of the proofs of the earth's rotatory motion, he says, "When these reasons, all upon different principles, are considered, they amount to a proof of the earth's rotation about its axis, which is as satisfactory to the mind as the most direct demonstration could be;" or, as he had said just before, "the mind rests equally satisfied, as if the matter was strictly proved." [1] That is, first there is no demonstration that the earth rotates; next there is a cluster of "reasons on *different* principles," that is, independent probabilities in cumulation; thirdly, these "*amount* to a proof," and "the mind" feels "*as if* the matter was strictly proved," that is, there is the equivalent of proof; lastly, "the mind rests *satisfied,*" that is, it is certain on the point. And though evidence of the fact is now obtained which was not known fifty years ago, that evidence on the whole has not changed its character.

Compare with this avowal the language of Butler, when discussing the proof of Revelation. "Probable proofs," he says,

[1] Pp. 84, 85.

"by being added, not only increase the evidence, but multiply it. The truth of our religion, like the truth of common matters, is to be judged by the whole evidence taken together ... in like manner as, if in any common case numerous events acknowledged were to be alleged in proof of any other event disputed, the truth of the disputed event would be proved, not only if any one of the acknowledged ones did of itself clearly imply it, but though no one of them singly did so, if the whole of the acknowledged events taken together could not in reason be supposed to have happened, unless the disputed one were true." [1] Here, as in Astronomy, is the same absence of demonstration of the thesis, the same cumulating and converging indications of it, the same indirectness in the proof, as being *per impossibile*, the same recognition nevertheless that the conclusion is not only probable, but true. One other characteristic of the argumentative process is given, which is unnecessary in a subject-matter so clear and simple as astronomical science, viz. the moral state of the parties inquiring or disputing. They must be "as much in earnest about religion, as about their temporal affairs, capable of being convinced, on real evidence, that there is a God who governs the world, and feel themselves to be of a moral nature and accountable creatures." [2]

This being the state of the case, the question arises, whether, granting that the personality (so to speak) of the parties reasoning is an important element in proving propositions in concrete matter, any account can be given of the ratiocinative method in such proofs, over and above that analysis into syllogism which is possible in each of its steps in detail. I think there can; though I fear, lest to some minds it may appear far-fetched or fanciful; however, I will hazard this imputation. I consider, then, that the principle of concrete reasoning is parallel to the method of proof which is the foundation of modern mathematical science, as contained in

[1] "Analogy," pp. 329, 330, ed. 1836.
[2] Ibid., p. 278.

the celebrated lemma with which Newton opens his *Principia*. We know that a regular polygon, inscribed in a circle, its sides being continually diminished, tends to become that circle, as its limit; but it vanishes before it has coincided with the circle, so that its tendency to be the circle, though ever nearer fulfilment, never in fact gets beyond a tendency. In like manner, the conclusion in a real or concrete question is foreseen and predicted rather than actually attained; foreseen in the number and direction of accumulated premisses, which all converge to it, and as the result of their combination, approach it more nearly than any assignable difference, yet do not touch it logically, (though only not touching it,) on account of the nature of its subject-matter, and the delicate and implicit character of at least part of the reasonings on which it depends. It is by the strength, variety, or multiplicity of premisses, which are only probable, not by invincible syllogisms,—by objections overcome, by adverse theories neutralized, by difficulties gradually clearing up, by exceptions proving the rule, by unlooked-for correlations found for received truths, by suspense and delay in the process issuing in triumphant re-actions,—by all these ways, and many others, it is that the practised and experienced mind is able to make a sure divination that a conclusion is inevitable, of which his lines of reasoning do not actually put him in possession. This is what is meant by a proposition being "as good as proved," a conclusion as undeniable "as if it were proved," and by the reasons for it "amounting to a proof," for a proof is the limit of converging probabilities.

It may be added, that, whereas the logical form of this argument, is, as I have already observed, indirect, viz. that "the conclusion cannot be otherwise," and Butler says that an event is proved, if its antecedents "could not in reason be supposed to have happened *unless* it were true," and law-books tell us that the principle of circumstantial evidence is the *reductio ad absurdum*, so Newton too is forced to the same mode of proof for the establishment of his lemma, about prime and ultimate ratios. "If you deny that they become ultimately equal," he says, "let them be ultimately unequal;" and the consequence follows, "which is against the supposition."

Such being the character of the mental process in concrete reasoning, I should wish to adduce some good instances of it in illustration, instances in which the person reasoning confesses that he is reasoning on this very process, as I have been stating it; but these are difficult to find, from the very circumstance that the process from first to last is carried on as much without words as with them. However, I will set down three such.

1. First, an instance in physics. Wood, treating of the laws of motion, thus describes the line of reasoning by which the mind is certified of them. "They are not indeed self-evident, nor do they admit of accurate proof by experiment, on account of the effects of friction and the air's resistance, which cannot entirely be removed. They are, however, constantly and invariably suggested to our senses, and they agree with experiment, as far as experiment can go; and the more accurately the experiments are made, and the greater care we take to remove all those impediments which tend to render the conclusions erroneous, the more nearly do the experiments coincide with these laws.

"Their truth is also established upon a different ground: from these general principles innumerable particular conclusions have been deduced; sometimes the deductions are simple and immediate, sometimes they are made by tedious and intricate operations; yet they are all, without exception, consistent with each other and with experiment. It follows thereby, that the principles upon which the calculations are founded are true." [1]

The reasoning of this passage (in which the uniformity of the laws of nature is assumed) seems to me a good illustration of what must be considered the principle or form of an induction. The conclusion, which is its scope, is, by its own con-

[1] "Mechanics," p. 31.

fession, not proved; but it ought to be proved, or is as good as proved, and a man would be irrational who did not take it to be virtually proved; first, because the imperfections in the proof arise out of its subject-matter and the nature of the case, so that it *is* proved *interpretative;* and next, because in the same degree in which these faults in the subject-matter are overcome here or there, are the involved imperfections here or there of the proof remedied; and further, because, when the conclusion is assumed as an hypothesis, it throws light upon a multitude of collateral facts, accounting for them, and uniting them together in one whole. Consistency is not always the guarantee of truth; but there may be a consistency in a theory so variously tried and exemplified as to lead to belief in it, as reasonably as a witness in a court of law may, after a severe cross-examination, satisfy and assure judge, jury, and the whole court, of his simple veracity.

2. And from the courts of law shall my second illustration be taken.

A learned writer says, "In criminal prosecutions, the circumstantial evidence should be such, as to produce nearly the same degree of certainty as that which arises from direct testimony, and to exclude a rational probability of innocence." [1] By degrees of certainty he seems to mean, together with many other writers, degrees of proof, or approximations towards proof, and not certitude, as a state of mind; and he says that no one should be pronounced guilty on evidence which is not equivalent in weight to direct testimony. So far is clear; but what is meant by the expression "*rational* probability"? for there can be no probability but what is rational. I consider that the "exclusion of a rational probability" means "the exclusion of any argument in the man's favour which has a rational claim to be called probable," or rather, "the rational exclusion of any supposition that he is innocent;" and "rational" is used in contradistinction to argumentative, and means "resting on implicit reasons," such as we feel, indeed, but

[1] Phillipps' "Law of Evidence," vol. i. p. 456.

which for some cause or other, because they are too subtle or
too circuitous, we cannot put into words so as to satisfy logic.
If this is a correct account of his meaning, he says that the
evidence against a criminal, in order to be decisive of his guilt,
to the satisfaction of our conscience, must bear with it, along
with the palpable arguments for that guilt, such a reasonableness, or body of implicit reasons for it in addition, as may
exclude any probability, really such, that he is not guilty,—
that is, it must be an evidence free from any thing obscure,
suspicious, unnatural, or defective, such as (in the judgment
of a prudent man) would hinder that summation and coales-
cence of the evidence into a proof, which I have compared to
the running into a limit, in the case of mathematical ratios.
Just as an algebraical series may be of a nature never to
terminate or admit of valuation, as being the equivalent of an
irrational quantity or surd, so there may be some grave imperfections in a body of reasons, explicit or implicit, which is
directed to a proof, sufficient to interfere with its successful
issue or resolution, and to balk us with an irrational, that is,
an indeterminate, conclusion.

So much as to the principle of conclusions made upon evidence in criminal cases; now let us turn to an instance of its
application in a particular instance. Some years ago there was
a murder committed, which unusually agitated the popular
mind, and the evidence against the culprit was necessarily
circumstantial. At the trial the Judge, in addressing the Jury,
instructed them on the kind of evidence necessary for a verdict
of *guilty*. Of course he could not mean to say that they must
convict a man, of whose guilt they were not certain, especially
in a case in which two foreign countries, Germany and the
American States, were attentively looking on. If the Jury had
any doubt, that is, reasonable doubt, about the man's guilt, of
course they would give him the benefit of that doubt. Nor
could the certitude, which would be necessary for an adverse
verdict, be merely that which is sometimes called a "practical
certitude," that is, a certitude indeed, but a certitude that it

was a "duty," "expedient," "safe," to bring in a verdict of guilty. Of course the Judge spoke of what is called a "speculative certitude," that is, a certitude of the fact that the man was guilty; the only question being, what evidence was sufficient for the proof, for the certitude of that fact. This is what the Judge meant; and these are among the remarks which, with this drift, he made upon the occasion:—

After observing that by circumstantial evidence he meant a case in which "the facts do not directly prove the actual crime, but lead to the conclusion that the prisoner committed that crime," he went on to disclaim the suggestion, made by counsel in the case, that the Jury could not pronounce a verdict of *guilty*, unless they were as much satisfied that the prisoner did the deed as if they had seen him commit it. "That is not the certainty," he said, "which is required of you to discharge your duty to the prisoner, whose safety is in your hands." Then he stated what was the "degree of certainty," that is, of certainty or perfection of proof, which was necessary to the question, "involving as it did the life of the prisoner at the bar,"—it was such as that "with which," he said, "you decide upon and conclude your own most important transactions in life. Take the facts which are proved before you, separate those you believe from those which you do not believe, and all the conclusions that naturally and almost necessarily result from those facts, you may confide in as much as in the facts themselves. The case on the part of the prosecution is the *story* of the murder, told by the *different* witnesses, who *unfold the circumstances one after another*, according to their occurrence, together with the *gradual* discovery of some apparent connexion between the property that was lost, and the possession of it by the prisoner."

Now here I observe, that whereas the conclusion which is contemplated by the Judge, is what may be pronounced (on the whole, and considering all things, and judging reasonably) a proved or certain conclusion, that is, a conclusion of the truth of the allegation against the prisoner, or of the fact of his guilt, on the other hand, the *motiva* constituting this reasonable, rational proof, and this satisfactory certitude, needed not, according to him, to be stronger than those on which we prudently act on matters of important interest to ourselves, that is, probable reasons viewed in their convergence and combination. And whereas the certitude is viewed by the Judge as following on converging probabilities, which constitute a real, though only a reasonable, not an argumentative, proof, so it will be observed in this particular instance, that, in illustration of the general doctrine which I have laid down, the process is one of "line upon line, and letter upon letter," of various details accumulating and of deductions fitting in to each other; for, in the Judge's words, there was a story—and that not told right out and by one witness, but taken up and handed on from witness to witness—gradually unfolded, and tending to a proof, which of course might have been ten times stronger than it was, but was still a proof for all that, and sufficient for its conclusion,—just as we see that two straight lines are meeting, and are certain they will meet at a given distance, though we do not actually see the junction.

3. The third instance I will take is one of a literary character, the divination of the authorship of a certain anonymous publication, as suggested mainly by internal evidence, as I found it in a critique written some twenty years ago. In the extract which I make from it, we may observe the same steady march of a proof towards a conclusion, which is (as it were) out of sight;—a reckoning, or a reasonable judgment, that the conclusion really is proved, and a personal certitude upon that judgment, joined with a confession that a logical argument could not well be made out for it, and that the various details in which the proof consisted were in no small measure implicit and impalpable.

"Rumour speaks uniformly and clearly enough in attributing it to the pen of a particular individual. Nor, although a cursory reader might well skim the book without finding in it any thing to suggest, &c., . . . will it appear improbable to the more attentive student of its internal evidence; and the improbability will decrease more and more, in proportion as the *reader is capable* of judging, and appreciating the *delicate, and at first invisible touches,* which limit, to *those who understand them,* the individuals who can have written it to a very small number indeed. The utmost scepticism as to its authorship (*which we do not feel ourselves*) cannot remove it farther from him than to that of some one among his most intimate friends; so that, leaving others to discuss antecedent probabilities," &c.

Here is a writer who professes to have no doubt at all about the authorship of a book,—which at the same time he cannot prove by mere argumentation set down in words. The reasons of his conviction are too delicate, too intricate; nay, they are in part invisible; invisible, except to those who from circumstances have an intellectual perception of what does not appear to the many. They are personal to the individual. This again is an instance, distinctly set before us, of the particular mode in which the mind progresses in concrete matter, viz. from merely probable antecedents to the sufficient proof of a fact or a truth, and, after the proof, to an act of certitude about it.

I trust the foregoing remarks may not deserve the blame of a needless refinement. I have thought it incumbent on me to illustrate the intellectual process by which we pass from conditional inference to unconditional assent; and I have had only the alternative of lying under the imputation of a paradox or of a subtlety.

3

NATURAL INFERENCE

I COMMENCED MY REMARKS upon Inference by saying that reasoning ordinarily shows as a simple act, not as a process, as if there were no medium interposed between antecedent and consequent, and the transition from one to the other were of the nature of an instinct,—that is, the process is altogether unconscious and implicit. It is necessary, then, to take some notice of this natural or material Inference, as an existing phenomenon of mind; and that the more, because I shall thereby be illustrating and supporting what I have been saying of the characteristics of inferential processes as carried on in concrete matter, and especially of their being the action of the mind itself, that is, by its ratiocinative or illative faculty, not a mere operation as in the rules of arithmetic.

I say, then, that our most natural mode of reasoning is, not from propositions to propositions, but from things to things, from concrete to concrete, from wholes to wholes. Whether the consequents, at which we arrive from the antecedents with which we start, lead us to assent or only towards assent, those antecedents commonly are not recognized by us as subjects for analysis; nay, often are only indirectly recognized as antecedents at all. Not only is the inference with its process ignored, but the antecedent also. To the mind itself the reasoning is a simple divination or prediction; as it literally is in the instance of enthusiasts, who mistake their own thoughts for inspirations.

This is the mode in which we ordinarily reason, dealing with things directly, and as they stand, one by one, in the concrete, with an intrinsic and personal power, not a conscious adoption of an artificial instrument or expedient; and it is especially exemplified both in uneducated men, and in men of genius,— in those who know nothing of intellectual aids and rules, and in those who care nothing for them,—in those who are either without or above mental discipline. As true poetry is a spontaneous outpouring of thought, and therefore belongs to rude as well as to gifted minds, whereas no one becomes a poet merely by the canons of criticism, so this unscientific reasoning, being sometimes a natural, uncultivated faculty, sometimes approaching to a gift, sometimes an acquired habit and second nature, has a higher source than logical rule,—"nascitur, non fit." When it is characterized by precision, subtlety, promptitude, and truth, it is of course a gift and a rarity: in ordinary minds it is biassed and degraded by prejudice, passion, and self-interest; but still, after all, this divination comes by nature, and belongs to all of us in a measure, to women more than to men, hitting or missing, as the case may be, but with a success on the whole sufficient to show that there is a method in it, though it be implicit.

A peasant who is weather-wise may yet be simply unable to assign intelligible reasons why he thinks it will be fine to-morrow; and if he attempts to do so he may give reasons wide of the mark; but that will not weaken his own confidence in his prediction. His mind does not proceed step by step, but he feels all at once and together the force of various combined phenomena, though he is not conscious of them. Again, there are physicians who excel in the *diagnosis* of complaints; though it does not follow from this, that they could defend their decision in a particular case against a brother physician who disputed it. They are guided by natural acuteness and varied experience; they have their own idiosyncratic modes of observing, generalizing, and concluding; when questioned, they can but rest on their own authority, or appeal to the future event. In a popular novel,[1] a lawyer is introduced, who "would know, almost by instinct, whether an accused person was or was not guilty; and he had already perceived by instinct" that the heroine was guilty. "I've no doubt she's a clever woman," he said, and at once named an attorney practising at the Old Bailey. So, again, experts and detectives, when employed to investigate mysteries, in cases whether of the civil or criminal law, discern and follow out indications which promise solution with a sagacity incomprehensible to ordinary men. A parallel gift is the intuitive perception of character possessed by certain men, while others are as destitute of it, as others again are of an ear for music. What common measure is there between the judgments of those who have this intuition, and those who have not? What but the event can settle any differences of opinion which occurs in their estimation of a third person?

[1] [Anthony Trollope's] "Orley Farm."

These are instances of a natural capacity, or of nature improved by practice and habit, enabling the mind to pass promptly from one set of facts to another, not only, I say, without conscious media, but without conscious antecedents.

Sometimes, I say, this illative faculty is nothing short of genius. Such seems to have been Newton's perception of truths mathematical and physical, though proof was absent. At least that is the impression left on my own mind by various stories which are told of him, one of which was stated in the public papers a few years ago. "Professor Sylvester," it was said, "has just discovered the proof of Sir Isaac Newton's rule for ascertaining the imaginary roots of equations.... This rule has been a Gordian-knot among algebraists for the last century and a half. The proof being wanting, authors became ashamed at length for advancing a proposition, the evidence for which rested on no other foundation than belief in Newton's sagacity." [1]

Such is the gift of the calculating boys who now and then make their appearance, who seem to have certain short-cuts to conclusions, which they cannot explain to themselves. Some are said to have been able to determine off-hand what numbers are prime,—numbers, I think, up to seven places.

In a very different subject-matter, Napoleon supplies us with an instance of a parallel genius in reasoning, by which he was enabled to look at things in his own province, and to interpret them truly, apparently without any ratiocinative media. "By long experience," says Alison, "joined to great natural quickness and precision of eye, he had acquired the power of judging, with extraordinary accuracy, both of the amount of the enemy's force opposed to him in the field, and of the probable result of the movements, even the most complicated, going forward in the opposite armies.... He looked around him for a little while with his telescope, and immediately formed a clear conception of the position, forces, and intention of the whole hostile array. In this way he could, with

[1] *Guardian*, June 28, 1865.

surprising accuracy, calculate in a few minutes, according to what he could see of their formation and the extent of the ground which they occupied, the numerical force of armies of 60,000 or 80,000 men; and if their troops were at all scattered, he knew at once how long it would require for them to concentrate, and how many hours must elapse before they could make their attack." [1]

It is difficult to avoid calling such clear presentiments by the name of instinct; and I think they may so be called, if by instinct be understood, not a natural sense, one and the same in all, and incapable of cultivation, but a perception of facts without assignable media of perceiving. There are those who can tell at once what is conducive or injurious to their welfare, who are their friends, who their enemies, what is to happen to them, and how they are to meet it. Presence of mind, fathoming of motives, talent for repartee, are instances of this gift. As to that divination of personal danger which is found in the young and innocent, we find a description of it in one of Scott's romances, in which the heroine, "without being able to discover what was wrong either in the scenes of unusual luxury with which she was surrounded, or in the manner of her hostess," is said nevertheless to have felt "an instinctive apprehension that all was not right,—a feeling in the human mind," the author proceeds to say, "allied perhaps to that sense of danger, which animals exhibit, when placed in the vicinity of the natural enemies of their race, and which makes birds cower when the hawk is in the air, and beasts tremble when the tiger is abroad in the desert." [2]

A religious biography, lately published, affords us an instance of this spontaneous perception of truth in the province of revealed doctrine. "Her firm faith," says the Author of the Preface, "was so vivid in its character, that it was almost like an intuition of the entire prospect of revealed truth. Let an error against faith be concealed under expressions however

[1] "History," vol. x. pp. 286, 287.
[2] "Peveril of the Peak."

abstruse, and her sure instinct found it out. I have tried this experiment repeatedly. She might not be able to separate the heresy by analysis, but she saw, and felt, and suffered from its presence." [1]

And so of the great fundamental truths of religion, natural and revealed, and as regards the mass of religious men: these truths, doubtless, may be proved and defended by an array of invincible logical arguments, but such is not commonly the method in which those same logical arguments make their way into our minds. The grounds, on which we hold the divine origin of the Church, and the previous truths which are taught us by nature—the being of a God, and the immortality of the soul—are felt by most men to be recondite and impalpable, in proportion to their depth and reality. As we cannot see ourselves, so we cannot well see intellectual motives which are so intimately ours, and which spring up from the very constitution of our minds; and while we refuse to admit the notion that religion has not irrefragable arguments in its behalf, still the attempts to argue, on the part of an individual *hic et nunc,* will sometimes only confuse his apprehension of sacred objects, and subtracts from his devotion quite as much as it adds to his knowledge.

This is found in the case of other perceptions besides that of faith. It is the case of nature against art: of course, if possible, nature and art should be combined, but sometimes they are incompatible. Thus, in the case of calculating boys, it is said, I know not with what truth, that to teach them the ordinary rules of arithmetic is to endanger or to destroy the extraordinary endowment. And men who have the gift of playing on an instrument by ear, are sometimes afraid to learn by rule, lest they should lose it.

There is an analogy, in this respect, between Ratiocination and Memory, though the latter may be exercised without antecedents or media, whereas the former requires them in its very idea. At the same time association has so much to do with

[1] "Life of Mother Margaret M. Hallahan," p. vii.

memory, that we may not unfairly consider memory, as well as reasoning, as depending on certain previous conditions. Writing, as I have already observed, is a *memoria technica,* or logic of memory. Now it will be found, I think, that, indispensable as is the use of letters, still, in fact, we weaken our memory in proportion as we habituate ourselves to commit all that we wish to remember to memorandums. Of course in proportion as our memory is weak or overburdened, and thereby treacherous, we cannot act otherwise; but in the case of men of strong memory, in any particular subject-matter, as in that of dates, all artificial expedients, from the "Thirty days has September," &c., to the more formidable formulas which are offered for their use, are as difficult and repulsive as the natural exercise of memory is healthy and easy to them; just as the clear-headed and practical reasoner, who sees conclusions at a glance, is uncomfortable under the drill of a logician, being oppressed and hampered, as David in Saul's armour, by what is intended to be a benefit.

I need not say more on this part of the subject. What is called reasoning is often only a peculiar and personal mode of abstraction, and so far, like memory, may be said to exist without antecedents. It is a power of looking at things in some particular aspect, and of determining their internal and external relations thereby. And according to the subtlety and versatility of their gift, are men able to read what comes before them justly, variously, and fruitfully. Hence, too, it is that in our intercourse with others, in business and family matters, in social and political transactions, a word or an act on the part of another is sometimes a sudden revelation; light breaks in upon us, and our whole judgment of a course of events, or of an undertaking, is changed. We determine correctly or otherwise, as it may be; but in either case it is by a sense proper to ourselves, for another may see the objects which we are thus using, and give them quite a different interpretation, inasmuch as he abstracts another set of general notions from those same phenomena which present themselves to us also.

What I have been saying of Ratiocination, may be said of Taste, and is confirmed by the obvious analogy between the two. Taste, skill, invention in the fine arts—and so, again, discretion or judgment in conduct—are exerted spontaneously, when once acquired, and could not give a clear account of themselves, or of their mode of proceeding. They do not go by rule, though to a certain point their exercise may be analyzed, and may take the shape of an art or method. But these parallels will come before us presently.

And now I come to a further peculiarity of this natural and spontaneous ratiocination. This faculty, as it is actually found in us, proceeding from concrete to concrete, is attached to a definite subject-matter, according to the individual. In spite of Aristotle, I will not allow that genuine reasoning is an instrumental art; and in spite of Dr. Johnson, I will assert that genius, as far as it is manifested in ratiocination, is not equal to all undertakings, but has its own peculiar subject-matter, and is circumscribed in its range. No one would for a moment expect that because Newton and Napoleon both had a genius for ratiocination, that, in consequence, Napoleon could have generalized the principle of gravitation, or Newton have seen how to concentrate a hundred thousand men at Austerlitz. The ratiocinative faculty, then, as found in individuals, is not a general instrument of knowledge, but has its province, or is what may be called departmental. It is not so much one faculty, as a collection of similar or analogous faculties under one name, there being really as many faculties as there are distinct subject-matters, though in the same person some of them may, if it so happen, be united,—nay, though some men have a sort of literary power in arguing in all subject matters, *de omni scibili*, a power extensive, but not deep or real.

This surely is the conclusion to which we are brought by our ordinary experience of men. It is almost proverbial that a hard-headed mathematician may have no head at all for what is called historical evidence. Successful experimentalists need not have talent for legal research or pleading. A shrewd man of business may be a bad arguer in philosophical questions. Able statesmen and politicians have been before now eccentric or superstitious in their religious views. It is notorious how ridiculous a clever man may make himself, who ventures to argue with professed theologians, critics, or geologists, though without positive defects in knowledge of his subject. Priestly, great in electricity and chemistry, was but a poor ecclesiastical historian. The Author of the Minute Philosopher is also the Author of the Analyst. Newton wrote not only his *Principia,* but his comments on the Apocalypse; Cromwell, whose actions savoured of the boldest logic, was a confused speaker. In these, and various similar instances, the defect lay, not so much in an ignorance of facts, as in an inability to handle those facts suitably; in feeble or perverse modes of abstraction, observation, comparison, analysis, inference, which nothing could have obviated, but that which was wanting,—a specific talent, and a ready exercise of it.

I have already referred to the faculty of memory in illustration; it will serve me also here. We can form an abstract idea of memory, and call it one faculty, which has for its subject-matter all past facts of our personal experience; but this is really only an illusion; for there is no such gift of universal memory. Of course, we all remember, in a way, as we reason, in all subject-matters; but I am speaking of remembering rightly, as I spoke of reasoning rightly. In real fact memory, as a talent, is not one indivisible faculty, but a power of retaining and recalling the past in this or that department of our experience, not in any whatever. Two memories, which are both specially retentive, may also be incommensurate. Some men can recite the canto of a poem, or good part of a speech, after once reading it, but have no head for dates. Others have great capacity for the vocabulary of languages, but recollect nothing of the small occurrences of the day or year. Others never forget any statement which they have read, and can give volume and page, but have no memory for faces. I have known those who could, without effort, run through the succession of days on which Easter fell for years back; or could say where they were, or what they were doing, on a given day, in a given year; or could recollect accurately the Christian names of friends and strangers; or could enumerate in exact order the names on all the shops from Hyde Park Corner to the Bank; or had so mastered the University Calendar as to be able to bear an examination in the academical history of any M.A. taken at random. And I believe in most of these cases the talent, in its exceptional character, did not extend beyond several classes of subjects. There are a hundred memories, as there are a hundred virtues. Virtue is one indeed in the abstract; but, in fact, gentle and kind natures are not therefore heroic, and prudent and self-controlled minds need not be open-handed. At the utmost such virtue is one only *in posse;* as developed in the concrete, it takes the shape of species which in no sense imply each other.

So is it with Ratiocination; and as we should betake ourselves to Newton for physical, not for theological conclusions, and to Wellington for his military experience, not for statesmanship, so the maxim holds good generally, "Cuique in arte suâ credendum est:" or, to use the grand words of Aristotle, "We are bound to give heed to the undemonstrated sayings and opinions of the experienced and aged, not less than to demonstrations; because, from their having the eye of experience, they behold the principles of things."[1] Instead of trusting logical science, we must trust persons, namely, those who by long acquaintance with their subject have a right to judge. And if we wish ourselves to share in their convictions and the grounds of them, we must follow their history, and learn as they have learned. We must take up their particular subject as they took it up, beginning at the beginning, give ourselves to it, depend on practice and experience more than on reasoning, and thus gain that mental insight into truth, whatever its subject-matter may be, which our masters have gained before us. By following this course, we may make ourselves of their

[1] Eth. Nicom. vi. 11, fin.

number, and then we rightly lean upon ourselves, directing ourselves by our own moral or intellectual judgment, not by our skill in argumentation.

This doctrine, stated in substance as above, by the great philosopher of antiquity, is more fully expounded in a passage which he elsewhere quotes from Hesiod. "Best of all is he," says that poet, "who is wise by his own wit; next best he who is wise by the wit of others; but whoso is neither able to see, nor willing to hear, he is a good-for-nothing fellow." Judgment then in all concrete matter is the architectonic faculty; and what may be called the Illative Sense, or right judgment in ratiocination, is one branch of it.

CHAPTER IX

THE ILLATIVE SENSE

MY OBJECT IN THE FOREGOING PAGES has been, not to form a theory which may account for those phenomena of the intellect of which they treat, viz. those which characterize inference and assent, but to ascertain what is the matter of fact as regards them, that is, when it is that assent is given to propositions which are inferred, and under what circumstances. I have never had the thought of an attempt which in me would be ambitious, and which has failed in the hands of others, if that attempt may unfairly be called unsuccessful, which, though made by the acutest minds, has not succeeded in convincing opponents. Especially have I found myself unequal to antecedent reasonings in the instance of a matter of fact. There are those, who, arguing à priori, maintain, that, since experience leads by syllogism only to probabilities, certitude is ever a mistake. There are others, who, while they deny this conclusion, grant the à priori principle assumed in the argument, and in consequence are obliged, in order to vindicate the certainty of our knowledge, to have recourse to the hypothesis of intuitions, intellectual forms, and the like, which belong to us by nature, and may be considered to elevate our experience into something more than it is in itself. Earnestly maintaining, as I would, with this latter school of philosophers, the certainty of knowledge, I think it enough to appeal to the common voice of mankind in proof of it. That is to be accounted a normal operation of our nature, which men in general do actually instance. That is a law of our minds, which is exemplified in action on a large scale, whether à priori it ought to be a law or no. Our hoping is a proof that hope, as such, is not an extravagance; and our possession of certitude is a proof that it is not a weakness or an absurdity to be certain. How it comes about that we can be certain is not my business to determine; for me it is sufficient that certitude is felt. This is what the schoolmen, I believe, call treating a subject *in facto esse,* in contrast with *in fieri.* Had I attempted the latter, I should have been falling into metaphysics; but my aim is of a practical character, such as that of Butler in his *Analogy,* with this difference, that he treats of probability, doubt, expedience, and duty, whereas in these pages, without excluding, far from it, the question of duty, I would confine myself to the truth of things, and to the mind's certitude of that truth.

Certitude is a mental state: certainty is a quality of propositions. Those propositions I call certain, which are such that I am certain of them. Certitude is not a passive impression made upon the mind from without, by argumentative compulsion, but in all concrete questions (nay, even in abstract, for though the reasoning is abstract, the mind which judges of it is concrete) it is an active recognition of propositions as true, such as it is the duty of each individual himself to exercise at the bidding of reason, and, when reason forbids, to withhold. And reason never bids us be certain except on an absolute proof; and such a proof can never be furnished to us by the logic of words, for as certitude is of the mind, so is the act of inference which leads to it. Every one who reasons, is his own centre; and no expedient for attaining a common measure of minds can reverse this truth;—but then the question follows, is there any *criterion* of the accuracy of an act of inference, such as may be our warrant that certitude is rightly elicited in favour of the proposition inferred, since our warrant cannot, as I have said, be scientific? I have already said that the sole and final judgment on the validity of an inference in concrete matter is committed to the personal action of the ratiocinative faculty, the perfection or virtue of which I have called the Illative Sense, a use of the word "sense" parallel to our use of

it in "good sense," "common sense," à "sense of beauty," etc.:—
and I own I do not see any way to go farther than this in
answer to the question. However, I can at least explain my
meaning more fully; and therefore I will now speak, first of
the sanction of the Illative Sense, next of its nature, and then
of its range.

1

THE SANCTION OF THE ILLATIVE SENSE

WE ARE IN A WORLD OF FACTS, and we use them; for there is
nothing else to use. We do not quarrel with them, but
we take them as they are, and avail ourselves of what they
can do for us. It would be out of place to demand of fire, water,
earth, and air their credentials, so to say, for acting upon us,
or ministering to us. We call them elements, and turn them to
account, and make the most of them. We speculate on them at
our leisure. But what we are still less able to doubt about or
annul, at our leisure or not, is that which is at once their
counterpart and their witness, I mean, ourselves. We are conscious of the objects of external nature, and we reflect and act
upon them, and this consciousness, reflection, and action we
call our own rationality. And as we use the (so called) elements without first criticizing what we have no command over,
so is it much more unmeaning in us, to criticize or find fault
with our own nature, which is nothing else than we ourselves,
instead of using it according to the use of which it ordinarily
admits. Our being, with its faculties, mind and body, is a fact
not admitting of question, all things being of necessity referred
to it, not it to other things.

If I may not assume that I exist, and in a particular way,
that is, with a particular mental constitution, I have nothing to
speculate about, and had better let speculation alone. Such as
I am, it is my all; this is my essential stand-point, and must
be taken for granted; otherwise, thought is but an idle amusement, not worth the trouble. There is no medium between

using my faculties, as I have them, and flinging myself upon the external world according to the random impulse of the moment, as spray upon the surface of the waves, and simply forgetting that I am.

I am what I am, or I am nothing. I cannot think, reflect, or judge about my being, without starting from the very point which I aim at concluding. My ideas are all assumptions, and I am ever moving in a circle. I cannot avoid being sufficient for myself, for I cannot make myself any thing else, and to change me is to destroy me. If I do not use myself, I have no other self to use. My only business is to ascertain what I am, in order to put it to use. It is enough for the proof of the value and authority of any function which I possess, to be able to pronounce that it is natural. What I have to ascertain is the laws under which I live. My first elementary lesson of duty is that of resignation to the laws of my nature, whatever they are; my first disobedience is to be impatient at what I am, and to indulge an ambitious aspiration after what I cannot be, to cherish a distrust of my powers, and to desire to change laws which are identical with myself.

Truths such as these, which are too obvious to be called irresistible, are illustrated by what we see in universal nature. Every being is in a true sense sufficient for itself, so as to be able to fulfil its particular needs. It is a general law that, whatever is found as a function or an attribute of any class of beings, or is natural to it, is in its substance suitable to it, and subserves its existence, and cannot be rightly regarded as a fault or enormity. No being could endure, of which the constituent parts were at war with each other. And more than this; there is that principle of vitality in every being, which is of a sanative and restorative character, and which brings all its parts and functions together into one whole, and is ever repelling and correcting the mischiefs which befall it, whether from within or without, while showing no tendency to cast off its belongings as if foreign to its nature. The brute animals are found severally with limbs and organs, habits, instincts, appetites, surroundings, which play together for the safety and welfare of the whole; and, after all exceptions, may be said each of them to have, after its own kind, a perfection of nature. Man is the highest of the animals, and more indeed than an animal, as having a mind; that is, he has a complex nature different from theirs, with a higher aim and a specific perfection; but still the fact that other beings find their good in the use of their particular nature, is a reason for anticipating that to use duly our own is our interest as well as our necessity.

What is the peculiarity of our nature, in contrast with the inferior animals around us? It is that, though man cannot change what he is born with, he is a being of progress with relation to his perfection and characteristic good. Other beings are complete from their first existence, in that line of excellence which is allotted to them; but man begins with nothing realized (to use the word), and he has to make capital for himself by the exercise of those faculties which are his natural inheritance. Thus he gradually advances to the fulness of his original destiny. Nor is this progress mechanical, nor is it of necessity; it is committed to the personal efforts of each individual of the species; each of us has the prerogative of completing his inchoate and rudimental nature, and of developing his own perfection out of the living elements with which his mind began to be. It is his gift to be the creator of his own sufficiency; and to be emphatically self-made. This is the law of his being, which he cannot escape; and whatever is involved in that law he is bound, or rather he is carried on, to fulfil.

And here I am brought to the bearing of these remarks upon my subject. For this law of progress is carried out by means of the acquisition of knowledge, of which inference and assent are the immediate instruments. Supposing, then, the advancement of our nature, both in ourselves individually and as regards the human family, is to every one of us in his place a sacred duty, it follows that that duty is intimately bound up with the right use of these two main instruments of fulfilling it. And as we do not gain the knowledge of the law of progress by any *à priori* view of man, but by looking at it as the interpretation which is provided by himself on a large scale in the ordinary action of his intellectual nature, so too we must appeal to himself, as a fact, and not to any antecedent theory, in order to find what is the law of his mind as regards the two faculties in question. If then such an appeal does bear me out in deciding, as I have done, that the course of inference is ever more or less obscure, while assent is ever distinct and definite, and yet that what is in its nature thus absolute does, in fact, follow upon what in outward manifestation is thus complex, indirect, and recondite, what is left to us but to take things as they are, and to resign ourselves to what we find? that is, instead of devising, what cannot be, some sufficient science of reasoning, which may compel certitude in concrete conclusions, to confess that there is no ultimate test of truth besides the testimony borne to truth by the mind itself, and that this phenomenon, perplexing as we may find it, is a normal and inevitable characteristic of the mental constitution of a being like man on a stage such as the world. His progress is a living growth, not a mechanism; and its instruments are mental acts, not the formulas and contrivances of language.

We are accustomed in this day to lay great stress upon the harmony of the universe; and we have well learned the maxim so powerfully inculcated by our own English philosopher, that in our inquiries into its laws, we must sternly destroy all idols of the intellect, and subdue nature by co-operating with her. Knowledge is power, for it enables us to use eternal principles which we cannot alter. So also is it in that microcosm, the human mind. Let us follow Bacon more closely than to distort its faculties according to the demands of an ideal optimism, instead of looking out for modes of thought proper to our nature, and faithfully observing them in our intellectual exercises.

Of course I do not stop here. As the structure of the universe speaks to us of Him who made it, so the laws of the mind are the expression, not of mere constituted order, but of His will.

I should be bound by them even were they not His laws; but
since one of their very functions is to tell me of Him, they
throw a reflex light upon themselves, and, for resignation to
my destiny, I substitute a cheerful concurrence in an over-
ruling Providence. We may gladly welcome such difficulties
as are to be found in our mental constitution, and in the interaction of our faculties, if we are able to feel that He gave them
to us, and He can overrule them for us. We may securely take
them as they are, and use them as we find them. It is He who
teaches us all knowledge; and the way by which we acquire
it is His way. He varies that way according to the subject-
matter; but whether He has set before us in our particular
pursuit the way of observation or of experiment, of speculation
or of research, of demonstration or of probability, whether we
are inquiring into the system of the universe, or into the elements of matter and of life, or into the history of human
society and past times, if we take the way, proper to our subject-matter, we have His blessing upon us, and shall find, besides abundant matter for mere opinion, the materials in due
measure of proof and assent.

And especially, by this disposition of things, shall we learn,
as regards religious and ethical inquiries, how little we can
effect, however much we exert ourselves, without that blessing; for, as if on set purpose, He has made this path of thought
rugged and circuitous above other investigations, that the very
discipline inflicted on our minds in finding Him, may mould
them into due devotion to Him when He is found. "Verily
Thou art a hidden God, the God of Israel, the Saviour," is
the very law of His dealings with us. Certainly we need a clue
into the labyrinth which is to lead us to Him; and who among
us can hope to seize upon the true starting-points of thought
for that enterprise, and upon all of them, who is to understand
their right direction, to follow them out to their just limits,
and duly to estimate, adjust, and combine the various reasonings in which they issue, so as safely to arrive at what it is
worth any labour to secure, without a special illumination

from Himself? Such are the dealings of Wisdom with the elect
soul. "She will bring upon him fear, and dread, and trial; and
She will torture him with the tribulation of Her discipline, till
She try him by Her laws, and trust his soul. Then She will
strengthen him, and make Her way straight to him, and give
him joy."

2

THE NATURE OF THE ILLATIVE SENSE

IT IS THE MIND that reasons, and that controls its own reasonings, not any technical apparatus of words and propositions.
This power of judging and concluding, when in its perfection,
I call the Illative Sense, and I shall best illustrate it by referring to parallel faculties, which we commonly recognize without difficulty.

For instance, how does the mind fulfil its function of supreme direction and control, in matters of duty, social intercourse, and taste? In all of these separate actions of the intellect, the individual is supreme, and responsible to himself,
nay, under circumstances, may be justified in opposing himself to the judgment of the whole world; though he uses rules
to his great advantage, as far as they go, and is in consequence
bound to use them. As regards moral duty, the subject is fully
considered in the well-known treatises of Aristotle.[1] He calls
the faculty which guides the mind in matters of conduct, by
the name of *phronesis,* or judgment. This is the directing, controlling, and determining principle in such matters, personal
and social. What it is to be virtuous, how we are to gain the
just idea and standard of virtue, how we are to approximate

---

[1] Though Aristotle, in his Nicomachean Ethics, speaks of φρόνησις as
the virtue of the δοξαστικὸν generally, and as being concerned generally
with contingent matter (vi. 4), or what I have called the concrete, and
of its function being, as regards that matter, ἀληθεύειν τῷ καταφάναι ἤ
ἀποφάναι (*ibid.* 3), he does not treat of it in that work in its general
relation to truth and the affirmation of truth, but only as it bears upon
τὰ πρακτά.

in practice to our own standard, what is right and wrong in a particular case, for the answers in fulness and accuracy to these and similar questions, the philosopher refers us to no code of laws, to no moral treatise, because no science of life, applicable to the case of an individual, has been or can be written. Such is Aristotle's doctrine, and it is undoubtedly true. An ethical system may supply laws, general rules, guiding principles, a number of examples, suggestions, landmarks, limitations, cautions, distinctions, solutions of critical or anxious difficulties; but who is to apply them to a particular case? whither can we go, except to the living intellect, our own, or another's? What is written is too vague, too negative for our need. It bids us avoid extremes; but it cannot ascertain for us, according to our personal need, the golden mean. The authoritative oracle, which is to decide our path, is something more searching and manifold than such jejune generalizations as treatises can give, which are most distinct and clear when we least need them. It is seated in the mind of the individual, who is thus his own law, his own teacher, and his own judge in those special cases of duty which are personal to him. It comes of an acquired habit, though it has its first origin in nature itself, and it is formed and matured by practice and experience; and it manifests itself, not in any breadth of view, any philosophical comprehension of the mutual relations of duty towards duty, or any consistency in its teachings, but it is a capacity sufficient for the occasion, deciding what ought to be done here and now, by this given person, under these given circumstances. It decides nothing hypothetical, it does not determine what a man should do ten years hence, or what another should do at this time. It may indeed happen to decide ten years hence as it does now, and to decide a second case now as it now decides a first; still its present act is for the present, not for the distant or the future.

State or public law is inflexible, but this mental rule is not only minute and particular, but has an elasticity, which, in its application to individual cases, is, as I have said, not studious to maintain the appearance of consistency. In old times the mason's rule which was in use at Lesbos was, according to Aristotle, not of wood or iron, but of lead, so as to allow of its adjustment to the uneven surface of the stones brought together for the work. By such the philosopher illustrates the nature of equity in contrast with law, and such is that *phronesis,* from which the science of morals forms its rules, and receives its complement.

In this respect of course the law of truth differs from the law of duty, that duties change, but truths never; but, though truth is ever one and the same, and the assent of certitude is immutable, still the reasonings which carry us on to truth and certitude are many and distinct, and vary with the inquirer; and it is not with assent, but with the controlling principle in inferences that I am comparing *phronesis.* It is with this drift that I observe that the rule of conduct for one man is not always the rule for another, though the rule is always one and the same in the abstract, and in its principle and scope. To learn his own duty in his own case, each individual must have recourse to his own rule; and if his rule is not sufficiently developed in his intellect for his need, then he goes to some other living, present authority, to supply it for him, not to the dead letter of a treatise or a code. A living, present authority, himself or another, is his immediate guide in matters of a personal, social, or political character. In buying and selling, in contracts, in his treatment of others, in giving and receiving, in thinking, speaking, doing, and working, in toil, in danger, in his recreations and pleasures, every one of his acts, to be praiseworthy, must be in accordance with this practical sense. Thus it is, and not by science, that he perfects the virtues of justice, self-command, magnanimity, generosity, gentleness, and all others. *Phronesis* is the regulating principle of every one of them.

These last words lead me to a further remark. I doubt whether it is correct, strictly speaking, to consider this *phronesis* as a general faculty, directing and perfecting all the virtues at once. So understood, it is little better than an abstract term, including under it a circle of analogous faculties, severally proper to the separate virtues. Properly speaking, there are as many kinds of *phronesis* as there are virtues; for the judgment, good sense, or tact which is conspicuous in a man's conduct in one subject-matter, is not necessarily traceable in another. As in the parallel cases of memory and reasoning, he may be great in one aspect of his character, and little-minded in another. He may be exemplary in his family, yet commit a fraud on the revenue; he may be just and cruel, brave and sensual, imprudent and patient. And if this be true of the moral virtues, it holds good still more fully when we compare what is called his private character with his public. A good man may make a bad king; profligates have been great statesmen, or magnanimous political leaders.

So, too, I may go on to speak of the various callings and professions which give scope to the exercise of great talents, for these talents also are matured, not by mere rule, but by personal skill and sagacity. They are as diverse as pleading and cross-examining, conducting a debate in Parliament, swaying a public meeting, and commanding an army; and here, too, I observe that, though the directing principle in each case is called by the same name,—sagacity, skill, tact, or prudence, —still there is no one ruling faculty leading to eminence in all these various lines of action in common, but men will excel in one of them, without any talent for the rest.

The parallel may be continued in the case of the Fine Arts, in which, though true and scientific rules may be given, no one would therefore deny that Phidias or Rafael had a far more subtle standard of taste and a more versatile power of embodying it in his works, than any which he could communicate to others in even a series of treatises. And here again genius is indissolubly united to one definite subject-matter; a poet is not therefore a painter, or an architect a musical composer.

And so, again, as regards the useful arts and personal accomplishments, we use the same word "skill," but proficiency in engineering or in ship-building, or again in engraving, or again in singing, in playing instruments, in acting, or in gymnastic exercises, is as simply one with its particular subject-matter, as the human soul with its particular body, and is, in its own department, a sort of instinct or inspiration, not an obedience to external rules of criticism or of science.

It is natural, then, to ask the question, why ratiocination should be an exception to a general law which attaches to the intellectual exercises of the mind; why it is held to be commensurate with logical science; and why logic is made an instrumental art sufficient for determining every sort of truth, while no one would dream of making any one formula, however generalized, a working rule at once for poetry, the art of medicine, and political warfare?

This is what I have to remark concerning the Illative Sense, and in explanation of its nature and claims; and on the whole, I have spoken of it in four respects,—as viewed in itself, in its subject-matter, in the process it uses, and in its function and scope.

First, viewed in its exercise, it is one and the same in all concrete matters, though employed in them in different measures. We do not reason in one way in chemistry or law, in another in morals or religion; but in reasoning on any subject whatever, which is concrete, we proceed, as far indeed as we can, by the logic of language, but we are obliged to supplement it by the more subtle and elastic logic of thought; for forms by themselves prove nothing.

Secondly, it is in fact attached to definite subject-matters, so that a given individual may possess it in one department of thought, for instance, history, and not in another, for instance, philosophy.

Thirdly, in coming to its conclusion, it proceeds, always in the same way, by a method of reasoning, which as I have observed above, is the elementary principle of that mathematical calculus of modern times, which has so wonderfully extended the limits of abstract science.

Fourthly, in no class of concrete reasonings, whether in experimental science, historical research, or theology, is there any ultimate test of truth and error in our inferences besides the trustworthiness of the Illative Sense that gives them its sanction; just as there is no sufficient test of poetical excellence, heroic action, or gentlemanlike conduct, other than the particular mental sense, be it genius, taste, sense of propriety, or the moral sense, to which those subject-matters are severally committed. Our duty in each of these is to strengthen and perfect the special faculty which is its living rule, and in every case as it comes to do our best. And such also is our duty and our necessity, as regards the Illative Sense.

3

THE RANGE OF THE ILLATIVE SENSE

GREAT AS ARE THE SERVICES of language in enabling us to extend the compass of our inferences, to test their validity, and to communicate them to others, still the mind itself is more versatile and vigorous than any of its works, of which language is one, and it is only under its penetrating and subtle action that the margin disappears, which I have described as intervening between verbal argumentation and conclusions in the concrete. It determines what science cannot determine, the limit of converging probabilities and the reasons sufficient for a proof. It is the ratiocinative mind itself, and no trick of art, however simple in its form and sure in operation, by which we are able to determine, and thereupon to be certain, that a moving body left to itself will never stop, and that no man can live without eating.

Nor, again, is it by any diagram that we are able to scrutinize, sort, and combine the many premisses which must be first run together before we answer duly a given question. It is to the living mind that we must look for the means of using correctly principles of whatever kind, facts or doctrines, experiences or testimonies, true or probable, and of discerning what conclusion from these is necessary, suitable, or expedient, when they are taken for granted; and this, either by means of a natural gift, or from mental formation and practice and a long familiarity with those various starting-points. Thus, when Laud said that he did not see his way to come to terms with the Holy See, "till Rome was other than she was," no Catholic would admit the sentiment: but any Catholic may understand that this is just the judgment consistent with Laud's actual condition of thought and cast of opinions, his ecclesiastical position, and the existing state of England.

Nor, lastly, is an action of the mind itself less necessary in relation to those first elements of thought which in all reasoning are assumptions, the principles, tastes, and opinions, very often of a personal character, which are half the battle in the inference with which the reasoning is to terminate. It is the mind itself that detects them in their obscure recesses, illustrates them, establishes them, eliminates them, resolves them into simpler ideas, as the case may be. The mind contemplates them without the use of words, by a process which cannot be analyzed. Thus it was that Bacon separated the physical system of the world from the theological; thus that Butler connected together the moral system with the religious. Logical formulas could never have sustained the reasonings involved in such investigations.

Thus the Illative Sense, that is, the reasoning faculty, as exercised by gifted, or by educated or otherwise well-prepared minds, has its function in the beginning, middle, and end of all verbal discussion and inquiry, and in every step of the process. It is a rule to itself, and appeals to no judgment beyond its own; and attends upon the whole course of thought from antecedents to consequents, with a minute diligence and unwearied presence, which is impossible to a cumbrous apparatus of verbal reasoning, though, in communicating with others, words are the only instrument we possess, and a serviceable, though imperfect instrument.

One function indeed there is of Logic, to which I have referred in the preceding sentence, which the Illative Sense does not and cannot perform. It supplies no common measure between mind and mind, as being nothing else than a personal gift or acquisition. Few there are, as I said above, who are good reasoners on all subject-matters. Two men, who reason well each in his own province of thought, may, one or both of them, fail and pronounce opposite judgments on a question belonging to some third province. Moreover, all reasoning being from premises, and those premises arising (if it so happen) in their first elements from personal characteristics, in which men are in fact in essential and irremediable variance one with another, the ratiocinative talent can do no more than point out where the difference between them lies, how far it is immaterial, when it is worth while continuing an argument between them, and when not.

Now of the three main occasions of the exercise of the Illative Sense, which I have been insisting on, and which are the measure of its range, the start, the course, and the issue of an inquiry, I have already, in treating of Informal Inference, shown the place it holds in the final resolution of concrete questions. Here then it is left to me to illustrate its presence and action in relation to the elementary premises, and, again, to the conduct of an argument. And first of the latter.

1

There has been a great deal written of late years, on the subject of the state of Greece and Rome during the pre-historic period; let us say before the Olympiads in Greece, and the war with Pyrrhus in the annals of Rome. Now, in a question like this, it is plain that the inquirer has first of all to decide on the point from which he is to start in the presence of the received accounts; on what side, from what quarter he is to approach them; on what principles his discussion is to be conducted; what he is to assume, what opinions or objections he is summarily to put aside as nugatory, what arguments, and when, he is to consider as apposite, what false issues are to be avoided, when the state of his arguments is ripe for a conclusion. Is he to commence with absolutely discarding all that has hitherto been received; or to retain it in outline; or to make selections from it; or to consider and interpret it as mythical, or as allegorical; or to hold so much to be trustworthy, or at least of *primâ facie* authority, as he cannot actually disprove; or never to destroy except in proportion as he can construct? Then, as to the kind of arguments suitable or admissible, how far are tradition, analogy, isolated monuments and records, ruins, vague reports, legends, the facts or sayings of later times, language, popular proverbs, to tell in the inquiry? what are marks of truth, what of falsehood, what is probable, what suspicious, what promises well for discriminating facts from fictions? Then, arguments have to be balanced against each other, and then lastly the decision is to be made, whether any conclusion at all can be drawn, or whether any before certain issues are tried and settled, or whether a probable conclusion or a certain. It is plain how incessant will be the call here or there for the exercise of a definitive judgment, how little that judgment will be helped on by logic, and how intimately it will be dependent upon the intellectual complexion of the writer.

This might be illustrated at great length, were it necessary, from the writings of any of those able men, whose names are so well known in connexion with the subject I have instanced; such as Niebuhr, Mr. Clinton, Sir George Lewis, Mr. Grote, and Colonel Mure. These authors have severally views of their own on the period of history which they have selected for investigation, and they are too learned and logical not to know and to use to the utmost the testimonies by which the facts which they investigate are to be ascertained. Why then do they differ so much from each other, whether in their estimate of those testimonies or of those facts? because that estimate is simply their own, coming of their own judgment; and that judgment coming of assumptions of their own, explicit, or implicit; and those assumptions spontaneously issuing out of the state of thought respectively belonging to each of them; and all these successive processes of minute reasoning superintended and directed by an intellectual instrument far too subtle and spiritual to be scientific.

What was Niebuhr's idea of the office he had undertaken? I suppose it was to accept what he found in the historians of Rome, to interrogate it, to take it to pieces, to put it together again, to re-arrange and interpret it. Prescription together with internal consistency was to him the evidence of fact, and if he pulled down he felt he was bound to build up. Very different is the spirit of another school of writers, with whom prescription is nothing, and who will admit no evidence which has not first proved its right to be admitted. "We are able," says Niebuhr, "to trace the history of the Roman constitution back to the beginning of the Commonwealth, as accurately as we wish, and even more perfectly than the history of many portions of the middle ages." But "we may rejoice," says Sir George Lewis, "that the ingenuity or learning of Niebuhr should have enabled him to advance many noble hypotheses and conjectures respecting the form of the early constitution of Rome, but, unless he can support those hypotheses by sufficient evidence, they are not entitled to our belief." "Niebuhr," says a writer nearly related to myself, "often expresses much contempt for mere incredulous criticism and negative conclusions; .. yet wisely to disbelieve is our first grand requisite in dealings with materials of mixed worth." And Sir George Lewis again, "It may be said that there is scarcely any of the leading conclusions of Niebuhr's work which has not been impugned by some subsequent writer."

Again, "It is true," says Niebuhr, "that the Trojan war belongs to the region of fable, yet undeniably it has an historical foundation." But Mr. Grote writes, "If we are asked whether the Trojan war is not a legend . . raised upon a basis of truth, . . our answer must be, that, as the possibility of it cannot be denied, so neither can the reality of it be affirmed." On the other hand, Mr. Clinton lays down the general rule, "We may acknowledge as real persons, all those whom there is no reason for rejecting. The presumption is in favour of the early tradition, if no argument can be brought to overthrow it." Thus he lodges the *onus probandi* with those who impugn the received accounts; but Mr. Grote and Sir George Lewis throw it upon those who defend them. "Historical evidence," says the latter, "is founded on the testimony of credible witnesses." And again, "It is perpetually assumed in practice, that historical evidence is different in its nature from other sorts of evidence. This laxity seems to be justified by the doctrine of taking the best evidence which can be obtained. The object of [my] inquiry will be to apply to the early Roman history the same rules of evidence which are applied by common consent to modern history." Far less severe is the judgment of Colonel Mure: "Where no positive historical proof is affirmable, the balance of historical probability must reduce itself very much to a reasonable indulgence to the weight of national conviction, and a deference to the testimony of the earliest native authorities." "Reasonable indulgence" to popular belief, "deference" to ancient tradition, are principles of writing history abhorrent to the judicial temper of Sir George Lewis. He considers the words "reasonable indulgence" to be "ambiguous," and observes that "the very point which cannot be taken for granted, and in which writers differ, is, as to the extent to which contemporary attestation may be presumed without direct and positive proof, . . the extent to which the existence of a popular belief concerning a supposed matter of fact authorizes the inference that it grew out of authentic testimony." And Mr. Grote observes to the same effect: "The word *tradition* is an equivocal word, and begs the whole question. It is tacitly understood to imply a tale descriptive of some real matter of fact, taking rise at the time when the fact happened, originally accurate, but corrupted by oral transmission." And Lewis, who quotes the passage, adds, "This *tacit understanding* is the key-stone of the whole argument."

I am not contrasting these various opinions of able men, who have given themselves to historical research, as if it were any reflection on them that they differ from each other. It is the cause of their differing on which I wish to insist. Taking the facts by themselves, probably these authors would come to no conclusion at all; it is the "tacit understandings" which Mr. Grote speaks of, the vague and impalpable notions of "reasonableness" on his own side as well as on that of others, which both make conclusions possible, and are the pledge of their being contradictory. The conclusions vary with the particular writer, for each writes from his own point of view and with his own principles, and these admit of no common measure.

This in fact is their own account of the matter: "The results of speculative historical inquiry," says Colonel Mure, "can rarely amount to more than fair presumption of the reality of the events in question, as limited to their general substance, not as extending to their details. Nor can there consequently be expected in the minds of different inquirers any such unity regarding the precise degree of reality, as may frequently exist in respect to events attested by documentary evidence." Mr. Grote corroborates this decision by the striking instance of the diversity of existing opinions concerning the Homeric Poems. "Our means of knowledge," he says, "are so limited, that no one can produce arguments sufficiently cogent to contend against opposing preconceptions, and it creates a painful sensation of diffidence, when we read the expressions of equal and absolute persuasion with which the two opposite conclusions have both been advanced." And again, "there is a difference of opinion among the best critics, which is probably not destined to be adjusted, since so much depends partly upon critical feeling, partly upon the general reasonings in respect to ancient epical unity, with which a man sits down to the study." Exactly so; every one has his own "critical feeling," his antecedent "reasonings," and in consequence his own "absolute persuasion, coming in fresh and fresh at every turn of the discussion;" and who, whether stranger or friend, is to reach and affect what is so intimately bound up with the mental constitution of each?

Hence the categorical contradictions between one writer and another, which abound. Colonel Mure appeals in defence of an historical thesis to the "fact of the Hellenic confederacy combining for the adoption of a common national system of chronology in 776 B.C." Mr. Grote replies: "Nothing is more at variance with my conception,"—he just now spoke of the preconceptions of others,—"of the state of the Hellenic world in 776 B.C., than the idea of a combination among all the members of the race for any purpose, much more for the purpose of adopting a common national system of chronology." Colonel Mure speaks of the "bigoted Athenian public;" Mr. Grote replies that "no public ever less deserved the epithet of 'bigoted' than the Athenian." Colonel Mure also speaks of Mr. Grote's "arbitrary hypothesis;" and again (in Mr. Grote's words), of his "unreasonable scepticism." He cannot disprove by mere argument the conclusions of Mr. Grote; he can but have recourse to a personal criticism. He virtually says, "We differ in our personal view of things." Men become personal when logic fails; it is their mode of appealing to their own primary elements of thought, and their own illative sense, against the principles and the judgment of another.

I have already touched upon Niebuhr's method of investigation, and Sir George Lewis's dislike of it: it supplies us with as apposite an instance of a difference in first principles as is afforded by Mr. Grote and Colonel Mure. "The main characteristic of his history," says Lewis, "is the extent to which he relies upon internal evidence, and upon the indications afforded by the narrative itself, independently of the testimony of its truth." And, "ingenuity and labour can produce nothing but hypotheses and conjectures, which may be supported by analogies, but can never rest upon the solid foundation of proof." And it is undeniable, that, rightly or wrongly, disdaining the scepticism of the mere critic, Niebuhr does consciously proceed by the high path of divination. "For my own part," he says, "I *divine* that, since the censorship of Fabius and Decius falls in the same year, that Cn. Flavius became mediator between his own class and the higher orders." Lewis considers this to be a process of guessing; and says, "Instead of employing those tests of credibility which are consistently applied to modern history," Niebuhr, and his followers, and most of his opponents, "attempt to guide their judgment by the indication of internal evidence, and assume that the truth is discovered by an occult faculty of historical divination." Niebuhr defends himself thus: "The real geographer has a tact which determines his judgment and choice among different statements. He is able from isolated statements to draw inferences respecting things that are unknown, which are closely approximate to results obtained from observation of facts, and may supply their place. He is able with limited data to form an image of things which no eyewitness has described." He applies this to himself. The principle set forth in this passage is obviously the same as I should myself advocate; but Sir George Lewis, though not simply denying it as a principle, makes little account of it, when applied to historical research. "It is not enough," he says, "for an historian to claim the possession of a retrospective second-sight, which is denied to the rest of the world—of a mysterious doctrine, revealed only to the initiated." And he pronounces, that "the history of Niebuhr has opened more questions than it has closed, and it has set in motion a large body of combatants, whose mutual variances are not at present likely to be settled by deference to a common principle." [1]

[1] Niebuhr, "Roman History," vol. i. p. 177; vol. iii. pp. 262, 318, 322. "Lectures," vol. iii. App. p. xxii. Lewis, "Roman History," vol. i. pp. 11–17; vol. ii. pp. 489–492. F. W. Newman, "Regal Rome," p. v. Grote, "Greece," vol. ii. pp. 67, 68, 218, 630–639. Mure, "Greece," vol. iii. p. 503; vol. iv. p. 318. Clinton, ap. Grote, suprà.

We see from the above extracts how a controversy, such as that to which they belong, is carried on from starting-points, and with collateral aids, not formally proved, but more or less assumed, the process of assumption lying in the action of the Illative Sense, as applied to primary elements of thought respectively congenial to the disputants. Not that explicit argumentation on these minute or minor, though important, points is not sometimes possible to a certain extent; but, as I have said, it is too unwieldy an expedient for a constantly recurring need, even when it is tolerably exact.

2

And now secondly, as to the first principles themselves. In illustration, I will mention under separate heads some of those elementary contrarieties of opinion, on which the Illative Sense has to act, discovering them, following them out, defending or resisting them, as the case may be.

1. As to the statement of the case. This depends on the particular aspect under which we view a subject, that is, on the abstraction which forms our representative notion of what it is. Sciences are only so many distinct aspects of nature; sometimes suggested by nature itself, sometimes created by the mind. (1) One of the simplest and broadest aspects under which to view the physical world, is that of a system of final causes, or, on the other hand, of initial or effective causes. Bacon, having it in view to extend our power over nature, adopted the latter. He took firm hold of the idea of causation (in the common sense of the word) as contrasted to that of design, refusing to mix up the two ideas in one inquiry, and denouncing such traditional interpretations of facts, as did but obscure the simplicity of the aspect necessary for his purpose. He saw what others before him might have seen in what they saw, but who did not see as he saw it. In this achievement of intellect, which has been so fruitful in results, lie his genius and his fame.

(2) So again, to refer to a very different subject-matter,

we often hear of the exploits of some great lawyer, judge or advocate, who is able in perplexed cases, when common minds see nothing but a hopeless heap of facts, foreign or contrary to each other, to detect the principle which rightly interprets the riddle, and, to the admiration of all hearers, converts a chaos into an orderly and luminous whole. This is what is meant by originality in thinking: it is the discovery of an aspect of a subject-matter, simpler, it may be, and more intelligible than any hitherto taken.

(3) On the other hand, such aspects are often unreal, as being mere exhibitions of ingenuity, not of true originality of mind. This is especially the case in what are called philosophical views of history. Such seems to me the theory advocated in a work of great learning, vigour, and acuteness, Warburton's *Divine Legation of Moses*. I do not call Gibbon merely ingenious; still his account of the rise of Christianity is the mere subjective view of one who could not enter into its depth and power.

(4) The aspect under which we view things is often intensely personal; nay, even awfully so, considering that, from the nature of the case, it does not bring home its idiosyncrasy either to ourselves or to others. Each of us looks at the world in his own way, and does not know that perhaps it is characteristically his own. This is the case even as regards the senses. Some men have little perception of colours; some recognize one or two; to some men two contrary colours, as red and green, are one and the same. How poorly can we appreciate the beauties of nature, if our eyes discern, on the face of things, only an Indian-ink or a drab creation!

(5) So again, as regards form: each of us abstracts the relation of line to line in his own personal way,—as one man might apprehend a curve as convex, another as concave. Of course, as in the case of a curve, there may be a limit to possible aspects; but still, even when we agree together, it is not perhaps that we learn one from another, or fall under any law of agreement, but that our separate idiosyncrasies happen to

concur. I fear I may seem trifling, if I allude to an illustration which has ever had a great force with me, and that for the very reason it is so trivial and minute. Children, learning to read, are sometimes presented with the letters of the alphabet turned into the figures of men in various attitudes. It is curious to observe from such representations, how differently the shape of the letters strikes different minds. In consequence I have continually asked the question in a chance company, which way certain of the great letters look, to the right or the left; and whereas nearly every one present had his own clear view, so clear that he could not endure the opposite view, still I have generally found that one half of the party considered the letters in question to look to the left, while the other half thought they looked to the right.

(6) This variety of interpretation in the very elements of outlines seems to throw light upon other cognate differences between one man and another. If they look at the mere letters of the alphabet so differently, we may understand how it is they form such distinct judgments upon handwriting; nay, how some men may have a talent for deciphering from it the intellectual and moral character of the writer, which others have not. Another thought that occurs is, that perhaps here lies the explanation why it is that family likenesses are so variously recognized, and how mistakes in identity may be dangerously frequent.

(7) If we so variously apprehend the familiar objects of sense, still more various, we may suppose, are the aspects and associations attached by us, one with another, to intellectual objects. I do not say we differ in the objects themselves, but that we may have interminable differences as to their relations and circumstances. I have heard say (again to take a trifling matter) that at the beginning of this century, it was a subject of serious, nay, of angry controversy, whether it began with January 1800, or January 1801. Argument, which ought, if in any case, to have easily brought the question to a decision, was but sprinkling water upon a flame. I am not clear that, if

it could be fairly started now, it would not lead to similar results; certainly I know those who studiously withdraw from giving an opinion on the subject, when it is accidentally mooted, from their experience of the eager feeling which it is sure to excite in some one or other who is present. This eagerness can only arise from an overpowering sense that the truth of the matter lies in the one alternative, and not in the other.

These instances, because they are so casual, suggest how it comes to pass, that men differ so widely from each other in religious and moral perceptions. Here, I say again, it does not prove that there is no objective truth, because not all men are in possession of it; or that we are not responsible for the associations which we attach, and the relations which we assign, to the objects of the intellect. But this it does suggest to us, that there is something deeper in our differences than the accident of external circumstances; and that we need the interposition of a Power greater than human teaching and human argument to make our beliefs true and our minds one.

2. Next I come to the implicit assumption of definite propositions in the first start of a course of reasoning, and the arbitrary exclusion of others, of whatever kind. Unless we had the right, when we pleased, of ruling that propositions were irrelevant or absurd, I do not see how we could conduct an argument at all; our way would be simply blocked up by extravagant principles and theories, gratuitous hypotheses, false issues, unsupported statements, and incredible facts. There are those who have treated the history of Abraham as an astronomical record, and have spoken of our Adorable Saviour as the sun in *Aries*. Arabian Mythology has changed Solomon into a mighty wizard. Noah has been considered the patriarch of the Chinese people. The ten tribes have been pronounced still to live in their descendants, the Red Indians; or to be the ancestors of the Goths and Vandals, and thereby of the present European races. Some have conjectured that the Apollos of the Acts of the Apostles was Apollonius Tyaneus. Able men have reasoned out, almost against their will, that Adam was a

negro. These propositions, and many others of various kinds, we should think ourselves justified in passing over, if we were engaged in a work of sacred history; and there are others, on the contrary, which we should assume as true by our own right, and without notice, and without which we could not set about or carry on our work.

(1) However, the right of making assumptions has been disputed; but, when the objections are examined, I think they only go to show that we have no right in argument to make any assumption we please. Thus, in the historical researches which just now came before us, it seems fair to say that no testimony should be received, except such as comes from competent witnesses, while it is not unfair to urge, on the other side, that tradition, though unauthenticated, being (what is called) in possession, has a prescription in its favour, and may, *primâ facie*, or provisionally, be received. Here are the materials of a fair dispute; but there are writers who seem to have gone far beyond this reasonable scepticism, laying down as a general proposition that we have no right in philosophy to make any assumption whatever, and that we ought to begin with a universal doubt. This, however, is of all assumptions the greatest, and to forbid assumptions universally is to forbid this one in particular. Doubt itself is a positive state, and implies a definite habit of mind, and thereby necessarily involves a system of principles and doctrines all its own. Again, if nothing is to be assumed, what is our very method of reasoning but an assumption? and what our nature itself? The very sense of pleasure and pain, which is one of the most intimate portions of ourselves, inevitably translates itself into intellectual assumptions.

Of the two, I would rather have to maintain that we ought to begin with believing every thing that is offered to our acceptance, than that it is our duty to doubt of every thing. The former, indeed, seems the true way of learning. In that case, we soon discover and discard what is contradictory to itself; and error having always some portion of truth in it, and the truth having a reality which error has not, we may expect, that when there is an honest purpose and fair talents, we shall somehow make our way forward, the error falling off from the mind, and the truth developing and occupying it. Thus it is that the Catholic religion is reached, as we see, by inquirers from all points of the compass, as if it mattered not where a man began, so that he had an eye and a heart for the truth.

(2) An argument has been often put forward by unbelievers, I think by Paine, to this effect, that "a revelation, which is to be received as true, ought to be written on the sun." This appeals to the common-sense of the many with great force, and implies the assumption of a principle which Butler, indeed, would not grant, and would consider unphilosophical, and yet I think something may be said in its favour. Whether abstractedly defensible or not, Catholic populations would not be averse, *mutatis mutandis,* to admitting it. Till these last centuries, the Visible Church was, at least to her children, the light of the world, as conspicuous as the sun in the heavens; and the Creed was written on her forehead, and proclaimed through her voice, by a teaching as precise as it was emphatical; in accordance with the text, "Who is she that looketh forth at the dawn, fair as the moon, bright as the sun, terrible as an army set in array?" It was not, strictly speaking, a miracle, doubtless; but in its effect, nay, in its circumstances, it was little less. Of course I would not allow that the Church fails in this manifestation of the truth now, any more than in former times, though the clouds have come over the sun; for what she has lost in her appeal to the imagination, she has gained in philosophical cogency, by the evidence of her persistent vitality. So far is clear, that if Paine's aphorism has a *primâ facie* force against Christianity, it owes this advantage to the miserable deeds of the fifteenth and sixteenth centuries.

(3) Another conflict of first principles or assumptions, which have often been implicit on either side, has been carried through in our day, and relates to the end and scope of civil

society, that is, whether government and legislation ought to be of a religious character, or not; whether the state has a conscience; whether Christianity is the law of the land; whether the magistrate, in punishing offenders, exercises a retributive office or a corrective; or whether the whole structure of society is raised upon the base of secular expediency. The relation of philosophy and the sciences to theology comes into the question. The old time-honoured theory has, during the last forty years, been vigorously contending with the new; and the new is in the ascendant.

(4) There is another great conflict of first principles, and that among Christians, which has occupied a large space in our domestic history, during the last thirty or forty years, and that is the controversy about the Rule of Faith. I notice it as affording an instance of an assumption so deeply sunk into the popular mind, that it is a work of great difficulty to obtain from its maintainers an acknowledgment that it is an assumption. That Scripture is the Rule of Faith is in fact an assumption so congenial to the state of mind and course of thought usual among Protestants, that it seems to them rather a truism than a truth. If they are in controversy with Catholics on any point of faith, they at once ask, "Where do you find it in Scripture?" and if Catholics reply, as they must do, that it is not necessarily in Scripture in order to be true, nothing can persuade them that such an answer is not an evasion, and a triumph to themselves. Yet it is by no means self-evident that all religious truth is to be found in a number of works, however sacred, which were written at different times, and did not always form one book; and in fact it is a doctrine very hard to prove. So much so, that years ago, when I was considering it from a Protestant point of view, and wished to defend it to the best of my power, I was unable to give any better account of it than the following, which I here quote from it appositeness to my present subject.

"It matters not," I said, speaking of the first Protestants, "whether or not they only happened to come right on what, in a logical point of view, are faulty premisses. They had no time for theories of any kind; and to require theories at their hand argues an ignorance of human nature, and of the ways in which truth is struck out in the course of life. Common sense, chance, moral perception, genius, the great discoverers of principles do not reason. They have no arguments, no grounds, they see the truth, but they do not know how they see it; and if at any time they attempt to prove it, it is as much a matter of experiment with them, as if they had to find a road to a distant mountain, which they see with the eye; and they get entangled, embarrassed, and perchance overthrown in the superfluous endeavour. It is the second-rate men, though most useful in their place, who prove, reconcile, finish, and explain. Probably, the popular feeling of the sixteenth century saw the Bible to be the Word of God, so as nothing else is His Word, by the power of a strong sense, by a sort of moral instinct, or by a happy augury." [1]

That is, I considered the assumption as an act of the Illative Sense;—I should now add, the Illative Sense, acting on mistaken elements of thought.

3. After the aspects in which a question is to be viewed, and the principles on which it is to be considered, come the arguments by which it is decided; among these are antecedent reasons, which are especially in point here, because they are in great measure made by ourselves and belong to our personal character, and to them I shall confine myself.

Antecedent reasoning, when negative, is safe. Thus no one would say that, because Alexander's rash heroism is one of the leading characteristics of his history, therefore we are justified, except in writing a romance, in asserting that at a particular time and place, he distinguished himself by a certain exploit about which history is altogether silent; but, on the other hand, his notorious bravery would be almost decisive against any charge against him of having on a particular occasion acted as a coward.

[1] "Prophetical Office of the Church," pp. 347, 348, ed. 1837.

In like manner, good character goes far in destroying the force of even plausible charges. There is indeed a degree of evidence in support of an allegation, against which reputation is no defence; but it must be singularly strong to overcome an established antecedent probability which stands opposed to it. Thus historical personages or great authors, men of high and pure character, have had imputations cast upon them, easy to make, difficult or impossible to meet, which are indignantly trodden under foot by all just and sensible men, as being as anti-social as they are inhuman. I need not add what a cruel and despicable part a husband or a son would play, who readily listened to a charge against his wife or his father. Yet all this being admitted, a great number of cases remain which are perplexing, and on which we cannot adjust the claims of conflicting and heterogeneous arguments except by the keen and subtle operation of the Illative Sense.

Butler's argument in his *Analogy* is such a presumption used negatively. Objection being brought against certain characteristics of Christianity, he meets it by the presumption in their favour derived from their parallels as discoverable in the order of nature, arguing that they do not tell against the Divine origin of Christianity, unless they tell against the Divine origin of the natural system also. But he could not adduce it as a positive and direct proof of the Divine origin of the Christian doctrines that they had their parallels in nature, or at the utmost as more than a recommendation of them to the religious inquirer.

Unbelievers use the antecedent argument from the order of nature against our belief in miracles. Here, if they only mean that the fact of that system of laws, by which physical nature is governed, makes it antecedently improbable that an exception should occur in it, there is no objection to the argument; but if, as is not uncommon, they mean that the fact of an established order is absolutely fatal to the very notion of an exception, they are using a presumption as if it were a proof. They are saying,—What has happened 999 times one way cannot possibly happen on the 1000th time another way, *because* what has happened 999 times one way is likely to happen in the same way on the 1000th. But unlikely things do happen sometimes. If, however, they mean that the existing order of nature constitutes a physical necessity, and that a law is an unalterable fact, this is to assume the very point in debate, and is much more than asserting its antecedent probability.

Facts cannot be proved by presumptions, yet it is remarkable that in cases where nothing stronger than presumption was even professed, scientific men have sometimes acted as if they thought this kind of argument taken by itself decisive of a fact which was in debate. Thus in the controversy about the Plurality of worlds, it has been considered, on purely antecedent grounds, as far as I see, to be so necessary that the Creator should have filled with living beings the luminaries which we see in the sky, and the other cosmical bodies which we imagine there, as that it almost amounts to a blasphemy to doubt it.

Theological conclusions, it is true, have often been made on antecedent reasoning; but then it must be recollected that theological reasoning professes to be sustained by a more than human power, and to be guaranteed by a more than human authority. It may be true, also, that conversions to Christianity have often been made on antecedent reasons; yet, even admitting the fact, which is not quite clear, a number of antecedent probabilities, confirming each other, may make it a duty in the judgment of a prudent man, not only to act as if a statement were true, but actually to accept and believe it. This is not unfrequently instanced in our dealings with others, when we feel it right, in spite of our misgivings, to oblige ourselves to believe their honesty. And in all these delicate questions there is constant call for the exercise of the Illative Sense.

CHAPTER X

INFERENCE AND ASSENT IN THE
MATTER OF RELIGION

A ND NOW I HAVE COMPLETED my review of the second
subject to which I have given my attention in this Essay,
the connexion existing between the intellectual acts of
Assent and Inference, my first being the connexion of Assent
with Apprehension; and as I closed my remarks upon Assent
and Apprehension by applying the conclusions at which I
had arrived to our belief in the truths of Religion, so now I
ought to speak of its evidences, before quitting the consideration of the dependence of Assent upon Inference. I shall
attempt to do so in this Chapter, not without much anxiety,
lest I should injure so large, momentous, and sacred a subject
by a necessarily cursory treatment.

I begin with expressing a sentiment, which is habitually in
my thoughts, whenever they are turned to the subject of
mental or moral science, and which I am as willing to apply
here to the Evidences of Religion as it properly applies to
Metaphysics or Ethics, viz. that in these provinces of inquiry
egotism is true modesty. In religious inquiry each of us can
speak only for himself, and for himself he has a right to speak.
His own experiences are enough for himself, but he cannot
speak for others: he cannot lay down the law; he can only
bring his own experiences to the common stock of psychological facts. He knows what has satisfied and satisfies himself; if
it satisfies him, it is likely to satisfy others; if, as he believes
and is sure, it is true, it will approve itself to others also, for

there is but one truth. And doubtless he does find in fact, that, allowing for the difference of minds and of modes of speech, what convinces him, does convince others also. There will be very many exceptions, but these will admit of explanation. Great numbers of men refuse to inquire at all; they put the subject of religion aside altogether; others are not serious enough to care about questions of truth and duty and to entertain them; and to numbers, from their temper of mind, or the absence of doubt, or a dormant intellect, it does not occur to inquire why or what they believe; many, though they tried, would not be able to do so in any satisfactory way. This being the case, it causes no uneasiness to any one who honestly attempts to set down his own view of the Evidences of Religion, that at first sight he seems to be but one among many who are all in opposition to each other. But, however that may be, he brings together his reasons, and relies on them, because they are his own, and this is his primary evidence; and he has a second ground of evidence, in the testimony of those who agree with him. But his best evidence is the former, which is derived from his own thoughts; and it is that which the world has a right to demand of him; and therefore his true sobriety and modesty consists, not in claiming for his conclusions an acceptance or a scientific approval which is not to be found any where, but in stating what are personally his own grounds for his belief in Natural and Revealed Religion,— grounds which he holds to be so sufficient, that he thinks that others do hold them implicitly or in substance, or would hold them, if they inquired fairly, or will hold if they listen to him, or do not hold from impediments, invincible or not as it may be, into which he has no call to inquire. However, his own business is to speak for himself. He uses the words of the Samaritans to their countrywoman, when our Lord had remained with them for two days, "Now we believe, not for thy saying, for we have heard Him ourselves, and know that this is indeed the Saviour of the world."

In these words it is declared both that the Gospel Revelation is divine, and that it carries with it the evidence of its divinity; and this is of course the matter of fact. However, these two attributes need not have been united; a revelation might have been really given, yet given without credentials. Our Supreme Master might have imparted to us truths which nature cannot teach us, without telling us that He had imparted them, as is actually the case now, as regards heathen countries, into which portions of revealed truth overflow and penetrate, without their populations knowing whence those truths came. But the very idea of Christianity in its profession and history, is something more than this; it is a "Revelatio revelata;" it is a definite message from God to man distinctly conveyed by His chosen instruments, and to be received as such a message; and therefore to be positively acknowledged, embraced, and maintained as true, on the ground of its being divine, not as true on intrinsic grounds, not as probably true, or partially true, but as absolutely certain knowledge, certain in a sense in which nothing else can be certain, because it comes from Him who neither can deceive nor be deceived.

And the whole tenor of Scripture from beginning to end is to this effect: the matter of revelation is not a mere collection of truths, not a philosophical view, not a religious sentiment or spirit, not a special morality, poured out upon mankind as a stream might pour itself into the sea, mixing with the world's thought, modifying, purifying, invigorating it;—but an authoritative teaching, which bears witness to itself, and keeps itself together as one, in contrast to the assemblage of opinions on all sides of it, and speaks to all men, as being ever and every where one and the same, and claiming to be received intelligently, by all whom it addresses, as one doctrine, discipline, and devotion directly given from above. In consequence, the exhibition of credentials, that is, of evidence, that it is what it professes to be, is essential to Christianity, as it comes to us; for we are not left at liberty to pick and choose out of its contents according to our judgment, but must receive it all, as we find it, if we accept it at all. It is a religion in addition to the religion of nature; and as nature has an intrinsic claim upon us to be obeyed and used, so what is over and above nature, or supernatural, must also bring with it valid testimonials of its right to demand our homage.

Next, as to its relation to nature. As I have said, Christianity is simply an addition to it; it does not supersede or contradict it; it recognizes and depends on it, and that of necessity: for how possibly can it prove its claims except by an appeal to what men have already? be it ever so miraculous, it cannot dispense with nature; this would be to cut the ground from under it; for what would be the worth of evidences in favour of a revelation which denied the authority of that system of thought, and those courses of reasoning, out of which those evidences necessarily grew?

And in agreement with this obvious conclusion we find in Scripture our Lord and His Apostles always treating Christianity as the completion and supplement of Natural Religion, and of previous revelations; as when He says that the Father testified of Him; that not to know Him was not to know the Father; and as St. Paul at Athens appeals to the "Unknown God," and says that "He that made the world" "now declareth to all men to do penance, because He hath appointed a day to judge the world by the man whom He hath appointed." As then our Lord and His Apostles appeal to the God of Nature, we must follow them in that appeal; and, to do this with the better effect, we must first inquire into the chief doctrines and the grounds of Natural Religion.

1

NATURAL RELIGION

BY RELIGION I MEAN the Knowledge of God, of His Will, and of our duties towards Him; and there are three main channels which Nature furnishes for our acquiring this knowledge, viz. our own minds, the voice of mankind, and the course of the world, that is, of human life and human affairs. The informations which these three convey to us teach us the Being and Attributes of God, our responsibility to Him, our dependence on Him, our prospect of reward or punishment, to be somehow brought about, according as we obey or disobey Him. And the most authoritative of these three means of knowledge, as being specially our own, is our own mind, whose informations give us the rule by which we test, interpret, and correct what is presented to us for belief, whether by the universal testimony of mankind, or by the history of society and of the world.

Our great internal teacher of religion is, as I have said in an earlier part of this Essay, our Conscience.[1] Conscience is a personal guide, and I use it because I must use myself; I am as little able to think by any mind but my own as to breathe with another's lungs. Conscience is nearer to me than any other means of knowledge. And as it is given to me, so also is it given to others; and being carried about by every individual in his own breast, and requiring nothing besides itself, it is thus adapted for the communication to each separately of that knowledge which is most momentous to him individually,—adapted for the use of all classes and conditions of men, for high and low, young and old, men and women, independently of books, of educated reasoning, of physical knowledge, or of philosophy. Conscience, too, teaches us, not only that God is, but what He is; it provides for the mind a real image of Him, as a medium of worship; it gives us a rule of right and wrong, as being His rule, and a code of moral duties. Moreover, it is so constituted that, if obeyed, it becomes clearer in its injunctions, and wider in their range, and corrects and completes the accidental feebleness of its initial teachings. Conscience, then, considered as our guide, is fully furnished for its office. I say all this without entering into the question how far external assistances are in all cases necessary to the action of the mind, because in fact man does not live in isola-

[1] *Supra*, p. 80, etc. *Vide* also Univ. Serm. II. 7–13.

tion, but is every where found as a member of society. I am not concerned here with abstract questions.

Now conscience suggests to us many things about that Master, whom by means of it we perceive, but its most prominent teaching, and its cardinal and distinguishing truth, is that He is our Judge. In consequence, the special Attribute under which it brings Him before us, to which it subordinates all other Attributes, is that of justice—retributive justice. We learn from its informations to conceive of the Almighty, primarily, not as a God of Wisdom, of Knowledge, of Power, of Benevolence, but as a God of Judgment and Justice; as One who, not simply for the good of the offender, but as an end good in itself, and as a principle of government, ordains that the offender should suffer for his offence. If it tells us any thing at all of the characteristics of the Divine Mind, it certainly tells us this; and, considering that our shortcomings are far more frequent and important than our fulfilment of the duties enjoined upon us, and that of this point we are fully aware ourselves, it follows that the aspect under which Almighty God is presented to us by Nature, is (to use a figure) of One who is angry with us, and threatens evil. Hence its effect is to burden and sadden the religious mind, and is in contrast with the enjoyment derivable from the exercise of the affections, and from the perception of beauty, whether in the material universe or in the creations of the intellect. This is that fearful antagonism brought out with such soul-piercing reality by Lucretius, when he speaks so dishonourably of what he considers the heavy yoke of religion, and the "æternas pœnas in morte timendum;" and, on the other hand, rejoices in his "Alma Venus," "quæ rerum naturam sola gubernas." And we may appeal to him for the fact, while we repudiate his view of it.

Such being the *primâ facie* aspect of religion which the teachings of Conscience bring before us individually, in the next place let us consider what are the doctrines, and what the influences, as we find it embodied in those various rites and devotions which have taken root in the many races of mankind, since the beginning of history, and before history, all over the earth. Of these also Lucretius gives us a specimen; and they accord in form and complexion with that doctrine about duty and responsibility, which he so bitterly hates and loathes. It is scarcely necessary to insist, that wherever religion exists in a popular shape, it has almost invariably worn its dark side outwards. It is founded in one way or other on the sense of sin; and without that vivid sense it would hardly have any precepts or any observances. Its many varieties all proclaim or imply that man is in a degraded, servile condition, and requires expiation, reconciliation, and some great change of nature. This is suggested to us in the many ways in which we are told of a realm of light and a realm of darkness, of an elect fold and a regenerate state. It is suggested in the almost ubiquitous and ever-recurring institution of a Priesthood; for wherever there is a priest, there is the notion of sin, pollution, and retribution, as, on the other hand, of intercession and mediation. Also, still more directly, is the notion of our guilt impressed upon us by the doctrine of future punishment, and that eternal, which is found in mythologies and creeds of such various parentage.

Of these distinct rites and doctrines embodying the severe side of Natural Religion, the most remarkable is that of atonement, that is, "a substitution of something offered, or some personal suffering, for a penalty which would otherwise be exacted;" most remarkable, I say, both from its close connexion with the notion of vicarious satisfaction, and, on the other hand, from its universality. "The practice of atonement," says the author, whose definition of the word I have just given, "is remarkable for its antiquity and universality, proved by the earliest records that have come down to us of all nations, and by the testimony of ancient and modern travellers. In the oldest books of the Hebrew Scriptures, we have numerous instances of expiatory rites, where atonement is the prominent feature. At the earliest date, to which we can carry our inquiries by means of the heathen records, we meet with the same notion of atonement. If we pursue our inquiries through the accounts left us by the Greek and Roman writers of the barbarous nations with which they were acquainted, from India to Britain, we shall find the same notions and similar practices of atonement. From the most popular portion of our own literature, our narratives of voyages and travels, every one, probably, who reads at all will be able to find for himself abundant proof that the notion has been as permanent as it is universal. It shows itself among the various tribes of Africa, the islanders of the South Seas, and even that most peculiar race, the natives of Australia, either in the shape of some offering, or some mutilation of the person." [1]

These ceremonial acknowledgments, in so many distinct forms of worship, of the existing degradation of the human race, of course imply a brighter, as well as a threatening aspect of Natural Religion; for why should men adopt any rites of deprecation or of purification at all, unless they had some hope of attaining to a better condition than their present? Of this happier side of religion I will speak presently; here, however, a question of another kind occurs, viz. whether the notion of atonement can be admitted among the doctrines of Natural Religion,—I mean, on the ground that it is inconsistent with those teachings of Conscience, which I have recognized above, as the rule and corrective of every other information on the subject. If there is any truth brought home to us by conscience, it is this, that we are personally responsible for what we do, that we have no means of shifting our responsibility, and that dereliction of duty involves punishment; how, it may be asked, can acts of ours of any kind—how can even amendment of life—undo the past? And if even our own subsequent acts of obedience bring with them no promise of reversing what has once been committed, how can external rites, or the actions of another (as of a priest), be substitutes for that punishment which is the connatural fruit and intrinsic development of

[1] *Penny Cyclopædia,* art. "Atonement" (abridged).

violation of the sense of duty? I think this objection avails as far as this, that amendment is no reparation, and that no ceremonies or penances can in themselves exercise any vicarious virtue in our behalf; and that, if they avail, they only avail in the intermediate season of probation, that in some way we must make them our own, and that, when the time comes, which conscience forebodes, of our being called to judgment, then, at least, we shall have to stand in and by ourselves, whatever we shall have by that time become, and must bear our own burden. But it is plain that in this final account, as it lies between us and our Master, He alone can decide how the past and the present will stand together who is our Creator and our Judge.

In thus making it a necessary point to adjust the religions of the world with the intimations of our conscience, I am suggesting the reason why I confine myself to such religions as have had their rise in barbarous times, and do not recognize the religion of what is called civilization, as having legitimately a part in the delineation of Natural Religion. It may at first sight seem strange, that, considering I have laid such stress upon the progressive nature of man, I should take my ideas of his religion from his initial, and not his final testimony about its doctrines; and it may be urged that the religion of civilized times is quite opposite in character to the rites and traditions of barbarians, and has nothing of that gloom and sternness, on which I have insisted as their characteristic. Thus the Greek Mythology was for the most part cheerful and graceful, and its new gods certainly more genial and indulgent than the old ones. And, in like manner, the religion of philosophy is more noble and more humane than those primitive conceptions which were sufficient for early kings and warriors. But my answer to this objection is obvious: the progress of which man's nature is capable is a development, not a destruction of its original state; it must subserve the elements from which it proceeds, in order to be a true development and not a perversion.[1] And those popular rituals do in fact subserve and complete that nature with which man is born. It is otherwise with the religion of so-called civilization; such religion does but contradict the religion of barbarism; and since this civilization itself is not a development of man's whole nature, but mainly of the intellect, recognizing indeed the moral sense, but ignoring the conscience, no wonder that the religion in which it issues has no sympathy either with the hopes and fears of the awakened soul, or with those frightful presentiments which are expressed in the worship and traditions of the heathen. This artificial religion, then, has no place in the inquiry; first, because it comes of a one-sided progress of mind, and next, for the very reason that it contradicts informants which speak with greater authority than itself.

Now we come to the third natural informant on the subject of Religion; I mean the system and the course of the world. This established order of things, in which we find ourselves, if it has a Creator, must surely speak of His will in its broad outlines and its main issues. This principle being laid down as certain, when we come to apply it to things as they are, our first feeling is one of surprise and (I may say) of dismay, that His control of this living world is so indirect, and His action so obscure. This is the first lesson that we gain from the course of human affairs. What strikes the mind so forcibly and so painfully is, His absence (if I may so speak) from His own world.[2] It is a silence that speaks. It is as if others had got possession of His work. Why does not He, our Maker and Ruler, give us some immediate knowledge of Himself? Why does He not write His Moral Nature in large letters upon the face of history, and bring the blind, tumultuous rush of its events into a celestial, hierarchical order? Why does He not

[1] On these various subjects I have written in "University Sermons" (Oxford), No. vi. "Idea of a University," Disc. viii. "History of Turks," ch. iv. "Development of Doctrine," ch. i. sect. 3.

[2] *Vide* "Apologia," pp. 218-219.

grant us in the structure of society at least so much of a revelation of Himself as the religions of the heathen attempt to supply? Why from the beginning of time has no one uniform steady light guided all families of the earth, and all individual men, how to please Him? Why is it possible without absurdity to deny His will, His attributes, His existence? Why does He not walk with us one by one, as He is said to have walked with His chosen men of old time? We both see and know each other; why, if we cannot have the sight of Him, have we not at least the knowledge? On the contrary, He is specially "a Hidden God;" and with our best efforts we can only glean from the surface of the world some faint and fragmentary views of Him. I see only a choice of alternatives in explanation of so critical a fact:—either there is no Creator, or He has disowned His creatures. Are then the dim shadows of His Presence in the affairs of men but a fancy of our own, or, on the other hand, has He hid His face and the light of His countenance, because we have in some special way dishonoured Him? My true informant, my burdened conscience, gives me at once the true answer to each of these antagonist questions:—it pronounces without any misgiving that God exists:—and it pronounces too quite as surely that I am alienated from Him; that "His Hand is not shortened, but that our iniquities have divided between us and our God." Thus it solves the world's mystery, and sees in that mystery only a confirmation of its own original teaching.

Let us pass on to another great fact of experience, bearing on Religion, which confirms this testimony both of conscience and of the forms of worship which prevail among mankind;— I mean, the amount of suffering, bodily and mental, which is our portion in this life. Not only is the Creator far off, but some being of malignant nature seems, as I have said, to have got hold of us, and to be making us his sport. Let us say there are a thousand millions of men on the earth at this time; who can weigh and measure the aggregate of pain which this one generation has endured and will endure from birth to death?

Then add to this all the pain which has fallen and will fall upon our race through centuries past and to come. Is there not then some great gulf fixed between us and the good God? Here again the testimony of the system of nature is more than corroborated by those popular traditions about the unseen state, which are found in mythologies and superstitions, ancient and modern; for those traditions speak, not only of present misery, but of pain and evil hereafter, and even without end. But this dreadful addition is not necessary for the conclusion which I am here wishing to draw. The real mystery is, not that evil should never have an end, but that it should ever have had a beginning. Even a universal restitution could not undo what had been, or account for evil being the necessary condition of good. How are we to explain it, the existence of God being taken for granted, except by saying that another will, besides His, has had a part in the disposition of His work, that there is a quarrel without remedy, a chronic alienation, between God and man?

I have implied that the laws on which this world is governed do not go so far as to prove that evil will never die out of the creation; nevertheless, they look in that direction. No experience indeed of life can assure us about the future, but it can and does give us means of conjecturing what is likely to be; and those conjectures coincide with our natural forebodings. Experience enables us to ascertain the moral constitution of man, and thereby to presage his future from his present. It teaches us, first, that he is not sufficient for his own happiness, but is dependent upon the sensible objects which surround him, and that these he cannot take with him when he leaves the world; secondly, that disobedience to his sense of right is even by itself misery, and that he carries that misery about him, wherever he is, though no divine retribution followed upon it; and thirdly, that he cannot change his nature and his habits by wishing, but is simply himself, and will ever be himself and what he now is, wherever he is, as long as he continues to be,—or at least that pain has no natural tendency to make him other than he is, and that the longer he lives, the more difficult he is to change. How can we meet these not irrational anticipations, except by shutting our eyes, turning away from them, and saying that we have no call, no right, to think of them at present, or to make ourselves miserable about what is not certain, and may be not true? [1]

Such is the severe aspect of Natural Religion: also it is the most prominent aspect, because the multitude of men follow their own likings and wills, and not the decisions of their sense of right and wrong. To them Religion is a mere yoke, as Lucretius describes it; not a satisfaction or refuge, but a terror and a superstition. However, I must not for an instant be supposed to mean, that this is its only, its chief, or its legitimate aspect. All Religion, so far as it is genuine, is a blessing, Natural as well as Revealed. I have insisted on its severe aspect in the first place, because, from the circumstances of human nature, though not by the fault of Religion, such is the shape in which we first encounter it. Its large and deep foundation is the sense of sin and guilt, and without this sense there is for man, as he is, no genuine religion. Otherwise, it is but counterfeit and hollow; and that is the reason why this so-called religion of civilization and philosophy is so great a mockery. However, true as this judgment is which I pass on philosophical religion, and troubled as are the existing relations between God and man, as both the voice of mankind and the facts of Divine Government testify, equally true are other general laws which govern those relations, and they speak another language, and compensate for what is stern in the teaching of nature, without tending to deny that sternness.

The first of these laws, relieving the aspect of Natural Religion, is the very fact that religious beliefs and institutions, of some kind or other, are of such general acceptance in all times and places. Why should men subject themselves to the tyranny which Lucretius denounces, unless they had either experience or hope of benefits to themselves by so doing?

[1] *Vide* "Calista," ch. xix.

Though it be mere hope of benefits, that alone is a great alleviation of the gloom and misery which their religious rites presuppose or occasion; for thereby they have a prospect, more or less clear, of some happier state in reserve for them, or at least the chances of it. If they simply despaired of their fortunes, they would not care about religion. And hope of future good, as we know, sweetens all suffering.

Moreover, they have an earnest of that future in the real and recurring blessings of life, the enjoyment of the gifts of the earth, and of domestic affection and social intercourse, which is sufficient to affect and subdue even the most guilty of men in his better moments, reminding him that he is not utterly cast off by Him whom nevertheless he is not given to know. Or, in the Apostle's words, though the Creator once "suffered all nations to walk in their own ways," still, "He left not Himself without testimony, doing good from heaven, giving rains and fruitful seasons, filling our hearts with food and gladness."

Nor are these blessings of physical nature the only tokens in the Divine System, which in that heathen time, and indeed in every age, bring home to our experience the fact of a Good God, in spite of the tumult and confusion of the world. It is possible to give an interpretation to the course of things, by which every event or occurrence in its order becomes providential: and though that interpretation does not hold good unless the world is contemplated from a particular point of view, in one given aspect, and with certain inward experiences, and personal first principles and judgments, yet these may be fairly pronounced to be common conditions of human thought, that is, till they are wilfully or accidentally lost; and they issue in fact, in leading the great majority of men to recognize the Hand of unseen power, directing in mercy or in judgment the physical and moral system. In the prominent events of the world, past and contemporary, the fate, evil or happy, of great men, the rise and fall of states, popular revolutions, decisive battles, the migration of races, the replenishing of the earth, earthquakes and pestilences, critical discoveries and inventions, the history of philosophy, the advancement of knowledge, in these the spontaneous piety of the human mind discerns a Divine Supervision. Nay, there is a general feeling, originating directly in the workings of conscience, that a similar governance is extended over the persons of individuals, who thereby both fulfil the purposes and receive the just recompenses of an Omnipotent Providence. Good to the good, and evil to the evil, is instinctively felt to be, even from what we see, amid whatever obscurity and confusion, the universal rule of God's dealings with us. Hence come the great proverbs, indigenous in both Christian and heathen nations, that punishment is sure, though slow, that murder will out, that treason never prospers, that pride will have a fall, that honesty is the best policy, and that curses fall on the heads of those who utter them. To the unsophisticated apprehension of the many, the successive passages of life, social, or political, are so many miracles, if that is to be accounted miraculous which brings before them the immediate Divine Presence; and should it be objected that this is an illogical exercise of reason, I answer, that since it actually brings them to a right conclusion, and was intended to bring them to it, if logic finds fault with it, so much the worse for logic.

Again, prayer is essential to religion, and, where prayer is, there is a natural relief and solace in all trouble, great or ordinary: now prayer is not less general in mankind at large than is faith in Providence. It has ever been in use, both as a personal and as a social practice. Here again, if, in order to determine what the Religion of Nature is, we may justly have recourse to the spontaneous acts and proceedings of our race, as viewed on a large field, we may safely say that prayer, as well as hope, is a constituent of man's religion. Nor is it a fair objection to this argument, to say that such prayers and rites as have obtained in various places and times, are in their character, object, and scope inconsistent with each other; because their contrarieties do not come into the idea of re-

ligion, as such, at all, and the very fact of their discordance
destroys their right to be taken into account, so far as they are
discordant; for what is not universal has no claim to be considered natural, right, or of divine origin. Thus we may
determine prayer to be part of Natural Religion, from such
instances of the usage as are supplied by the priests of Baal
and by dancing Dervishes, without therefore including in our
notions of prayer the frantic excesses of the one, or the artistic
spinning of the other, or sanctioning their respective objects
of belief, Baal or Mahomet.

As prayer is the voice of man to God, so Revelation is the
voice of God to man. Accordingly, it is another alleviation of
the darkness and distress which weigh upon the religions of
the world, that in one way or other such religions are founded
on some idea of express revelation, coming from the unseen
agents whose anger they deprecate; nay, that the very rites
and observances, by which they hope to gain the favour of
these beings, are by these beings themselves communicated
and appointed. The Religion of Nature has not been a deduction of reason, or the joint, voluntary manifesto of a multitude
meeting together and pledging themselves to each other, as
men move resolutions now for some political or social purpose,
but it has been a tradition or an interposition vouchsafed to a
people from above. To such an interposition men even
ascribed their civil polity or citizenship, which did not orig-
inate in any plebiscite, but in *dii minores* or heroes, and was
inaugurated with portents or palladia, and protected and
prospered by oracles and auguries. Here is an evidence, too,
how congenial the notion of a revelation is to the human mind,
so that the expectation of it may truly be considered an
integral part of Natural Religion.

Among the observances imposed by these professed revelations, none is more remarkable, or more general, than the rite
of sacrifice, in which guilt was removed or blessing gained by
an offering, which availed instead of the merits of the offerer.
This too, as well as the notion of divine interpositions, may be

considered almost an integral part of the Religion of Nature and an alleviation of its gloom. But it does not stand by itself; I have already spoken of the doctrine of atonement, under which it falls, and which, if what is universal is natural, enters into the idea of religious service. And what the nature of man suggests, the providential system of the world sanctions by enforcing. It is the law, or the permission, given to our whole race, to use the Apostle's words, to "bear one another's burdens;" and this, as I said when on the subject of Atonement, is quite consistent with his antithesis that "every one must bear his own burden." The final burden of responsibility when we are called to judgment is our own; but among the media by which we are prepared for that judgment are the exertions and pains taken in our behalf by others. On this vicarious principle, by which we appropriate to ourselves what others do for us, the whole structure of society is raised. Parents work and endure pain, that their children may prosper; children suffer for the sin of their parents, who have died before it bore fruit. "Delirant reges, plectuntur Achivi." Sometimes it is a compulsory, sometimes a willing mediation. The punishment which is earned by the husband falls upon the wife; the benefits in which all classes partake are wrought out by the unhealthy or dangerous toil of the few. Soldiers endure wounds and death for those who sit at home; and ministers of state fall victims to their zeal for their countrymen, who do little else than criticize their actions. And so in some measure or way this law embraces all of us. We all suffer for each other, and gain by each other's sufferings; for man never stands alone here, though he will stand by himself one day hereafter; but here he is a social being, and goes forward to his long home as one of a large company.

Butler, it need scarcely be said, is the great master of this doctrine, as it is brought out in the system of nature. In answer to the objection to the Christian doctrine of satisfaction, that it "represents God as indifferent whether He punishes the innocent or the guilty," he observes that "the world is a constitution or system, whose parts have a mutual reference to each other; and that there is a scheme of things gradually carrying on, called the course of nature, to the carrying on of which God has appointed us, in various ways, to contribute. And in the daily course of natural providence, it is appointed that innocent people should suffer for the faults of the guilty. Finally, indeed and upon the whole, every one shall receive according to his personal deserts; but during the progress, and, for aught we know, even in order to the completion of this moral scheme, vicarious punishments may be fit, and absolutely necessary. We see in what variety of ways one person's sufferings contribute to the relief of another; and being familiarized to it, men are not shocked with it. So the reason of their insisting on objections against the [doctrine of] satisfaction is, either that they do not consider God's settled and uniform appointments as His appointments at all; or else they forget that vicarious punishment is a providential appointment of every day's experience." [1] I will but add, that, since all human suffering is in its last resolution the punishment of sin, and punishment implies a Judge and a rule of justice, he who undergoes the punishment of another in his stead may be said in a certain sense to satisfy the claims of justice towards that other in his own person.

One concluding remark has to be made here. In all sacrifices it was especially required that the thing offered should be something rare, and unblemished; and in like manner in all atonements and all satisfactions, not only was the innocent taken for the guilty, but it was a point of special importance that the victim should be spotless, and the more manifest that spotlessness, the more efficacious was the sacrifice. This leads me to a last principle which I shall notice as proper to Natural Religion, and as lightening the prophecies of evil in which it is founded; I mean the doctrine of meritorious intercession. The man in the Gospel did but speak for the human race every where, when he said, "God heareth not sinners; but if a man

[1] "Analogy," Pt. ii. ch. 5 (abridged).

be a worshipper of God, and doth His will, him He heareth."
Hence every religion has had its eminent devotees, exalted
above the body of the people, mortified men, brought nearer
to the Source of good by austerities, self-inflictions, and
prayer, who have influence with Him, and extend a shelter
and gain blessings for those who become their clients. A belief
like this has been, of course, attended by numberless superstitions; but those superstitions vary with times and places,
and the belief itself in the mediatorial power of the good and
holy has been one and the same every where. Nor is this belief an idea of past times only or of heathen countries. It is
one of the most natural visions of the young and innocent. And
all of us, the more keenly we feel our own distance from holy
persons, the more are we drawn near to them, as if forgetting
that distance, and proud of them because they are so unlike
ourselves, as being specimens of what our nature may be, and
with some vague hope that we, their relations by blood, may
profit in our own persons by their holiness.

Such, then, in outline is that system of natural beliefs and
sentiments, which, though true and divine, is still possible to
us independently of Revelation, and is the preparation for it;
though in Christians themselves it cannot really be separated
from their Christianity, and never is possessed in its higher
forms in any people without some portion of those inward aids
which Christianity imparts to us, and those endemic traditions
which have their first origin in a paradisiacal illumination.

2

REVEALED RELIGION

IN DETERMINING, as above, the main features of Natural Religion, and distinguishing it from the religion of philosophy
or civilization, I may be accused of having taken a course of
my own, for which I have no sufficient warrant. Such an accus-
ation does not give me much concern. Every one who thinks

on these subjects takes a course of his own, though it will also happen to be the course which others take besides himself. The minds of many separately bear them forward in the same direction, and they are confirmed in it by each other. This I consider to be my own case; if I have mis-stated or omitted notorious facts in my account of Natural Religion, if I have contradicted or disregarded any thing which He who speaks through my conscience has told us all directly from Heaven, then indeed I have acted unjustifiably and have something to unsay; but, if I have done no more than view the notorious facts of the case in the medium of my primary mental experiences, under the aspects which they spontaneously present to me, and with the aid of my best illative sense, I only do on one side of the question what those who think differently do on the other. As they start with one set of first principles, I start with another. I gave notice just now that I should offer my own witness in the matter in question; though of course it would not be worth while my offering it, unless what I felt myself agreed with what is felt by hundreds and thousands besides me, as I am sure it does, whatever be the measure, more or less, of their explicit recognition of it.

In thus speaking of Natural Religion as in one sense a matter of private judgment, and that with a view of proceeding from it to the proof of Christianity, I seem to give up the intention of demonstrating either. Certainly I do; not that I deny that demonstration is possible. Truth certainly, as such, rests upon grounds intrinsically and objectively and abstractedly demonstrative, but it does not follow from this that the arguments producible in its favour are unanswerable and irresistible. These latter epithets are relative, and bear upon matters of fact; arguments in themselves ought to do, what perhaps in the particular case they cannot do. The fact of revelation is in itself demonstrably true, but it is not therefore true irresistibly; else, how comes it to be resisted? There is a vast distance between what it is in itself, and what it is to us. Light is a quality of matter, as truth is of Christianity; but light is

not recognized by the blind, and there are those who do not
recognize truth, from the fault, not of truth, but of themselves.
I cannot convert men, when I ask for assumptions which they
refuse to grant me; and without assumptions no one can prove
any thing about any thing.

I am suspicious then of scientific demonstrations in a question of concrete fact, in a discussion between fallible men.
However, let those demonstrate who have the gift; "unusquis-
que in suo sensu abundet." For me, it is more congenial to my
own judgment to attempt to prove Christianity in the same
informal way in which I can prove for certain that I have been
born into this world, and that I shall die out of it. It is pleasant to my own feelings to follow a theological writer, such as
Amort, who has dedicated to the great Pope, Benedict XIV.,
what he calls "a new, modest, and easy way of demonstrating
the Catholic Religion." In this work he adopts the argument
merely of the *greater* probability; [1] I prefer to rely on that of
an *accumulation* of various probabilities; but we both hold
(that is, I hold with him), that from probabilities we may
construct legitimate proof, sufficient for certitude. I follow him

[1] "Scopus operis est, planiorem Protestantibus aperire viam ad veram
Ecclesiam. Cùm enim hactenus Polemici nostri insudarint toti in
demonstrandis singulis Religionis Catholicæ articulis, in id ego unum
incumbo, ut hæc tria evincam. Primo: Articulos fundamentales Religionis Catholicæ esse evidenter credibiliores oppositis, &c. &c. . . . .
Demonstratio autem hujus novæ modestæ, ac facilis viæ, quâ ex articulis
fundamentalibus solùm probabilioribus adstruitur summa Religionis
certitudo, hæc est: Deus, cùm sit sapiens ac providus, tenetur, Religionem à se revelatam reddere evidenter credibiliorem religionibus falsis.
Imprudenter enim vellet, suam Religionem ab hominibus recipi, nisi
eam redderet evidenter credibiliorem religionibus cæteris. Ergo illa
religio, quæ est evidenter credibilior cæteris, est ipsissima religio a Deo
revelata, adeoque certissimè vera, seu demonstrata. Atqui, &c. . . . .
Motivum aggrediendi novam hanc, modestam, ac facilem viam illud
præcipuum est, quòd observem, Protestantium plurimos post innumeros
concertationum fluctus, in iis tandem consedisse syrtibus, ut credant,
nullam dari religionem undequaque demonstratam, &c. . . . Ratiociniis
denique opponunt ratiocinia; præjudiciis præjudicia ev majoribus
sua," &c.

in holding, that since a Good Providence watches over us, He blesses such means of argument as it has pleased Him to give us, in the nature of man and of the world, if we use them duly for those ends for which He has given them; and that, as in mathematics we are justified by the dictate of nature in withholding our assent from a conclusion of which we have not yet a strict logical demonstration, so by a like dictate we are not justified, in the case of concrete reasoning and especially of religious inquiry, in waiting till such logical demonstration is ours, but on the contrary are bound in conscience to seek truth and to look for certainty by modes of proof, which, when reduced to the shape of formal propositions, fail to satisfy the severe requisitions of science.[1]

Here then at once is one momentous doctrine or principle, which enters into my own reasoning, and which another ignores, viz. the providence and intention of God; and of course there are other principles, explicit or implicit, which are in like circumstances. It is not wonderful then, that, while I can prove Christianity divine to my own satisfaction, I shall not be able to force it upon any one else. Multitudes indeed I ought to succeed in persuading of its truth without any force at all, because they and I start from the same principles, and what is a proof to me is a proof to them; but if any one starts from any other principles but ours, I have not the power to change

---

[1] "Docet naturalis ratio, Deum, ex ipsâ naturâ bonitatis ac providentiæ suæ, si velit in mundo habere religionem puram, eamque instituerc ac conservare usque in finem mundi, teneri ad eam religionem reddendam evidenter credibiliorem ac verisimiliorem cæteris, &c. &c. . . . Ex hoc sequitur ulterius; certitudinem moralem de verâ Ecclesiâ elevari posse ad certitudinem metaphysicam, si homo advertat, certitudinem moralem absolutè fallibilem substare in materiâ religionis circa ejus constitutiva fundamentalia speciali providentiæ divinæ, præservatrici ab omni errore. . . . . Itaque homo semel ex serie historicâ actorum perductus ad moralem certitudinem de auctore, fundatione, propagatione, et continuatione Ecclesiæ Christianæ, per reflexionem ad existentiam certissimam providentiæ divinæ in materiâ religionis, à priori lumine naturæ certitudine metaphysicâ notam, eo ipso eadem infallibili certitudine intelliget, argumenta de acutore, &c."—Amort. Ethica Christiana, p. 252.

his principles or the conclusion which he draws from them, any more than I can make a crooked man straight. Whether his mind will ever grow straight, whether I can do any thing towards its becoming straight, whether he is not responsible, responsible to his Maker, for being mentally crooked, is another matter; still the fact remains, that in any inquiry about things in the concrete men differ from each other, not so much in the soundness of their reasoning as in the principles which govern its exercise, that those principles are of a personal character, that where there is no common measure of minds, there is no common measure of arguments, and that the validity of proof is determined, not by any scientific test, but by the illative sense.

Accordingly, instead of saying that the truths of Revelation depend on those of Natural Religion, it is more pertinent to say that belief in revealed truths depends on belief in natural. Belief is a state of mind; belief generates belief; states of mind correspond to each other; the habits of thought and the reasonings which lead us on to a higher state of belief than our present, are the very same which we already possess in connexion with the lower state. Those Jews became Christians in Apostolic times who were already what may be called crypto-Christians; and those Christians in this day remain Christian only in name, and (if it so happen) at length fall away, who are nothing deeper or better than men of the world, *savants*, literary men, or politicians.

That a special preparation of mind is required for each separate department of inquiry and discussion (excepting, of course, that of abstract science) is strongly insisted upon in well-known passages of the *Nicomachean Ethics*. Speaking of the variations which are found in the logical perfection of proof in various subject-matters, Aristotle says, "A well-educated man will expect exactness in every class of subject, according as the nature of the thing admits; for it is much the same mistake to put up with a mathematician using probabilities, and to require demonstration of an orator. Each man judges skilfully in those things about which he is well-informed; it is of these that he is a good judge; viz. he, in each subject-matter, is a judge, who is well-educated in that subject-matter, and he is in an absolute sense a judge, who is in all of them well-educated." Again: "Young men come to be mathematicians and the like, but they cannot possess practical judgment; for this talent is employed upon individual facts, and these are learned only by experience; and a youth has not experience, for experience is only gained by a course of years. And so, again, it would appear that a boy may be a mathematician, but not a philosopher, or learned in physics, and for this reason,—because the one study deals with abstractions, while the other studies gain their principles from experience, and in the latter subjects youths do not give assent, but make assertions, but in the former they know what it is that they are handling."

These words of a heathen philosopher, laying down broad principles about all knowledge, express a general rule, which in Scripture is applied authoritatively to the case of revealed knowledge in particular;—and that not once or twice only, but continually, as is notorious. For instance:—"I have understood," say the Psalmist, "more than all my teachers, because Thy testimonies are my meditation." And so our Lord: "He that hath ears, let him hear." "If any man will do His will, He shall know of the doctrine." And "He that is of God, heareth the words of God." Thus too the Angels at the Nativity announce "Peace to men of good will." And we read in the Acts of the Apostles of "Lydia, whose heart the Lord opened to attend to those things which were said by Paul." And we are told on another occasion, that "as many as were ordained," or disposed by God, "to life everlasting, believed." And St. John tells us, "He that knoweth God, heareth us; he that is not of God, heareth us not; by this we know the spirit of truth, and the spirit of error."

1

Relying then on these authorities, human and Divine, I have no scruple in beginning the review I shall take of Christianity by professing to consult for those only whose minds are properly prepared for it; and by being prepared, I mean to denote those who are imbued with the religious opinions and sentiments which I have identified with Natural Religion. I do not address myself to those, who in moral evil and physical see nothing more than imperfections of a parallel nature; who consider that the difference in gravity between the two is one of degree only, not of kind; that moral evil is merely the offspring of physical, and that as we remove the latter so we inevitably remove the former; that there is a progress of the human race which tends to the annihilation of moral evil; that knowledge is virtue, and vice is ignorance; that sin is a bugbear, not a reality; that the Creator does not punish except in the sense of correcting; that vengeance in Him would of necessity be vindictiveness; that all that we know of Him, be it much or little, is through the laws of nature; that miracles are impossible; that prayer to Him is a superstition; that the fear of Him is unmanly; that sorrow for sin is slavish and abject; that the only intelligible worship of Him is to act well our part in the world, and the only sensible repentance to do better in future; that if we do our duties in this life, we may take our chance for the next; and that it is of no use perplexing our minds about the future state, for it is all a matter of guess. These opinions characterize a civilized age; and if I say that I will not argue about Christianity with men who hold them, I do so, not as claiming any right to be impatient or peremptory with any one, but because it is plainly absurd to attempt to prove a second proposition to those who do not admit the first.

I assume then that the above system of opinion is simply false, inasmuch as it contradicts the primary teachings of nature in the human race, wherever a religion is found and its workings can be ascertained. I assume the Presence of God in our conscience, and the universal experience, as keen as our experience of bodily pain, of what we call a sense of sin, or guilt. This sense of sin, as of something not only evil in itself, but an affront to the good God, is chiefly felt as regards one or other of three violations of His Law. He Himself is Sanctity, Truth, and Love; and the three offences against His Majesty are impurity, inveracity, and cruelty. All men are not distressed at these offences alike; but the piercing pain and sharp remorse which one or other inflicts upon the mind, till habituated to them, brings home to it the notion of what sin is, and is the vivid type and representative of its intrinsic hatefulness.

Starting from these elements, we may determine without difficulty the class of sentiments, intellectual and moral, which constitute the formal preparation for entering upon what are called the Evidences of Christianity. These Evidences, then, presuppose a belief and perception of the Divine Presence, a recognition of His attributes and an admiration of His Person viewed under them, a conviction of the worth of the soul and of the reality and momentousness of the unseen world, an understanding that, in proportion as we partake in our own persons of the attributes which we admire in Him, we are dear to Him, a consciousness on the contrary that we are far from exemplifying them, a consequent insight into our guilt and misery, an eager hope of reconciliation to Him, a desire to know and to love Him, and a sensitive looking-out in all that happens, whether in the course of nature or of human life, for tokens, if such there be, of His bestowing on us what we so greatly need. These are specimens of the state of mind for which I stipulate in those who would inquire into the truth of Christianity; and my warrant for so definite a stipulation lies in the teaching, as I have described it, of conscience and the moral sense, in the testimony of those religious rites which have ever prevailed in all parts of the world, and in the character and conduct of those who have commonly been selected by the popular instinct as the special favourites of Heaven.

2

I have appealed to the popular ideas on the subject of religion, and to the objects of popular admiration and praise, as illustrating my account of the preparation of mind which is necessary for the inquirer into Christianity. Here an obvious objection occurs, in noticing which I shall be advanced one step farther in the work which I have undertaken.

It may be urged, then, that no appeal will avail me, which is made to religions so notoriously immoral as those of paganism; nor indeed can it be made without an explanation. Certainly, as regards ethical teaching, various religions, which have been popular in the world, have not supplied any; and in the corrupt state in which they appear in history, they are little better than schools of imposture, cruelty, and impurity. Their objects of worship were immoral as well as false, and their founders and heroes have been in keeping with their gods. This is undeniable, but it does not destroy the use that may be made of their testimony. There is a better side of their teaching; purity has often been held in reverence, if not practised; ascetics have been in honour; hospitality has been a sacred duty; and dishonesty and injustice have been under a ban. Here then, as before, I take our natural perception of right and wrong as the standard for determining the characteristics of Natural Religion, and I use the religious rites and traditions which are actually found in the world, only so far as they agree with our moral sense.

This leads me to lay down the general principle, which I have all along implied:—that no religion is from God which contradicts our sense of right and wrong. Doubtless; but at the same time we ought to be quite sure that, in a particular case which is before us, we have satisfactorily ascertained what the dictates of our moral nature are, and that we apply them rightly, and whether the applying them or not comes into question at all. The precepts of a religion certainly may be absolutely immoral; a religion which simply commanded us to lie, or to have a community of wives, would *ipso facto* forfeit all claim to a divine origin. Jupiter and Neptune, as represented in the classical mythology, are evil spirits, and nothing can make them otherwise. And I should in like manner repudiate a theology which taught that men were created in order to be wicked and wretched.

I alluded just now to those who consider the doctrine of retributive punishment, or of divine vengeance, to be incompatible with the true religion; but I do not see how they can maintain their ground. In order to do so, they have first to prove that an act of vengeance must, as such, be a sin in our own instance; but even this is far from clear. Anger and indignation against cruelty and injustice, resentment of injuries, desire that the false, the ungrateful, and the depraved should meet with punishment, these, if not in themselves virtuous feelings, are at least not vicious; but, first from the certainty that, if habitual, it will run into excess and become sin, and next because the office of punishment has not been committed to us, and further because it is a feeling unsuitable to those who are themselves so laden with imperfection and guilt, therefore vengeance, in itself allowable, is forbidden to us. These exceptions do not hold in the case of a perfect being, and certainly not in the instance of the Supreme Judge. Moreover, we see that even men on earth have different duties, according to their personal qualifications and their positions in the community. The rule of morals is the same for all; and yet, notwithstanding, what is right in one is not necessarily right in another. What would be a crime in a private man to do, is a crime in a magistrate not to have done: still wider is the difference between man and his Maker. Nor must it be forgotten, that, as I have observed above, retributive justice is the very attribute under which God is primarily brought before us in the teachings of our natural conscience.

And further, we cannot determine the character of particular actions, till we have the whole case before us out of which they arise; unless, indeed, they are in themselves distinctively vicious. We all feel the force of the maxim, "Audi alteram partem." It is difficult to trace the path and to determine the scope of Divine Providence. We read of a day when the Almighty will condescend to place His actions in their completeness before His creatures, and "will overcome when He is judged." If, till then, we feel it to be a duty to suspend our judgment concerning certain of His actions or precepts, we do no more than what we do every day in the case of an earthly friend or enemy, whose conduct in some point requires explanation. It surely is not too much to expect of us that we should act with parallel caution, and be "memores conditionis nostræ" as regards the acts of our Creator. There is a poem of Parnell's which strikingly brings home to us how differently the divine appointments will look in the light of day, from what they appear to be in our present twilight. An Angel, in disguise of a man, steals a golden cup, strangles an infant, and throws a guide into the stream, and then explains to his horrified companion, that acts which would be enormities in man, are in him, as God's minister, deeds of merciful correction or of retribution.

Moreover, when we are about to pass judgment on the dealings of Providence with other men, we shall do well to consider first His dealings with ourselves. We cannot know about others, about ourselves we do know something; and we know that He has ever been good to us, and not severe. Is it not wise to argue from what we actually know to what we do not know? It may turn out in the day of account, that unforgiven souls, while charging His laws with injustice in the case of others, may be unable to find fault with His dealings severally towards themselves.

As to those various religions which, together with Christianity, teach the doctrine of eternal punishment, here again we ought, before we judge, to understand, not only the whole state of the case, but what is meant by the doctrine itself. Eternity, or endlessness, is in itself mainly a negative idea, though the idea of suffering is positive. Its fearful force, as an element of future punishment, lies in what it excludes; it means never any change of state, no annihilation or restoration; what, considered positively, it adds to suffering, we do not know. For what we know, the suffering of one moment may in itself have no bearing, or but a partial bearing, on the suffering of the next; and thus, as far as its intensity is concerned, it may vary with every lost soul. This may be so, unless we assume that the suffering is necessarily attended by a consciousness of duration and succession, by a present imagination of its past and its future, by a sustained power of realizing its continuity.[1] As I have already said, the great mystery is, not that evil has no end, but that it had a beginning. But I submit the whole subject to the Theological School.

3

One of the most important effects of Natural Religion on the mind, in preparation for Revealed, is the anticipation which it creates, that a Revelation will be given. That earnest desire of it, which religious minds cherish, leads the way to the expectation of it. Those who know nothing of the wounds of the soul, are not led to deal with the question, or to consider its circumstances; but when our attention is roused, then, the more steadily we dwell upon it, the more probable does it seem that a revelation has been or will be given to us. This presentiment is founded on our sense, on the one hand, of the infinite goodness of God, and, on the other, of our own extreme misery and need—two doctrines which are the primary con-

---

[1] "De hac damnatorum saltem hominum respiratione, nihil adhuc certi decretum est ab Ecclesiâ Catholicâ: ut propterea non temerè, tanquam absurda, sit explodenda sanctissimorum Patrum hæc opinio: quamvis à communi sensu Catholicorum hoc tempore sit aliena."—Petavius de Angelis, fin. *Vide* Note III.

stituents of Natural Religion. It is difficult to put a limit to the legitimate force of this antecedent probability. Some minds will feel it to be so powerfully, as to recognize in it almost a proof, without direct evidence, of the divinity of a religion claiming to be the true, supposing its history and doctrine are free from positive objection, and there be no rival religion with plausible claims of its own. Nor ought this trust in a presumption to seem preposterous to those who are so confident, on *à priori* grounds, that the moon is inhabited by rational beings, and that the course of nature is never crossed by miraculous agency. Any how, very little positive evidence seems to be necessary, when the mind is penetrated by the strong anticipation which I am supposing. It was this instinctive apprehension, as we may conjecture, which carried on Dionysius and Damaris at Athens to a belief in Christianity, though St. Paul did no miracle there, and only asserted the doctrines of the Divine Unity, the Resurrection, and the universal judgment, while, on the other hand, it had no tendency to attach them to any of the mythological rites in which the place abounded.

Here my method of argument differs from that adopted by Paley in his *Evidences of Christianity*. This clearheaded and almost mathematical reasoner postulates, for his proof of its miracles, only thus much, that, under the circumstances of the case, a revelation is not improbable. He says, "We do not assume the attributes of the Deity, or the existence of a future state." "It is not necessary for our purpose that these propositions (viz. that a future existence should be destined by God for His human creation, and that, being so destined, He should have acquainted them with it,) be capable of proof, or even that, by arguments drawn from the light of nature, they can be made out as probable; it is enough that we are able to say of them, that they are not so violently improbable, so contradictory to what we already believe of the divine power and character, that [they] ought to be rejected at first sight, and to be rejected by whatever strength or complication of evidence they be attested." He has such confidence in the strength, of the testimony which he can produce in favour of the Christian miracles, that he only asks to be allowed to bring it into court.

I confess to much suspicion of legal proceedings and legal arguments, when used in questions whether of history or of philosophy. Rules of court are dictated by what is expedient on the whole and in the long run; but they incur the risk of being unjust to the claims of particular cases. Why am I to begin with taking up a position not my own, and unclothing my mind of that large outfit of existing thoughts, principles, likings, desires, and hopes, which make me what I am? If I am asked to use Paley's argument for my own conversion, I say plainly I do not want to be converted by a smart syllogism; [1] if I am asked to convert others by it, I say plainly I do not care to overcome their reason without touching their hearts. I wish to deal, not with controversialists, but with inquirers.

I think Paley's argument clear, clever, and powerful; and there is something which looks like charity in going out into the highways and hedges, and compelling men to come in; but in this matter some exertion on the part of the persons whom I am to convert is a condition of a true conversion. They who have no religious earnestness are at the mercy, day by day, of some new argument or fact, which may overtake them, in favour of one conclusion or the other. And how, after all, is a man better for Christianity, who has never felt the need of it or the desire? On the other hand, if he has longed for a revelation to enlighten him and to cleanse his heart, why may he not use, in his inquiries after it, that just and reasonable anticipation of its probability, which such longing has opened the way to his entertaining?

Men are too well inclined to sit at home, instead of stirring themselves to inquire whether a revelation has been given; they expect its evidences to come to them without their

[1] *Vide supra*, p. 229.

trouble; they act, not as suppliants, but as judges.[1] Modes of argument such as Paley's, encourage this state of mind; they allow men to forget that revelation is a boon, not a debt on the part of the Giver; they treat it as a mere historical phenomenon. If I was told that some great man, a foreigner, whom I did not know, had come into town, and was on his way to call on me, and to go over my house, I should send to ascertain the fact, and meanwhile should do my best to put my house into a condition to receive him. He would not be pleased if I left the matter to take its chance, and went on the maxim that seeing was believing. Like this is the conduct of those who resolve to treat the Almighty with dispassionateness, a judicial temper, clearheadedness, and candour. It is the way with some men, (surely not a good way,) to say, that without these lawyerlike qualifications conversion is immoral. It is their way, a miserable way, to pronounce that there is no religious love of truth where there is fear of error. On the contrary, I would maintain that the fear of error is simply necessary to the genuine love of truth. No inquiry comes to good which is not conducted under a deep sense of responsibility, and of the issues depending upon its determination. Even the ordinary matters of life are an exercise of conscientiousness; and where conscience is, fear must be. So much is this acknowledged just now, that there is almost an affectation, in popular literature, in the case of criticisms on the fine arts, on poetry, and music, of insisting upon conscientiousness in writing, painting, or singing; and that earnestness and simplicity of mind, which makes men fear to go wrong in these minor matters, has surely a place in the most serious of all undertakings.

It is on these grounds that, in considering Christianity, I start with conditions different from Paley's; not, however, as undervaluing the force and serviceableness of his argument, but as preferring inquiry to disputation in a question about truth.

[1] *Vide* the author's "Occasional Sermons," No. 5.

4

There is another point on which my basis of argument differs from Paley's. He argues on the principle that the credentials, which ascertain for us a message from above, are necessarily in their nature miraculous; nor have I any thought of saying otherwise. In fact, all professed revelations have been attended, in one shape or another, with the professions of miracles; and we know how direct and unequivocal are the miracles of both the Jewish Covenant and of our own. However, my object here is to assume as little as possible as regards facts, and to dwell only on what is patent and notorious; and therefore I will only insist on those coincidences and their cumulations, which, though not in themselves miraculous, do irresistibly force upon us, almost by the law of our nature, the presence of the extraordinary agency of Him whose being we already acknowledge. Though coincidences rise out of a combination of general laws, there is no law of those coincidences; [1] they have a character of their own, and seem left by Providence in His own Hands, as the channel by which, inscrutable to us, He may make known to us His will.

For instance, if I am a believer in a God of Truth and Avenger of dishonesty, and know for certain that a market-woman, after calling on Him to strike her dead if she had in her possession a piece of money not hers, did fall down dead on the spot, and that the money was found in her hand, how can I call this a blind coincidence, and not discern in it an act of Providence over and above its general laws? So, certainly, thought the inhabitants of an English town, when they erected a pillar as a record of such an event at the place where it occurred. And if a Pope excommunicates a great conqueror; and he, on hearing the threat, says to one of his friends, "Does he think the world has gone back a thousand years? does he suppose the arms will fall from the hands of my soldiers?" and within two years, on the retreat over the snows of Russia, as

[1] *Vide supra,* p. 64.

two contemporary historians relate, "famine and cold tore their arms from the grasp of the soldiers," "they fell from the hands of the bravest and most robust," and "destitute of the power of raising them from the ground, the soldiers left them in the snow;" is not this, too, though no miracle, a coincidence so special, as rightly to be called a Divine judgment? So thinks Alison, who avows with religious honesty, that "there is something in these marvellous coincidences beyond the operation of chance, and which even a Protestant historian feels himself bound to mark for the observation of future years." [1] And so, too, of a cumulation of coincidences, separately less striking; when Spelman sets about establishing the fact of the ill-fortune which in many instances has followed upon acts of sacrilege, among us, even though in many instances it has not followed, and in many instances he exaggerates, still there may be a large residuum of cases which cannot be properly resolved into the mere accident of concurrent causes, but must in reason be considered the warning voice of God. So, at least, thought Gibson, Bishop of London, when he wrote, "Many of the instances, and those too well-attested, are so terrible in the event, and in the circumstances so surprising, that no considering person can well pass them over."

I think, then, that the circumstances under which a professed revelation comes to us, may be such as to impress both our reason and our imagination with a sense of its truth, even though no appeal be made to strictly miraculous intervention—in saying which I do not mean of course to imply that those circumstances, when traced back to their first origins, are not the outcome of such intervention, but that the miraculous intervention addresses us at this day in the guise of those circumstances; that is, of coincidences, which are indications, to the illative sense of those who believe in a Moral Governor, of His immediate Presence, especially to those who in addition hold with me the strong antecedent probability that, in His

[1] History, vol. viii.

mercy, He will thus supernaturally present Himself to our apprehension.

5

Now as to the fact; has what is so probable in anticipation actually been granted to us, or have we still to look out for it? It is very plain, supposing it has been granted, which among all the religions of the world comes from God: and if it is not that, a revelation is not yet given, and we must look forward to the future. There is only one religion in the world which tends to fulfil the aspirations, needs, and foreshadowings of natural faith and devotion. It may be said, perhaps, that, educated in Christianity, I merely judge of it by its own principles; but this is not the fact. For, in the first place, I have taken my idea of what a revelation must be, in good measure, from the actual religions of the world; and as to its ethics, the ideas with which I come to it are derived not simply from the Gospel, but prior to it from heathen moralists, whom Fathers of the Church and Ecclesiastical writers have imitated or sanctioned; and as to the intellectual position from which I have contemplated the subject, Aristotle has been my master. Besides, I do not here single out Christianity with reference simply to its particular doctrines or precepts, but for a reason which is on the surface of its history. It alone has a definite message addressed to all mankind. As far as I know, the religion of Mahomet has brought into the world no new doctrine whatever, except, indeed, that of its own divine origin; and the character of its teaching is too exact a reflection of the race, time, place, and climate in which it arose, to admit of its becoming universal. The same dependence on external circumstances is characteristic, so far as I know, of the religions of the far East; nor am I sure of any definite message from God to man which they convey and protect, though they may have sacred books. Christianity, on the other hand, is in its idea an announcement, a preaching; it is the depository of truths beyond human discovery, momentous, practical, maintained one and the same in substance in every age from its first, and addressed to all mankind. And it has actually been embraced and is found in all parts of the world, in all climates, among all races, in all ranks of society, under every degree of civilization, from barbarism to the highest cultivation of mind. Coming to set right and to govern the world, it has ever been, as it ought to be, in conflict with large masses of men, with the civil power, with physical force, with adverse philosophies; it has had successes, it has had reverses; but it has had a grand history, and has effected great things, and is as vigorous in its age as in its youth. In all these respects it has a distinction in the world and a pre-eminence of its own; it has upon it *primâ facie* signs of divinity; I do not know what can be advanced by rival religions to match prerogatives so special; so that I feel myself justified in saying either Christianity is from God, or a revelation has not yet been given to us.

It will not surely be objected, as a point in favour of some of the Oriental religions, that they are older than Christianity by some centuries; yet, should it be so said, it must be recollected that Christianity is only the continuation and conclusion of what professes to be an earlier revelation, which may be traced back into pre-historic times, till it is lost in the darkness that hangs over them. As far as we know, there never was a time when that revelation was not,—a revelation continuous and systematic, with distinct representatives and an orderly succession. And this, I suppose, is far more than can be said for the religions of the East.

6

Here, then, I am brought to the consideration of the Hebrew nation and the Mosaic religion, as the first step in the direct evidence for Christianity.

The Jews are one of the few Oriental nations who are known in history as a people of progress, and their line of progress is the development of religious truth. In that their own line they stand by themselves among all the populations, not only of the East, but of the West. Their country may be called the classical home of the religious principle, as Greece is the home of intellectual power, and Rome that of political and practical wisdom. Theism is their life; it is emphatically their national religion, for they never were without it, and were made a people by means of it. This is a phenomenon singular and solitary in history, and must have a meaning. If there be a God and Providence, it must come from Him, whether immediately or indirectly; and the people themselves have ever maintained that it has been His direct work, and has been recognized by Him as such. We are apt to treat pretences to a divine mission or to supernatural powers as of frequent occurrence, and on that score to dismiss them from our thoughts; but we cannot so deal with Judaism. When mankind had universally denied the first lesson of their conscience by lapsing into polytheism, is it a thing of slight moment that there was just one exception to the rule, that there was just one people who, first by their rulers and priests, and afterwards by their own unanimous zeal, professed, as their distinguishing doctrine, the Divine Unity and Government of the world, and that, moreover, not only as a natural truth, but as revealed to them by that God Himself of whom they spoke,—who so embodied it in their national polity, that a Theocracy was the only name by which it could be called? It was a people founded and set up in Theism, kept together by Theism, and maintaining Theism for a period from first to last of 2000 years, till the dissolution of their body politic; and they have maintained it since in their state of exile and wandering for 2000 years more. They begin with the beginning of history, and the preaching of this august dogma begins with them. They are its witnesses and confessors, even to torture and death; on it and its revelation are moulded their laws and government; on this their politics, philosophy, and literature are founded; of this truth their poetry is the voice, pouring itself out in devotional compositions which Christianity, through all its many countries and ages, has been unable to rival; on this aboriginal truth, as time goes on, prophet after prophet bases his further revelations, with a sustained reference to a time when, according to the secret counsels of its Divine Object and Author, it is to receive completion and perfection,—till at length that time comes.

The last age of their history is as strange as their first. When that time of destined blessing came, which they had so accurately marked out, and were so carefully waiting for—a time which found them, in fact, more zealous for their Law, and for the dogma it enshrined, than they ever had been before—then, instead of any final favour coming on them from above, they fell under the power of their enemies, and were overthrown, their holy city razed to the ground, their polity destroyed, and the remnant of their people cast off to wander far and away through every land except their own, as we find them at this day; lasting on, century after century, not absorbed in other populations, not annihilated, as likely to last on, as unlikely to be restored, as far as outward appearances go, now as a thousand years ago. What nation has so grand, so romantic, so terrible a history? Does it not fulfil the idea of, what the nation calls itself, a chosen people, chosen for good and evil? Is it not an exhibition in a course of history of that primary declaration of conscience, as I have been determining it, "With the upright Thou shalt be upright, and with the froward Thou shalt be froward"? It must have a meaning, if there is a God. We know what was their witness of old time; what is their witness now?

Why, I say, was it that, after so memorable a career, when their sins, and sufferings were now to come to an end, when they were looking out for a deliverance and a Deliverer, suddenly all was reversed for once and for all? They were the favoured servants of God, and yet a peculiar reproach and note of infamy is affixed to their name. It was their belief that His protection was unchangeable, and that their Law would last for ever;—it was their consolation to be taught by an uninter-

rupted tradition, that it could not die, except by changing into
a new self, more wonderful than it was before;—it was their
faithful expectation that a promised King was coming, the
Messiah, who would extend the sway of Israel over all people;
—it was a condition of their covenant, that, as a reward to
Abraham, their first father, the day at length should dawn
when the gates of their narrow land should open, and they
should pour out for the conquest and occupation of the whole
earth;—and, I repeat, when the day came, they did go forth,
and they did spread into all lands, but as hopeless exiles, as
eternal wanderers.

Are we to say that this failure is a proof that, after all, there
was nothing providential in their history? For myself, I do not
see how a second portent obliterates a first; and, in truth, their
own testimony and their own sacred books carry us on towards
a better solution of the difficulty. I have said they were in
God's favour under a covenant,—perhaps they did not fulfil
the conditions of it. This indeed seems to be their own account
of the matter, though it is not clear what their breach of en-
gagement was. And that in some way they did sin, whatever
their sin was, is corroborated by the well-known chapter in
the Book of Deuteronomy, which so strikingly anticipates the
nature of their punishment. That passage, translated into
Greek as many as 350 years before the siege of Jerusalem by
Titus, has on it the marks of a wonderful prophecy; but I am
not now referring to it as such, but merely as an indication
that the disappointment, which actually overtook them at the
Christian era, was not necessarily out of keeping with the
original divine purpose, or again with the old promise made
to them, and their confident expectation of its fulfilment. Their
national ruin, which came instead of aggrandizement, is described in that book, in spite of all promises, with an emphasis
and minuteness which prove that it was contemplated long
before, at least as a possible issue of the fortunes of Israel.
Among other inflictions which should befall the guilty people,
it was told them that they should fall down before their

enemies, and should be scattered throughout all the kingdoms of the earth; that they never should have quiet in those nations, or have rest for the sole of their foot; that they were to have a fearful heart and languishing eyes, and a soul consumed with heaviness; that they were to suffer wrong, and to be crushed at all times, and to be astonished at the terror of their lot; that their sons and daughters were to be given to another people, and they were to look and to sicken all the day, and their life was ever to hang in doubt before them, and fear to haunt them day and night; that they should be a proverb and a by-word of all people among whom they were brought; and that curses were to come on them, and to be signs and wonders on them and their seed for ever. Such are some portions, and not the most terrible, of this extended anathema; and its partial accomplishment at an earlier date of their history was a warning to them, when the destined time drew near, that, however great the promises made to them might be, those promises were dependent on the terms of the covenant which stood between them and their Maker, and that, as they had turned to curses at that former time, so they might turn to curses again.

This grand drama, so impressed with the characters of supernatural agency, concerns us here only in its bearing upon the evidence for the divine origin of Christianity; and it is at this point that Christianity comes upon the historical scene. It is a notorious fact that it issued from the Jewish land and people; and, had it no other than this historical connexion with Judaism, it would have some share in the prestige of its original home. But it claims to be far more than this; it professes to be the actual completion of the Mosaic Law, the promised means of deliverance and triumph to the nation, which that nation itself, as I have said, has since considered to be on account of some sin or other, withheld or forfeited. It professes to be, not the casual, but the legitimate offspring, heir, and successor of the Mosaic covenant, or rather to be Judaism itself, developed and transformed. Of course it has to prove its claim, as well as to prefer it; but if it succeeds in doing so, then all those tokens of the Divine Presence, which distinguish the Jewish history, at once belong to it, and are a portion of its credentials.

And at least the *primâ facie* view of its relations towards Judaism is in favour of these pretensions. It is an historical fact, that, at the very time that the Jews committed their unpardonable sin, whatever it was, and were driven out from their home to wander over the earth, their Christian brethren, born of the same stock, and equally citizens of Jerusalem, did also issue forth from the same home, but in order to subdue that same earth and make it their own; that is, they undertook the very work which, according to the promise, their nation actually was ordained to execute; and, with a method of their own indeed, and with a new end, and only slowly and painfully, but still really and thoroughly, they did it. And since that time the two children of the promise have ever been found together—of the promise forfeited and the promise fulfilled; and whereas the Christian has been in high place, so the Jew has been degraded and despised—the one has been "the head," and the other "the tail;" so that, to go no farther, the fact that Christianity actually has done what Judaism was to have done, decides the controversy, by the logic of facts, in favour of Christianity. The prophecies announced that the Messiah was to come at a definite time and place; Christians point to Him as coming then and there, as announced; they are not met by any counter claim or rival claimant on the part of the Jews, only by their assertion that He did not come at all, though up to the event they had said He was then and there coming. Further, Christianity clears up the mystery which hangs over Judaism, accounting fully for the punishment of the people, by specifying their sin, their heinous sin. If, instead of hailing their Messiah, they crucified Him, then the strange scourge which has pursued them after the deed, and the energetic wording of the curse before it, are explained by the very strangeness of their guilt;—or rather, their sin is their punishment; for in rejecting their Divine King, they *ipso facto* lost the living principle and tie of their nationality. Moreover, we see what led them into error; they thought a triumph and an empire were to be given to them at once, which were given indeed eventually, but by the slow and gradual growth of many centuries and a long warfare.

On the whole, then, I observe, on the one hand, that, Judaism having been the channel of religious traditions which are lost in the depth of their antiquity, of course it is a great point for Christianity to succeed in proving that it is the legitimate heir to that former religion. Nor is it, on the other, of less importance to the significance of those early traditions to be able to determine that they were not lost together with their original storehouse, but were transferred, on the failure of Judaism, to the custody of the Christian Church. And this apparent correspondence between the two is in itself a presumption for such correspondence being real. Next, I observe, that if the history of Judaism is so wonderful as to suggest the presence of some special divine agency in its appointments and fortunes, still more wonderful and divine is the history of Christianity; and again it is more wonderful still, that two such wonderful creations should span almost the whole course of ages, during which nations and states have been in existence, and should constitute a professed system of continued intercourse between earth and heaven from first to last amid all the vicissitudes of human affairs. This phenomenon again carries on its face, to those who believe in a God, the probability that it has that divine origin which it professes to have; and, (when viewed in the light of the strong presumption which I have insisted on, that in God's mercy a revelation from Him will be granted to us, and of the contrast presented by other religions, no one of which professes to be a revelation direct, definite, and integral as this is,)—this phenomenon, I say, of cumulative marvels raises that probability, both for

·Judaism and Christianity, in religious minds, almost to a certainty.

7

If Christianity is connected with Judaism as closely as I have been supposing, then there have been, by means of the two, direct communications between man and his Maker from time immemorial down to this day—a great prerogative such, that it is nowhere else even claimed. No other religion but these two professses to be the organ of a formal revelation, certainly not of a revelation which is directed to the benefit of the whole human race. Here it is that Mahometanism fails, though it claims to carry on the line of revelation after Christianity: for it is the mere creed and rite of certain races, bringing with it, as such, no gifts to our nature, and is rather a reformation of local corruptions, and a return to the ceremonial worship of earlier times, than a new and larger revelation. And while Christianity was the heir to a dead religion, Mahometanism was little more than a rebellion against a living one. Moreover, though Mahomet professed to be the Paraclete, no one pretends that he occupies a place in the Christian Scriptures as prominent as that which the Messiah fills in the Jewish. To this especial prominence of the Messianic idea I shall now advert; that is, to the prophecies of the Old Scriptures, and to the argument which they furnish in favour of Christianity; and though I know that argument might be clearer and more exact than it is, and I do not pretend here to do much more than refer to the fact of its existence, still so far forth as we enter into it, will it strengthen our conviction of the claim to divinity both of the Religion which is the organ of those prophecies, and of the Religion which is their object.

Now that the Jewish Scriptures were in existence long before the Christian era, and were in the sole custody of the Jews, is undeniable; whatever then their Scriptures distinctly say of Christianity, if not attributable to chance or to happy conjecture, is prophetic. It is undeniable too, that the Jews gathered from those books that a great Personage was to be born of their stock and to conquer the whole world and to become the instrument of extraordinary blessings to it; moreover, that he would make his appearance at a fixed date, and that, the very date when, as it turned out, our Lord did actually come. This is the great outline of the prediction, and if we are able to prove nothing else, to prove as much as this is far from unimportant. And it is undeniable, I say, both that the Jewish Scriptures contain thus much, and that the Jews actually understood them as containing it.

First, then, as to what Scripture declares. From the book of Genesis we learn that the chosen people was set up in this one idea, viz. to be a blessing to the whole earth, and that, by means of one of their own race, "a greater than their father Abraham." This was the meaning and drift of their being chosen. There is no room for mistake here; the divine purpose is stated from the first with the utmost precision. At the very time of Abraham's call, he is told of it:—"I will make of thee a great nation, and in thee shall all tribes of the earth be blessed." Thrice is this promise and purpose announced in Abraham's history; and after Abraham's time it is repeated to Isaac, "In thy seed shall all the nations of the earth be blessed;" and after Isaac to Jacob, when a wanderer from his home, "In thee and in thy seed shall all the tribes of the earth be blessed." And from Jacob the promise passes on to his son Judah, and that with an addition, viz. with a reference to the great Person who was to be the world-wide blessing, and to the date when He should come. Judah was the chosen son of Jacob, and his staff or sceptre, that is his patriarchal authority, was to endure till a greater than Judah came, so that the loss of the sceptre, when it took place, was the sign of His near approach. "The sceptre," says Jacob on his death-bed, "shall not be taken away from Judah, until He come for whom it is reserved," or "who is to be sent," "and He shall be the expectation of the nations." [1]

Such was the categorical prophecy, literal and unequivocal in its wording, direct and simple in its scope. One man, born of the chosen tribe, was the destined minister of blessing to the whole world; and the race, as represented by that tribe, was to lose its old self in gaining a new self in Him. Its destiny was sealed upon it in its beginning. An expectation was the measure of its life. It was created for a great end, and in that end it had its ending. Such were the initial communications made to the chosen people, and there they stopped;—as if the outline of promise, so sharply cut, had to be effectually imprinted on their minds, before more knowledge was given to them; as if, by the long interval of years which passed before the more varied prophecies in type and figure, after the manner of the East, were added, the original notices might stand out in the sight of all in their severe explicitness, as archetypal truths, and guides in interpreting whatever else was obscure in its wording or complex in its direction.

---

[1] Before and apart from Christianity the Samaritan Version reads, "donec veniat Pacificus, et ad ipsum congregabuntur populi." The Targum, "donec veniat Messias, cujus est regnum, et obedient populi." The Septuagint, "donec veniant quæ reservata sunt illi" (or "donec veniat cui reservatum est"), "et ipse expectatio gentium." And so again the Vulgate, "donec veniat qui mittendus est, et ipse erit expectatio gentium."

The ingenious translation of some learned men ("donec venerit Juda Siluntem," i.e. "the tribe-sceptre shall not depart from Judah till Judah comes to Shiloh"), with the explanation that the tribe of Judah had the leadership in the war against the Canaanites, *vide* Judges i. 1, 2; xx. 18 (i.e. after Joshua's *death*), and that possibly, and for what we know, the tribe gave up that war-command at Shiloh, *vide* Joshua xviii. (i.e. in Joshua's *life-time*), labours under three grave difficulties: 1. That the patriarchal sceptre is a temporary war-command. 2. That this command belonged to Judah at the very time that it belonged to Joshua. And 3. That it was finally lost to Judah (Joshua living) before it had been committed to Judah (Joshua dead).

And in the second place it is quite clear that the Jews did thus understand their prophecies, and did expect their great Ruler, in the very age in which our Lord came, and in which they, on the other hand, were destroyed, losing their old self without gaining their new. Heathen historians shall speak for the fact. "A persuasion had possession of most of them," says Tacitus, speaking of their resistance to the Romans, "that it was contained in the ancient books of the priests that at that very time the East should prevail, and that men who issued from Judea should obtain the empire. The common people, as is the way with human cupidity, having once interpreted in their own favour this grand destiny, were not even by their reverses brought round to the truth of facts." And Suetonius extends the belief:—"The whole East was rife with an old and persistent belief, that at that time persons who issued from Judea, should possess the empire." After the event of course the Jews drew back, and denied the correctness of their expectation, still they could not deny that the expectation had existed. Thus the Jew Josephus, who was of the Roman party, says that what encouraged them in the stand they made against the Romans was "an ambiguous oracle, found in their sacred writings, that at that date some one of them from that country should rule the world." He can but pronounce that the oracle was ambiguous; he cannot state that they thought it so.

Now, considering that at that very time our Lord did appear as a teacher, and founded not merely a religion, but (what was then quite a new idea in the world) a system of religious warfare, an aggressive and militant body, a dominant Catholic Church, which aimed at the benefit of all nations by the spiritual conquest of all; and that this warfare, then begun by it, has gone on without cessation down to this day, and now is as living and real as ever it was; that that militant body has from the first filled the world, that it has had wonderful successes, that its successes have on the whole been of extreme benefit to the human race, that it has imparted an intelligent notion about the Supreme God to millions who would have lived and died in irreligion, that it has raised the tone of morality wherever it has come, has abolished great social anomalies and miseries, has elevated the female sex to its proper dignity, has protected the poorer classes, has destroyed slavery, encouraged literature and philosophy, and had a principal part in that civilization of human kind, which with some evils, still has on the whole been productive of far greater good,—considering, I say, that all this began at the destined, expected, recognized season when the old prophecy said that in one Man, born of the tribe of Judah, all the tribes of the earth were to be blessed, I feel I have a right to say (and my line of argument does not lead me to say more), that it is at the very least a remarkable coincidence,—that is, one of those coincidences which, when they are accumulated, come close upon the idea of miracle, as being impossible without the Hand of God directly and immediately in them.

When we have got as far as this, we may go on a great deal farther. Announcements, which could not be put forward in the front of the argument, as being figurative, vague, or ambiguous, may be used validly and with great effect, when they have been interpreted for us, first by the prophetic outline, and still more by the historical object. It is a principle which applies to all matters on which we reason, that what is only a maze of facts, without order or drift prior to the due explanation, may, when we once have that explanation, be located and adjusted with great facility in all its separate parts, as we know is the case as regards the motions of the heavenly bodies since the hypothesis of Newton. In like manner the event is the true key to prophecy, and reconciles conflicting and divergent descriptions by embodying them in one common representative. Thus it is that we learn how, as the prophecies said, the Messiah could both suffer, yet be victorious; His kingdom be Judaic in structure, yet evangelic in spirit; and His people the children of Abraham, yet "sinners of the Gentiles." These seeming paradoxes, are only parallel and akin to those others which form so prominent a feature in the teaching of our Lord and His Apostles.

As to the Jews, since they lived before the event, it is not wonderful, that, though they were right in their general interpretation of Scripture as far as it went, they stopped short of the whole truth; nay, that even when their Messiah came, they could not recognize Him as the promised King as we recognize Him now;—for we have the experience of His history for nearly two thousand years, by which to interpret their Scriptures. We may partly understand their position towards those prophecies, by our own at present towards the Apocalypse. Who can deny the superhuman grandeur and impressiveness of that sacred book! yet, as a prophecy, though some outlines of the future are discernible, how differently it affects us from the predictions of Isaiah! either because it relates to undreamed-of events still to come, or because it has been fulfilled long ago in events which in their detail and circumstance have never become history. And the same remark applies doubtless to portions of the Messianic prophecies still; but, if their fulfilment has been thus gradual in time past, we must not be surprised though portions of them still await their slow but true accomplishment in the future.

8

When I implied that in some points of view Christianity has not answered the expectations of the old prophecies, of which it claims to be the fulfilment, I had in mind principally the contrast which is presented to us between the picture which they draw of the universality of the kingdom of the Messiah, and that partial development of it through the world, which is all the Christian Church can show; and again the contrast between the rest and peace which they said He was to introduce, and the Church's actual history,—the conflicts of opinion which have raged within its pale, the violent acts and unworthy lives of many of its rulers, and the moral degradation of great masses of its people. I do not profess to meet these difficulties here, except by saying that the failure of Christianity in one respect in corresponding to those prophecies cannot destroy the force of its correspondence to them in others; just as we may allow that the portrait of a friend is a faulty likeness to him, and yet be quite sure that it is his portrait. What I shall actually attempt to show here is this,— that Christianity was quite aware from the first of its own prospective future, so unlike the expectations which the prophets would excite concerning it, and that it meets the difficulty thence arising and by anticipation, by giving us its own predictions of what it was to be in historical fact, predictions which are at once explanatory comments upon the Jewish Scriptures, and direct evidences of its own prescience.

I think it observable then, that, though our Lord claims to be the Messiah, He shows so little of conscious dependence on the old Scriptures, or of anxiety to fulfil them; as if it became Him, who was the Lord of the Prophets, to take His own course, and to leave the prophets to adjust themselves to Him as they could, and not to be careful to accommodate Himself to them. The Evangelists do indeed show some such natural zeal in His behalf, and thereby illustrate what I notice in Him by the contrast. They betray an earnestness to trace in His Person and history the accomplishment of prophecy, as when they discern it in His return from Egypt, in His life at Nazareth, in the gentleness and tenderness of His mode of teaching, and in the various minute occurrences of His passion; but He Himself goes straight forward on His way, of course claiming to be the Messiah of the Prophets,[1] still not so much recurring to past prophecies, as uttering new ones, with an antithesis not unlike that which is so impressive in the Sermon on the Mount, when He first first says, "It has

---

[1] He appeals to the prophecies in evidence of His Divine mission, in addressing the people of Nazareth (Luke iv.18), St. John's disciples (Matt. xi.5), and the Pharisees (Matt. xxi.42, and John v.39), but not in details. The appeal to details He reserves for his disciples. *Vide* Matt. xi.10; xxvi.24.31.54; Luke xxii.37; xxiv.27, 46.

been said by them of old time," and then adds, "But I say unto you." Another striking instance of this is seen in the Names under which He spoke of Himself, which have little or no foundation in any thing which was said of Him before-hand in the Jewish Scriptures. They speak of Him as Ruler, Prophet, King, Hope of Israel, Offspring of Judah, and Messiah; and His Evangelists and Disciples call Him Master, Lord, Prophet, Son of David, King of Israel, King of the Jews, and Messiah or Christ; but He Himself, though, I repeat, He acknowledges these titles as His own, especially that of the Christ, chooses as His special designations these two, Son of God and Son of Man, the latter of which is only once given Him in the Old Scriptures, and by which He corrects any narrow Judaic interpretation of them; while the former was never distinctly used of Him before He came, and seems first to have been announced to the world by the Angel Gabriel and St. John the Baptist. In those two Names, Son of God and Son of Man, declaratory of the two natures of Emmanuel, He separates Himself from the Jewish Dispensation, in which He was born, and inaugurates the New Covenant.

This is not an accident, and I shall now give some instances of it, that is, of what I may call the independent autocratic view which He takes of His own religion, into which the old Judaism was melting, and of the prophetic insight into its spirit and its future which that view involves. In quoting His own sayings from the Evangelists for this purpose, I assume (of which there is no reasonable doubt) that they wrote before any historical events had happened of a nature to cause them unconsciously to modify or to colour the language which their Master used.

1. First, then, the fact has been often insisted on as a bold conception, unheard of before, and worthy of divine origin, that He should even project a universal religion, and that to be effected by what may be called a propagandist movement from one centre. Hitherto it had been the received

notion in the world, that each nation had its own gods. The Romans legislated upon that basis, and the Jews had held it from the first, holding of course also, that all gods but their own God were idols and demons. It is true that the Jews ought to have been taught by their prophecies what was in store for the world and for them, and that their first dispersion through the empire centuries before Christ came, and the proselytes which they collected around them in every place, were a kind of comment on the prophecies larger than their own; but we see what was, in fact, when our Lord came, their expectation from those prophecies, in the passages which I have quoted above from the Roman historians of His day. But He from the first resisted those plausible, but mistaken interpretations of Scripture. In His cradle indeed He had been recognized by the Eastern sages as their King; the Angel announced that He was to reign over the house of Jacob; Nathanael, too, owned Him as the Messiah with a regal title; but He, on entering upon His work, interpreted these anticipations in His own way, and that not the way of Theudas and Judas of Galilee, who took the sword, and collected soldiers about them,—nor the way of the Tempter, who offered Him "all the kingdoms of the world." In the words of the Evangelists, He began, not to fight, but "to preach;" and further, to "preach the kingdom of heaven," saying, "The time is accomplished, and the kingdom of God is at hand; repent, and believe the Gospel." This is the significant title, "the kingdom of heaven,"—the more significant, when explained by the attendant precept of repentence and faith,—on which he founds the polity which he was establishing from first to last. One of His last sayings before He suffered was, "My kingdom is not of this world." And His last words, before He left the earth, when His disciples asked Him about His kingdom, were that they, preachers as they were, and not soldiers, should "be His witnesses to the end of the earth," should "preach to all nations, beginning with Jerusalem," should "go into the world and preach the Gospel to every creature," should "go and make disciples of all nations till the consummation of all things."

The last Evangelist of the four is equally precise in recording the initial purpose with which our Lord began His ministry, viz. to create an empire, not by force, but by persuasion. "Light is come into the world; every one that doth evil, hateth the light, but he that doth truth cometh to the light." "Lift up your eyes, and see the countries, for they are white already to harvest." "No man can come to Me, except the Father, who hath sent Me, draw him." "And I, if I be lifted up from the earth, will draw all things to Myself."

Thus, while the Jews, relying on their Scriptures with great appearance of reason, looked for a deliverer who should conquer with the sword, we find that Christianity, from the first, not by an after-thought upon trial and experience, but as a fundamental truth, magisterially set right that mistake, transfiguring the old prophecies, and bringing to light, as St. Paul might say, "the mystery which had been hidden from ages and generations, but now was made manifest in His saints, the glory of this mystery among the Gentiles, which is Christ in you," not simply over you, but in you, by faith and love, "the hope of glory."

2. I have partly anticipated my next remark, which relates to the means by which the Christian enterprise was to be carried into effect. That preaching was to have a share in the victories of the Messiah was plain from Prophet and Psalmist; but then Charlemagne preached, and Mahomet preached, with an army to back them. The same Psalm which speaks of those "who preach good tidings," speaks also of their King's "foot being dipped in the blood of His enemies;" but what is so grandly original in Christianity is, that on its broad field of conflict its preachers were to be simply unarmed, and to suffer, but to prevail. If we were not so familiar with our Lord's words, I think they would astonish us. "Behold I send you as sheep in the midst of wolves." This was to be their

normal state, and so it was; and all the promises and directions given to them imply it. "Blessed are they that suffer persecution;" "blessed are ye when they revile you;" "the meek shall inherit the earth;" "resist not evil;" "you shall be hated of all men for My Name's sake;" "a man's enemies shall be they of his own household;" "he that shall persevere to the end, he shall be saved." What sort of encouragement was this for men who were to go about an immense work? Do men in this way send out their soldiers to battle, or their sons to India or Australia? The King of Israel hated Michaiah, because he always "prophesied of him evil." "So persecuted they the Prophets that were before you," says our Lord. Yes, and the Prophets failed; they were persecuted, and they lost the battle. "Take, my brethren," says St. James, "for an example of suffering evil, of labour and patience, the Prophets, who spake in the Name of the Lord." They were "racked, mocked, stoned, cut asunder, they wandered about,—of whom the world was not worthy," says St. Paul. What an argument to encourage them to aim at success by suffering, to put before them the precedent of those who suffered and who failed!

Yet the first preachers, our Lord's immediate disciples, saw no difficulty in a prospect to human eyes so appalling, so hopeless. How connatural this strange, unreasoning, reckless courage was with their regenerate state is shown most signally in St. Paul, as having been a convert of later vocation. He was no personal associate of our Lord's, yet how faithfully he echoes back our Lord's language! His instrument of conversion is "the foolishness of preaching;" "the weak things of the earth confound the strong;" "we hunger and thirst, and are naked, and are buffeted, and have no home;" "we are reviled and bless, we are persecuted, and blasphemed, and are made the refuse of this world, and the offscouring of all things." Such is the intimate comprehension, on the part of one who had never seen our Lord on earth, and knew little from His original disciples, of the genius of His teaching;— and considering that the prophecies, upon which he had lived

from his birth, for the most part bear on their surface a contrary doctrine, and that the Jews of that day did commonly
understand them in that contrary sense, we cannot deny that
Christianity, in tracing out the method by which it was to
prevail in the future, took its own, independent line, and, in
assigning from the first a rule and a history to its propagation,
a rule and a history which have been carried out to this day,
rescues itself from the charge of but partially fulfilling those
Jewish prophecies, by the assumption of a prophetical character of its own.

3. Now we come to a third point, in which the Divine
Master explains, and in a certain sense corrects, the prophecies
of the Old Covenant, by a more exact interpretation of them
from Himself. I have granted that they seemed to say that His
coming would issue in a period of peace and religiousness.
"Behold," says the Prophet, "a king shall reign in justice, and
princes shall rule in judgment. The fool shall no more be
called prince, neither shall the deceitful be called great. The
wolf shall dwell with the lamb, and the leopard lie down with
the kid. They shall not hurt nor kill in all My holy mountain,
for the earth is filled with the knowledge of the Lord, as the
covering waters of the sea."

These words seem to predict a reversal of the consequences
of the fall, and that reversal has not yet been granted to us,
it is true; but let us consider how distinctly Christianity warns
us against any such anticipation. While it is so forcibly laid
down in the Gospels that the history of the kingdom of heaven
begins in suffering and sanctity, it is as plainly said that it
results in unfaithfulness and sin; that is to say, that, though
there are at all times many holy, many religious men in it,
and that sanctity, as at the beginning, is ever the life and the
substance and the germinal seed of the Divine Kingdom, yet
there will ever be many too, there will be more, who by their
lives are a scandal and injury to it, not a defence. This again,
is an astonishing announcement, and the more so when viewed
in contrast with the precepts delivered by our Lord in His

Sermon on the Mount, and His description to the Apostles of their weapons and their warfare. So perplexing to Christians was the fact when fulfilled, as it was in no long time on a large scale, that three of the early heresies more or less originated in obstinate, unchristian refusal to readmit to the privileges of the Gospel those who had fallen into sin. Yet our Lord's words are express: He tells us that "Many are called, few are chosen;" in the parable of the Marriage Feast, the servants who are sent out gather together "all that they found, both bad and good;" the foolish virgins "had no oil in their vessels;" amid the good seed an enemy sows seed that is noxious or worthless; and "the kingdom is like to a net which gathered together all kind of fishes;" and "at the end of the world the Angels shall go forth, and shall separate the wicked from among the just."

Moreover, He not only speaks of His religion as destined to possess a wide temporal power, such that, as in the case of the Babylonian, "the birds of the air should dwell in its branches," but He opens on us the prospect of ambition and rivalry in its leading members, when He warns His disciples against desiring the first places in His kingdom; nay, of grosser sins, in His description of the Ruler, who "began to strike his fellow-servants, and to eat and drink and be drunken,"—passages which have an awful significance, considering what kind of men have before now been His chosen representatives, and have sat in the chair of His Apostles.

If then it be objected that Christianity does not, as the old prophets seem to promise, abolish sin and irreligion within its pale, we may answer, not only that it did not engage to do so, but that actually in a prophetical spirit it warned its followers against the expectation of its so doing.

9

According to our Lord's announcements before the event, Christianity was to prevail and to become a great empire, and to fill the earth; but it was to accomplish this destiny, not as other victorious powers had done, and as the Jews expected, by force of arms or by other means of this world, but by the novel expedient of sanctity and suffering. If some aspiring party of this day, the great Orleans family, or a branch of the Hohenzollern, wishing to found a kingdom, were to profess, as their only weapon, the practice of virtue, they would not startle us more than it startled a Jew eighteen hundred years ago, to be told that his glorious Messiah was not to fight, like Joshua or David, but simply to preach. It is indeed a thought so strange, both in its prediction and in its fulfilment, as urgently to suggest to us that some Divine Power went with him who conceived and proclaimed it. This is what I have been saying;—now I wish to consider the fact, which was predicted, in itself, without reference to its being the subject whether of a prediction or of a fulfilment; that is, the history of the rise and establishment of Christianity; and to inquire whether it is a history that admits of being resolved, by any philosophical ingenuity, into the ordinary operation of moral, social, or political causes.

As is well known, various writers have attempted to assign human causes in explanation of the phenomenon: Gibbon especially has mentioned five, viz. the zeal of Christians, inherited from the Jews, their doctrine of a future state, their claim to miraculous power, their virtues, and their ecclesiastical organization. Let us briefly consider them.

He thinks these five causes, when combined, will fairly account for the event; but he has not thought of accounting for their combination. If they are ever so available for his purpose, still that availableness arises out of their coincidence, and out of what does that coincidence arise? Until this is explained, nothing is explained, and the question had better have been let alone. These presumed causes are quite distinct from each other, and, I say, the wonder is, what made them come together. How came a multitude of Gentiles to be influenced with Jewish zeal? How came zealots to submit to a strict, ecclesiastical *régime*? What connexion has a secular *régime* with the immortality of the soul? Why should immortality, a philosophical doctrine, lead to belief in miracles, which is a superstition of the vulgar? What tendency had miracles and magic to make men austerely virtuous? Lastly, what power was there in a code of virtue, as calm and enlightened as that of Antoninus, to generate a zeal as fierce as that of Maccabæus? Wonderful events before now have apparently been nothing but coincidences, certainly; but they do not become less wonderful by cataloguing their constituent causes, unless we also show how these came to be constituent.

However, this by the way; the real question is this,—are these historical characteristics of Christianity, also in matter of fact, historical causes of Christianity? Has Gibbon given proof that they are? Has he brought evidence of their operation, or does he simply conjecture in his private judgment that they operated? Whether they were adapted to accomplish a certain work, is a matter of opinion; whether they did accomplish it is a question of fact. He ought to adduce instances of their efficiency before he has a right to say that they are efficient. And the second question is, what is this effect, of which they are to be considered as causes? It is no other than this, the conversion of bodies of men to the Christian faith. Let us keep this in view. We have to determine whether these five characteristics of Christianity were efficient causes of bodies of men becoming Christians? I think they neither did effect such conversions, nor were adapted to do so, and for these reasons:—

1. For first, as to zeal, by which Gibbon means party spirit, or *esprit de corps*; this doubtless is a motive principle when men are already members of a body, but does it operate in bringing them into it? The Jews were born in Judaism, they had a long and glorious history, and would naturally feel and show *esprit de corps*; but how did party spirit tend to transplant Jew or Gentile out of his own place into a new society, and that a society which as yet scarcely was formed in a society? Zeal, certainly, may be felt for a cause, or for a per-

son; on this point I shall speak presently; but Gibbon's idea
of Christian zeal is nothing better than the old wine of Judaism decanted into new Christian bottles, and would be too
flat a stimulant, even if it admitted of such a transference, to
be taken as a cause of conversion to Christianity without definite evidence in proof of the fact. Christians had zeal for
Christianity after they were converted, not before.

2. Next, as to the doctrine of a future state. Gibbon seems
to mean by this doctrine the fear of hell; now certainly in this
day there are persons converted from sin to a religious life,
by vivid descriptions of the future punishment of the wicked;
but then it must be recollected that such persons already
believe in the doctrine thus urged upon them. On the contrary, give some Tract upon hell-fire to one of the wild boys
in a large town, who has had no education, who has no faith;
and, instead of being startled by it, he will laugh at it as
something frightfully ridiculous. The belief in Styx and Tar-
tarus was dying out of the world at the time that Christianity
came in, as the parallel belief now seems to be dying out in
all classes of our own society. The doctrine of eternal punishment does only anger the multitude of men in our large towns
now, and make them blaspheme; why should it have had any
other effect on the heathen populations in the age when our
Lord came? Yet it was among those populations, that He and
His made their way from the first. As to the hope of eternal
life, that doubtless, as well as the fear of hell, was a most
operative doctrine in the case of men who had been actually
converted, of Christians brought before the magistrate, or
writhing under torture, but the thought of eternal glory does
not keep bad men from a bad life now, and why should it
convert them then from their pleasant sins, to a heavy, mortified, joyless existence, to a life of ill-usage, fright, contempt,
and desolation?

3. That the claim to miracles should have any wide influence in favour of Christianity among heathen populations,
who had plenty of portents of their own, is an opinion in curi-

ous contrast with the objection against Christianity which has provoked an answer from Paley, viz. that "Christian miracles are not recited or appealed to, by early Christian writers themselves, so fully or so frequently as might have been expected." Paley solves the difficulty as far as it is a fact, by observing, as I have suggested, that "it was their lot to contend with magical agency, against which the mere production of these facts was not sufficient for the convincing of their adversaries: "I do not know," he continues, "whether they themselves thought it quite decisive of the controversy." A claim to miraculous power on the part of Christians, which was so unfrequent as to become now an objection to the fact of their possessing it, can hardly have been a principal cause of their success.

4. And how is it possible to imagine with Gibbon that what he calls the "sober and domestic virtues" of Christians, their "aversion to the luxury of the age," their "chastity, temperance, and economy," that these dull qualities were persuasives of a nature to win and melt the hard heathen heart, in spite too of the dreary prospect of the *barathrum*, the amphitheatre, and the stake? Did the Christian morality by its severe beauty make a convert of Gibbon himself? On the contrary, he bitterly says, "It was not in this world that the primitive Christians were desirous of making themselves either agreeable or useful." "The virtue of the primitive Christians, like that of the first Romans, was very frequently guarded by poverty and ignorance." "Their gloomy and austere aspect, their abhorrence of the common business and pleasures of life, and their frequent predictions of impending calamities, inspired the Pagans with the apprehension of some danger which would arise from the new sect." Here we have not only Gibbon hating their moral and social bearing, but his heathen also. How then were those heathen overcome by the amiableness of that which they viewed with such disgust? We have here plain proof that the Christian character repelled the heathen; where is the evidence that it converted them?

5. Lastly, as to the ecclesiastical organization, this, doubtless, as time went on, was a special characteristic of the new religion; but how could it directly contribute to its extension? Of course it gave it strength, but it did not give it life. We are not born of bones and muscles. It is one thing to make conquests, another to consolidate an empire. It was before Constantine, that Christians made their great conquests. Rules are for settled times, not for time of war. So much is this contrast felt in the Catholic Church now, that, as is well known, in heathen countries and in countries which have thrown off her yoke, she suspends her diocesan administration and her Canon Law, and puts her children under the extraordinary, extra-legal jurisdiction of Propaganda.

This is what I am led to say on Gibbon's Five Causes. I do not deny that they might have operated now and then; Simon Magus came to Christianity in order to learn the craft of miracles, and Peregrinus from love of influence and power; but Christianity made its way, not by individual, but by broad, wholesale conversions, and the question is, how they originated?

It is very remarkable that it should not have occurred to a man of Gibbon's sagacity to inquire, what account the Christians themselves gave of the matter. Would it not have been worth while for him to have let conjecture alone, and to have looked for facts instead? Why did he not try the hypothesis of faith, hope, and charity? Did he never hear of repentance towards God, and faith in Christ? Did he not recollect the many words of Apostles, Bishops, Apologists, Martyrs, all forming one testimony? No; such thoughts are close upon him, and close upon the truth; but he cannot sympathize with them, he cannot believe in them, he cannot even enter into them, *because* he needs the due formation for such an exercise of mind.[1] Let us see whether the facts of the case do not come out clear and unequivocal, if we will but have the patience to endure them.

[1] *Vide supra*, pp. 259, 284, 314–16.

A Deliverer of the human race through the Jewish nation had been promised from time immemorial. The day came when He was to appear, and He was eagerly expected; moreover, One actually did make His appearance at that date in Palestine, and claimed to be He. He left the earth without apparently doing much for the object of His coming. But when He was gone, His disciples took upon themselves to go forth to preach to all parts of the earth with the object of preaching *Him,* and collecting converts *in His name.* After a little while they are found wonderfully to have succeeded. Large bodies of men in various places are to be seen, professing to be His disciples, owning Him as their King, and continually swelling in number and penetrating into the populations of the Roman Empire; at length they convert the Empire itself. All this is historical fact. Now, we want to know the farther historical fact, viz. the cause of their conversion; in other words, what were the topics of that preaching which was so effective? If we believe what is told us by the preachers and their converts, the answer is plain. They "preached Christ;" they called on men to believe, hope, and place their affections, in that Deliverer who had come and gone; and the moral instrument by which they persuaded them to do so, was a description of the life, character, mission, and power of that Deliverer, a promise of His invisible Presence and Protection here, and of the Vision and Fruition of Him hereafter. From first to last to Christians, as to Abraham, He Himself is the centre and fulness of the dispensation. They, as Abraham, "see His day, and are glad."

A temporal sovereign makes himself felt by means of his subordinate administrators, who bring his power and will to bear upon every individual of his subjects who personally know him not; the universal Deliverer, long expected, when He came, instead of making and securing subjects by a visible graciousness or majesty, departs;—*but* is found, through His preachers, to have imprinted the Image [1] or Idea of Himself

---

[1] *Vide supra,* pp. 19—24 and 57—61.

in the minds of His subjects individually; and that Image, apprehended and worshipped in individual minds, becomes a principle of association, and a real bond of those subjects one with another, who are thus united to the body by being united to that Image; and moreover that Image, which is their moral life, when they have been already converted, is also the original instrument of their conversion. It is the Image of Him who fulfils the one great need of human nature, the Healer of its wounds, the Physician of the soul, this Image it is which both creates faith, and then rewards it.

When we recognize this central Image as the vivifying idea both of the Christian body and of individuals in it, then, certainly, we are able to take into account at least two, of Gibbon's causes, as having, in connexion with that idea, some influence both in making converts and in strengthening them to persevere. It was the Thought of Christ, not a corporate body or a doctrine, which inspired that zeal which the historian so poorly comprehends; and it was the Thought of Christ which gave a life to the promise of that eternity, which without Him would be, in any soul, nothing short of an intolerable burden.

Now a mental vision such as this, perhaps, will be called cloudy, fanciful, unintelligible; that is, in other words, miraculous. I think it is so. How, without the Hand of God, could a new idea, one and the same, enter at once into myriads of men, women, and children of all ranks, especially the lower, and have power to wean them from their indulgences and sins, and to nerve them against the most cruel tortures, and to last in vigour as a sustaining influence for seven or eight generations, till it founded an extended polity, broke the obstinacy of the strongest and wisest government which the world has ever seen, and forced its way from its first caves and catacombs to the fulness of imperial power?

In considering this subject, I shall confine myself to the proof, as far as my limits allow, of two points,—first, that this Thought or Image of Christ was the principle of conversion

and fellowship; and next, that among the lower classes, who
had no power, influence, reputation, or education, lay its
principal success [1].

As to the vivifying idea, this is St. Paul's account of it: "I
make known to you the gospel which I preached to you, which
also you have received, and wherein you stand; by which also
you are saved. For I delivered to you first of all that which
I also received, how that Christ died for our sins according to
the Scriptures," &c., &c. "I am the least of the Apostles; but,
whether I or they, so we preached, and so you believed." "It
has pleased God by the foolishness of preaching to save them
that believe." "We preach Christ crucified." "I determined to
know nothing among you, but Jesus Christ, and Him crucified." "Your life is hid with Christ in God. When Christ, who
is your life, shall appear, then you also shall appear with Him
in glory." "I live, but now not I, but Christ liveth in me."

St. Peter, who has been accounted the master of a separate
school, says the same: "Jesus Christ, whom you have not seen,
yet love; in whom you now believe, and shall rejoice."

And St. John, who is sometimes accounted a third master
in Christianity: "It hath not yet appeared what we shall be;
but we know that, when He shall appear, we shall be like
to Him, because we shall see Him as He is."

That their disciples followed them in this sovereign devotion to an Invisible Lord, will appear as I proceed.

And next, as to the worldly position and character of His
disciples, our Lord, in the well-known passage, returns thanks
to His Heavenly Father "because," He says, "Thou hast hid
these things"—the mysteries of His kingdom—"from the wise
and prudent, and hast revealed them to little ones." And, in
accordance with this announcement, St. Paul says that "not

---

[1] Had my limits allowed it, I ought, as a third subject, to have described the existing system of impure idolatry and the wonderful
phenomenon of such multitudes, who had been slaves to it, escaping
from it by the power of Christianity,—under the guidance of the great
work ("On the Gentile and the Jew") of Dr. Döllinger.

many wise men according to the flesh, not many mighty, not many noble," became Christians. He, indeed, is one of those few; so were others his contemporaries, and, as time went on, the number of these exceptions increased, so that converts were found, not a few, in the high places of the empire, and in the schools of philosophy and learning; but still the rule held, that the great mass of Christians were to be found in those classes which were of no account in the world, whether on the score of rank or of education.

We all know this was the case with our Lord and His Apostles. It seems almost irreverent to speak of their temporal employments, when we are so simply accustomed to consider them in their spiritual associations; but it is profitable to remind ourselves that our Lord Himself was a sort of smith, and made ploughs and cattle-yokes. Four Apostles were fishermen, one a petty tax collector, two husbandmen, and another is said to have been a market-gardener.[1] When Peter and John were brought before the Council, they are spoken of as being, in a secular point of view, "illiterate men, and of the lower sort," and thus they are spoken of in a later age by the Fathers.

That their converts were of the same rank as themselves, is reported, in their favour or to their discredit, by friends and enemies, for four centuries. "If a man be educated," says Celsus in mockery, "let him keep clear of us Christians; we want no men of wisdom, no men of sense. We account all such as evil. No; but, if there be one who is inexperienced, or stupid, or untaught, or a fool, let him come with good heart." "They are weavers," he says elsewhere, "shoemakers, fullers, illiterate, clowns." "Fools, low-born fellows," says Trypho. "The greater part of you," says Cæcilius, "are worn with want, cold, toil, and famine; men collected from the lowest dregs of the

---

[1] On the subjects which follow, *vide* Lami, *De Eruditione Apostolorum;* Mamachius, *Origines Christ.;* Ruinart, *Act. Mart.;* Lardner, *Credibility,* &c.; Fleury, *Eccles. Hist.;* Kortholt, *Calumn. Pagan.;* and *De Morib. Christ.,* &c.

people; ignorant, credulous women;" "unpolished, boors, illiterate, ignorant even of the sordid arts of life; they do not understand even civil matters, how can they understand divine?" "They have left their tongs, mallets, and anvils, to preach about the things of heaven," says Libanius. "They deceive women, servants, and slaves," says Julian. The author of Philopatris speaks of them as "poor creatures, blocks, withered old fellows, men of downcast and pale visages." As to their religion, it had the reputation popularly, according to various Fathers, of being an anile superstition, the discovery of old women, a joke, a madness, an infatuation, an absurdity, a fanaticism.

The Fathers themselves confirm these statements, so far as they relate to the insignificance and ignorance of their brethen. Athenagoras speaks of the virtue of their "ignorant men, mechanics, and old women." "They are gathered," says St. Jerome, "not from the Academy or Lyceum, but from the low populace." "They are whitesmiths, servants, farm-labourers, woodmen, men of sordid trades, beggars," says Theodoret. "We are engaged in the farm, in the market, at the baths, wine-shops, stables, and fairs; as seamen, as soldiers, as peasants, as dealers," says Tertullian. How came such men to be converted? and, being converted, how came such men to overturn the world? Yet they went forth from the first, "conquering and to conquer."

The first manifestation of their formidable numbers is made just about the time when St. Peter and St. Paul suffered martyrdom, and was the cause of a terrible persecution. We have the account of it in Tacitus. "Nero," he says, "to put an end to the common talk [that Rome had been set on fire by his order], imputed it to others, visiting with a refinement of punishment those detestable criminals who went by the name of Christians. The author of that denomination was Christus, who had been executed in Tiberius's time by the procurator, Pontius Pilate. The pestilent superstition, checked for a while, burst out again, not only throughout Judea, the first seat of the

evil, but even throughout Rome, the centre both of confluence
and outbreak of all that is atrocious and disgraceful from every
quarter. First were arrested those who made no secret of their
sect; and by this clue a vast multitude of others, convicted, not
so much of firing the city, as of hatred to the human race.
Mockery was added to death; clad in skins of beasts, they
were torn to pieces by dogs; they were nailed up to crosses;
they were made inflammable, so that, when day failed, they
might serve as lights. Hence, guilty as they were, and deserv-
ing of exemplary punishment, they excited compassion, as
being destroyed, not for the public welfare, but from the
cruelty of one man."

The two Apostles suffered, and a silence follows of a whole
generation. At the end of thirty or forty years, Pliny, the friend
of Trajan, as well as of Tacitus, is sent as that Emperor's
Proprætor into Bithynia, and is startled and perplexed by the
number, influence, and pertinacity of the Christians whom he
finds there, and in the neighbouring province of Pontus. He
has the opportunity of being far more fair to them than his
friend the historian. He writes to Trajan to know how he
ought to deal with them, and I will quote some portions of
his letter.

He says he does not know how to proceed with them, as
their religion has not received toleration from the state. He
never was present at any trial of them; he doubted whether
the children among them as well as grown people, ought to
be accounted as culprits; whether recantation would set
matters right, or whether they incur punishment all the same;
whether they were to be punished, merely because Christians,
even though no definite crime was proved against them. His
way had been to examine them, and put questions to them;
if they confessed the charge, he gave them one or two chances,
threatening them with punishment; then, if they persisted, he
gave orders for their execution. "For," he argues, "I felt no
doubt that, whatever might be the character of their opinions,
stubborn and inflexible obstinacy deserved punishment. Others

there were of a like infatuation, whom, being citizens, I sent
to Rome."

Some satisfied him; they repeated after him an invocation
to the gods, and offered wine and incense to the Emperor's
image, and in addition, cursed the name of Christ. "Accordingly," he says, "I let them go; for I am told nothing can
compel a real Christian to do any of these things." There were
others, too, who sacrificed, who had been Christians, some of
them for as many as twenty years.

Then he is curious to know something more definite about
them. "This, the informers told me, was the whole of their
crime or mistake, that they were accustomed to assemble on
a stated day before dawn, and to say together a hymn to Christ
as a god, and to bind themselves by an oath [sacramento]
(not to any crime, but on the contrary) to keep from theft,
robbery, adultery, breach of promise, and making free with
deposits. After this they used to separate, and then to meet
again for a meal, which was social and harmless. However,
they left even that off, after my Edict against their meeting."

This information led him to put to the torture two maid-
servants, "who were called ministers," in order to find out
what was true, what was false in it; but he says he could make
out nothing, except a depraved and excessive superstition.
This is what led him to consult the Emperor, "especially because of the number who were implicated in it; for these are,
or are likely to be, many, of all ages, nay, of both sexes. For
the contagion of this superstition has spread, not only in the
cities, but about the villages and the open country." He adds
that already there was some improvement. "The almost for-
saken temples begin to be filled again, and the sacred solem-
nities after a long intermission are revived. Victims, too, are
again on sale, purchasers having been most rare to find."

The salient points in this account are these, that, at the
end of one generation from the Apostles, nay, almost in the
lifetime of St. John, Christians had so widely spread in a large
district of Asia, as nearly to suppress the Pagan religions there;

that they were people of exemplary lives; that they had a name for invincible fidelity to their religion; that no threats or sufferings could make them deny it; and that their only tangible characteristic was the worship of our Lord.

This was at the beginning of the second century; not a great many years after, we have another account of the Christian body, from an anonymous Greek Christian, in a letter to a friend whom he was anxious to convert. It is far too long to quote, and difficult to compress; but a few sentences will show how strikingly it agrees with the account of the heathen Pliny, especially in two points,—first, in the numbers of the Christians, secondly, on devotion to our Lord as the vivifying principle of their association.

"Christians," says the writer, "differ not from other men in country, or speech, or customs. They do not live in cities of their own, or speak in any peculiar dialect, or adopt any strange modes of living. They inhabit their native countries, but as sojourners; they take their part in all burdens, as if citizens, and in all sufferings, as if they were strangers. In foreign countries they recognize a home, and in every home they see a foreign country. They marry like other men, but do not disown their children. They obey the established laws, but they go beyond them in the tenor of their lives. They love all men, and are persecuted by all; they are not known, and they are condemned; they are poor, and make many rich; they are dishonoured, yet in dishonour they are glorified; they are slandered, and they are cleared; they are called names, and they bless. By the Jews they are assailed as aliens, by the Greeks they are persecuted, nor can they who hate them say why.

"Christians are in the world, as the soul in the body. The soul pervades the limbs of the body, and Christians the cities of the world. The flesh hates the soul, and wars against it, though suffering no wrong from it; and the world hates Christians. The soul loves the flesh that hates it, and Christians love their enemies. Their tradition is not an earthly invention, nor

is it a mortal thought which they so carefully guard, nor a
dispensation of human mysteries which is committed to their
charge; but God Himself, the Omnipotent and Invisible
Creator, has from heaven established among men His Truth
and His Word, the Holy and Incomprehensible, and has
deeply fixed the same in their hearts; not, as might be expected, sending any servant, angel, or prince, or administrator
of things earthly or heavenly, but the very Artificer and De-
miurge of the Universe. Him God hath sent to man, not to
inflict terror, but in clemency and gentleness, as a King sending a King who was His Son; He sent Him as God to men, to
save them. He hated not, nor rejected us, nor remembered our
guilt, but showed Himself long-suffering, and, in His own
words, bore our sins. He gave His own Son as a ransom for
us, the just for the unjust. For what other thing, except His
Righteousness, could cover our guilt? In whom was it possible
for us, lawless sinners, to find justification, save in the Son of
God alone? O sweet interchange! O heavenly workmanship
past finding out! O benefits exceeding expectation! Sending,
then, a Saviour, who is able to save those who of themselves
are incapable of salvation, He has willed that we should
regard Him as our Guardian, Father, Teacher, Counsellor,
Physician; our Mind, Light, Honour, Glory, Strength, and
Life." [1]

The writing from which I have been quoting is of the early
part of the second century. Twenty or thirty years after it St.
Justin Martyr speaks as strongly of the spread of the new
Religion: "There is not any one race of men," he says, "bar-
barian or Greek, nay, of those who live in waggons, or who
are Nomads, or Shepherds in tents, among whom prayers and
eucharists are not offered to the Father and Maker of the
Universe, through the name of the crucified Jesus."

Towards the end of the century, Clement:—"The word of
our Master did not remain in Judea, as philosophy remained
in Greece, but has been poured out over the whole world,

[1] Ep. ad Diognet.

persuading Greeks and Barbarians alike, race by race, village by village, every city, whole houses, and hearers one by one, nay, not a few of the philosophers themselves."

And Tertullian, at the very close of it, could in his *Apologia*, even proceed to threaten the Roman Government:—"We are a people of yesterday," he says; "and yet we have filled every place belonging to you, cities, islands, castles, towns, assemblies, your very camp, your tribes, companies, palaces, senate, forum. We leave you your temples only. We can count your armies, and our numbers in a single province will be greater. In what war with you should we not be sufficient and ready, even though unequal in numbers, who so willingly are put to death, if it were not in this Religion of ours more lawful to be slain than to slay?"

Once more, let us hear the great Origen, in the early part of the next century:—"In all Greece and in all barbarous races within our world, there are tens of thousands who have left their national laws and customary gods for the law of Moses and the word of Jesus Christ; though to adhere to that law is to incur the hatred of idolaters, and the risk of death besides to have embraced that word. And considering how, in so few years, in spite of the attacks made on us, to the loss of life or property, and with no great store of teachers, the preaching of that word has found its way into every part of the world, so that Greek and barbarians, wise and unwise, adhere to the religion of Jesus, doubtless it is a work greater than any work of man."

We need no proof to assure us that this steady and rapid growth of Christianity was a phenomenon which startled its contemporaries, as much as it excites the curiosity of philosophic historians now; and they too had their own ways then of accounting for it, different indeed from Gibbon's, but quite as pertinent, though less elaborate. These were principally two, both leading them to persecute it,—the obstinacy of the Christians and their magical powers, of which the former was the explanation adopted by educated minds, and the latter chiefly by the populace.

As to the former, from first to last, men in power magisterially reprobate the senseless obstinacy of the members of the new sect, as their characteristic offence. Pliny, as we have seen, found it to be their only fault, but one sufficient to merit capital punishment. The Emperor Marcus seems to consider obstinacy the ultimate motive-cause to which their unnatural conduct was traceable. After speaking of the soul, as "ready, if it must now be separated from the body, to be extinguished, or dissolved, or to remain with it;" he adds, "but the readiness must come of its own judgment, not from simple perverseness, as in the case of Christians, but with considerateness, with gravity, and without theatrical effect, so as to be persuasive." And Diocletian, in his Edict of persecution, professes it to be his "earnest aim to punish the depraved persistence of those most wicked men."

As to the latter charge, their founder, it was said, had gained a knowledge of magic in Egypt, and had left behind him in his sacred books the secrets of the art. Suetonius himself speaks of them as "men of a magical superstition;" and Celsus accuses them of "incantations in the name of demons." The officer who had custody of St. Perpetua, feared her escape from prison "by magical incantations." When St. Tiburtius had walked barefoot on hot coals, his judge cried out that Christ had taught him magic. St. Anastasia was thrown into prison as dealing in poisons; the populace called out against St. Agnes, "Away with the witch! away with the sorceress!" When St. Bonosus and St. Maximilian bore the burning pitch without shrinking, Jews and heathen cried out, "Those wizards and sorcerers." "What new delusion," says the magistrate concerning St. Romanus, in the Hymn of Prudentius, "has brought in these sophists who deny the worship of the Gods? how doth this chief sorcerer mock us, skilled by his Thessalian charm to laugh at punishment?" [1]

It is indeed difficult to enter into the feelings of irritation and fear, of contempt and amazement, which were excited, whether in the town populace or in the magistrates in the

[1] Essay on Development of Doctrine, ch. vi. § 1, 18.

presence of conduct so novel, so unvarying, so absolutely beyond their comprehension. The very young and the very old, the child, the youth in the heyday of his passions, the sober man of middle age, maidens and mothers of families, boors and slaves as well as philosophers and nobles, solitary confessors and companies of men and women,—all these were seen equally to defy the powers of darkness to do their worst. In this strange encounter it became a point of honour with the Roman to break the determination of his victim, and it was the triumph of faith when his most savage expedients for that purpose were found to be in vain. The martyrs shrank from suffering like other men, but such natural shrinking was incommensurable with apostasy. No intensity of torture had any means of affecting what was a mental conviction; and the sovereign Thought in which they had lived was their adequate support and consolation in their death. To them the prospect of wounds and loss of limbs was not more terrible than it is to the combatant of this world. They faced the implements of torture as the soldier takes his post before the enemy's battery. They cheered and ran forward to meet his attack, and as it were dared him, if he would, to destroy the numbers who kept closing up the foremost rank, as their comrades who had filled it fell. And when Rome at last found she had to deal with a host of Scævolas, then the proudest of earthly sovereignties, arrayed in the completeness of her material resources, humbled herself before a power which was founded on a mere sense of the unseen.

In the colloquy of the aged Ignatius, the disciple of the Apostles, with the Emperor Trajan, we have a sort of type of what went on for three, or rather four centuries. He was sent all the way from Antioch to Rome to be devoured by the beasts in the amphitheatre. As he travelled, he wrote letters to various Christian Churches, and among others to his Roman brethren, among whom he was to suffer. Let us see whether, as I have said, the Image of that Divine King, who had been

promised from the beginning, was not the living principle of
his obstinate resolve. The old man is almost fierce in his
determination to be martyred. "May those beasts," he says to
his brethren, "be my gain, which are in readiness for me! I
will provoke and coax them to devour me quickly, and not to
be afraid of me, as they are of some whom they will not touch.
Should they be unwilling, I will compel them. Bear with me;
I know what is my gain. Now I begin to be a disciple. Of
nothing of things visible or invisible am I ambitious, save to
gain Christ. Whether it is fire or the cross, the assault of wild
beasts, the wrenching of my bones, the crunching of my limbs,
the crushing of my whole body, let the tortures of the devil
all assail me, if I do but gain Christ Jesus." Elsewhere in the
same Epistle he says, "I write to you, still alive, but longing to
die. My Love is crucified! I have no taste for perishable food.
I long for God's Bread, heavenly Bread, Bread of life, which
is Flesh of Jesus Christ, the Son of God. I long for God's
draught, His Blood, which is Love without corruption, and
Life for evermore." It is said that, when he came into the
presence of Trajan, the latter cried out, "Who are you, poor
devil, who are so eager to transgress our rules?" "That is no
name," he answered, "for Theophorus." "Who is Theophorus?"
asked the Emperor. "He who bears Christ in his breast." In
the Apostle's words, already cited, he had "Christ in him, the
hope of glory." All this may be called enthusiasm; but enthusiasm affords a much more adequate explanation of the
confessorship of an old man, than do Gibbon's five reasons.

Instances of the same ardent spirit, and of the living faith
on which it was founded, are to be found wherever we open
the *Acta Martyrum*. In the outbreak at Smyrna in the middle
of the second century, amid tortures which even moved the
heathen bystanders to compassion, the sufferers were conspicuous for their serene calmness. "They made it evident to
us all," says the Epistle of the Church, "that in the midst of
those sufferings they were absent from the body, or rather,

that the Lord stood by them, and walked in the midst of them."

At that time Polycarp, the familiar friend of St. John, and a contemporary of Ignatius, suffered in his extreme old age. When, before his sentence, the Proconsul bade him "swear by the fortunes of Cæsar, and have done with Christ," his answer betrayed that intimate devotion to the self-same Idea, which had been the inward life of Ignatius. "Eighty and six years," he answered, "have I been His servant, and He has never wronged me, but ever has preserved me; and how can I blaspheme my King and my Saviour?" When they would have fastened him to the stake, he said, "Let alone; He who gives me to bear the fire, will give me also to stand firm upon the pyre without your nails."

Christians felt it as an acceptable service to Him who loved them, to confess with courage and to suffer with dignity. In this chivalrous spirit, as it may be called, they met the words and deeds of their persecutors, as the children of men return bitterness for bitterness, and blow for blow. "What soldier," says Minucius, with a reference to the invisible Presence of our Lord, "does not challenge danger more daringly under the eye of his commander?" In that same outbreak at Smyrna, when the Proconsul urged the young Germanicus to have mercy on himself and on his youth, to the astonishment of the populace he provoked a wild beast to fall upon him. In like manner, St. Justin tells us of Lucius, who, when he saw a Christian sent off to suffer, at once remonstrated sharply with the judge, and was sent off to execution with him; and then another presented himself, and was sent off also. When the Christians were thrown into prison, in the fierce persecution at Lyons, Vettius Epagathus, a youth of distinction who had given himself to an ascetic life, could not bear the sight of the sufferings of his brethren, and asked leave to plead their cause. The only answer he got was to be sent off the first to die. What the contemporary account sees in his conduct is, not that he was zealous for his brethren, though zealous he was, nor that he believed in miracles, though he doubtless did believe; but that he "was a gracious disciple of Christ, following the Lamb whithersoever He went."

In that memorable persecution, when Blandina, a slave, was seized for confessorship, her mistress and her fellow Christians dread lest, from her delicate make, she should give way under the torments; but she even tired out her tormentors. It was a refreshment and relief to her to cry out amid her pains, "I am a Christian." They remanded her to prison, and then brought her out for fresh suffering a second day and a third. On the last day she saw a boy of fifteen brought into the amphitheatre for death; she feared for him, as others had feared for her; but he too went through his trial generously, and went to God before her. Her last sufferings were to be placed in the notorious red-hot chair, and then to be exposed in a net to a wild bull; they finished by cutting her throat. Sanctus, too, when the burning plates of brass were placed on his limbs, all through his torments did but say, "I am a Christian," and stood erect and firm, "bathed and strengthened," say his brethren who write the account, "in the heavenly well of living water which flows from the breast of Christ," or, as they say elsewhere of all the martyrs, "refreshed with the joy of martyrdom, the hope of blessedness, love towards Christ, and the spirit of God the Father." How clearly do we see all through this narrative what it was which nerved them for the combat! If they love their brethren, it is in the fellowship of their Lord; if they look for heaven, it is because He is the Light of it.

Epipodius, a youth of gentle nurture, when struck by the Prefect, on the mouth while blood flowed from it, cried out, "I confess that Jesus Christ is God, together with the Father and the Holy host." Symphorian, of Autun, also a youth, and of noble birth, when told to adore an idol, answered, "Give me leave, and I will hammer it to pieces." When Leonidas, the father of the young Origen, was in prison for his faith, the boy, then seventeen, burned to share his martyrdom, and his mother had to hide his clothes to prevent him from executing his purpose. Afterwards he attended the confessors in prison, stood by them at the tribunal, and gave them the kiss of peace when they were led out to suffer, and this, in spite of being several times apprehended and put upon the rack. Also in Alexandria, the beautiful slave, Potamiæna, when about to be stripped in order to be thrown into the cauldron of hot pitch, said to the Prefect, "I pray you rather let me be dipped down slowly into it with my clothes on, and you shall see with what patience I am gifted by Him of whom you are ignorant, Jesus Christ." When the populace in the same city had beaten out the aged Apollonia's teeth, and lit a fire to burn her, unless she would blaspheme, she leaped into the fire herself, and so gained her crown. When Sixtus, Bishop of Rome, was led to martyrdom, his deacon, Laurence, followed him weeping and complaining, "O my father, whither goest thou without thy son?" And when his own turn came, three days afterwards, and he was put upon the gridiron, after a while he said to the Prefect, "Turn me; this side is done." Whence came this tremendous spirit, scaring, nay, offending, the fastidious criticism of our delicate days? Does Gibbon think to sound the depths of the eternal ocean with the tape and measuring-rod of his merely literary philosophy?

When Barulas, a child of seven years old, was scourged to blood for repeating his catechism before the heathen judge— viz. "There is but one God, and Jesus Christ is true God"—his mother encouraged him to persevere, chiding him for asking for some drink. At Merida, a girl of noble family, of the age of twelve, presented herself before the tribunal, and over- turned the idols. She was scourged and burned with torches; she neither shed a tear, nor showed other signs of suffering. When the fire reached her face, she opened her mouth to receive it, and was suffocated. At Cæsarea, a girl, under eight- een, went boldly to ask the prayers of some Christians who were in chains before the Prætorium. She was seized at once, and her sides torn open with the iron rakes, preserving the while a bright and joyous countenance. Peter, Dorotheus, Gorgonius, were boys of the imperial bed-chamber; they were highly in favour with their masters, and were Christians. They too suffered dreadful torments, dying under them, without a shadow of wavering. Call such conduct madness, if you will, or magic; but do not mock us by ascribing it in such mere children to simple desire of immortality, or to any ecclesiastical organization.

When the persecution raged in Asia, a vast multitude of Christians presented themselves before the Proconsul, challenging him to proceed against them. "Poor wretches!" half in contempt and half in affright, he answered, "if you must die, cannot you find ropes or precipices for the purpose?" At Utica, a hundred and fifty Christians of both sexes and all ages were martyrs in one company. They are said to have been told to burn incense to an idol, or they should be thrown into a pit of burning lime; they without hesitation leapt into it. In Egypt a hundred and twenty confessors, after having sustained the loss of eyes or of feet, endured to linger out their lives in the mines of Palestine and Cilicia. In the last persecution, according to the testimony of the grave Eusebius, a contemporary, the slaughter of men, women, and children, went on by twenties, sixties, hundreds, till the instruments of execution were worn out, and the executioners could kill no more. Yet he tells us, as an eye-witness, that, as soon as any Christians were condemned, others ran from all parts, and surrounded the tribunals, confessing the faith, and joyfully receiving their condemnation, and singing songs of thanksgiving and triumph to the last.

Thus was the Roman power overcome. Thus did the Seed of Abraham, and the Expectation of the Gentiles, the meek Son of man, "take to Himself His great power and reign" in the hearts of His people, in the public theatre of the world. The mode in which the primeval prophecy was fulfilled is as marvellous, as the prophecy itself is clear and bold.

"So may all Thy enemies perish, O Lord; but let them that love Thee shine, as the sun shineth in his rising!"

I will add the memorable words of the two great Apologists of the period:—

"Your cruelty," says Tertullian, "though each act be more refined than the last, doth profit you nothing. To our sect it is rather an inducement. We grow up in great numbers, as often as you cut us down. The blood of the martyrs is their seed for the harvest."

Origen even uses the language of prophecy. To the objection of Celsus that Christianity from its principles would, if let alone, open the whole empire to the irruption of the barbarians, and the utter ruin of civilization, he replies, "If all Romans are such as we, then too the barbarians will draw near to the Word of God, and will become the most observant of the Law. And every worship shall come to nought, and that of the Christians alone obtain the mastery, for the Word is continually gaining possession of more and more souls."

One additional remark:—It was fitting that those mixed unlettered multitudes, who for three centuries had suffered and triumphed by virtue of the inward Vision of their Divine Lord, should be selected, as we know they were, in the fourth, to be the special champions of His Divinity and the victorious foes of its impugners, at a time when the civil power, which had found them too strong for its arms, attempted, by means of a portentous heresy in the high places of the Church, to rob them of that Truth which had all along been the principle of their strength.

10

I have been forestalling all along the thought with which I shall close these considerations on the subject of Christianity; and necessarily forestalling it, because it properly comes first, though the course which my thoughts have taken has not allowed me to introduce it in its natural place. Revelation begins where Natural Religion fails. The Religion of Nature is a mere inchoation, and needs a complement,—it can have but one complement, and that very complement is Christianity.

Natural Religion is based upon the sense of sin; it recognizes the disease, but it cannot find, it does but look out for the remedy. That remedy, both for guilt and for moral impotence, is found in the central doctrine of Revelation, the Mediation of Christ. I need not go into a subject so familiar to all men in a Christian country.

Thus it is that Christianity is the fulfilment of the promise made to Abraham and of the Mosaic revelations; this is how it has been able from the first to occupy the world and gain a hold on every class of human society to which its preachers reached; this is why the Roman power and the multitude of religions which it embraced could not stand against it; this is the secret of its sustained energy, and its never-flagging martyrdoms; this is how at present it is so mysteriously potent, in spite of the new and fearful adversaries which beset its path. It has with it that gift of staunching and healing the one deep wound of human nature, which avails more for its success than a full encyclopedia of scientific knowledge and a whole library of controversy, and therefore it must last while human nature lasts. It is a living truth which never can grow old.

Some persons speak of it as if it were a thing of history, with only indirect bearings upon modern times; I cannot allow that it is a mere historical religion. Certainly it has its foundations in past and glorious memories, but its power is in the present. It is no dreary matter of antiquarianism; we do not contemplate it in conclusions drawn from dumb documents and dead events, but by faith exercised in ever-living objects, and by the appropriation and use of ever-recurring gifts.

Our communion with it is in the unseen, not in the obsolete. At this very day its rites and ordinances are continually eliciting the active interposition of that Omnipotence in which the

Religion long ago began. First and above all is the Holy Mass, in which He who once died for us upon the Cross, brings back and perpetuates, by His literal presence in it, that one and the same sacrifice which cannot be repeated. Next, there is the actual entrance of Himself, soul and body, and divinity, into the soul and body of every worshipper who comes to Him for the gift, a privilege more intimate than if we lived with Him during His long-past sojourn upon earth. And then, moreover, there is His personal abidance in our churches, raising earthly service into a foretaste of heaven. Such is the profession of Christianity, and, I repeat, its very divination of our needs is in itself a proof that it is really the supply of them.

Upon the doctrines which I have mentioned as central truths, others, as we all know, follow, which rule our personal conduct and course of life, and our social and civil relations. The promised Deliverer, the Expectation of the nations, has not done His work by halves. He has given us Saints and Angels for our protection. He has taught us how by our prayers and services to benefit our departed friends, and to keep up a memorial of ourselves when we are gone. He has created a visible hierarchy and a succession of sacraments, to be the channels of His mercies, and the Crucifix secures the thought of Him in every house and chamber. In all these ways He brings Himself before us. I am not here speaking of His gifts as gifts, but as memorials; not as what Christians know they convey, but in their visible character; and I say that, as human nature itself is still in life and action as much as ever it was, so He too lives, to our imaginations, by His visible symbols, as if He were on earth, with a practical efficacy which even unbelievers cannot deny, so as to be the corrective of that nature, and its strength day by day, and that this power of perpetuating His Image, being altogether singular and special, and the prerogative of Him and Him alone, is a grand evidence how well He fulfils to this day that Sovereign Mission which, from the first beginning of the world's history, has been in prophecy assigned to Him.

I cannot better illustrate this argument than by recurring to a deep thought on the subject of Christianity, which has before now attracted the notice of philosophers and preachers,[1] as coming from the wonderful man who swayed the destinies of Europe in the first years of this century. It was an argument not unnatural in one who had that special passion for human glory, which has been the incentive of so many heroic careers and of so many mighty revolutions in the history of the world. In the solitude of his imprisonment, and in the view of death, he seems to have expressed himself to the following effect:—

"I have been accustomed to put before me the examples of Alexander and Cæsar, with the hope of rivalling their exploits, and living in the minds of men for ever. Yet, after all, in what sense does Cæsar, in what sense does Alexander live? Who knows or cares any thing about them? At best, nothing but their names is known; for who among the multitude of men, who hear or who utter their names really knows any thing about their lives or their deeds, or attaches to those names any definite idea? Nay, even their names do but flit up and down the world like ghosts, mentioned only on particular occasions, or from accidental associations. Their chief home is the schoolroom; they have a foremost place in boys' grammars and exercise-books; they are splendid examples for themes; they form writing-copies. So low is heroic Alexander fallen, so low is imperial Cæsar, 'ut pueris placeat et declamatio fiat.'

"But, on the contrary" (he is reported to have continued), "there is just One Name in the whole world that lives; it is the Name of One who passed His years in obscurity, and who died a malefactor's death. Eighteen hundred years have gone since that time, but still it has its hold upon the human mind. It has possessed the world, and it maintains possession. Amid the most varied nations, under the most diversified circumstances, in the most cultivated, in the rudest races and intel-

[1] Fr. Lacordaire and M. Nicolas.

lects, in all classes of society, the Owner of that great Name reigns. High and low, rich and poor, acknowledge Him. Millions of souls are conversing with Him, are venturing on His word, are looking for His presence. Palaces, sumptuous, innumerable, are raised to His honour; His image, as in the hour of His deepest humiliation, is triumphantly displayed in the proud city, in the open country, in the corners of streets, on the tops of mountains. It sanctifies the ancestral hall, the closet, and the bed-chamber; it is the subject for the exercise of the highest genius in the imitative arts. It is worn next the heart in life; it is held before the failing eyes in death. Here, then, is One who is *not* a mere name, who is not a mere fiction, who is a reality. He is dead and gone, but still He lives,—lives as the living, energetic thought of successive generations, as the awful motive-power of a thousand great events. He has done without effort what others with life-long struggles have not done. Can He be less than Divine? Who is He but the Creator Himself; who is sovereign over His own works, towards whom our eyes and hearts turn instinctively, because He is our Father and our God?"

Here I end my specimens, among the many which might be given, of the arguments adducible for Christianity. I have dwelt upon them, in order to show how I would apply the principles of this Essay to the proof of its divine origin. Christianity is addressed, both as regards its evidences and its contents, to minds which are in the normal condition of human nature, as believing in God and in a future judgment. Such minds it addresses both through the intellect and through the imagination; creating a certitude of its truth by arguments too various for direct enumeration, too personal and deep for words, too powerful and concurrent for refutation. Nor need reason come first and faith second (though this is the logical order), but one and the same teaching is in different aspects both object and proof, and elicits one complex act both of inference and of assent. It speaks to us one by one, and it is received by us one by one, as the counterpart, so to say, of ourselves, and is real as we are real.

In the sacred words of its Divine Author and Object concerning Himself, "I am the Good Shepherd, and I know Mine, and Mine know Me. My sheep hear My voice, and I know them, and they follow Me. And I give them everlasting life, and they shall never perish; and no man shall pluck them out of My hand."

NOTE I

On Hooker and Chillingworth, vid. supr. 171

1. ON the first publication of this volume, a Correspondent did me the favour of marking for me a list of passages in Chillingworth's celebrated work, besides that which I had myself quoted, in which the argument was more or less brought forward, on which I have animadverted in ch. vii. § 2, p. 171. He did this with the purpose of showing, that Chillingworth's meaning, when carefully inquired into, would be found to be in substantial agreement with the distinction I had myself made between infallibility and certitude; those inaccuracies of language into which he fell, being necessarily involved in the *argumentum ad hominem*, which he was urging upon his opponent, or being the accidental result of the peculiar character of his intellect, which, while full of ideas, was wanting in the calmness and caution which are conspicuous in Bishop Butler. Others more familiar with Chillingworth than I am must decide on this point; but I can have no indisposition to accept an explanation, which deprives controversialists of this day of the authority of a vigorous and acute mind in their use of an argument, which is certainly founded on a great confusion of thought.

I subjoin the references with which my Correspondent has supplied me:—

(1.) Passages tending to show an agreement of Chillingworth's opinion on the distinction between certitude and infallibility with that laid down in the foregoing essay:

1. "Religion of Protestants," ch. ii. § 121 (vol. i. p. 243, Oxf. ed. 1838), "For may not a private man," &c.
2. *Ibid.* § 152 (p. 265). The last sentence, however, after "when they thought they dreamt," is a fall into the error which he had been exposing.
3. *Ibid.* § 160 (p. 275).
4. Ch. iii. § 26 (p. 332), "Neither is your argument," &c.
5. *Ibid.* § 36 (p. 346).
6. *Ibid.* § 50 (p. 363), "That Abraham," &c.
7. Ch. v. § 63 (vol. ii. p. 215).

8. *Ibid.* § 107 (p. 265).
9. Ch. vii. § 13 (p. 452).
      Vide. also vol. i. pp. 115, 121, 196, 236, 242, 411.
(2.) Passages inconsistent with the above:—
1. Ch. ii. § 25 (vol. i. p. 177) An *argumentum ad hominem.*
2. *Ibid.* § 28 (p. 180).
3. *Ibid.* § 45 (p. 189). An *argumentum ad hominem.*
4. *Ibid.* § 149 (p. 263). An *argumentum ad hominem.*
5. *Ibid.* § 154 (p. 267). Quoted in the text, p. 226.
6. Ch. v. § 45 (vol. ii. p. 391). He is arguing on his opponent's principles.

2. Also, I have to express my obligation to another Correspondent, who called my attention to a passage of Hooker ("Eccles. Pol." ii. 7) beginning "An earnest desire," &c., which seemed to anticipate the doctrine of Locke about certitude. It is so difficult to be sure of the meaning of a writer whose style is so foreign to that of our own times, that I am shy of attempting to turn this passage into categorical statements. Else, I should ask, does not Hooker here assume the absolute certainty of the inspiration and divine authority of Scripture, and believe its teaching as the very truth unconditionally and without any admixture of doubt? Yet what had he but probable evidence as a warrant for such a view of it? Again, did he receive the Athanasian Creed on any logical demonstration that its articles were in Scripture? Yet he felt himself able without any misgiving to say aloud in the congregation, "Which faith except every one do keep whole and undefiled, *without doubt* he shall perish everlastingly." In truth it is the happy inconsistency of his school to be more orthodox in their conclusions than in their premises; to be sceptics in their paper theories, and believers in their own persons.

3. Also, a friend sends me word, as regards the controversy on the various readings of Shakespeare to which I have referred (*supra,* ch. viii. § 1, p. 206) in illustration of the shortcomings of Formal Inference, that, since the date of the article in the magazine, of which I have there availed myself, the verdict of critics has been unfavourable to the authority and value of the Annotated Copy, discovered twenty years ago. I may add, that, since my first edition, I have had the pleasure of reading Dr. Ingleby's interesting dissertation on the "Traces of the Authorship of the Works attributed to Shakespeare."

NOTE II

On the alternative intellectually between Atheism and Catholicity, vid. supr. p. 107, &c.

December, 1880

As I am sending the last pages of the New Edition of this Essay to the press, I avail myself of an opportunity which its subject makes apposite, to explain a misunderstanding, as appearing in a London daily print, of a statement of mine used in controversy, which has elicited within the last few days a prompt and effective defence from the kind zeal of Mr. Lilly. I should not think it necessary to make any addition to what he has said so well, except that it may be expected that what is a great mistake concerning me should be set right under my own hand and in my own words.

It has been said of me that "Cardinal Newman has *confined* his defence of his own *creed* to the proposition that it is *the only possible* alternative to Atheism." I understand this to mean, that I have given up, both in my religious convictions and my controversial efforts, any thought of bringing arguments from reason to bear upon the question of the truth of the Catholic faith, and that I do but rely upon the threat and the consequent scare, that, unless a man be a Catholic he ought to be an Atheist. And I consider it to be said, not only that I use no argument in controversy in behalf of my creed besides the threat of atheism as its alternative; but also that I have not even attempted to prove by argument the reasonableness of that threat.

Now, what do I hold, and what do I not hold? The present volume supplies an answer to this question. From beginning to end it is full of arguments, of which the scope is the truth of the Catholic religion, yet no one of them introduces or depends upon the alternative of Catholicity or Atheism; how, then, can it be said that that alternative is the only defence that I have proposed for my creed? The Essay begins with refuting the fallacies of those who say that we cannot believe what we cannot understand. No appeal to the argument from *Atheism* here. Incidentally and *obiter* reasons are given for saying that causation and law, as we find them in the universe, bespeak an infinite Creator; still no *argumentum ab*

378

atheismo. This portion of the work finished, I proceed to justify certitude as exercised upon a cumulation of proofs, short of demonstration separately; nothing about atheism. Then I go to a direct proof of theism (which, indeed, has been in a great measure anticipated in a former chapter) as a conclusion drawn from three departments of phenomena; still the threat of atheism is away. I pass on to the proof of Christianity; and where does the threat of atheism come in here? I begin it with prophecy; then I proceed to the coincident testimony of the two covenants, and thence to the overpowering argument from the testimony borne to the divinity of Catholicism by the bravery and endurance of the primitive martyrs. And there I end.

Nor is this my only argumentative work in defence of my "creed" which I have given to the public. I have published an "Essay on Development of Doctrine," "Theological Tracts," "A Letter to Dr. Pusey," "A Letter to the Duke of Norfolk," works all more or less controversial, all defences of the Catholic creed; does the very word "atheism" occur in any one of them?

So much, then, on what I do not hold and have not said:—now as to what I have avowed and do adhere to. This brings me at once to the saying to which I have committed myself in "Apologia," page 179, viz., 'that there is no medium, in true philosophy, between Atheism and Catholicity, and that a perfectly consistent mind, under those circumstances in which it finds itself here below must embrace either the one or the other;"—a saying which doubtless my critic has in mind, and which, I am aware, has been before now a difficulty with readers whom I should be sorry to perplex.

Now, if we found it asserted in Butler's Analogy that there is no consistent standing or logical *medium* between the acceptance of the Gospel and the denial of a Moral Governor, for the same difficulties can be brought against both beliefs, and if they are fatal as against Christianity, they are fatal against natural religion, should we not have understood what was meant? It might be taken, indeed, as a threat against denying Christianity, but would it not have an argumentative basis and meaning, and would such an interpretation be fair? It would be quite fair indeed to say, as some have said, "It drives me the wrong way," and its advocates could only reply, "What is one man's meat is another man's poison," but would it be fair to accuse Butler of putting aside all scientific reasoning for a threat? No one would say, "Butler *confines* the defence of his own creed to the proposition that it is the only possible alternative of the denial of the Moral Law," putting aside as nothing to the purpose his Sermons at the Rolls' Chapel. Yet what have I said more dangerous or more obscure than Butler's argument? Could he be said to destroy all logical proof of a God, because he paralleled the difficulties of grace to the difficulties of nature? Nay, even should he go on to say with me, "if on account of difficulties we give up the gospel, then on account of parallel difficulties we must give up nature; for there is no standing-ground between putting up with the one trial of faith, and putting up with the other?"

Nor is this all. It seems, insistence on this analogy between the mysteries of nature and those of grace is my *sole* argument for the truth of my creed. How can this be, from the very nature of the case? The argument from Analogy is mainly negative, but argument which tends to prove must be positive. Butler does not prove Christianity to be true by his famous argument, but he removes a great obstacle of a *primâ facie* character to listening to the proofs of Christianity. It is like the trenches soldiers dig to shield them when they propose to storm a fort. No one would say that such trenches dispense with soldiers. So far, then, from "confining" myself to the argument from Analogy in behalf of my creed, I absolutely imply the presence and the use of independent arguments, positive arguments, by the fact of using what is mainly a negative one. And that I was quite aware of this, and acted upon it, the following passage from my Sermon on Mysteries shows beyond mistake:

"If I must submit my reason to mysteries, it is not much matter whether it is a mystery more or a mystery less; the main difficulty is to believe at all; the main difficulty for an inquirer is firmly to hold that there is a living God, in spite of the darkness which surrounds Him, the Creator, Witness, and Judge of men. When once the mind is broken in, as it must be, to the belief of a Power above it, when once it understands that it is not itself the measure of all things in heaven and earth, it will have little difficulty in going forward. *I do not say it will, or can, go on to other truths without conviction; I do not say it ought to believe the Catholic Faith without grounds and motives;* but I say that, when once it believes in God, the great obstacle to faith has been taken away, a proud, self-sufficient spirit, &c."—(Discourses.) [1]

I must somewhat enlarge what I have last been saying, but it is in order to increase the force and fulness of this explanation. There is a certain sense in which Analogy may be said to supply a positive argument, though it is not its primary and direct purpose. The coincidence of two witnesses independently giving the same account of a transaction is an argument for its truth; the likeness of two effects argues one cause for both. The fact of Mediation so prominent in Scripture and in the world, as Butler illustrates it, is a positive argument that the God of Scripture is the God of the world. This is the immediate sense in which I speak in the "Apologia" of the objective matter of Religion, Natural and Revealed, of the character of the evidence, and of the legitimate position and exercise of the intellect relatively towards it. Religion has, as such, certain definite belongings and surroundings, and it calls for what Aristotle would call a πεπαιδευμένος investigator, and a process of investigation *sui similis*. This peculiarity I first found in the history of doctrinal development; in the first instance it had presented itself to me as a mode of accounting for a difficulty, viz. for what are called "the Variations of Popery," but next I found it a law, which was instanced in the successive developments through which revealed truth has passed. And then I reflected that a law implied a lawgiver, and that so orderly and majestic a growth of doctrine in the Catholic Church, contrasted with the deadness and helplessness, or the vague changes and contradictions in the teaching of other religious bodies, argued a spiritual Presence in Rome, which was nowhere else, and which constituted a presumption that Rome was right; if the doctrine of the Eucharist was not from heaven, why should the doctrine of Original Sin be? If the Athanasian Creed was from heaven, why not the Creed of Pope Pius? This was a use of Analogy beside and beyond Butler's use of it; and then, when I had recognized its force in the development of doctrine, I was led to apply it to the Evidences of Religion, and in this sense I came to say what I have said in the "Apologia." "There is no *medium* in true philosophy," "to a perfectly consistent mind," "between Atheism and Catholicity."

[1] *Discourses to Mixed Congregations*, Discourse XIII, "Mysteries of Nature and of Grace."

The multitude of men indeed are not consistent, logical, or thorough; they obey no law in the course of their religious views; and while they cannot reason without premises, and premises demand first principles, and first principles must ultimately be (in one shape or other) assumptions, they do not recognize what this involves, and are set down at this or that point in the ascending or descending scale of thought, according as their knowledge of facts, prejudices, education, domestic ties, social position, and opportunities for inquiry determine; but nevertheless there is a certain ethical character, one and the same, a system of first principles, sentiments and tastes, a mode of viewing the question and of arguing, which is formally and normally, naturally and divinely, the *organum investigandi* given us for gaining religious truth, and which would lead the mind by an infallible succession from the rejection of atheism to theism, and from theism to Christianity, and from Christianity to Evangelical Religion, and from these to Catholicity. And again when a Catholic is seriously wanting in this system of thought, we cannot be surprised if he leaves the Catholic Church, and then in due time gives up religion altogether. I will add, that a main reason for my writing this Essay on Assent, to which I am adding these last words, was, as far as I could, to describe the *organum investigandi* which I thought the true one, and thereby to illustrate and explain the saying in the "Apologia" which has been the subject of this Note.

I have only one remark more before concluding. I have said of course there was a descending as well as an ascending course of inquiry and of faith. However, speaking in my "Apologia" of Evidences, and, following the lead of what I have said there about doctrinal development, I have mainly in view the ascending scale, not the descending. I have meant to say, "I am a Catholic, for the reason that I am not an Atheist." This makes the misinterpretation of my words which I am exposing the more striking, for it paraphrases me into a threat and nothing else, viz. "If you are not a Catholic, you must be an Atheist, and will go to hell." Mr. Lilly, in his letter in my defence, sees this, and most happily adopts the positive interpretation which is the true one.

This explanation, also, is an answer to some good, but easily frightened men, who have fancied that I was denying that the Being of a God was a natural truth, because I said that to deny

revelation was the way to deny natural religion. I have but argued
that the same sophistry which denies the one may deny the other.

That the ascending scale of my abstract alternative has been the
prominent idea in my mind, may be argued from the following
passage of a Lecture delivered many years before the "Apologia:"—

"A Protestant is already reaching forward to the whole truth,
from the very circumstance of his really grasping any part of it.
So strongly do I feel this, that I account it no paradox to say that,
let a man but master the one doctrine of the Being of a God, let
him really and truly, and not in words only, or by inherited profession, or in the conclusions of reason, but by a direct apprehension
be a Monotheist," (that is, with what in the foregoing Essay I
have called a "real assent" as following upon "Inference," and
acting as a fresh start) "and he is already three-fourths of the way
towards Catholicism."

I end by placing before the reader Mr. Lilly's apposite Letter,
dated Nov. 18.

"Sir,—I observe in your issue of this evening a statement against
which I must beg your permission to protest in the strongest
manner as a most serious, although, I am quite sure, an uninten-
tional, misrepresentation of my deeply venerated friend Cardinal
Newman. The statement is that 'he has confined his defence
of his own creed to the proposition that it is the only possible
alternative to atheism.' It certainly is true that Cardinal Newman
has said, 'There is no medium, in true philosophy, between
Atheism and Catholicism' ('Apologia,' p. 179, ed. 1947); and
it as certainly is not true that he *confines* his defence of his creed
to this proposition. He expressly recognizes 'the formal proofs on
which the being of a God rests' (they may be seen in any text-book
of Catholic theology) as affording 'irrefragable demonstration'
('Discourses to Mixed Congregations,' p. 262, Fourth Edition);
but the great argument which comes home to him personally with
supreme force is that derived from the witness of Conscience—
'the aboriginal Vicar of Christ, a prophet in its informations,
a monarch in its peremptoriness, a priest in its blessings and
anathemas.' The existence of God, 'borne in upon him irresistibly'
by the voice within, is 'the great truth of which his whole being
is full' ('Apologia,' pp. 218-19, ed. 1947).'

After quoting the words of M. Renan, Mr. Lilly proceeds, "This is the point from which he (Cardinal Newman) starts. Conscience, the 'great internal teacher,' 'nearer to us than any other means of knowledge,' informs us (as he judges) that God is; 'the special Attribute under which it brings Him before us, to which it sub-ordinates all other Attributes, being that of justice—retributive justice' ('Grammar of Assent,' p. 319, ed. 1947). 'The sense of right and wrong' he considers to be 'the first element' in natural religion ('Letter to the Duke of Norfolk,' § 5). And Catholicism, which he regards as the sole form of Christianity historically or philosophically tenable, is for him the only possible complement of natural religion. I cannot venture to ask you to allow me space to do more than thus indicate the nature of the argument by which he ascends from his first to his final religious idea. I would refer those who would follow it step by step to his 'Grammar of Assent,' 'Apologia,' and 'Discourses to Mixed Congregations;' or, if a mere summary will suffice, to an article of my own in the *Fortnightly Review* of July, 1879. Cardinal Newman's main defence—not his sole defence—of his creed amounts, then, to this: that religion is an integral part of our nature, and that Catholicism alone ade-quately fulfils the expectation of a revelation which natural religion raises. This may be a good or a bad defence; but, whether good or bad, it is very different from the nude proposition 'that Catholicism is the only possible alternative to atheism.' " He ends with a few kind words about myself personally.

Vid. my answer to Principal Fairbairn in the *Contemporary Review* of October, 1885.

NOTE III

On the punishment of the wicked having no termination,
vid. supr. 321.

December, 1882

A serious misrepresentation of a passage in this volume, which appeared last year in a Review of great name, calls for some notice here.

Petavius says, that, according to Fathers of high authority, a *refrigerium* or *refrigeria* may be conceived as granted to the lost, amid their endless penal suffering; that is, that their punishment, though without end, is not without cessation. I have quoted his words in the footnote on p. 321; and in the text I have ventured on a suggestion of my own, but short of his, to the effect that a *refrigerium* was conceivable, which was not strictly a cessation of punishment, though it acted as such; I mean, the temporary absence in the lost soul of the consciousness of its continuity or duration.

The story is well known of the monk who, going out into the wood to meditate, was detained there by the song of a bird for three hundred years, which to his consciousness passed as only one hour. Now pain as well as joy, may be an ecstasy, and destroy for the time the sense of succession; even in this life, and when not great, it sometimes has this effect; and, supposing such an insensibility to time to last for three hundred years, for three hundred years pain might be gathered up into a point; and there would be for that interval a *refrigerium*. And, if for three hundred years, so it might be for three million, or million million, according to the degrees of guilt with which individual souls were severally laden.

It may be objected, that such a view of future punishment explains away its severity, and blunts its moral force as a threat and restraint upon crime. Not so; on this view the facts of suffering and of its eternity remains intact; and of suffering, it may be, "as by fire." Also, the eternity of punishment remains in its negative aspect, viz., that there never will be change of state, annihilation or restoration. Mere eternity, though without suffering, if realized in the soul's consciousness, is formidable enough; it would be insupportable even to the good, except for, and as involved in, the Beatific Vision; it would be a perpetual solitary confinement. It is this which makes the prospect of a future life so dismal to our present agnostics, who have no God to give them "mansions" in the unseen world.

On the other hand, it may be objected, that the longest possible series of *refrigeria*, to whatever extent, added together, they may run, is as nothing after all compared with an eternity of punishment. But this is to misconceive what I have been advancing. As belonging to an eternity, the *refrigeria* which I contemplate match in their recurrence, and reach as far as, that eternity, and are themselves in number infinite, as being exceptions in a course which is infinite.

Further, it may be objected that this view of future punishment is at first sight inconsistent with the teaching of St. Thomas, 2. 2, qu. xviii. 3, where he says that, if the lost are condemned to eternal punishment, they must know that it is eternal, because such knowledge is necessarily a part of their punishment.

I understand him to argue thus:

1. It is de ratione pœnæ that it should voluntati repugnare.

2. But there cannot be this repugnantia, unless there is present to the party punished a consciousness of the fact of that pœna.

3. Therefore pœna implies a consciousness of the fact of the pœna.

4. And, if the pœna is perpetual, so is its consciousness.

Certainly: but I do not predicate anything of the pœna, nor of the consciousness of the pœna, nor of its perpetuity, nor of the consciousness of its perpetuity; I do but speak of the consciousness (perpetuity apart,) of the lapse of time or successiveness of moments, through which that pœna and consciousness of pœna passes. The lost may be conscious of their lost state and of its irreversibility, yet it may be a further question, whether, however conscious that it is irreversible, they are always or ever conscious of the fact of its long course, in memory and in prospect, through periods and æons.

The song of the bird, which the monk heard without taking note of the passage of time, might have been, "And they shall reign for ever and ever;" though of the many thousand times of the bird's repeating the words, there sounded in the monk's ear but one song once sung. And if this may be in the case of holy souls, why not, if it should so please God, in the instance of the unholy?

In what I have been saying, I have considered eternity as infinite time, because this is the received assumption.

And I have been speaking all along under correction, as submitting absolutely all I have said to the judgment of the Church and its head.

Vid. my article in the *Contemporary* above referred to.

INDEX

Abraham, 285, 331, 336, 339, 353, 369, 371.
Adam, 285.
Addison, J., xv.
Adeste Fideles, 20.
Aeschylus, 207.
Alexander, Bishop of Alexandria, 107, 108.
Alexander the Great, 8, 114, 289, 373.
Alexandrians, xii.
Alison, Sir A., 253, 326.
Amort, 141, 312, 313.
Analogy (Bishop Butler), 243, 262, 290, 309, 379.
Angels, 39, 43, 103.
Apollonius Tyaneus, 285.
Apologia (Newman), 379, 381, 382, 383.
Appollonia, 368.
Apprehension, xviii, 11 ff., 16 ff., 68, 75 ff., notional, 30; real, 19 ff., 30; relation of assent to, 119.
Arguments, 127 ff.
Arians, 114.
Arians of the Fourth Century, The (Newman), xii.
Aries, 285.
Aristotle, 257, 259, 268 ff., 314, 381.
Arius, 107, 108.
Arnold, Matthew, xiii.
Assent, xv, xvi, xvii, xviii, 4 ff., 75 ff., 120 ff., 129 ff., 154 ff., 184 ff., 197; assent and certitude contrasted, 159 ff., 184;

as apprehensive, 11 ff., 119 ff.; complex, 142 ff., conditional, 137; degrees of, 121 ff., 131 ff.; deliberate, 138; hesitating, 138; notional, 29 ff., 57, 68 ff., 75; notional and real contrasted, 68 ff.; real, 29, 57ff., 68 ff., 75; simple, 120 ff., 154 ff.; unconditional, 119 ff.
Assertion (modes of holding propositions), 3.
Athanasian Creed, the, 94, 95, 100, 101, 104, 106, 186, 377.
Atheism, 182, 378.
Atheism and Catholicity, 378 ff.
Athenagoras, 357.
Atonement, 299.
Augustus, 8.
"Auld Lang Syne," 23.

Baal, 307.
Bacon, Lord, 266, 274, 282.
Balaam, 140.
Barulas, 368.
Beautiful, sense of the, 82 ff., 93.
Beethoven, xv.
Belief, 68 ff., 76, 146 ff., 314.
Benedict XIV, Pope, 312.
Benthamism, 70.
Beveridge, Bishop W., 43.
"Bible Religion," 43.
Blandina, 367.
Blessed Virgin, the, 43, 44.
Brougham, Lord, 69, 73.
Buddhism, 112.

Date Due

	PRINTED	IN U. S. A.	